MW01625559

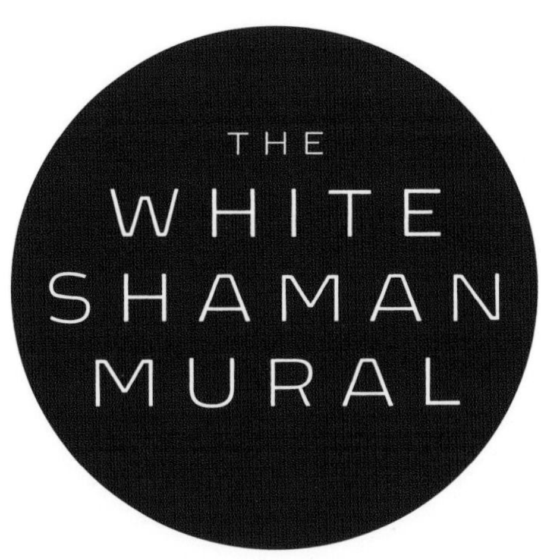
THE
WHITE
SHAMAN
MURAL

THE LINDA SCHELE SERIES IN MAYA AND PRE-COLUMBIAN STUDIES

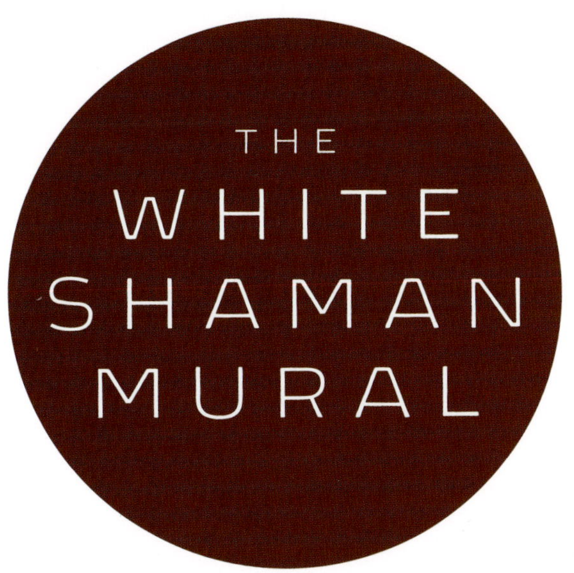

The White Shaman Mural

An Enduring Creation Narrative in the Rock Art of the Lower Pecos

CAROLYN E. BOYD, WITH CONTRIBUTIONS BY KIM COX

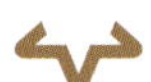

UNIVERSITY OF TEXAS PRESS AUSTIN

Copyright © 2016 by the University of Texas Press
All rights reserved
Printed in China
Third reprint, 2024

All illustrations are by the author.
All photographs are by Shumla Archaeological Research and Education Center unless otherwise noted.

Requests for permission to reproduce material from this work should be sent to:
Permissions
University of Texas Press
P.O. Box 7819
Austin, TX 78713-7819
utpress.utexas.edu

♾ The paper used in this book meets the minimum requirements of ANSI/NISO Z39.48-1992 (R1997) (Permanence of Paper).

Library of Congress Cataloging-in-Publication Data

Boyd, Carolyn E., 1958– author. Cox, Kim, contributor.

The White Shaman mural : an enduring creation narrative in the rock art of the Lower Pecos / Carolyn E. Boyd ; with contributions by Kim Cox.

Linda Schele series in Maya and pre-Columbian studies.

First edition. Austin : University of Texas Press, 2016.
Includes bibliographical references and index.

LCCN 2016003032 (print) LCCN 2016004114 (ebook)

ISBN 9781477310304 (cloth : alk. paper)
ISBN 9781477311196 (library e-book)
ISBN 9781477311202 (non-library e-book)

Indians of North America—Pecos River Valley (N.M. and Tex.)—Antiquities. Indian art—Pecos River Valley (N.M. and Tex.) Petroglyphs—Pecos River Valley (N.M. and Tex.) Rock paintings—Pecos River Valley (N.M. and Tex.) Pecos River Valley (N.M. and Tex.)—Antiquities.

LCC E78.T4 B69 2016 (print) LCC E78.T4 (ebook)
DDC 976.4/901—dc23
LC record available at http://lccn.loc.gov/2016003032

doi:10.7560/310304

TO ALFREDO LÓPEZ AUSTIN,
WHOSE BRILLIANT SCHOLARSHIP LAID THE FOUNDATION
FOR THIS BOOK. THANK YOU FOR YOUR GUIDANCE AND
ENCOURAGEMENT IN OUR SEARCH FOR THE ARCHAIC CORE.

IN MEMORY OF LINDA SCHELE,
WHO ENCOURAGED ME TO LOOK SOUTH AND WHOSE
TENACIOUS SPIRIT SPURRED ME ON.

AND IN LOVING MEMORY OF MY DEAR FRIEND AND COUNSELOR,
JO ANN HARRIS.

CONTENTS

ILLUSTRATIONS

FIGURES

TABLES

ACKNOWLEDGMENTS

First and foremost I thank my collaborator, Kim A. Cox. Without him, this book would never have been possible. In 2007 Kim began encouraging me to publish a monograph about the White Shaman mural. His encouragement turned to dogged insistence, and here we are, eight years later, with a finished manuscript. Kim's keen intellect and knowledge of Mesoamerican mythology led to many of the discoveries presented in the pages that follow. He has been a tireless editor: reading, commenting on, and contributing to each chapter more times than I can count. He is a true friend and colleague to whom I am eternally grateful.

Kim and I thank Gale Galloway and the Rock Art Foundation for their preservation and protection of the White Shaman site. Without their early, continuing, and often thankless efforts, there would be no White Shaman mural. The archaeological community and, indeed, the world owe them a huge debt of gratitude. We would especially like to thank Greg Williams, executive director of the Rock Art Foundation, for his friendship and his gracious and unfailing support.

There are no words to express the depth of gratitude I have for the incredible people who helped with the documentation and analysis of the White Shaman mural. First and foremost is the staff, both past and present, of the Shumla Archaeological Research and Education Center. I especially thank Amanda Castañeda, Charles Koenig, Ben Dwyer, Vicky Muñoz, and Jerod Roberts, who not only worked tirelessly with me in the field and in the lab, but also carried Shumla's documentation efforts forward while I was sequestered to write. Amanda and Charles were instrumental in developing and refining Shumla's rock art recording methods. Their gentle spirits, good humor, and incredible talent made even the hottest day in the desert not only bearable, but delightful. Vicky, building on the foundation established by Ben Dwyer, created a powerful searchable rock art database. Her abilities never cease to amaze me. Jerod, who took almost all the photographs accompanying my illustrations in chapters 5 and 6, worked tirelessly to make certain the graphics were the very best they could be for the book. I consider it a privilege to work alongside these talented young people.

I also greatly appreciate the Shumla IT specialist, Keith Mann, for keeping the computers and servers operational, and for making sure every version of the manuscript was backed up in several locations. I will always be indebted to Brenda Norman, who managed the Shumla offices with the utmost care while we were writing the book, and to Missy Harrington, who worked tirelessly on edits to the bibliography.

I thank Karen Steelman (Department of Chemistry at the University of Central Arkansas) for her help documenting and analyzing the White Shaman mural, and for her camaraderie and life-giving encouragement. Mark Willis, the MacGyver of archaeology, introduced us to virtually all of the innovative technologies we are using today to record rock art. I am forever grateful to Mark and Karen for all that they have done and continue to do not just for Shumla, but for the global rock art community. Bill Sontag conducted extensive background research into the White Shaman Galloway Preserve and conducted hours of interviews with past and present stakeholders of the property. The audio recordings he produced of these oral histories are irreplaceable.

I would also like to thank the multitude of volunteers, students, and student interns that have worked with us in the Lower Pecos. Their numbers are too great to mention here, but I remember the contributions of each with special fondness and gratitude. They were not only helpful, but also inspirational.

If not for the support and understanding of the Shumla board of directors, this work would never have been completed: Emil Zuberbueler, Elton Prewitt, David Graf, Bill Cauthorn, Lacy Jemmott, Judy VanCleve, and the late, but never forgotten, Jo Ann Harris. Jo Ann, who served as Shumla vice president since 2004, was a continual source of moral support and sage advice. She was a dear friend and my love for her is woven throughout the pages of this book.

Jessica Lee, former Shumla board member and now executive director, was of invaluable assistance. She read and edited the manuscript, and gently spurred me on over the past years. Several wonderful individuals contributed maps and photographs for the book: Mark Willis, Kerza Prewitt, Bob Mark, Evelyn Billo, Jack Johnson, Chester Leeds, Dean Liu, and Jean Clottes.

This work benefitted greatly from the comments offered by several scholars. David Madsen provided very helpful organization recommendations. Elton Prewitt was a reliable sounding board, encourager, and advisor throughout the writing process. Francisco Marcos-Marín contributed greatly to our discussion of linguistics and was always there to challenge us, inspire us, and answer questions. We would especially like to thank Robert A. Ricklis for comments on the manuscript and for his lifelong inspiration in the pursuit of archaeology. We thank Steve Black for his camaraderie and collaboration in the archaeology of the Lower Pecos, and for offering comments on an earlier version of the manuscript. We feel honored to be working alongside him in the cause. We are deeply grateful to Thomas Guderjan and Carolyn Tate for their astute and helpful comments on the original manuscript submitted to the University of Texas Press, and to Alma Nabhan for her assistance with the index. Last, but far from least, is Alfredo López Austin, whose encouragement and insights have been a source of immeasurable inspiration and to whom this book is dedicated.

We are immensely grateful to Jack and Missy Harrington of Comstock, Texas, who have been a part of this project from the start, first donating their land for the establishment of Shumla and then giving their hearts to ensure its success. And to Jack and Wilmuth Skiles, as well as numerous other landowners, we extend our sincerest appreciation for their passionate stewardship of the archaeology of the Lower Pecos.

To the anonymous donor who provided significant financial support and a contagious enthusiasm for our work, no words can express our gratitude.

Finally, we thank our families. My father, Walker Boyd, has been a pillar of support throughout the writing of the book. He read and critiqued every version, questioned every idea relentlessly, and loved me unconditionally. It is because of him that I was able to accomplish this monumental undertaking. And to our spouses, Phil Dering and Beverly Miller-Cox, there is no end of gratitude. You have stood by us through this long and often tortuous journey. You have endured our frenzied excitement as we made new discoveries and our frustrations when it seemed there was no end to the writing. You endured our long hours at the computer, noses buried in books piled high around the house, and the sleepless nights. You are our rock. Thank you.

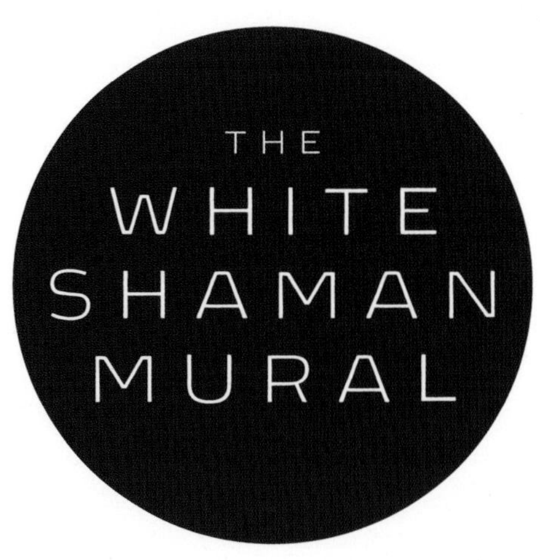
THE
WHITE
SHAMAN
MURAL

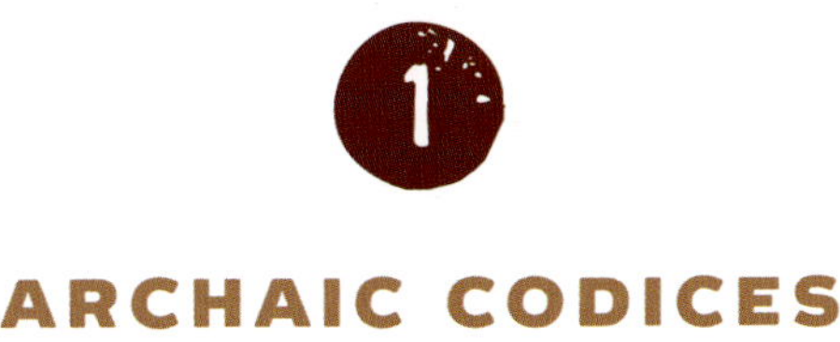

ARCHAIC CODICES

Life is short, art is long.
HIPPOCRATES

If you look upriver as you cross the Pecos River bridge heading west toward the historic town of Langtry, Texas, you will see nestled high on the canyon wall a small, shallow cave (figure 1.1). Near dusk on a winter's day the sun fills this rockshelter with light, illuminating the images painted thousands of years ago in red, yellow, black, and white. Those of us who know the paintings are there wave a greeting as we pass. Hundreds of thousands of people, however, cross the bridge and never know they are within a stone's throw of perhaps the oldest known "book" in North America: the rock art mural in White Shaman Shelter (41VV124).[1]

The few surviving prehistoric and early historic books of the Mixtec, Zapotec, Maya, and Nahua (Aztec)—ancient manuscripts composed of beautifully illustrated graphic writing—are called "codices." In the pages that follow, I will demonstrate that the White Shaman rock art mural functioned much like a pre-Columbian Mesoamerican codex. Produced by hunters and gatherers living in the Lower Pecos Canyonlands of southwest Texas and Coahuila, Mexico, perhaps as far back as 2000 BC, it was an Archaic form of communicating complex ideas through a graphic medium and was a precursor to what would eventually become the pre-Columbian codices. This Archaic "codex" documents cosmological concepts as sophisticated as those recorded in the codices of later agricultural societies.

Nothing about the White Shaman mural is random. As with words on a page, every image was intentionally placed. It is a visual text communicating a narrative by means of a graphic vocabulary—a narrative that has multiple levels of meaning and function. First and foremost, as with the Mesoamerican codices, it is about cycles of time and the spiritual meanings that adhere to time.[2] It is a creation story detailing the birth of the sun and the dawn of time. Second, it details protocols for a ritual reenactment of this cosmic event. And last, it creates a visible context within which the structure of the cosmos and its supernatural inhabitants can be seen as tangibly present. The work performed by the imagery extended beyond a simple graphic representation of forager cosmovision; it also instructed, informed, and socialized the community and members of the society.

First Encounters

On my first visit to the White Shaman site, I arrived by boat. It was 1989. Near its mouth, the river was deep, slow-moving, and wide. It pressed hard against sheer canyon walls reaching upward hundreds of feet, guiding the Pecos to its nearby confluence with the Rio Grande. But this is not the way it would have looked thousands of years ago or, for that matter, even a hundred years ago. The Rio Grande was dammed several miles downstream in 1968. The resulting Amistad Reservoir flooded thousands of acres of land, including an untold number of archaeological sites. When you cross the Pecos River bridge today, you are really crossing the reservoir, which extends about 14 miles up the Pecos River gorge.

For countless generations the shelter was accessed by climbing down from the canyon rim or up from the bottom of the deep gorge. The canyon floor now lies about 80 feet below the reservoir. I stepped from the boat onto limestone boulders bleached white by an un-

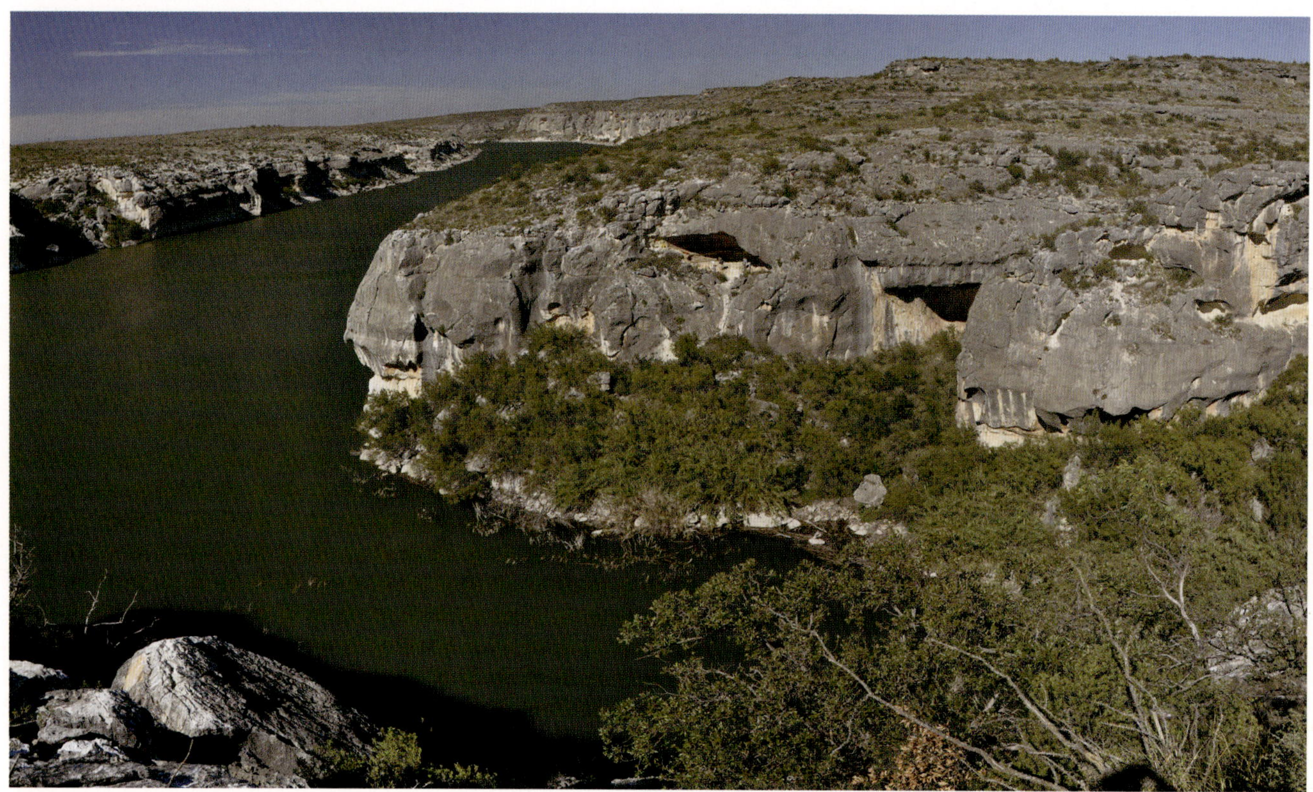

Figure 1.1. View of the Pecos River and White Shaman Shelter from across the canyon. Photo by Rupestrian Cyberservices. Courtesy of Shumla Archaeological Research and Education Center.

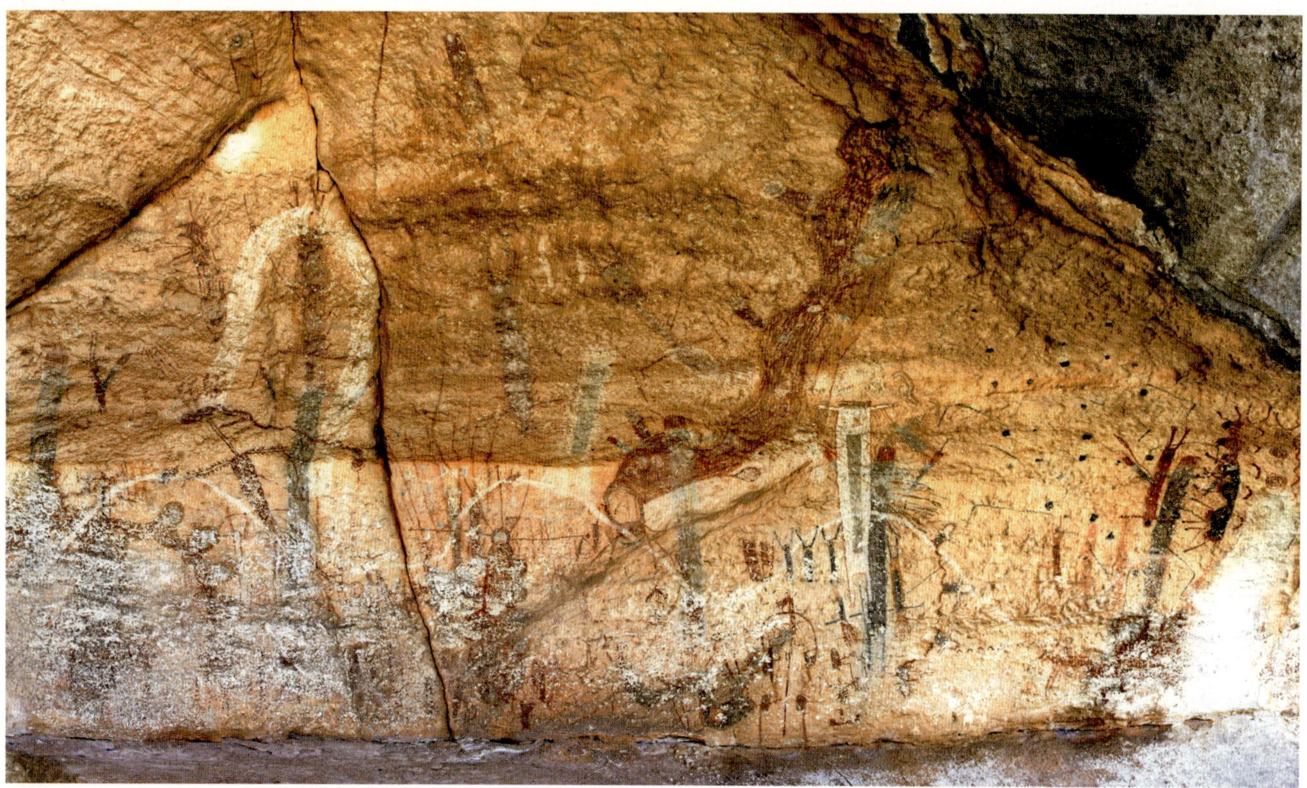

Figure 1.2. The polychromatic Pecos River style mural at the White Shaman site is approximately 26 feet long and 13 feet high. Photo by Chester Leeds.

relenting west Texas sun and began my ascent to the shelter, navigating a slippery talus of burned rock obscured by dense, thorny vegetation: black brush acacia, mesquite, and prickly pear. Just below the canyon rim I maneuvered up a vertical wall, searching out foot- and handholds, hoping they were free of rattlesnakes. Today a series of stone steps with a chain handrail makes access to the site much easier, but admittedly less authentic; I am thankful to have experienced it before the steps. When I reached the end of the climb, my focus shifted from the cold, gray limestone to the warm, cream-colored walls of the small rockshelter. Looking down at me were a myriad of humanlike and enigmatic figures, images that had seen the sun and moon set in the western sky for thousands of years (figure 1.2).

I am often asked who discovered the White Shaman site. The first person of European ancestry who had the opportunity to see the mural might have been someone in the Spanish expedition of 1590 led by Gaspar Castaño de Sosa. This expedition of 170 daring men, women, and children traveled up the Pecos River all the way into New Mexico (Foster 2008:176). Sadly, there is no mention of rock art by the Spanish chroniclers of that expedition. During an 1849 expedition into the Lower Pecos Canyonlands, US Army captain Samuel Gibbs French reported "rude Indian paintings on the rocks" but offered no descriptive details. Not long afterward Lieutenant Francis Henry French, who commanded the 19th Infantry's Black Seminole Indian Scouts in 1882, showed curiosity and speculation about the local rock art in his diary.[3] At Meyer's Spring, about 60 miles northwest of the White Shaman site, he noted the presence of solid red Indian paintings and lamented that the vandalism of modern man was severely impacting the art. The railroad, built later that decade, greatly increased the non-Native presence in the region. In its original location, it passed less than a mile from White Shaman Shelter.

Not even in 1931, when Emma Gutzeit and Mary Virginia Carson from the Witte Museum in San Antonio conducted their systematic survey of Lower Pecos rock art, did they include any mention of the White Shaman site. Soon after Gutzeit and Carson, Forrest Kirkland and his wife, Lula, made incredibly accurate watercolor renderings of forty-three rock art panels in the Lower Pecos. The Kirklands didn't record the White Shaman panel either, although they did record a site almost directly across the Pecos River. In retrospect, it seems odd that none of these early individuals were aware of the White Shaman panel. It is not well camouflaged from either the river or the roadway.

The earliest known documentation of White Shaman Shelter was in 1957, when archaeologists John A. Graham and William A. Davis visited the site. It was owned at that time by Mr. Fate Bell. They submitted an unremarkable one-page site survey form to the National Park Service River Basins Survey on February 19, 1958, and assigned its archaeological site number: 41VV124. It was the 124th archaeological site reported for Val Verde County. Today there are over two thousand reported sites. Graham and Davis painted VV124 on the shelter wall in bright green paint. Interestingly, this number is less visible today than the ancient paintings.

On July 12, 1966, archaeologist Mark Parsons visited the White Shaman site and, after acknowledging the prior documentation of Graham and Davis, recorded many more detailed observations. Parsons also named it the Jefferson Davis site due to its proximity to the Jefferson Davis Memorial Highway (US Hwy. 90).

By the early 1990s the newly formed Rock Art Foundation (RAF) had turned its attention to the acquisition of the shelter and surrounding lands. One of its founders, Jim Zintgraff (credited with giving the White Shaman site its present name), along with D. J. Sibley and Solveig Turpin, approached Texas oilman and philanthropist Gale Galloway about purchasing the site from the heirs of Fate Bell. On April 19, 1993, Galloway bought the property surrounding the White Shaman Shelter and on June 1, 1993, donated 265 acres, including the White Shaman site, to the Rock Art Foundation. The RAF has owned and managed the site since that time, offering tours from the park headquarters at Seminole Canyon State Park and Historic Site. The White Shaman mural may not have existed today had it not been for the dedicated efforts of the Rock Art Foundation. Jim Zintgraff once told me that he was offered a million dollars for the rock art panel. The buyer intended to cut the limestone canvas away from the shelter wall and display the art in a museum. You can imagine Jim's response. Over the years the RAF has protected the artwork and paved the way for rock art research and documentation.[4]

Art in Place

The shallow rockshelter housing the paintings was carved out of the cliff face by wind and water erosion millennia ago. The shelter stretches 65 feet across and 26 feet deep (figure 1.3). Powdery white cave dust and small, wafer-thin limestone fragments litter the otherwise bare bedrock floor—evidence that formation processes are still at work. Most of the walls are rough and deeply pitted, unsuitable for use as a canvas; however, on the right side of the shelter, in its own small alcove, is a comparatively smooth surface. It is here that the artists elected to paint the mural, which is approximately 26 feet long and 13 feet high (figure 1.4). It rests above a narrow, slick limestone bench reaching from the floor of the shelter up a few feet to the paintings. Remnants of paint stain the bench, but the imagery portrayed is no longer discernible. This natural feature served as a workstation from which most of the mural was painted, although scaffolding or ladders would have been required to complete the panel. Shallow grinding depressions, some with remnants of red paint, can be seen on the bench and nearby floor of the shelter. Deeper bedrock mortars—some as deep as an arm is long—are located on the opposite side of the shelter.

Unlike art and artifacts displayed in museums around the world, this art is not "art out of place." It was created here, to be viewed here, and to remain here. We have the unique opportunity to view it in the spatial and environmental context within which it was created,

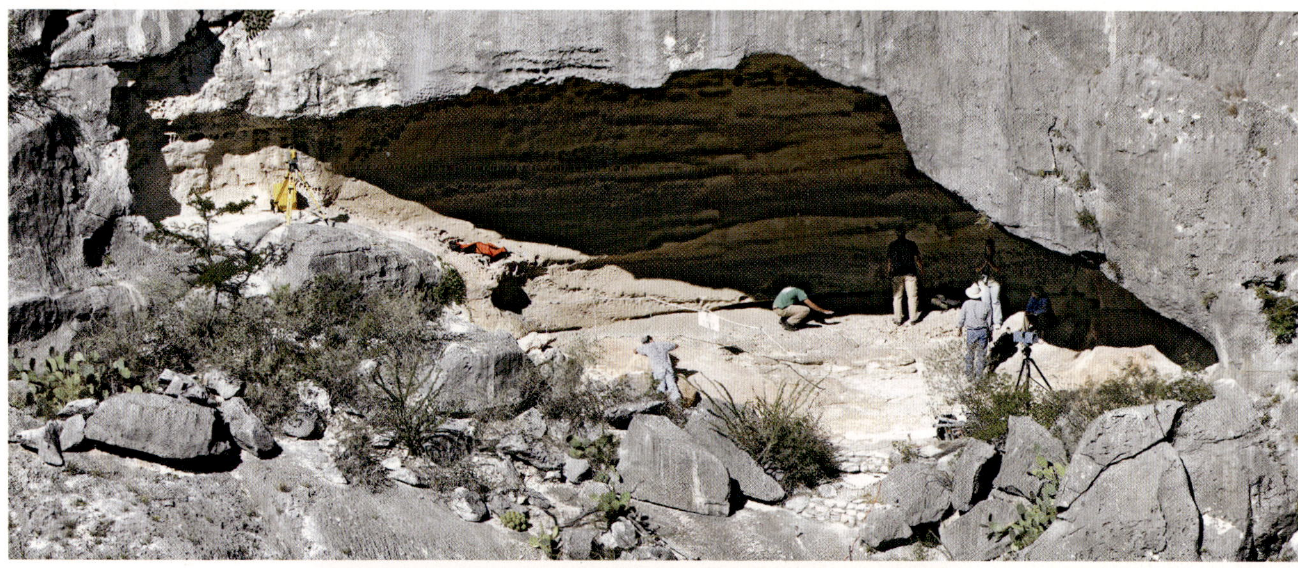

Figure 1.3. *(above)* The rockshelter housing the White Shaman mural is 65 feet across, 23 feet high, and 26 feet deep. Photo by Rupestrian Cyberservices. Courtesy of Shumla Archaeological Research and Education Center.

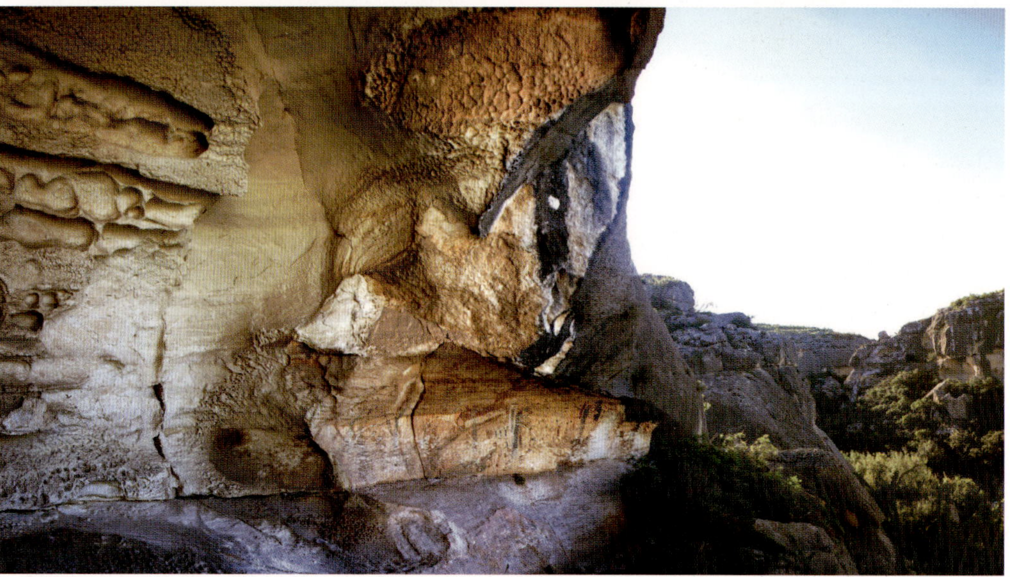

Figure 1.4. *(right)* The White Shaman mural is on the east wall of the southwest-facing shelter, so the paintings face due west. Photo by Chester Leeds.

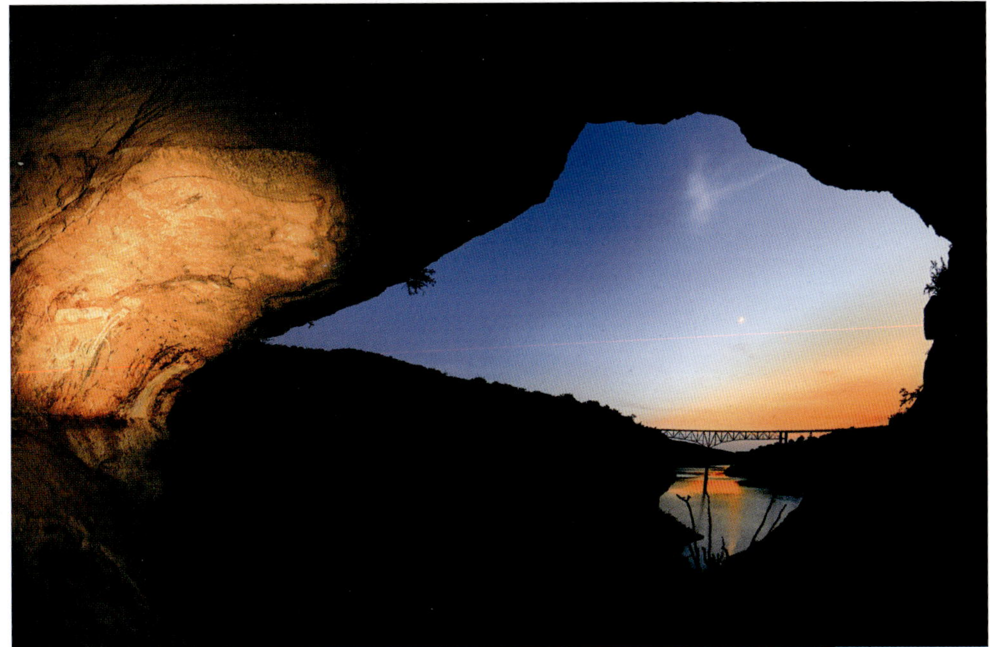

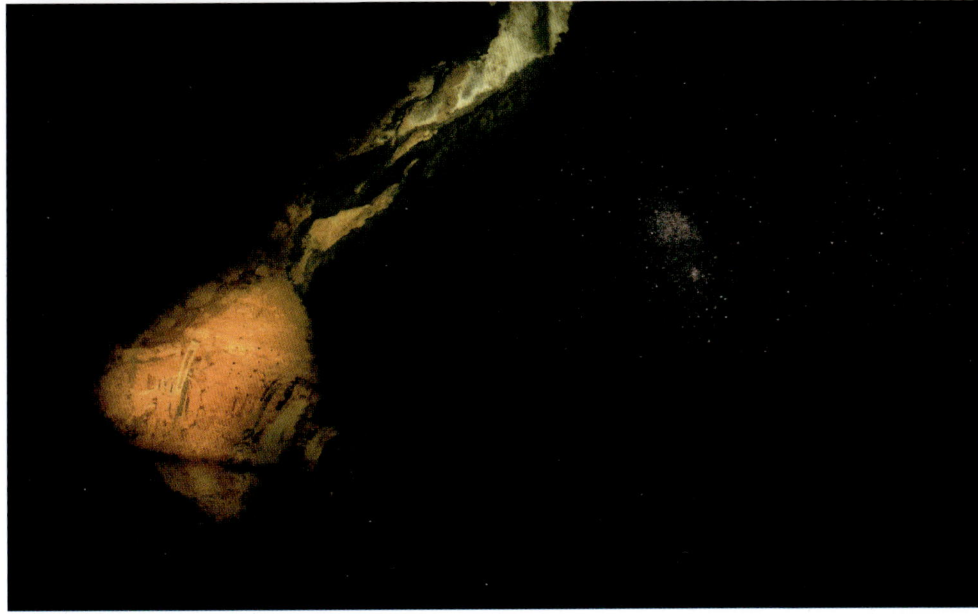

Figure 1.5. Viewscapes from White Shaman Shelter: (a) Sunset view on September 11, 2010, with the moon and Venus visible on the horizon above the mountains of Mexico. Photo by Dean Liu. (b) White Shaman Shelter serves as a natural observatory for breathtaking views of the night sky throughout the year. The Milky Way is visible in this photo taken September 11, 2010. Photo by Dean Liu.

albeit not the cultural context. The smell of wild oregano carried into the shelter on hot, dry summer breezes and the cascading whistles of canyon wrens were experienced by the artists of the panel just as they are by us today. There is, however, one notable difference. The artists did not experience the sound of eighteen-wheelers crossing the Pecos River bridge, magnified by the acoustics of this natural amphitheater, which are remarkable. The single strike of a drum travels out of the shelter and returns to form a heartbeat; a single hand clap returns like applause. Words spoken in a natural tone can be easily heard 400 feet across the canyon in a small shelter facing the White Shaman site. If the wind is out of the southwest, people talking on the bridge, 1,400 feet away, can be heard inside the shelter.

Although the rockshelter faces southwest, the paintings face due west, looking out toward the Pecos River and, beyond that, to the Burro Mountains in Coahuila, Mexico. Each evening, as the sun sets, the paintings and their limestone canvas are bathed in golden light, enhancing the red and yellow pigments. The cool light of a full moon subdues these earth colors, but intensifies images in white that are otherwise virtually invisible. On a moonlit night the panel becomes so illuminated that flash is not required for photography. The shelter serves as a natural planetarium, providing a perfect location to watch the sun, moon, and stars set each night (figure 1.5).

The Journey Begins

When I first visited the White Shaman site, I brought only a Pentax K1000 camera and sketchbook, two items I was rarely without. I remember sitting in front of the panel, recognizing the complexity of the composition and wondering how the artists produced such fine lines and rich earth colors thousands of years ago. I was working as an artist at the time, putting food on the table as a commissioned muralist, so the large scale was not unfamiliar to me. Recently I came across the sketches and notes I made during this visit to the site—a humbling experience. Some of my observations were astute. For example, I recognized the mural was a composition. But my imaginings of what the panel portrayed were naive. I saw the upside-down, dart-impaled, humanlike figures and declared the artist must have been commemorating a battle. Just for the pure joy of it, I replicated the mural on a 5-foot-long piece of butcher paper.[5] This twenty-five-year-old rendering is in deplorable condition today, replete with tiny footprints left behind by my daughter after she got into the strawberries.

Frederick Franck, author of *The Zen of Seeing* (1973), once wrote, "I have learned that what I have not drawn I have never really seen, and that when I start drawing an ordinary thing, I realize how extraordinary it is, sheer miracle" (6). As I reconstructed the panel in pastels and colored pencils, I was forced—or, more appropriately, given the privilege—to connect with each individual image and to experience some of the challenges the artist faced as he—or she—wove the individual figures into a composition. I recognized the hand, or at least the influence, of a single artist, the skillful use of space, and the thoughtful placement of imagery to move the eye across the panel.[6] It was just as Frederick Franck stated: extraordinary. I was hooked. I wanted to learn all that I could about the artist(s) and their work. What did the paintings communicate? How were they created—and why? So I returned to Texas A&M University in 1991 to finish my undergraduate degree and pursue a PhD in archaeology (1998a).

That same year Jim Zintgraff and Solveig Turpin published a beautiful photographic essay entitled *Pecos River Rock Art* (1991). In it they presented the first interpretation of the White Shaman mural—or more specifically, the striking white figure in the center of the rock art panel for which the shelter was named (figure 1.6). This complex panel, they wrote, "embodies several of the key attributes that confirm the shamanic origins of these cave paintings. The white shaman is in his ascendancy, leaving behind his black counterpart, his mortal body" (Zintgraff and Turpin 1991:40).

Labeling such figures as shamans was in vogue with the general American view of rock art in the 1960s. Mircea Eliade published his now famous *Shamanism: Archaic Techniques of Ecstasy* in English in 1964 (it had been published in French in 1951) and popularized both the term and the concept among American social scientists. Shamans, he argued, were magico-religious specialists that existed in almost every primitive society and were distinguished by being able to enter a state of ecstasy, usually taking the form of a trance. Frequently they were attended by an animal helper and could access the upperworld and underworld through various mind-altering techniques. Peter Furst, in *Shamanistic Survivals in Mesoamerican Religion* (1976), emphasized the role of hallucinogenic plants in shamanism and was one of the first to discuss in depth the widespread belief in human-animal transformations. This, in turn, led to David Carrasco's textbook *Religions of Mesoamerica* (1990) and the groundbreaking and immensely popular book by David Freidel, Linda Schele, and Joy Parker, *Maya Cosmos: Three Thousand Years of the Shaman's Path* (1993), in which they put forth the idea that shamanism was neither elitism nor limited to a fringe element, but was instead woven into the very fabric of society.

Rock art study at that time was not taken seriously. It was considered a stepchild of archaeology. Some would say it still is. There were many discussions about whether the study of rock art even belonged within archaeology. Archaeologists argued it was art and therefore couldn't be approached through traditional

Figure 1.6. *(facing page)* The White Shaman site was named in the 1980s for this striking 3-foot-tall, white anthropomorphic figure. Photo by Jean Clottes. Courtesy of Shumla Archaeological Research and Education Center.

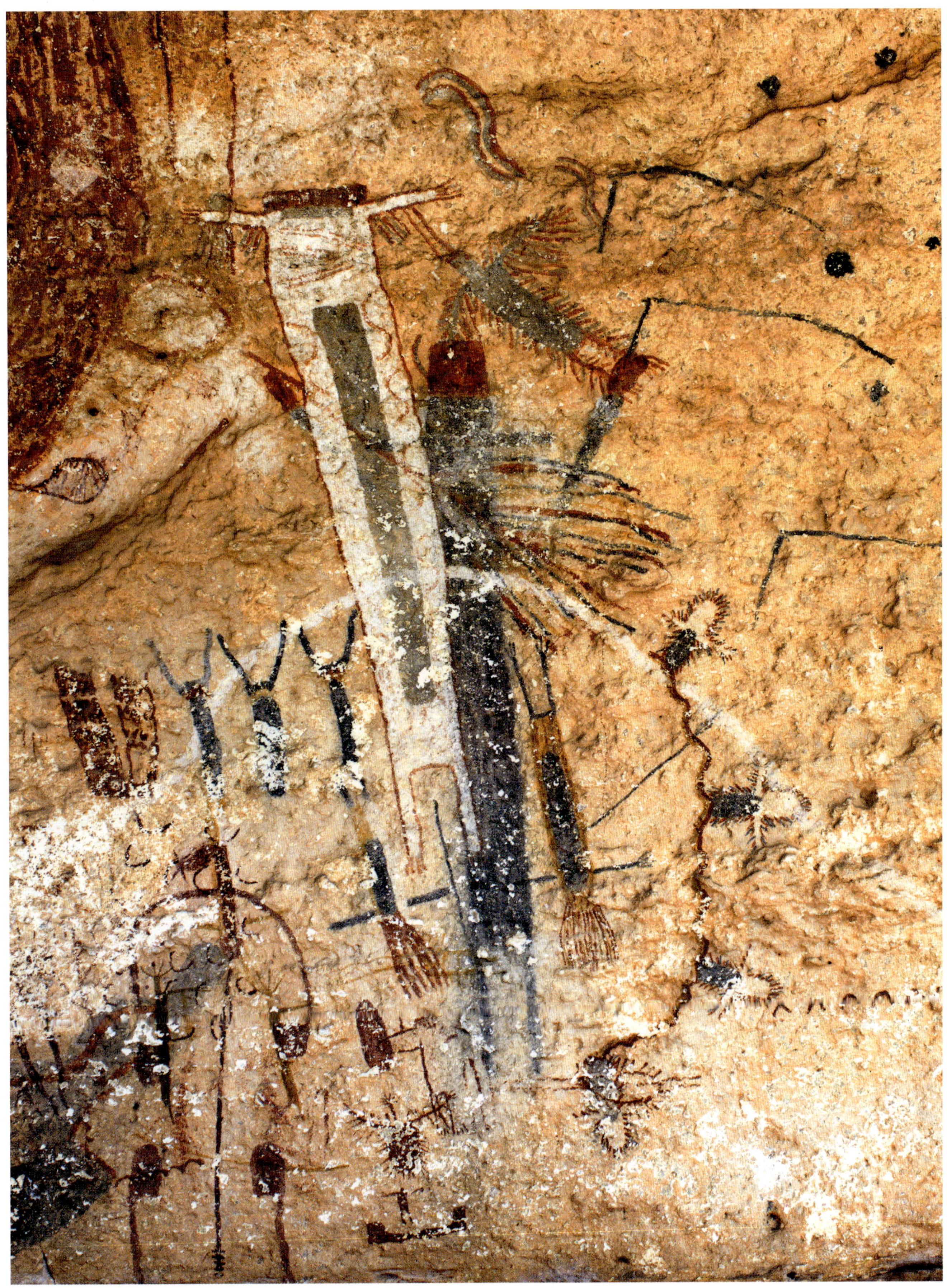

archaeological methods. I knew that if I wanted the archaeological community to recognize the insights that rock art studies could provide into the region's prehistory, I had to learn to speak their language and develop a systematic means of studying the rock art. And so it began—a journey into the science of art and an analysis of the White Shaman mural.

Inspired and encouraged by art historian and epigrapher Linda Schele, as well as Harry Shafer at Texas A&M, I developed an approach to document and analyze Lower Pecos rock art. Just as detectives look for patterns to solve crimes and cryptologists look for patterns to break codes, archaeologists look for patterns to interpret the archaeological record. I thus set out to determine if there were patterns that could shed light on the function and meaning of the art. To get at those patterns, however, required meticulous documentation and a systematic approach to data collection. I began with a formal analysis of the Pecos River style murals at Panther Cave (41VV83), Rattlesnake Canyon (41VV180), Cedar Springs (41VV696), Mystic Shelter (41VV612), and the White Shaman site (41VV124). Drawing each pictographic element increased my familiarity with imagery content and helped me identify variations and consistencies in artistic styles. It revealed recurring patterns and artistic conventions, as well as anomalies in the art. I used this information to document the distribution of pictographic elements and figure attributes within and among the five panels. The results revealed distinct patterns in the distribution and association of specific motifs across the landscape. The imagery had not been randomly placed on the walls of these magnificent sites, but rather appeared to be organized into compositionally intricate, highly patterned murals. At the White Shaman site, regionwide patterns coalesced: they were not only concentrated at this one site, but conjoined—linked together like pieces of a puzzle to form a complex narrative. These qualities begged explanation, and the patterns at the White Shaman site provided the first interpretive clues. The next steps proved to be the most challenging: interpreting, explaining, and reconstructing past lifeways and beliefs from the patterns.

I decided to approach the rock art as I would approach any other aspect of the archaeological record. To interpret that record, archaeologists develop bridging arguments that link the past to the present (Kelly and Thomas 2013:172). For my purposes this involved identifying and documenting patterns or motifs in ethnographic, ethnohistoric, and other literary sources that corresponded to patterns identified in the rock art. I mined the literature on myths and rituals of past and present peoples living in Mesoamerica and the American Southwest and much to my surprise found affinities with the patterns I had identified in the art. Most notable were inescapable parallels between patterns in the rock art and their analogues in Huichol myths and rituals associated with the peyote cactus, an important medicinal and sacramental plant for numerous indigenous groups (Boyd and Dering 1996; Boyd 1998b). Not only did this provide insight into several regional patterns, but it also provided a possible explanation for the coalescing and conjoining of the patterns at the White Shaman site. The pieces of the puzzle were falling into place.

Based on these findings, I offered the hypothesis that the patterns portrayed in the art are associated with peyotism, the ritual use of *Lophophora williamsii* (peyote cactus). I then assessed this hypothesis within the context of other aspects of regional material culture, such as three effigy peyote buttons with radiocarbon assays dating to six thousand years ago (Terry et al. 2006). These specimens were recovered by George Martin in the 1930s from deposits of the Shumla Caves, located only a couple of miles from the White Shaman site.[7] According to Martin Terry et al. (2006:1017), "The three Shumla Caves' specimens are not simply desiccated crowns of peyote cacti. . . , but are aggregates of ground peyote mixed with C_3 plant materials to form flattened hemispheres vaguely resembling peyote buttons." The three "buttons" contain comparable amounts of alkaloids and have statistically indistinguishable radiocarbon ages, with a weighted mean of 5195 ± 20 ^{14}C years BP, approximately one thousand years prior to the earliest dates for the Pecos River style paintings (Terry et al. 2006).

Examining the art in conjunction with artifacts helped to explain both assemblages. I continued developing cablelike arguments by intertwining distinct, separate strands of evidence from areas such as the social and biophysical environment, animal behavior, and cognitive neuroscience. This led me to believe that the rock art instructed foragers of the Lower Pecos about ecological relationships, such as the effects of rain on animal and plant behavior—knowledge that was necessary to successfully exploit their hunting and gathering niche. As such, the rock art and associated rituals may have influenced social cooperation regarding the control of scarce resources. This strongly suggested the art could be explained in the broader context within which it was produced, beyond that of shamanism. The White Shaman mural functioned as a direct form of communication, not simply as a record of altered cognitive states.

Ultimately, after an intensive study of Huichol myths and rituals, as well as further analysis of the rock art, I suggested that the White Shaman mural functioned as a prescription for ritual. It shows the process of a peyote ceremony, including the transformation of the mortal to the immortal, the cleansing and binding together (the uniting) of the pilgrims, the slaying of the peyote/deer, and the offering of fire to the ascending sun. This analysis introduced other possible functions for Pecos River style anthropomorphs beyond the stereotype of their being merely representations of shamans. Shamanism was certainly an integral component of hunter-gatherer religion; however, it was expressed in the rock art alongside and interwoven with a constellation of myths, histories, and ritual practices involving a myriad of spirit beings and mythological characters. Just as the meaning of the word *bow* depends on the context within which it is used, the meaning of each rock art motif is context-dependent. Its full meaning can be understood only within the context of the panel's other imagery.

My understanding of the White Shaman mural had expanded far beyond that of a random collection of images painted as a result of shamanic trance experiences. I had come to recognize the panel as a well-ordered composition documenting an ancient ritual similar in many respects to the modern-day Huichol peyote pilgrimage. This research formed the basis for my dissertation, which was subsequently published by Texas A&M University Press in 2003 under the title *Rock Art of the Lower Pecos*. What I had not yet realized, however, was the extraordinary depth with which myth had informed ritual.

The Journey Continues

After completing my doctoral studies in 1998, I founded the Shumla School, a nonprofit archaeological research and education center located in the Lower Pecos. For the next ten years my time was devoted to building the organization and our rock art documentation program; however, in 2008 I returned to the documentation and analysis of the White Shaman mural, this time joined by a talented team of Shumla archaeologists, students, and volunteers. We were also joined by Kim Cox, a lawyer and Mesoamericanist, who recognized parallels between the rock art of the Lower Pecos and Maya iconography. Working together, Kim and I expanded the ethnographic analysis beyond the Huichol to include the Nahua (popularly referred to as the Aztec) and the Maya.

Back in 1989, my first efforts to document the White Shaman mural began with the simple tools of an artist. Now, after years of intensive fieldwork with my colleagues at Shumla, our investigations incorporate 3D laser mapping, drone mapping, structure from motion (SfM) photogrammetry, portable X-ray fluorescence, handheld digital microscopes, total data stations, and Wacom Cintiq Interactive Pen Displays. We returned to the White Shaman site equipped with these state-of-the-art tools and years of experience to redocument the mural. Each visit was rewarded with new discoveries.

Working with Kim, I shifted my analytical emphasis to the myths from which the peyote rituals emerged. The task was daunting. We could identify repetitive symbols, but we were not sure that we would ever be able to put them into a context where they could be understood holistically as they contributed to the overall meaning of the panel. We returned to the historic ethnographies written about the Huichol and continued correlating patterns in the rock art with Huichol mythology. We were in search of the next layer of meaning—the origin myth from which the ritual emerged. With amazing rapidity the pieces began falling into place.

We discovered that the White Shaman mural contains the basic themes, the essential core elements, of not only the Huichol peyote ceremony, but also Huichol creation stories. But as patterns continued to emerge, we wondered how we could account for such strong parallels between contemporary ethnography and ancient iconography, separated not only temporally, but also spatially. The Huichol, after all, live about 600 miles south of the Lower Pecos Canyonlands.

The major objection to interpreting Lower Pecos rock art has always focused on the implausibility of using modern ethnography to explain concepts that are possibly thousands of years old.[8] Although it is true that the artists who painted these magnificent murals are no longer with us, their myths and belief systems live on. They endure in the shared symbolic language of the Native peoples living today in Mesoamerica and the American Southwest (P. Furst 1974:134). López Austin (1997:5) argues that this shared symbolic world is a manifestation of an archaic core, an almost unchangeable "hard nucleus" of ancient Mesoamerican traditions. This web of interrelated and intermeshed ideas forms a continuum still evident in Native American expressive culture. The actors and details may change, but at the core, basic story lines and concepts are amazingly resilient to change.

To explore this possibility, we turned to historical accounts and ethnographic observations of other Native American groups. Foremost among them was the Nahua, whose language, Nahuatl, is very closely related to that of the Huichol. To a lesser degree we examined ethnographies of several other Uto-Aztecan speakers outside Mesoamerica, including the Hopi and various small groups from the American Southwest and northwestern Mexico. Finally we turned to the region's non-Uto-Aztecan speakers, principally the Maya. Our goal was to see if the White Shaman panel fit into the basic structure of the broader continuum.

We found that, as with the Huichol, there were numerous connections relating to the actual structure of myths and ceremonies of all these people. At the mythological core, they incorporate similar patterns, reveal similar (if not identical) actions and symbols, and share a common function. Our revised hypothesis thus became that the White Shaman mural was not only a prescription for ritual, but a visual creation narrative containing many of the elements fundamental to an Archaic religious system widely practiced throughout much of Mesoamerica and the American Southwest. Similarities between the iconography of the mural and Nahua art and ethnography were particularly striking. This was not mere coincidence.

Theoretical Framework

We examined this phenomenon within two frameworks. The first involved the field of linguistics—tracing the symbology inherent in languages passed down from one generation to the next. The second involved semiotics—the study of how symbols (signs or metaphors) are acquired and operate within and across cultures. Here we transitioned from trying to understand *what* the visual text means, to *how* it means—how meaning was communicated through the art and how it formed part of the culture within which it was produced. This final level of analysis provided insights into not just the symbology of the panel, but its inherent meaning. We began to gain insights into the framework of ideas and beliefs through which the culture interpreted and interacted with the world: their worldview.

For reasons explained throughout the book, we believe the artist(s) who painted the White Shaman mural spoke a Southern Uto-Aztecan language. We believe certain identifiable ideas, symbols, iconographies, story lines, cosmovisions, and philosophies dominated the worldview of these people from some ill-defined Archaic time period before the creation of the White Shaman panel up until historical time or, in some cases, up until the present.

Our attempts to decipher the iconographies are systemic, meaning we require our explanations to fit into the greater Southern Uto-Aztecan ideological universe. Consequently, we propose no theory that lacks a counterpart in the ethnological, historical, or archaeological records. Our interpretations correspond to those previously identified ideas, symbols, iconographies, story lines, cosmovisions, and/or philosophies of either Corachol-Aztecan-speaking peoples or of a greater cultural area sharing some of those same ideals. We also take noted exception to any theory for the explanation of the Pecos River style iconographies that does not fit into that ideological universe. We do not believe that ideas originated, manifested themselves in obvious ways, and then completely disappeared from the historical or ethnographic record. Therefore, in the pages that follow, we attempt to explain at great length the worldview of the people who we believe painted the rock art of the Lower Pecos Canyonlands thousands of years ago.

Structure of the Book

Chapter 2 begins with a brief introduction to the Lower Pecos: its environment, cultural history, and magnificent visual culture. This includes a summary of the monumental efforts undertaken to document, date, and interpret the rock art over the past several decades. It is a fascinating story, and one to which I wish I could devote more time, but only the key players and their contributions are introduced here.

Chapter 3 provides a discussion of the definition and role of visual culture, and the methods used by art historians, iconographers, and archaeologists to extrapolate meaning from visual media. I also present an introduction to the recording techniques we use at Shumla Archaeological Research and Education Center to document rock art, as well as our approach to its iconographic analysis.

Chapter 4 provides an introduction to key concepts and terms used in subsequent chapters. It is a primer, of sorts, in which I discuss the Mesoamerican world vision identified by López Austin and other Mesoamerican scholars. I define core concepts of the shared symbolic world of Native America, such as replication, complementary dualism, and the sharing of divine essences. This chapter lays the foundation for the rest of the book.

Chapter 5 begins the iconographic analysis of the White Shaman mural. In this chapter I present an analysis of the art as informed by ethnohistoric and ethnographic observations of the Huichols. This is where I offer hypothetical meanings for the art by connecting the artistic motifs identified in chapter 5 with concepts discussed in chapter 4 and, more specifically, with Huichol myths and rituals. Chapter 5 opens with a brief introduction to the Huichols' creation story and their ritual reenactment of the birth of the sun, peyote, and the creation of time. This is followed by a reading of the mural, beginning with a detailed description of pictographic motifs and their correlation to Huichol cosmology and elements of the Mesoamerican core.

Chapter 6 presents an iconographic analysis of the art as informed by historical accounts and ethnographic observations of other Native American groups—in particular, the Nahuatl-speaking people of central Mexico. This chapter is, in a sense, a test of the hypothesis that the rock art is a graphic manifestation of ancient interrelated and intermeshed Mesoamerican ideas. If it is, it should fit into the basic structure of that broader continuum and be "readable" using historical accounts and ethnographic observations of indigenous groups living in Mesoamerica beyond the Huichol. I follow the same process used in chapter 6, beginning with a detailed description of the pictographs followed by their analogues in Nahua myth and ritual.

Chapter 7 synthesizes and examines the results of chapters 5 and 6, which I use to reconstruct the narrative and propose a general myth that informed production of the White Shaman mural. This reading is then assessed within the framework of linguistics and semiotics. Here we are no longer concerned with identifying the narrative of the White Shaman mural, but with the underlying ideological assumptions of the society within which the visual narrative operated. We examine the mural's intrinsic meaning and gain insight into the worldview of Lower Pecos artists.

The reader will note that throughout the book I often use the words *we* and *our*. This book is the result of hundreds of hours of collaborative research with Kim Cox and innumerable brainstorming sessions with Shumla staff. It is *we* who developed the ideas woven throughout this text, not just *I*.

THE PAINTED LANDSCAPE

> Not only do we find a pleasing variety and combination of colors on individual pictures, but the arrangement of color masses in large groups is much more than accidental. It indicates a sense of color balance unsurpassed by painters of our own time.
>
> FORREST KIRKLAND (1938:31–32)

Lower Pecos Canyonlands

White Shaman Shelter is located at the heart of the Lower Pecos Canyonlands. Due to a unique combination of ecological and geological factors, rockshelters here contain some of the best-preserved and longest records of Native American lifeways—from 11,000 years ago to European contact. As a result, the Lower Pecos Canyonlands is considered one of the most significant archaeological regions in the world. Although its boundaries are ill-defined, the visual and material culture characterizing the region and its prehistoric inhabitants extends approximately 70 miles north and 90 miles south of the United States–Mexico border, from near the hamlet of Sheffield, Texas, to the Arroyo de la Babia in Coahuila, Mexico. East and west the region stretches approximately 80 miles between the tiny communities of Carta Valley and Dryden, Texas. At the region's center, the Pecos River converges with the Rio Grande. White Shaman Shelter is located here in a small tributary canyon of the Pecos River (figure 2.1).

Over the millennia these rivers and their tributaries have sliced through masses of gray and white limestone. It is a dramatic landscape incised by deep, narrow gorges. Along the upper reaches of canyons grow succulents and rosette-stemmed evergreens such as prickly pear, tasajillo, yucca, and lechuguilla. These are joined by small trees such as mesquite, acacia, buckthorn, Texas persimmon, and spiny hackberry. When William Whiting traveled through the region in 1849 while exploring a new trade route between Missouri and Mexico, he painted a different picture of the vegetation. As he approached the divide between the Devils and Pecos Rivers, about 15 miles east of the White Shaman site, Whiting ([1849] 1938:340) described the area as a succession of valleys and hills, "the valleys covered with luxuriant crops of fine grass and the hills no longer obstructed by the limestone bluffs which hindered our march yesterday." During the last hundred years of overgrazing, the "luxuriant crops of fine grass" have been replaced by thorny scrub.

Beyond the Pecos to the west are rolling hills covered in shallow soils supporting vegetation commonly associated with the Chihuahuan Desert, such as sotol, lechuguilla, and creosote bush. To the east, past the Devils River, are the coastal plains. The vegetation here transitions into the mesquite-blackbrush acacia, shortgrass savannah typical of southern Texas. About 10 miles north of the White Shaman site the vegetation grades into the juniper-oak, shortgrass savanna characteristic of the Edwards Plateau. Looking south into Mexico one can see the Planos del Coahuila and, rising out of the plains less than 75 miles from the Rio Grande, the Serranías del Burro, an impressive mountain range with elevations exceeding 5,000 feet. Vegetation changes substantially within the Burros, transitioning from Chihuahuan desert scrub to oak chaparral, to piñon woodland, and finally to a mixed-conifer forest with Ponderosa pine and Douglas fir. Today the mountains are often obscured by a yellow haze of pollution from both sides of the border. Locals say that fifty years ago you could see the Burros clearly all the time and, in the winter, their snow-capped peaks (figure 2.2).

Climate in the region varies significantly between the north and south. The semiarid region surrounding White Shaman Shelter experiences extreme annual variability in climate with frequent droughts as well as unpredictable, catastrophic floods. Average annual rain-

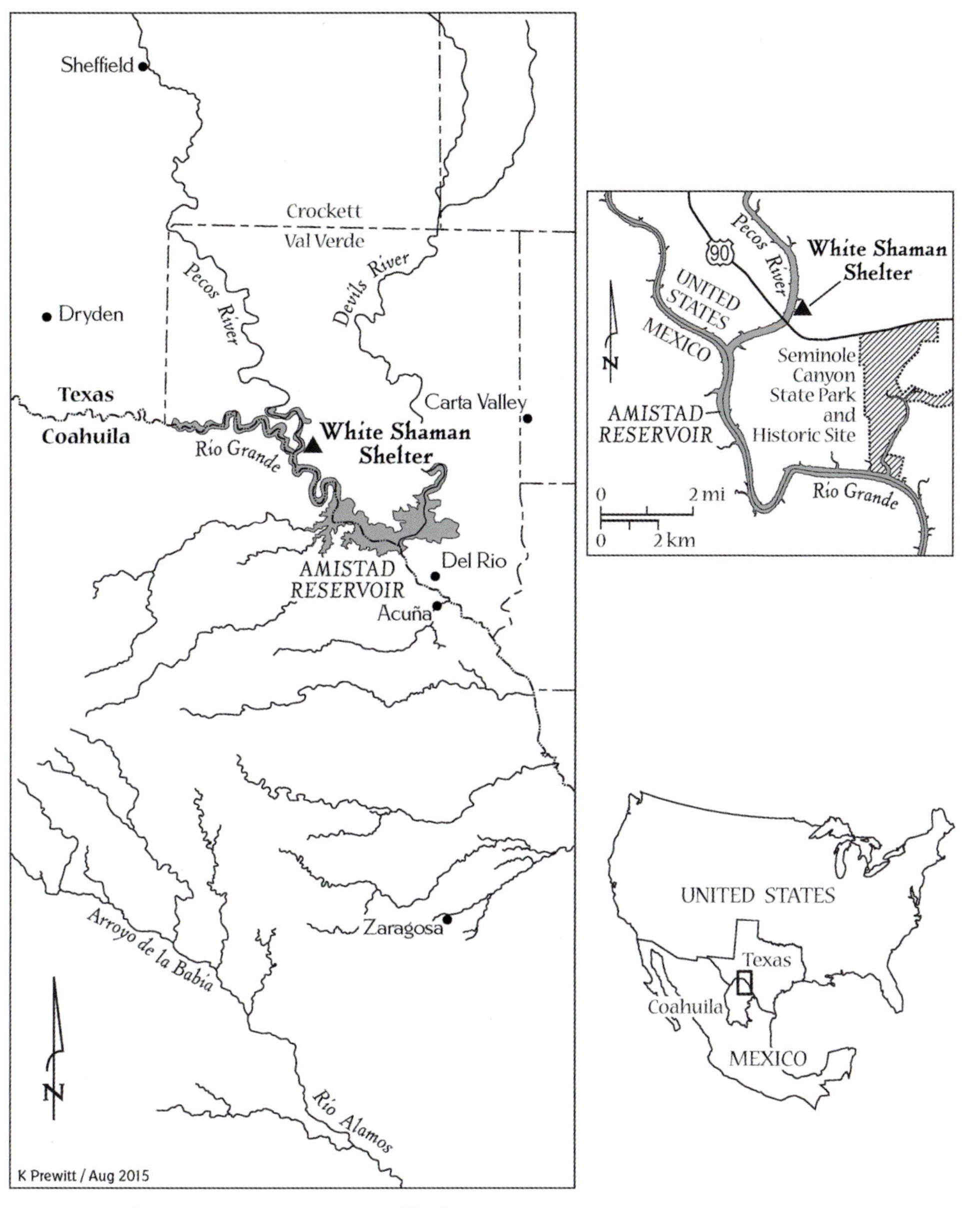

Figure 2.1. Map of the Lower Pecos cultural area. Map by Kerza Prewitt. Courtesy of Shumla Archaeological Research and Education Center.

fall is only about 17 inches, most of which occurs in two peaks: in spring (April–May) and early fall (September–October). The summer months (June–August) are very dry unless a hurricane tracks across south Texas and up the Rio Grande. In contrast, in the foothills of the Serranías del Burro, just a two-day walk south, the monsoon brings up to 16 inches of rain between June and September, but there is little to no precipitation from January through May. From the White Shaman site you can see the summer rains falling on the Burros. The artists who created the mural would have been intimately familiar with this entire region, including its vegetation and changing climate.

Cultural History of *el Despoblado*

People traveling west from Del Rio along Highway 90 often consider the landscape desolate and unwelcoming: a rough, dry, prickly, forsaken land with little to offer in the way of creature comforts. Early Spanish explorers apparently viewed the landscape surrounding

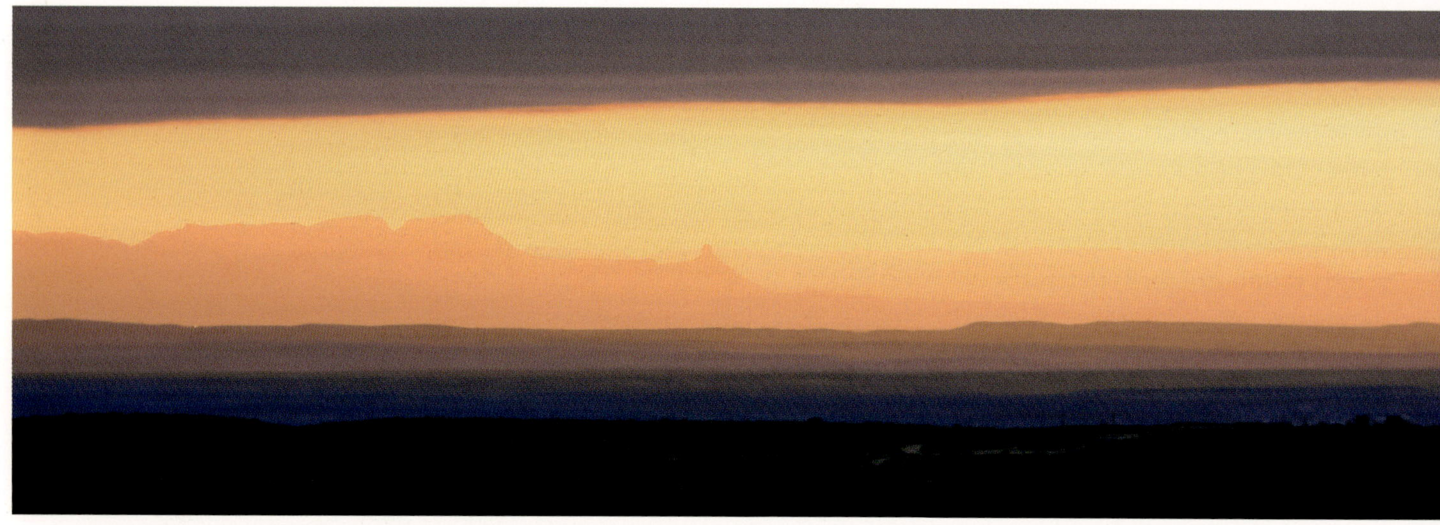

Figure 2.2. The Serranías del Burro at sunset. From the Galloway Preserve and the White Shaman site, the mountains of Mexico are visible on the horizon. Photo by Jack Johnson.

the junction of the Pecos and Devils Rivers with the Rio Grande similarly, referring to it as *el despoblado*, the uninhabited place. Some have speculated that the Indians fled from the Spaniards to avoid enslavement. Although slavery was forbidden by the Crown's laws, *Leyes nuevas*, in 1542, the laws were often disregarded. It seems reasonable to suppose that local residents were not eager to encounter the Spaniards, but there is no documented proof that they fled the region to avoid contact with them. Equally, if not more, plausible is the possibility that the Native population was decimated by European diseases arriving in advance of the Spanish explorers as they moved northward.

In 1590 Gaspar Castaño de Sosa's expedition traveled through the Lower Pecos on the way to New Mexico. In his journal, he provides little information about Native peoples encountered in this region, with one notable exception: a large group of "Tepeguan" camped along the Pecos River near what is now the Val Verde–Crockett County line (Schroeder and Matson 1965:50; Sosa 1871).[1] They reportedly had traveled 325 miles north from their homeland in Durango, Mexico, to hunt the bison that were in abundance there during the sixteenth century (Foster 2008:177; Schroeder and Matson 1965:50). One of the favored crossing points for groups traveling back and forth across the Rio Grande was around what is now the city of Del Rio, less than 50 miles east of the White Shaman site.

By the mid-seventeenth century, accounts mentioned significant numbers of Native Americans either occupying or traveling through the region.[2] Substantive information about them is, however, minimal at best. According to Wade (2003:xx), the archival information is "fragmentary, disjointed, and reflective of the lack of value attributed by Europeans to the social and cultural practices of these groups." Out of the hundreds of groups noted in Spanish records, the Gueiquesale (known also as Hueyquetzales, Quesale, and Quetzal, among a long list of other names) were one of the largest of those inhabiting the Lower Pecos Canyonlands during the seventeenth century.[3] Like all other Native groups in the region, they were mobile hunters and gatherers. Their territory was centered somewhere around Del Rio, extending north and west to the canyons of the Devils and Pecos Rivers and south into Coahuila. It is important to remember that aboriginal territories were not static, fixed points on the landscape, and Native groups did not live in isolation.

Foster (2008:243) describes these Native groups as "cosmopolitan" because they were multilingual and well-traveled, with incredible knowledge of geography. Native guides hired by Spanish explorers led expeditions along well-established trade routes between Mexico and Texas. These routes connected distant territories and distant peoples, providing interregional and intercontinental corridors along which material goods and ideas traveled for millennia.

Lower Pecos Prehistory

People were living in the Lower Pecos Canyonlands thousands of years before Europeans arrived, and they likely wore out many sandals establishing trade routes later traveled by the Spaniards. What we know of these people we have learned from what they left behind. Preserved within dry rockshelters are deeply stratified deposits and polychromatic murals providing a window into Native American lifeways in the Lower Pecos.

Paleoindian Period (12,500–8000 BC)

Although we do not yet know when people first arrived in the Lower Pecos, the archaeological record firmly establishes a human presence in the region by ten thousand years ago. At the famous bison-jump site of Bonfire Shelter, Folsom and Plainview dart points, which were made only during the Paleoindian period, were recovered (Dibble and Lorraine 1968; Turpin 1991). This same deposit contained butchered remains of an estimated 120 to 200 *Bison antiquus*, a species that has been extinct for thousands of years.

As documented by the region's artifact assemblage dating to around nine thousand years ago, by this time the lifeways of Paleoindian groups had changed. The Pleistocene megafauna had mostly become extinct, resulting in a Late Paleoindian subsistence economy emphasizing smaller game and more plant foods. The environment was also warming rapidly during this period. It is quite likely that the region was already experiencing modern climatic conditions (Bryant and Holloway 1985).

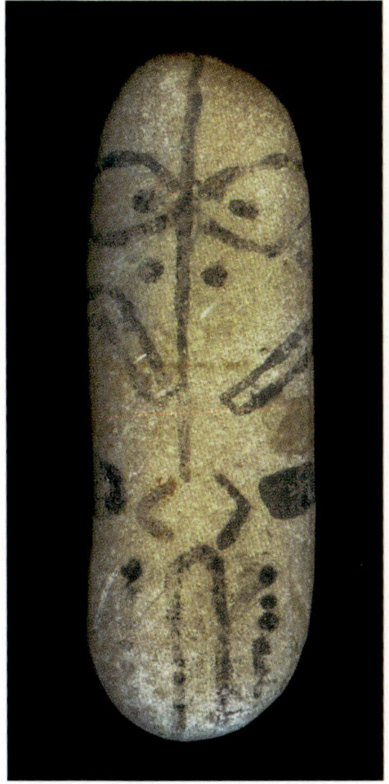
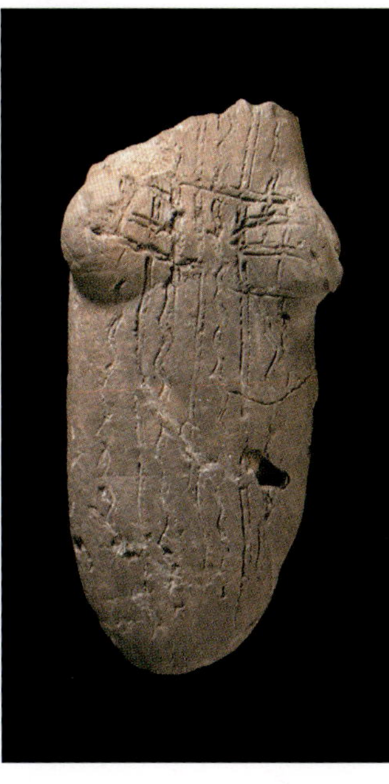

Figure 2.3. Portable visual culture: (a) Stream-rolled limestone pebble painted with designs extending around lateral edges onto reverse face (5 1/4 inches x 1 1/2 inches). Specimen no. 0411, Skiles Collection. Photo by Elton R. Prewitt. b) Clay female figurine (2 inches x 4/5 inch) from Coontail Spin (41VV82). Courtesy of Amistad National Recreation Area Collection at Texas Archeological Research Laboratory, AMIS 27620.

Early Archaic Period (8000–4000 BC)

Climate records are not entirely clear, but apparently the climate continued to dry out during the Early Archaic period (Bryant and Holloway 1985). The cultural record, however, is much more vivid. The combination of a semiarid climate, deep canyons, and dry rockshelters created perfect conditions for preserving the archaeological record of the region's Archaic hunter-gatherers. Both coiled and plaited basketry and various tool forms—including oval unifacial tools, manos, metates, and bedrock mortars—have been documented. Cordage made from lechuguilla and yucca was utilized in nets, snares, tools, and sandals. The technology of basketry and sandal manufacture was so similar to that documented at sites in northern Mexico that affiliation with groups to the south and west in Coahuila has been postulated (Andrews and Adovasio 1980; McGregor 1992).

Two types of portable art are known from the Early Archaic: painted pebbles (Parsons 1986) and clay figurines (Shafer 1975) (figure 2.3). Many of the painted pebbles are thought to represent human figures, usually female, and the clay figurines have exaggerated feminine attributes (Shafer 1975).

Middle Archaic Period (4000–1500 BC)

As population increased and the region became more arid, people grew increasingly reliant on small animals and a greater variety of plant resources (Hester 1980). A definitive change in how people lived off the land is documented by an increased presence of earth ovens to cook lechuguilla (*Agave lechuguilla*) and sotol (*Dasylirion texanum*) (Dering 1999; Shafer and Bryant 1977).

Reduced mobility during this period is suggested by increased diversity in artifact assemblages (Turpin 1995). An increase in population density is indicated by higher numbers of both upland and lowland sites in the region (Marmaduke 1978). This apparent increase in population density was accompanied by the appearance of a complex, polychrome pictographic art form, termed the Pecos River style. This art form is considered a hallmark of the Archaic in the Lower Pecos and can be found as far south as Arroyo de la Babia in Coahuila, Mexico (Turpin 2010).

Late Archaic Period (1500 BC–AD 1000)

At the beginning of the Late Archaic the environment is thought to have become cooler and wetter, promoting the expansion of grasslands, which allowed bison to return to the region. By the final one thousand years of this period, however, a steady increase in aridity is implied by a drop in percentages of grass and tree pollen and by disappearance of bison from archaeological deposits (Bryant and Holloway 1985; Turpin 1995). This time period also is marked by the presence of the Shumla point type. Since this type of point has also been recovered from Cueva de la Zona in Nuevo León, Mexico, it has been suggested that people from the plains of Coahuila and surrounding mountains moved into the Lower Pecos Canyonlands following the withdrawal of bison hunters (Turpin 1991, 1995).

Late Prehistoric (AD 1000–1500)

The Late Prehistoric period is marked by the appearance of the bow and arrow in the Lower Pecos (Hester 1995; Turpin 1995). The earliest appearance of arrow points in the region occurred around AD 650 (Turpin 1991). To the south, in Nuevo León, Mexico, arrow points date to around AD 950 at La Calsada (Nance 1992) and to around AD 800 at Cueva de la Zona. The practice of mural painting continued during this period. Red Monochrome style rock art portrays people wielding bows and arrows, and realistically depicted animals (Turpin 1991).

Social Organization in the Lower Pecos

Throughout prehistory, inhabitants of the Lower Pecos lived in small, mobile groups often referred to as "bands." Band size among foragers varies from small, single-family groups to as many as 150 to 200 people. The number of people constituting a band depends on several factors, such as the nature and quantity of available resources and the number of times a group changes residence. In the Lower Pecos, band size was probably limited to no more than twenty-five to thirty people, with smaller, family-sized bands of ten to fifteen individuals during the winter or lean seasons (Shafer 1988, 2013). Generally, band-organized societies are egalitarian, meaning all individuals of a particular age-sex category have equal access to prestige and resources. The concept of private property would have been alien to Lower Pecos folk, with sharing of virtually all resources the rule.

Band mobility was determined by local resource availability, including small and large game and, to a lesser extent, plant resources. Although larger game animals, such as deer, provided a more substantial source of protein, they were not always available and were not a regular part of the diet. Studies of coprolites (desiccated human feces) and middens (prehistoric trash dumps) indicate that the people of the Lower Pecos ate a very wide variety of foods; no single resource occurred in sufficient abundance to be relied upon for a majority of the diet. The unpredictable, semiarid climate, shallow soils, and deep canyons with narrow terraces prone to catastrophic floods limited the means by which people could live off the land. As a result, during the entire history of the region they were hunters of game, gatherers of wild plants, and fishers. Unlike areas to the south and west, which actually had less (but more predictable) rainfall, farming was seldom, if ever, practiced in the Lower Pecos (Dering 1999).

Eating a wide variety of foods is one way to reduce risk of starvation in an unpredictable environment (K. Brown 1991); however, certain stable resources made a very important contribution to diet and technology in the Lower Pecos. These resources included the xeric evergreen rosette plants—lechuguilla, sotol, beargrass, and several species of yucca—and various cacti, oaks, and grasses, as well as small game such as fish, rabbits, and rodents. In addition to providing nutrients, agave, sotol, and yucca were used to make baskets, sandals, netting, and textiles, as well as for fuel, bedding, and floor covering. In fact, at least thirty-five wild plant foods and fifty to sixty types of small animals provided the caloric intake for the hunter-gatherers of the Lower Pecos (Dering 1999; Lord 1984).

In part because they consumed a wide variety of plant foods and small game, and in part because the locally available resources were quickly exhausted, the Lower Pecos folk ranged widely across the landscape and changed residence often. Sobolik (1996) suggests a seasonal round covering more than 100 miles. Dering (1999) maintains that they moved frequently as they exhausted food and fuel resources in the narrow canyons. Although no one can describe exactly how often they moved or where their annual movements took them, we understand that these people were quite mobile. They remained in one place long enough, however, to paint elaborate murals on the walls of canyons and rockshelters. And they returned to these places repeatedly to conduct rituals and to affirm other social contracts.

It is not unusual for people to think of these prehistoric hunters and gatherers as being vastly different from us. In some ways they certainly were. They didn't have agriculture, houses with central air and heat, cars, or the Internet. But they were more like us than they were different. They awoke in the morning to the sounds of their children's laughter and, after getting the sleep out of their eyes, went about the work of providing for their family's needs. They made plans for the future, shared memories of the past, and took care of the business before them each day. They loved; they hated; they had successes and failures. They had good days and bad. They worshipped, sang songs, played instruments, and told stories. But, unlike us, they didn't live in a self-contained, built environment. They were part of the land; they belonged to the land.

These were anatomically modern humans with the same cognitive capacity and capabilities as you and I have. They had the same brain that put a man on the moon. Yes, they had an oral language—likely one with a vocabulary far richer than we can ever imagine when it comes to describing life, death, the land, and the heavens. Still, people have a hard time accepting that these prehistoric hunters and gatherers were thinking, feeling, and intellectually capable humans. In *The Land of the Tejas* (2012), John Arnn writes:

> Imagine humans so sophisticated that they were capable of adapting to any situation and overcoming any obstacle . . . Thousands of years before agriculture was developed, the first cities built, and the first armies formed, *families* had successfully conquered almost every inhabitable niche on Earth . . . The triumphs and tragedies of these migrations were not the achievements of "simple" or "primitive" humans, but rather the culmination of tens of thousands of years of application, experience, and assimilation by the modern human mind. [Arnn 2012:21]

That these prehistoric residents were socially well organized and intellectually capable is amply demonstrated in the archaeological record. The most compelling evidence, however, comes from their visual culture.

Visual Culture of the Lower Pecos Canyonlands

What is *visual culture*? The term is best defined by looking at each word individually. First, it applies to artifacts whose meaning is primarily *visual*, and second, *culture* refers to the context within which the visual artifact operated. According to Duncum (2001:106–107), the term "suggests an interest in the social conditions in which visual artifacts have their being, including their production, distribution, and use."[4] In the Lower Pecos, visual culture includes such artifacts as small painted pebbles and stone plaquettes, engraved freshwater mussel shells, painted and engraved objects made of wood or bone, painted baskets, clay figurines, and the magnificent rock paintings (pictographs) and engravings (petroglyphs) found throughout the region. I refer to pictographs and petroglyphs collectively as "rock art" in this book. I recognize that the term *art* is problematic, fraught with highly variable and often hotly contested definitions. I will not enter into the "Is rock art really 'Art'?" debate here.

Pictographs are the most common type of rock art found in the Lower Pecos, and these have been classified into five categories: Pecos River, Red Linear, Bold Line Geometric, Red Monochrome, and Historic Period. By far the most abundant and visually impressive is the Pecos River style. Easily recognized by its multicolored designs and striking anthropomorphic (humanlike), zoomorphic (animal-like), and enigmatic figures, Pecos River panels are ambitious in their scale and technical in their execution (figure 2.4). For more than twenty years archaeologists thought this was the oldest style in the region; however, Pecos River imagery overlays diminutive Red Linear pictographs (Boyd et al. 2013). Perhaps W. W. Newcomb (1976:181) was correct when he stated that Red Linear "is probably a product of the same artist, although produced for a different purpose." Regardless, Red Linear pictographs, which are interspersed throughout the extensive Pecos

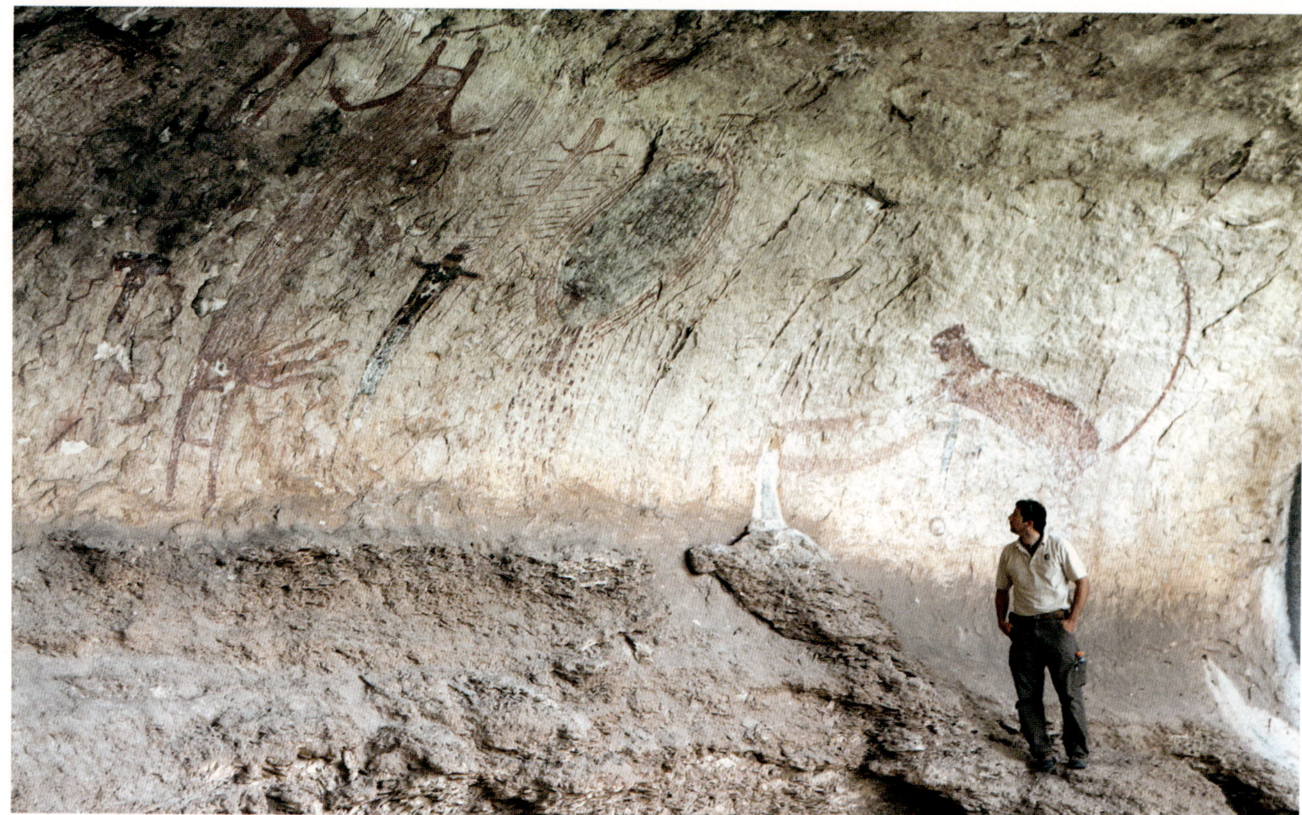

Figure 2.4. *(above)* The Pecos River style mural at Panther Cave (41VV83) is approximately 150 feet long and 15 feet high. This photograph shows only a small section of the shelter. The anthropomorph with upraised arms at the left side of the photo stands 10 1/2 feet tall. Photo by Michael Amador. Courtesy of the Texas Department of Transportation.

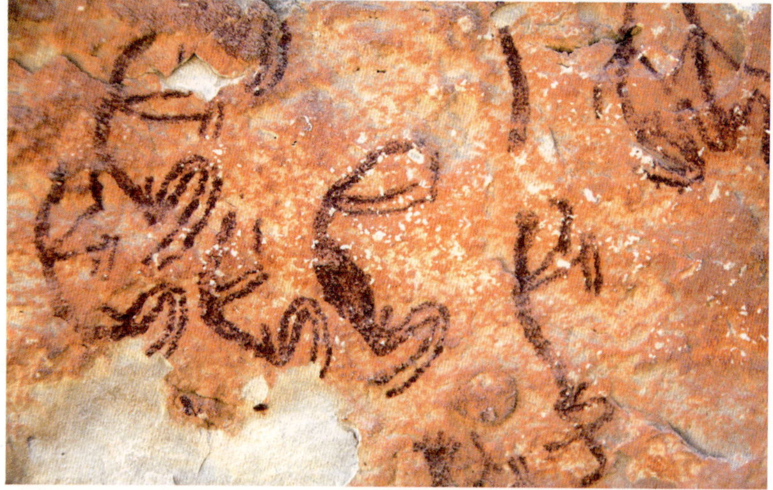

Figure 2.5. *(right, top)* Red Linear style pictographs at the Red Linear type site (41VV201). Each anthropomorph is approximately 4 inches high.

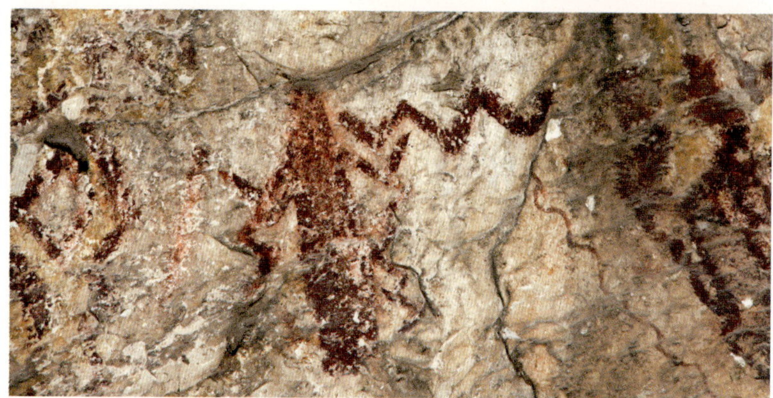

Figure 2.6. *(right, bottom)* Bold Line Geometric style at Parida Cave (41VV187).

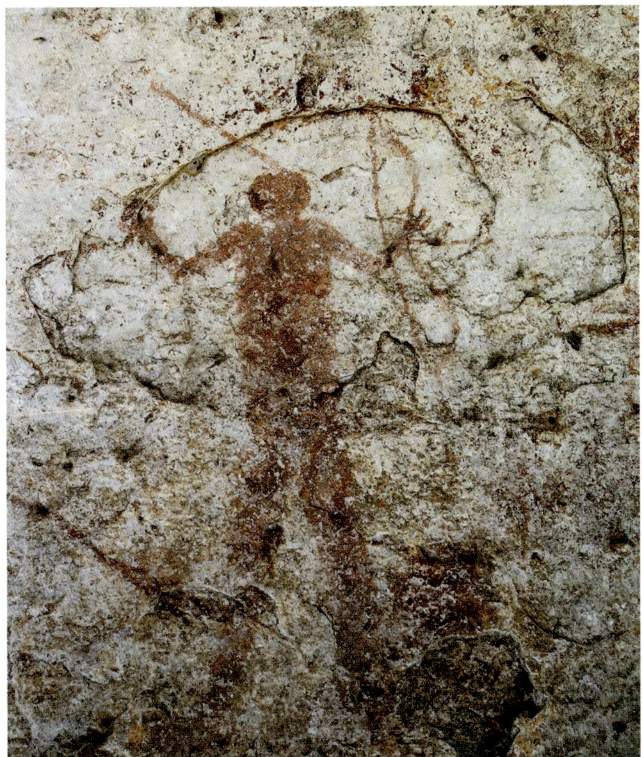

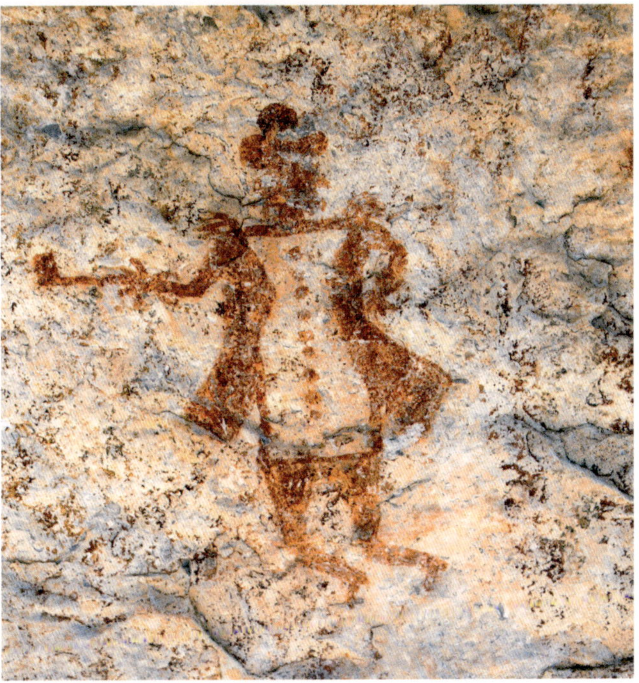

Figure 2.7. *(top)* Red Monochrome style anthropomorph from Painted Shelter (41VV78). It is approximately 5 feet tall and is holding a recurved bow in its left hand.

Figure 2.8. *(bottom)* Historic period rock art. A Spanish military officer wearing a uniform and holding a pipe is portrayed at Vaquero Shelter (41VV77) in Seminole Canyon State Park and Historic Site.

River panels, are smaller on average than all other defined styles in the region (figure 2.5). Both styles were produced during the Middle and Late Archaic periods. Bold Line Geometric contains abstract patterns including zigzags, lattices, and herringbones along with small anthropomorphic and zoomorphic figures (figure 2.6). Turpin (1986) proposes that this style was produced during the Late Prehistoric, the same period in which the Red Monochrome style begins. Red Monochrome paintings show front-facing human figures carrying bows and arrows, and animals realistically rendered in profile or dorsal view (figure 2.7). Historic Period rock art is the most accessible to direct interpretation because it contains figures easily recognizable to most audiences: the cattle, horses, missions, and robed figures emblematic of European contact (figure 2.8).

Pecos River Style Rock Art

The pictographs of White Shaman Shelter are classified as Pecos River style. This is the most complex and compositionally intricate of the regional rock art styles. An array of earth colors were used to create murals that are extraordinary in the level of skill required to produce them, as well as sheer size and complexity. Some of the panels are massive, measuring over 100 feet long and 30 feet high; others are small, tucked away in secluded alcoves high above the canyon floor (figure 2.9).

More than two hundred rockshelters north of the Rio Grande contain Pecos River style imagery. South of the border, in Coahuila, Mexico, at least thirty-five Pecos River style sites have been identified. Solveig Turpin (2010:41), who recently published a book on Coahuila rock art, maintains that "there are surely scores more in the secluded canyons and caves in the sierras north of Arroyo de la Babia."

Pictographic elements in Pecos River style murals on both sides of the border include anthropomorphs, zoomorphs, a wide range of geometric imagery, and enigmatic figures that are not identifiable as human or animal. Anthropomorphs are the most frequently depicted element (figure 2.10). Although these figures share many characteristics—such as elongated, rectangular bodies with disproportionally short arms and legs—among them there is incredible diversity. They typically average in size between 3 and 7 feet; however,

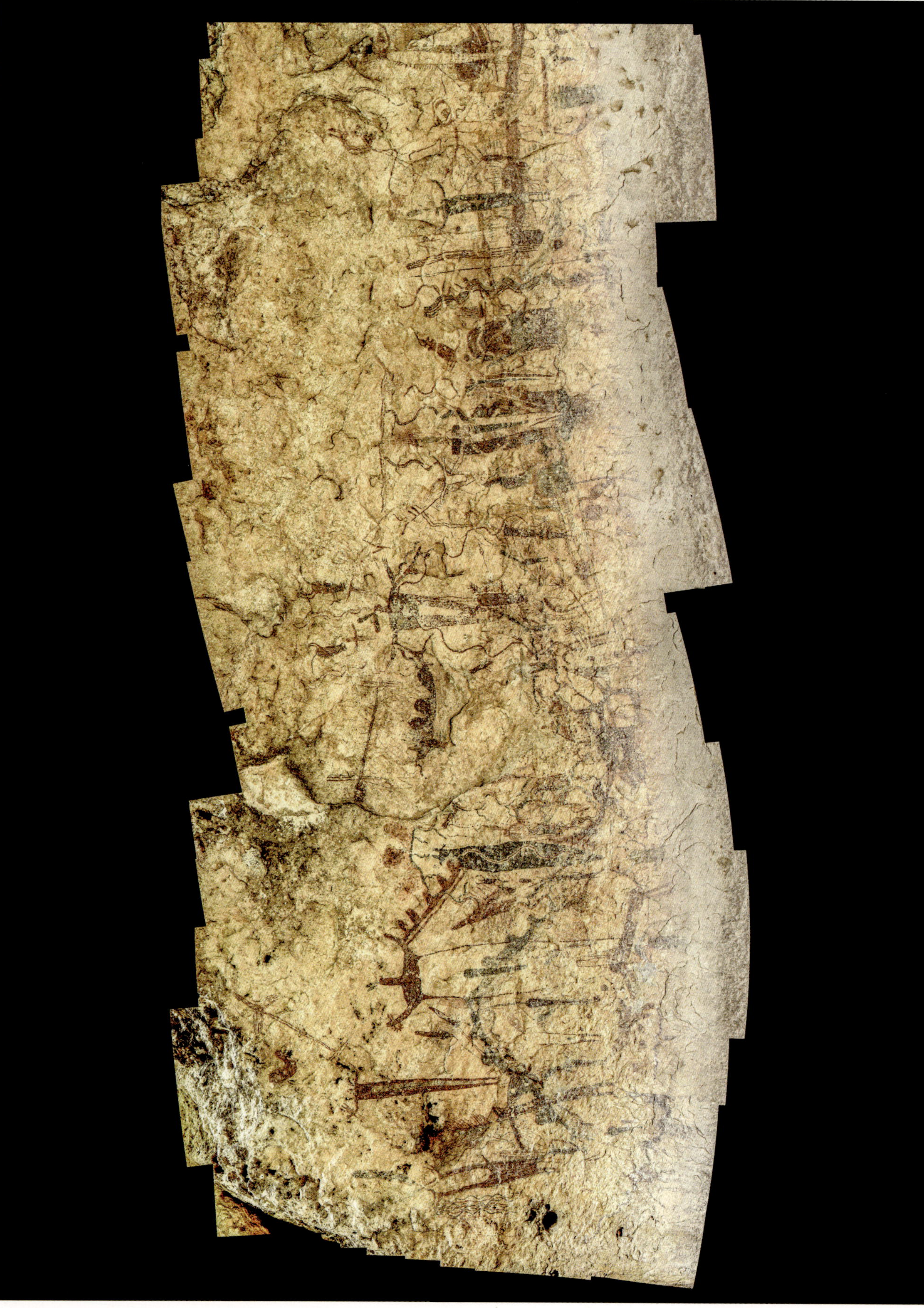

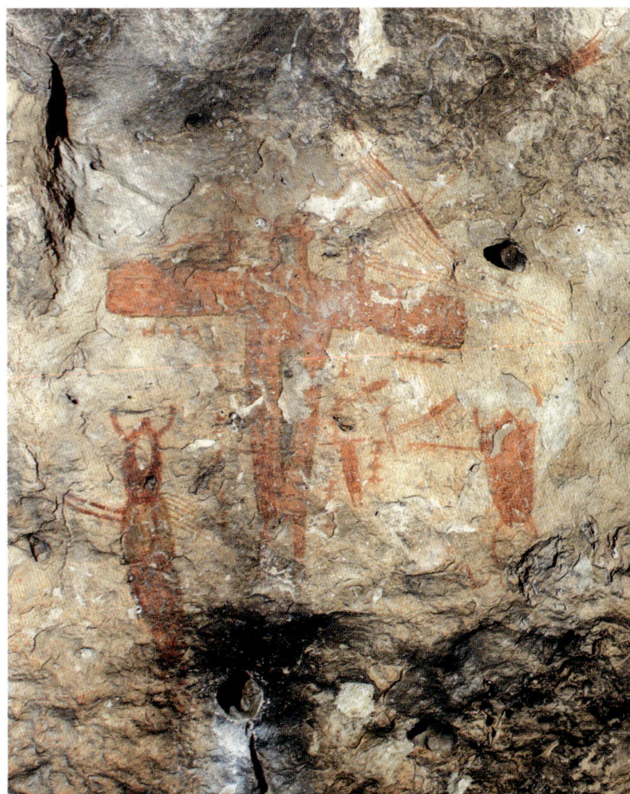

Figure 2.9. Pecos River style murals: (a) *(facing page)* Gigapan image of approximately a quarter of the Rattlesnake Canyon mural (41VV180), which is 106 feet long and contains more than 250 figures. Photo by Rupestrian Cyberservices. Courtesy of Amistad National Recreation Area. (b) *(above)* Raymond's Shelter is a small mural (less than 10 feet long) portraying only a dozen or so figures.

some are monumental, towering more than 20 feet high, while others are pocket-sized, standing only 3 inches tall.

These fascinating figures often are elaborately executed in red, yellow, black, and white, but at other times plainly painted in only one color. Not only is there variability in the form and color of these figures, but also in the accoutrements and paraphernalia associated with them. Headdresses of varying types, clusters of feathers at the waist, and wrist or elbow tassels often adorn these humanlike figures. Generally the artists portrayed anthropomorphs wielding paraphernalia such as atlatls and darts in their right hand. In the left hand they frequently hold staffs, feathered darts, and rabbit sticks. But sometimes none of these items are present, or they are associated with the opposite hand.

Animals are also portrayed in the paintings and, as do anthropomorphs, exhibit significant diversity. Deer and felines are the most visually prominent (figure 2.11). Deer are typically painted red, but also can be yellow, black, white, or a combination of colors. Some are portrayed with antlers, tails, hooves, and dew claws, but others with only antlers or hooves. Most of the time, but not always, they are impaled with a dart. Felines tend to be painted larger than life. A few are massive, measuring over 8 feet from the tip of the tail to the tip of the nose. Although most frequently painted red, they are also portrayed in yellow, black, and white, or a combination thereof. Birds are small, easily overlooked, and often painted in more than one color. Some imagery resembles insects, such as caterpillars, dragonflies, and moths or butterflies. Sinuous, snakelike figures are also portrayed. Some appear to be spewing venom, and others are incredibly long, spanning up to 20 feet and bedecked with dots and horns (figure 2.12).

For decades conventional wisdom held that these murals represented numerous painting episodes executed by different artists over hundreds or even thousands of years. We now know that most are not a random collection of images painted over the course of time but, rather, compositionally intricate, highly patterned, and rule-governed visual texts. The Lower Pecos artists used pieces of ochre or charcoal to sketch out and organize the elements of their compositions. Vestiges of these preliminary sketches still can be seen today. At Cedar Springs, red paint was sprayed around a stencil to produce a finely executed negative image of a 3 1/2-foot-tall anthropomorph. And at numerous sites, long, crisp lines with slightly raised paint along the outer perimeter suggest the use of a straightedge. Production of these panels was no small undertaking. Significant time and effort went into planning the composition, obtaining resources to make paint, creating the artist's tools, and constructing scaffolds or ladders, not to mention the rituals that likely accompanied each step in the process. The rock art of the Lower Pecos Canyonlands was part of the living landscape that provided food, shelter, and a connection with the spirit world. The canvases provided by rockshelter walls, such as those at the White Shaman site, played a significant role in how these people depicted and recorded their knowledge, revealing a deep, complex cosmology that we are now beginning to understand.

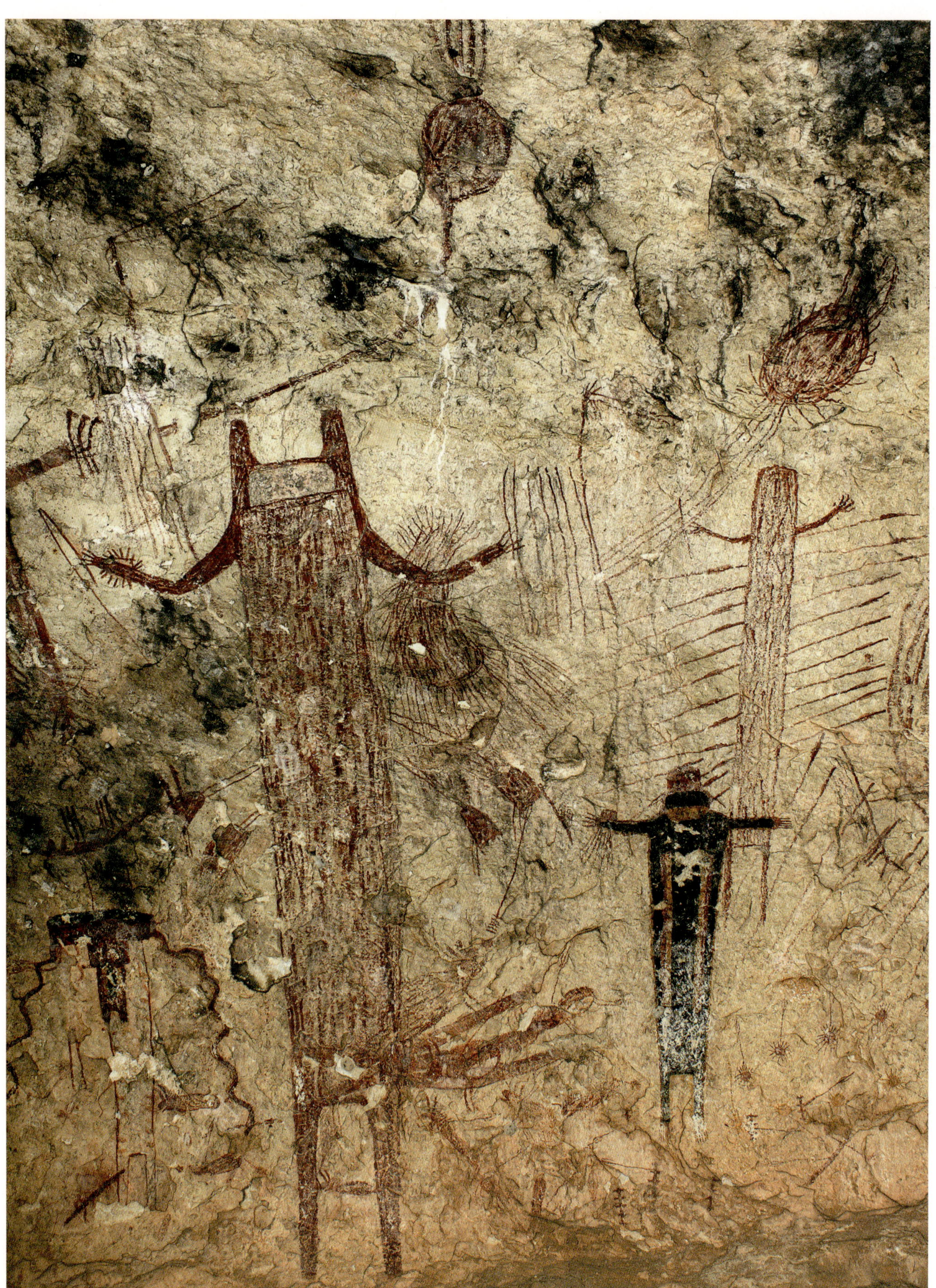

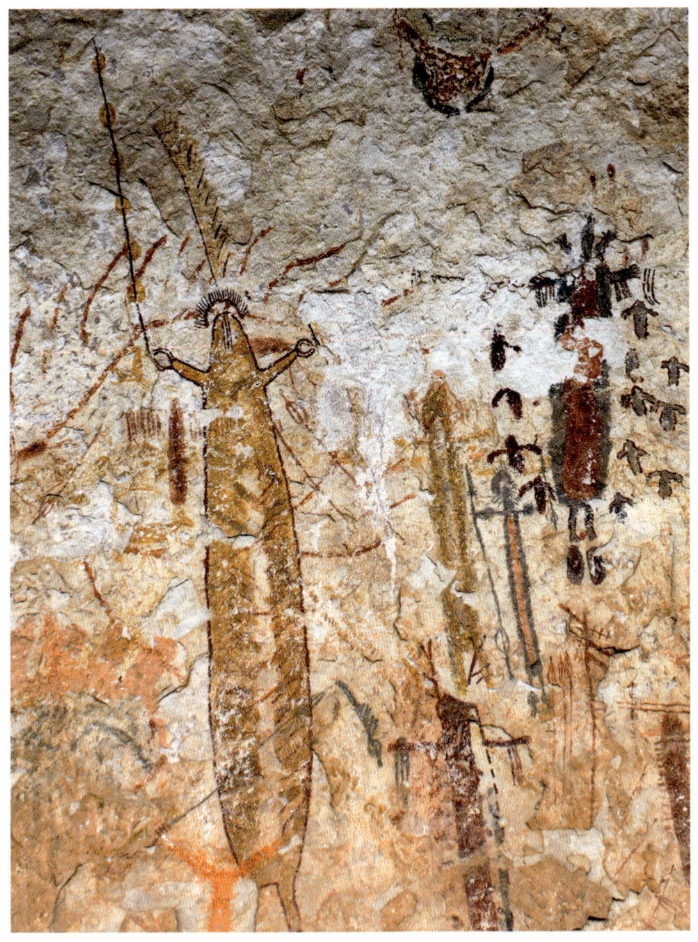

Figure 2.10. Pecos River style anthropomorphs: (a) *(facing page)* A 10-foot-tall anthropomorph in Panther Cave (41VV83) with upraised arms, U-shaped head, and a feather hip-cluster-like adornment on its left side. An atlatl loaded with a dart is portrayed in the figure's right hand, and in its left hand are additional darts as well as other paraphernalia. Photo by Jean Clottes. Courtesy of Shumla Archaeological Research and Education Center. (b) *(left)* Halo Shelter (41VV1230) houses this beautiful polychromatic anthropomorph measuring 3 feet from head to toe. A large, stafflike object is held in the figure's right hand by pincherlike fingers. A complex headdress extends another foot above the halo crowning the head of this finely executed figure. (c) *(below)* This 4-foot-tall, white anthropomorph at Cedar Springs (41VV696) is outlined in red with faint red lines running vertically down its center alongside a wide, central black band. The figure's red head and open mouth face the two atlatls held in its right hand. Two staffs are in its left hand.

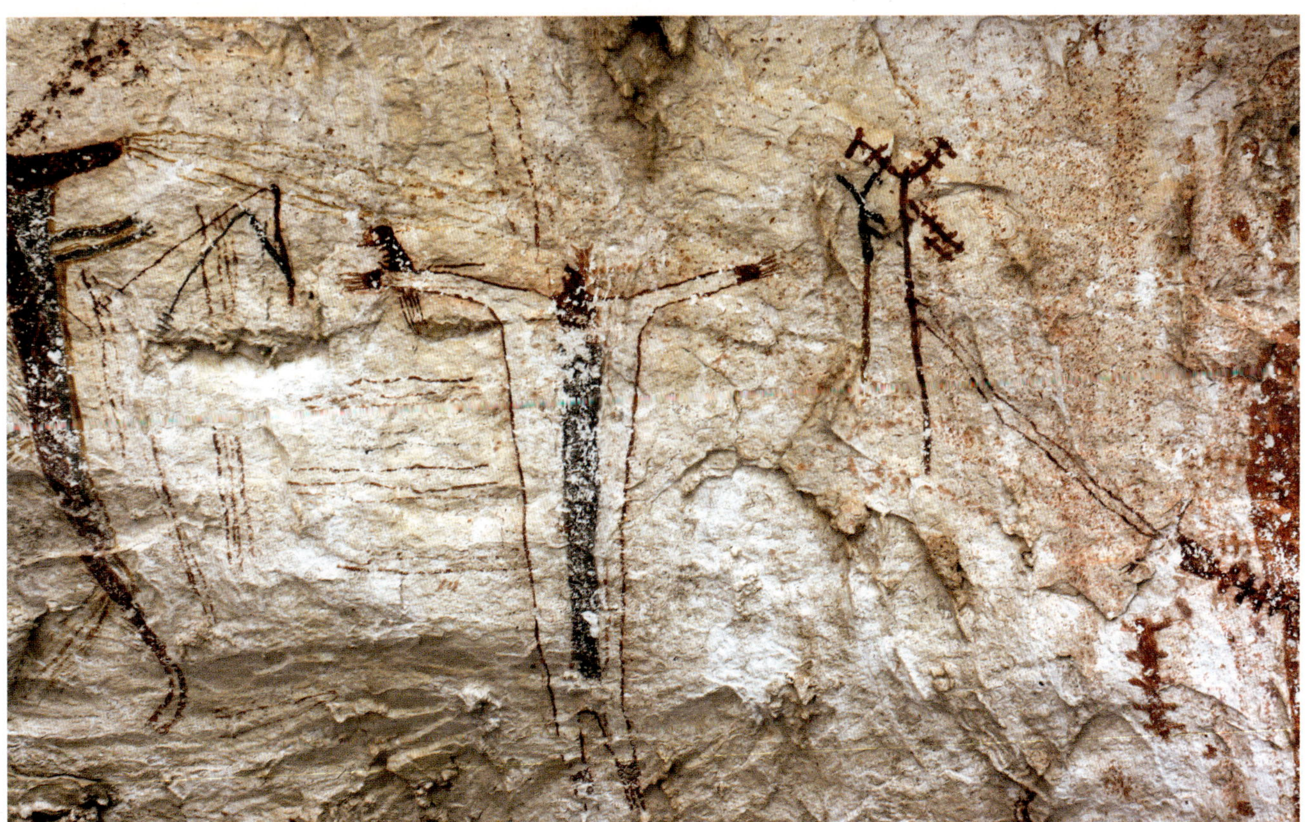

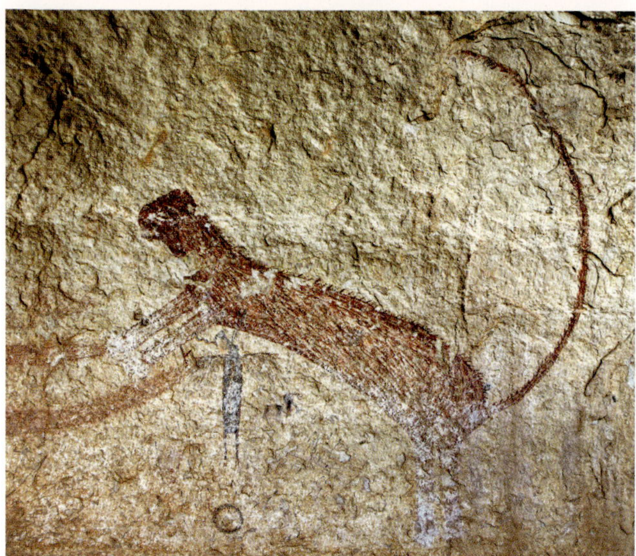

Figure 2.11. Pecos River style zoomorphs: (a) An antlered deer from Mystic Shelter (41VV612) measuring 1 1/2 feet long and impaled in its underbelly by a spear. Small Red Linear style figures are barely visible just below the deer. (b) Panther Cave (41VV83) was named for the many feline figures portrayed in the mural, including this 9-foot-long "panther" located at the downstream end of the shelter.

Dating Pecos River Style

In the late 1980s, Marvin Rowe, his student Jon Russ, and their colleagues in the chemistry laboratory at Texas A&M University pioneered the radiocarbon dating of pictographs (Rowe 2013; Russ et al. 1990). The Lower Pecos served as their initial study area. Russ et al. (1990) obtained the first radiocarbon date for an inorganic-pigmented rock painting anywhere in the world, and their results were published in *Nature*. The paint sample came from a Pecos River style panel in Seminole Canyon State Park and Historic Site. Since this pioneering work, thirty radiocarbon assays have been obtained from seventeen Pecos River style figures distributed across nine sites (Steelman et al., forthcoming).[5] The dates obtained for these seventeen figures range from 4200 ± 90 to 1465 ± 50 RCYBP (radiocarbon years before present). If accurate, the 4,200-year-old painting is the oldest dated pictograph in North America (Bates et al. 2015).[6] In calendar years this translates to approximately 2700 BC; however, as Rowe (2005:262) cautions, "[C]are must be taken when interpreting radiocarbon ages of pictographs."

There are significant limitations in using radiocarbon dating to estimate the age of rock paintings. Radiocarbon assays are obtained by extracting datable organic materials from a small sample of the pictograph, about the size of your thumbnail. Because of damage to the paintings, it is often difficult to collect a sample large enough to extract organic material for dating. Additionally, we do not yet know what organic material in the paint produced the carbon being dated. This is further complicated by the potential of contamination by organic material introduced into the sample

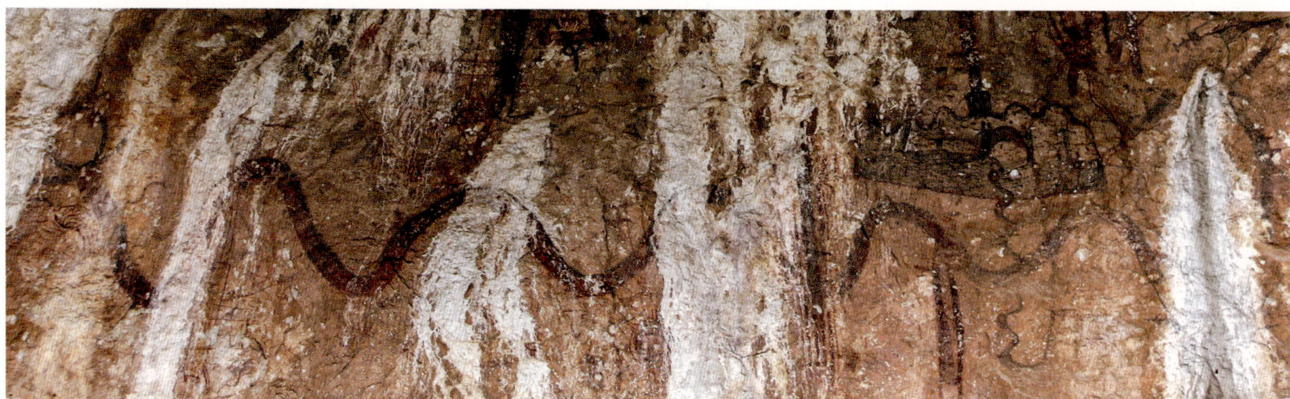

Figure 2.12. Horned serpent at Mystic Shelter. An undulating horned serpent spans 20 feet of the mural at 41VV612. Red, black, and possibly yellow dots form the underbelly of this massive horned snake.

(Rowe 2005; Steelman et al., forthcoming). For example, David Gebhard (1960:16) reports treating thirteen rock art panels with kerosene to enhance the imagery for photography. We do not know which sites or which figures he treated, but if we were to inadvertently collect a sample from one of the treated figures, the fossil fuels in the kerosene could return a date of 30,000 RCYBP or more. Obviously we would know this was a bad date, but other contaminants, such as organic materials in the carbon-containing limestone of the shelter wall, can subtly skew dates and go undetected.

The need for further dating studies in the Lower Pecos was recently made evident after an intriguingly young date was obtained for a Pecos River style deer at Black Cave (41VV76) (Bates et al. 2015). The paint sample from this figure yielded a date of 1465 ± 40 RCYBP or, in calendar years, around AD 600. Interestingly, in the 1990s, Marvin Rowe (2004:150–151) obtained younger-than-expected dates for Pecos River style paintings from two samples collected at the San Vicente site in northern Mexico (1930 + 149/-480 and 2500 ± 255 RCYBP) and from four samples collected at the White Shaman site.

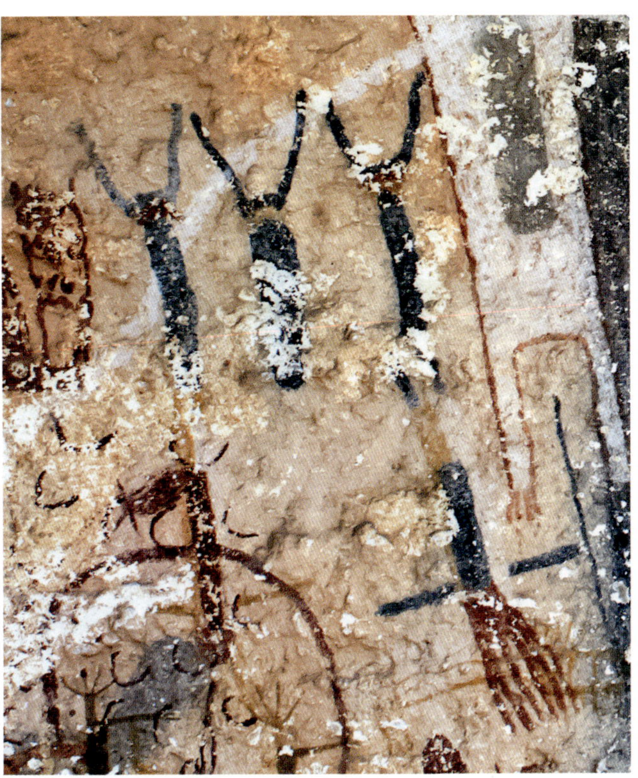

Figure 2.13. In the late 1990s Marvin Rowe collected black paint for radiocarbon dating from the three figures with upraised "arms" and the upside-down anthropomorph with red hair.

Five samples of black pigment were collected at White Shaman Shelter. One of the samples did not have sufficient carbon for a radiocarbon date, but the other four contained 75 to 175 µg carbon for AMS measurement. Rowe recalls that these four dates were obtained from a grouping of three enigmatic figures and an upside-down polychromatic anthropomorph (figure 2.13). These images at White Shaman are four of only seven dated Pecos River style paintings where the provenance of the sample is known. The samples were dated to 1970 ± 80, 1460 ± 80, 1960 ± 60, and 2420 ± 80 years BP (Rowe 2004:150). The three enigmatic figures are sequentially painted and morphologically identical; therefore, contemporaneous ages were expected. The anthropomorph is not stylistically different than the three figures located directly above it and appears to have been painted at the same time.

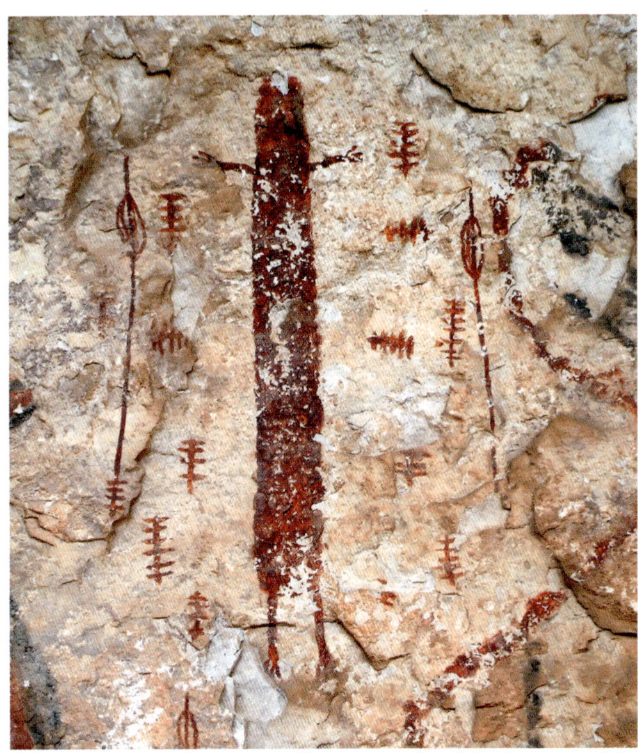

Figure 2.14. Single-pole ladders and stylized darts surround a 10-inch-tall Pecos River style anthropomorph at Halo Shelter (41VV1230).

The results were more recent than anticipated for the Pecos River style. Modern contamination from sheep rubbing against the imagery was suspected, and for that reason these dates were considered questionable. Adjacent to these images, however, is an unpainted rock background containing negligible amounts of organic carbon, revealing that the rock substrate contained minimal contamination. Also, it is unlikely that sheep would have been able to reach this location on the panel.

Karen Steelman, another of Marvin Rowe's students, has compiled and reviewed all dates obtained for Pecos River style paintings, including those discussed above (Steelman et al., forthcoming). She and her coauthors note that for replicate studies such as this, an average of the dates is typically better. They offer a mean and standard deviation of 2000 ± 400 RCYBP for the White Shaman mural, which is younger than other Pecos River paintings but has a similar magnitude of error compared to other replicate analyses.

The recently obtained new date from Black Cave brings the San Vicente and White Shaman dates back into the discussion. Did the Pecos River style endure for three thousand years? Are the younger dates inaccurate? Are the older dates inaccurate? The contributions of W. W. Newcomb and David Gebhard may provide some insight into these questions.

Newcomb (Kirkland and Newcomb 1967; Newcomb 1976) and Gebhard (1965) offered an internal chronology for Pecos River paintings based on superpositioning of figures and diagnostic attributes. Newcomb (Kirkland and Newcomb 1967:46) categorized the paintings into Periods 1 through 4, and Gebhard into Types 1 through 3, with Type 1 representing the oldest paintings. Both authors identified stylized dart tips as one of the diagnostic characteristics of younger Pecos River paintings: Period 3 for Newcomb (1976:184) and Type 3 for Gebhard (1965:10). The paintings at Black Cave and White Shaman both contain darts with stylized tips as well as other characteristics of this younger period (figure 2.14). It is likely that both the young and old dates for Pecos River paintings are correct, and the style did span three thousand years, but at this time we simply lack the data to know for sure.

Observations and Interpretations of Pecos River Style Rock Art

Unlocking the meanings of the Pecos River style paintings is a task that has been as daunting as it has been controversial. The conventional wisdom applied to the study and interpretation of Pecos River pictographs was, and in some cases continues to be, predicated on three points: (1) the rock art represents hunting and medicine cults; (2) anthropomorphs and accompanying imagery represent shamanistic documentations of visions and glimpses of the supernatural otherworld; and (3) attempts to decipher the art are nothing more than exercises in speculation. Before we discuss these three interpretive views, let's take a look at some early observations made by trained artists who pioneered rock art recording in the Lower Pecos. These individuals knew art. They knew how to produce it and how to analyze it. We recognize the valuable contributions they made through their tireless efforts to document the rock art, but in some cases we have failed to heed their written accounts.

Early Observations

In 1931 artists Emma Gutzeit and Virginia Carson were sent by the Witte Memorial Museum of San Antonio on an archaeological expedition to the Lower Pecos to produce artistic reproductions of the pictographs in the region. The two adventurous women recorded pictographs at eighteen sites, producing over a hundred watercolor sketches. I include the Gutzeit and Carson expedition not because they offered any interpretations of the paintings but because of an observation made by Gutzeit in her journal dated June 14, 1931. In her description of a site in Seminole Canyon, she writes, "The walls and roof are elaborately decorated with what seemingly is the picturing of a tribal epic or a ceremonial, for the pictures are very evidently a continuous story." Gutzeit was thus the first to recognize, at least in writing, that the paintings were "a continuous story"—a visual narrative.

A few years later Forrest Kirkland and his wife, Lula, both professional artists, launched what is now regarded as one of the most valuable contributions to Texas archaeology. Over the course of less than eight years they produced amazingly accurate watercolor renderings of rock art panels at ninety-one sites in Texas, forty-three of these in the Lower Pecos (figure 2.15). Severe weathering of the paintings limited the number of panels the Kirklands were able to reproduce. Describing the deterioration within Presa Canyon, Kirkland (1939:52) wrote, "In this canyon which is about two miles long, we found 522 feet of wall space on which the pictures had weathered so much that only bits of designs remained here and there; and there was only 176 feet where copies could be made." He surmised that conservatively half the pictures painted by the people of the Lower Pecos had been lost to weathering or, to a lesser degree, vandalism (Kirkland 1939:52). One can only imagine what it must have been like thousands of years ago to walk the canyons lined with vibrant polychromatic paintings.

Many people don't realize that Forrest Kirkland not only copied the rock art panels, he also wrote about them (Kirkland 1937a, 1937b, 1938, 1939). In 1938 he provided the first formal analysis of the paintings, including a discussion of color harmony, picture arrangement, rhythm, movement, and action. These astute observations were made by a trained artist who had spent years meticulously copying and analyzing the art. No one knew the art better or was more qualified to provide an analysis than Kirkland.

> Color harmony, which is unquestionably an important quality of art, was highly developed by the Val Verde Dry Shelter Culture [Pecos River style] . . . Not only do we find a pleasing variety and combination of colors on individual pictures, but the arrangement of color masses in large groups, is much more than accidental. It indicates a sense of color balance unsurpassed by painters of our own time . . .
>
> Closely related to color balance is the arrangement of objects, or picture composition as it is usually called . . . Like color harmony, we must go to Val Verde County to find the finest examples of pictorial arrangement. There, on spaces defined by imperfections of the cave wall, are designs so perfectly adapted to their respective areas, that to move a single important element, would seriously injure their delicate balance and detract from their artistic merit. [Kirkland 1938:31–32]

Like Gutzeit, Kirkland recognized the compositional nature of the paintings. He also maintained that many of the Pecos River style murals illustrated mythologies rather than "individual ideas of the artist" (Kirkland 1939:71). In 1942, Forrest Kirkland died at the early age of forty-nine from a heart attack. Twenty-five years later W. W. Newcomb (Kirkland and Newcomb 1967) wrote *The Rock Art of Texas Indians*, showcasing Kirkland's beautiful reproductions and acknowledging his contribution. "He had attempted what no one else had dared, and he had succeeded beyond the dreams of any. He had copied most of the rock art then known in Texas. His heroic, self-imposed task was completed" (Kirkland and Newcomb 1967:13).

Before his untimely death, Kirkland left us with the following observation and a question we have yet to answer, although I hope this book brings us at least one step closer.

> These firmly fixed mythological ideas and the highly conventionalized forms with which they are illustrated, along with the extremely individual style of painting seem to point to a very long period of development. The question naturally arises: was this culture with its elaborate paintings slowly evolved in the district around the mouth of the Pecos, or was it evolved elsewhere and brought in fully developed? [Kirkland 1939:72]

Kirkland's (1939:72) close examination of the murals and his inability to identify internal development led him to suggest that "the present evidence . . . although by no means conclusive, points to an outside development." And if this is the case, he argued, we should be able to find "the pictures from whence it came" in areas outside the Lower Pecos. Although there is inadequate data to satisfactorily answer Kirkland's question of origins and affiliations, researchers have noted some interesting parallels with other Archaic great mural rock art traditions.

In 1971, while looking for stylistic relationships between the Archaic Barrier Canyon pictographs of Utah and other rock art styles, Polly Schaafsma identified visual affinities with the Pecos River style. She notes that "as strange as it may seem at first, certain rather significant parallels can be drawn between the Barrier Canyon Style of the Colorado River drainage and the Western Archaic Pecos River Style paintings in Texas" (Schaafsma 1971:131).[7]

Others have since noted stylistic parallels not only between the Barrier Canyon and Pecos River styles, but with the great murals of Baja California in Mexico (Hays-Gilpin 2004:21). All three of these Archaic period rock art styles share visual counterparts: complex murals portraying tall anthropomorphs with elongated, tapering bodies accompanied by animals, birds, and enigmatic figures. However, simply identifying visual similarities among the great mural traditions produced during the Archaic period is insufficient for establishing cultural affiliations: instead, "solid archae-

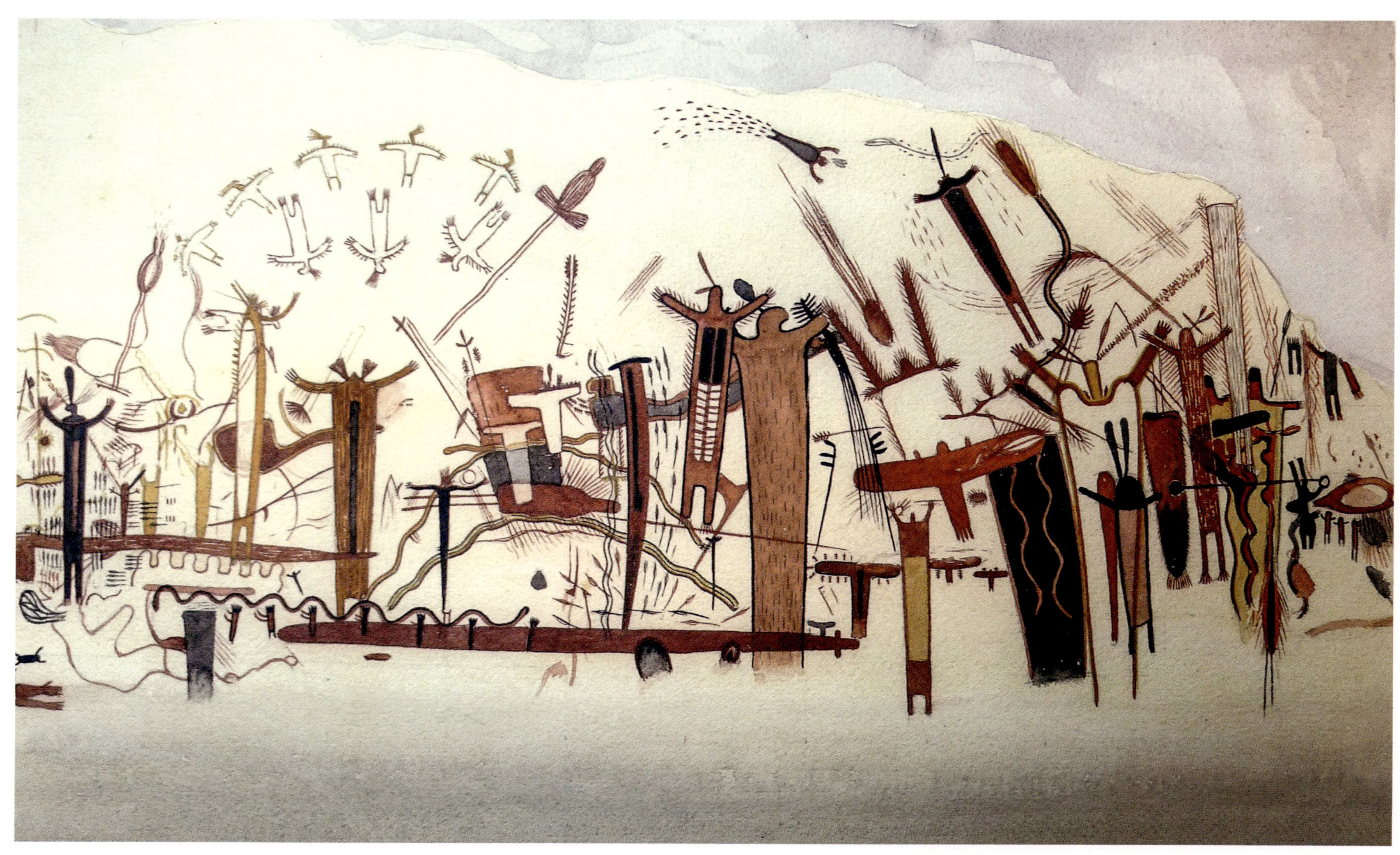

Figure 2.15. Forrest Kirkland's watercolor painting of a section of the mural at Rattlesnake Canyon (41VV180). Courtesy of Texas Archeological Research Laboratory, The University of Texas at Austin.

ological investigations will have to be made" (Schaafsma 1971:135).

To adequately address the question posed by Kirkland and establish cultural affiliations will require rigorous, systematic analyses and dating of pictograph *and* petroglyph assemblages on both sides of the US/Mexico border. Although excellent strides have been made in the documentation and analysis of rock art in northern and northwestern Mexico (e.g., Amador Bech 2010; Murray 2007; Rivera Estrada 2012; Turpin 2010; Viramontes Anzures 2005; and many others), there are vast areas south of the border that are scarcely known to archaeologists (Turpin 2010:27). Investigations into these unexplored regions and continued work in those areas currently under study should engage researchers from both countries. Working collaboratively, we can begin to identify not simply broad stylistic similarities (and dissimilarities) among rock art traditions, but cognitive patterns across media, space, and time that are not necessarily stylistically similar.

Early Interpretations

The first anthropological interpretations for Pecos River rock art were offered in the 1950s by J. Charles Kelley (1950) and T. N. Campbell (1958). Kelley (1950:73) argued that "in all probability this art style expresses pictorially the existence of a well-organized ceremonial hunting cult." Campbell agreed with Kelley's interpretation and further suggested that the consumption of mescal beans (*Sophora secundiflora*) was likely involved. "Even a cursory examination of the Pecos River-style pictographs reveals a number of parallels to the mescal bean cult . . . The historic cult is frequently linked with hunting and with the deer . . . and this also seems to be true of the Pecos River Focus cult" (Campbell 1958:158).

W. W. Newcomb, however, felt the hunting-cult hypothesis was too narrow an interpretation (Kirkland and Newcomb 1967:79). In *Rock Art of Texas Indians*, Newcomb offered an alternative shamanistic-society hypothesis to explain the association of animals and anthropomorphs in the panels. He divided anthropomorphic figures into two descriptive categories: those that were elaborately costumed, and those that were not.

> In order to name and distinguish between the two kinds of anthropomorphic beings, the intricately costumed and ornamented central figures have been designated "shamans." The probability is good . . . that these figures were in fact intended to represent shamans, that is, individuals who possessed special knowledge of the supernatural world and more than ordinary ability to deal with it. It is possible, however, that they were intended as something else, so this designation is in part a matter of convenience. [Kirkland and Newcomb 1967:46–47]

Nevertheless, he still agreed with Campbell's identification of a mescal bean cult. "If the shamanistic-society hypothesis is pursued a bit further," Newcomb argued, "one can readily imagine that the custom of painting shelter walls in the Lower Pecos country may have originated when a shaman emerging from a trance, very possibly induced by mescal beans, attempted to visualize his hallucinations or dreams" (Kirkland and Newcomb 1967:79–80). He further suggested the distinct possibility that peyote (*Lophophora williamsii*) was used interchangeably with mescal beans (Kirkland and Newcomb 1967:70).

It was archaeologist Solveig Turpin, however, who fully developed the shamanism hypothesis. Turpin has devoted decades of her life to the study of rock art in the Lower Pecos Canyonlands, including sites in Mexico. Turpin (1990:263) takes issue with the idea that rock art is only understandable in its vaguest form, arguing that this view exonerates archaeologists from ever engaging in the general anthropological discussion of how rock art relates to the field of hunter-gatherer archaeology. She maintains that most of the Pecos River style anthropomorphs are shamans and has argued that putting the art on rock walls for all to see was a reinforcement of the idea of "the shaman as spirit incarnate, promoter of his faith and protector of his community" (Turpin 1994:93). She also proposes that the rock art was produced in response to population density and scalar stress, "interpersonal conflicts that are resolved by the emergence of leaders, whether individuals—such as the shamans—or groups—such as the medicine societies characteristic of the Plains Indians. An increased emphasis on ritual would reify these changes in the social order and the rock art served to channel that information to the public" (Turpin 2010:53).

The idea that Pecos River rock art was a manifestation of shamanic visions fettered archaeological inquiry into alternative explanations. It wasn't long after Newcomb's original shamanism hypothesis that the term *shaman* became a catchall for Pecos River anthropomorphs. And by the late 1980s it was generally accepted that any attempt to interpret Pecos River rock art—beyond shamanism—would be at best speculative. The obstacles faced by archaeologists trying to interpret the art proved almost insurmountable. There obviously were no ethnographic studies made of the people who painted the panels, and no one was really sure who the artists were, where they had come from, or what had become of them. Harry Shafer (1986:146) expressed the prevailing view at the time when he wrote, "The paintings cannot be interpreted or understood from a modern perspective. Contemporary values are so far removed from those of the ancient artists that any attempt at an interpretation can only be speculative . . . The meanings are lost when the culture comes to an end." In all fairness, Shafer probably does not share that same view today, but many remain skeptical (e.g., Bednarik 2011; Greco 2011; Biesele 2013). The rock art of the Lower Pecos, however, is not beyond interpretation. Its meaning is lost only to those who believe that a symbol or idea expressed visually is beyond human comprehension. Visual texts can be read. In fact, they can be analyzed with the same logic, rigor, and success as printed texts.

In the following chapter I present a brief discussion of visual media and the methods used by art historians and iconographers to analyze this important form of communication. This is immediately followed by a presentation of the methods we used in our analysis of the White Shaman mural.

TRANSCRIBING AND READING VISUAL TEXTS

> By recognizing the attributes, we recognize the characters and the stories, and so help to crack the codes of much mythological and religious painting. The attribute isn't there because it is a casual part of the scene, but because it is deliberately included to indicate significance beyond its physical existence.
>
> HOWELLS AND NEGREIROS [2012:18]

Today we teach our children how to read and write the printed word. Once they have mastered the basics, they are taught to read a text critically. They learn to recognize sentence structure, isolate and classify patterns, identify relationships of one sentence to other sentences in the paragraph and each paragraph to other paragraphs in the chapter, and so on. From this they infer the overall meaning of the text. All of this seems pretty straightforward, and no one would question that this is a worthwhile endeavor; however, before the printed word, which is a relatively recent phenomenon, information was communicated visually.[1] Our not-so-distant ancestors taught their children how to read and write *visual* texts, how to encode meaning in and extrapolate meaning from visual media. With the advent of the printed word we have become, to some extent, visually illiterate (Howells and Negreiros 2012). In 1965, Gyorgy Kepes argued in the *Education of Vision* that "We have to get back to our roots . . . we have to re-educate our vision and reclaim our lost sensibilities" (Kepes 1965:ii).

In their book *Visual Culture* (2012), Howells and Negreiros argue it is not too late; we can learn how to analyze visual texts with the same logic and rigor used in the analysis of printed texts.

> . . . "visual texts" can be "read" with just the same rigour—and with just the same reward—as the printed word. We really can get to work on them—to wrestle with them, almost—to begin to discover both how and what they mean. And just as with the printed word, it is best if we begin with deliberate strategies for analysis if we want to get a text to unlock its secrets as revealingly as possible. [Howells and Negreiros 2012:1]

The key to unlocking visual texts, such as the rock art of the Lower Pecos, lies in utilizing "deliberate strategies for analysis." Two strategies that Howells and Negreiros (2012:xii) cite as solid bases for the analysis of a wide variety of visual texts are iconology and semiotics, both of which we employed in our analysis of the White Shaman mural. The former will be discussed below, and the latter toward the end of this chapter.

Iconology, as defined by the renowned art historian Erwin Panofsky ([1939] 1972:3), "is that branch of the history of art which concerns itself with the subject matter or meaning of works of art, as opposed to form." Panofsky believed art carries three levels of meaning: natural, conventional, and intrinsic. Natural meaning is understood, in part, by identifying visible forms and objects known to us from practical experience, and by identifying the change in their relations through actions or events. Panofsky uses the example of a man lifting his hat off his head as he passes someone on the street. The man and hat are *objects* and the lifting of the hat is the *event*. Although most people in Western societies understand that lifting one's hat represents a form of greeting, it is not universal. To interpret the hat-lifting event requires insights into a different level of meaning: the conventional meaning. "One must not only be familiar with the practical world of objects and events, but also with the more-than-practical world of customs and traditions peculiar to a certain civilization" (Panofsky [1939] 1972:4).

The final level identified by Panofsky is intrinsic meaning, which is the deepest and most difficult to establish. It is apprehended by "ascertaining those underlying principles which reveal the basic attitude of a nation, a period, a class, a religious or philosophical persuasion—unconsciously qualified by one personality and condensed into one work" (Panofsky [1939] 1972:7). Returning to the hat-lifting example, he writes that we can't get at the "personality" of the man based on this one event, "but only by coordinating a large number of similar observations and interpreting them in connection with our general information as to the gentleman's period, nationality, class, intellectual traditions and so forth" (Panofsky [1939] 1972:5). And he argues that we can apprehend through the subject matter of a work of art all three levels of meaning.

The method we used to analyze the White Shaman mural, which to some extent follows Panofsky's system, is summarized below.[2] In the chapters that follow, the method is operationalized and the results presented.

Formal Feature Analyses and Pre-Iconographical Descriptions

Panofksy's primary level of analysis involves identifying "pure forms": configurations of line, color, and shape that are combined to represent natural objects such as humans, plants, and animals. Relations between forms represent events. The world of forms, which Panofsky ([1939] 1972:5) calls "artistic motifs," are carriers of natural meanings. The enumeration, or inventory, of these motifs represents a pre-iconographical description of the artwork. For example, a pre-iconographical description of Leonardo da Vinci's *The Last Supper* might read something like this:

> The Last Supper mural is 29 feet long and 15 feet high. It portrays thirteen people situated along one side of a long table covered with a white tablecloth. On top of the table there are thirteen small dinner plates, ten glasses partially filled with a red liquid, and ten small loaves of bread. Twelve of the people appear shocked or upset; however, the central figure, whose head is located at the vanishing point in the painting, appears tranquil. His upper torso and outstretched arms resting on the table form a triangle. This central figure is slightly more illuminated than the other twelve, who are divided in half, with six to the right and six to the left of the illuminated figure. They are further subdivided into groupings of three. Almost all are portrayed wearing blue. There are three windows along the back wall and three doors on either side of the room. The person in the second seat to the right of the central figure appears to have knocked over a salt shaker. He is holding a small bag in his right hand.

Obviously a detailed description of *The Last Supper* would include far more detail, but the point is that at the pre-iconographic level of analysis we are not engaged in interpretation. We are engaged in observation, description, and data collection. We are identifying attributes of characters and of stories—attributes intentionally "penned" by the artist to communicate information critical to a reading of the art. I refer to this stage in our investigations as a "formal feature analysis." During this stage in our investigations at the White Shaman site we documented and described the structure and context of the rock art panel, characteristics of individual figures within the panel, and stratigraphic relationships between and among figures.

Site Documentation and Mapping

Although I had previously conducted a formal analysis of the White Shaman mural, the results of which became the basis for my dissertation, I lacked the technology available to us today. This new technology greatly increased the number of types and quantity of data we were able to collect. Each visit to the site was met with a new discovery.

The benefit of rock art research, in contrast to "dirt" archaeology, is that we *can* return. Traditional dirt archaeology is destructive and not repeatable: once a site is excavated, it is—for all intents and purposes—gone. Rock art archaeology, however, is preservative and repeatable. We don't excavate, label, bag, and take artifacts back to the lab for analysis. In fact, effort is made to not even touch the imagery. In the past, and regrettably still today, some people have applied anything from water to kerosene to the paintings to enhance their visibility.[3] It is heartbreaking to see photographs of rock art in scholarly books with water streaking down the walls. Are the paintings more visible? Sometimes, but this is absolutely not an accepted practice—the damage to the paintings is irreversible. If done properly, the documentation of a rock art site should have minimal to no impact on the art or the surrounding archaeological deposits. Researchers can and should return to a site to verify data they or others collected, and to implement new technologies as they become available. Ultimately, the rock art is preserved for future generations.

The daunting task of rock art recording involves not only preservation or description, however, but collection of data in such a way that it is useful for answering questions about our human past. This means detecting patterns, which are the clues to making sense of past human behavior. To do this requires documenting and describing the structure and context of the rock art panel, characteristics of individual figures within the panel, and stratigraphic relationships between and among figures.

The White Shaman site has benefited from this level of investigation.[4] It is the most intensively documented rock art assemblage in the region, likely in the New World. We mapped White Shaman Shelter using LiDAR (light detection and ranging) and SfM (structure from motion) technologies. Western Mapping was contracted for the LiDAR mapping, which included geodetic surveying, 3D laser scanning, and laser reflectivity analysis. From this data they produced planimetric maps, profiles, and elevations for the shelter (figure 3.1). Shumla's research team constructed a 3D color model of the shelter using SfM photogrammetry (figure 3.2). This data will be used in the future to develop predictive models incorporating the broader context of the site, such as astronomy and acoustics.

We are fortunate to have the opportunity to view and study the paintings at the White Shaman site in the physical context within which they were produced thousands of years ago. Context is more than just a point on the landscape or morphology of the shelter, although these are certainly important. It is also the soundscape: the natural and human-made acoustical properties of the site that change with wind direction or variations in humidity. It is the skyscape: a night sky that is ever-changing and yet forever constant. It is the viewscape: the river below and the mountains beyond. It is the interplay of light and shadow on the panel created by the sun, a full moon, or no moon at all. These combine to form the context within which the rock art was produced, experienced, and consumed. The physical context has changed very little over the millennia. It is the same night sky, the same mountains in the distance, and the same natural acoustic environment. Although there is much work yet to be done, we have begun documenting this broader context photographically on the solstices and equinoxes. Preliminary results of this analysis will be presented in subsequent chapters.

Figure Identification and Documentation

Description of individual figures in a rock art panel, just like analysis of artifacts from any other archaeological site, provides data for inter- and intrasite patterning. We categorized figures at White Shaman Shelter as anthropomorphic, zoomorphic, or enigmatic based on the presence or absence of specific attributes. For example, to qualify as an anthropomorph, a figure must possess at least three human characteristics, such as head, arms, legs, and torso. If a figure lacked characteristics of either a human or an animal, it was classified as enigmatic.

We identified forty-two anthropomorphs, six zoomorphs, and sixty-nine enigmatics in the shelter's main panel. While these are by far the most striking and best-preserved pictographs at the site, very faint remnants of pigment are observable high on the northwest wall opposite the main panel. Sadly, whatever images were there in prehistory are now lost beyond categorization. A thick layer of mineral accretion or calcium oxalate has completely obscured these pictographs.[5] Below the northwest wall, painted on the slick, limestone floor to the left of the steps leading into the shelter, is a poorly preserved red, comb-shaped pictograph. This area is exposed to the elements and has been trodden upon for thousands of years. It is highly likely that at some point in the distant past this figure was joined by other paintings on this slick limestone surface. An isolated small, red triangular shape is located high on the north wall. It is immediately visible as one enters the site by way of the steps. Below and to the right of this figure are smudges of dry-applied black pigment. With the exception of the site trinomial, which was painted in green on the north wall in 1958, these images make up the currently identified rock art assemblage at the White Shaman site.

Each discernible figure was assigned a reference code consisting of the archaeological site designation, its figure classification (A for anthropomorph; Z for zoomorph; and E for enigmatic), and its own unique number. For example, the first anthropomorph identified at the White Shaman Shelter, whose archaeological site number is 41VV124, is named 41VV0124_A001. This identification number is now the permanent name by

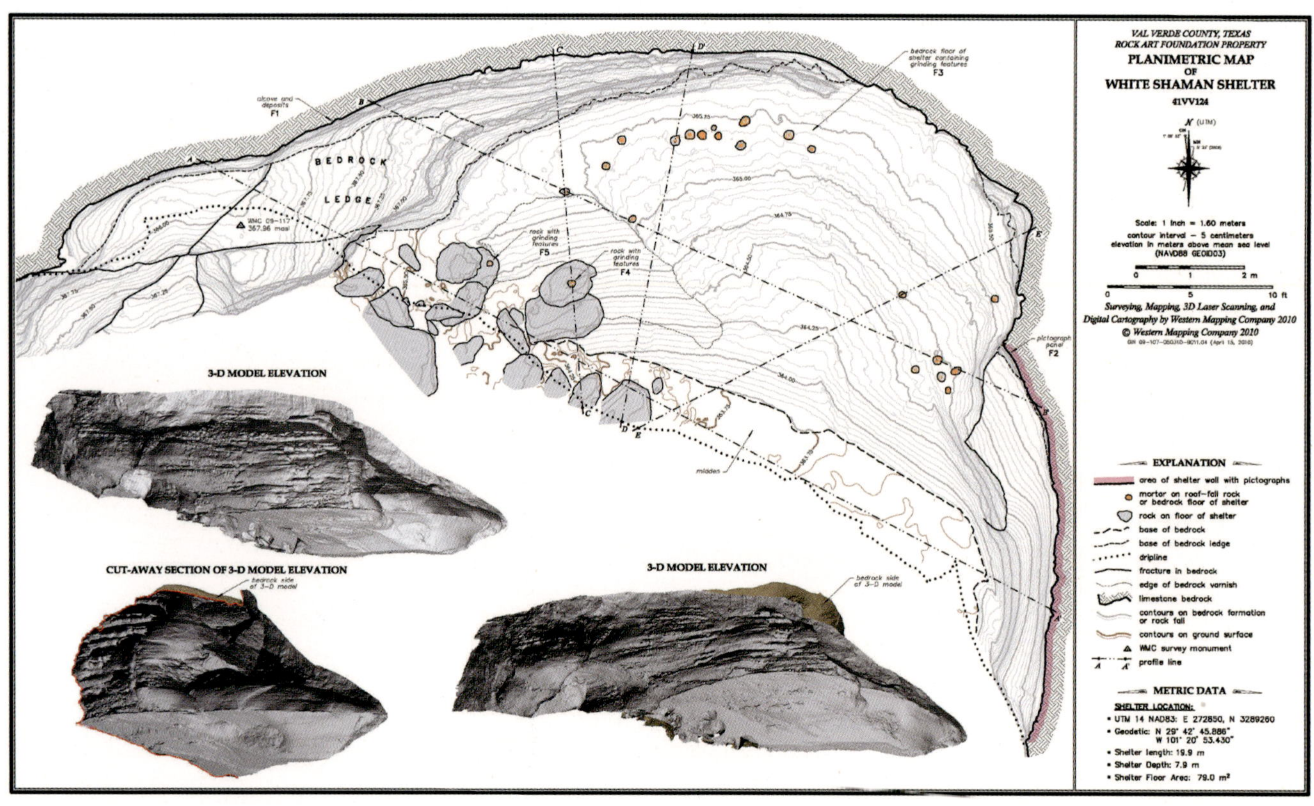

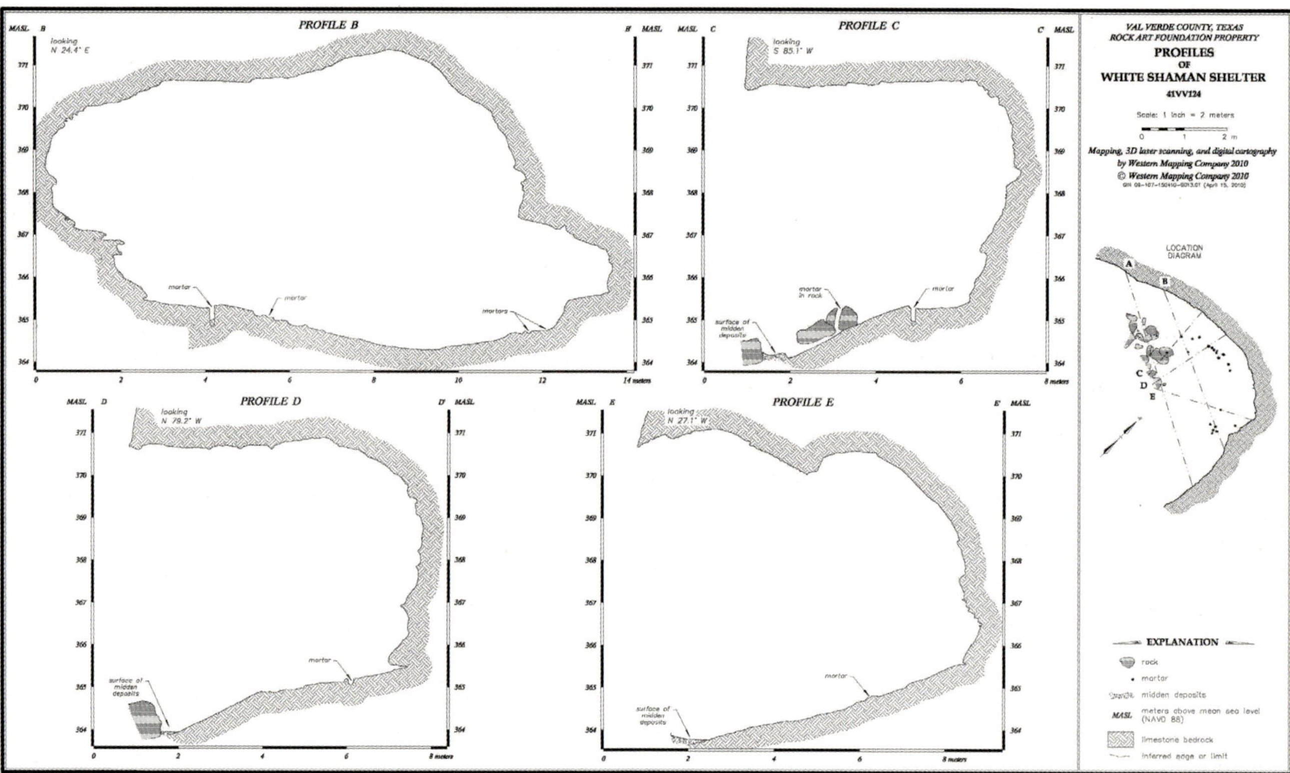

Figure 3.1. White Shaman site maps: (a) planimetric map, with the mural location highlighted in pink; (b) profile maps. Maps produced for Shumla Archaeological Research and Education Center by Western Mapping Company.

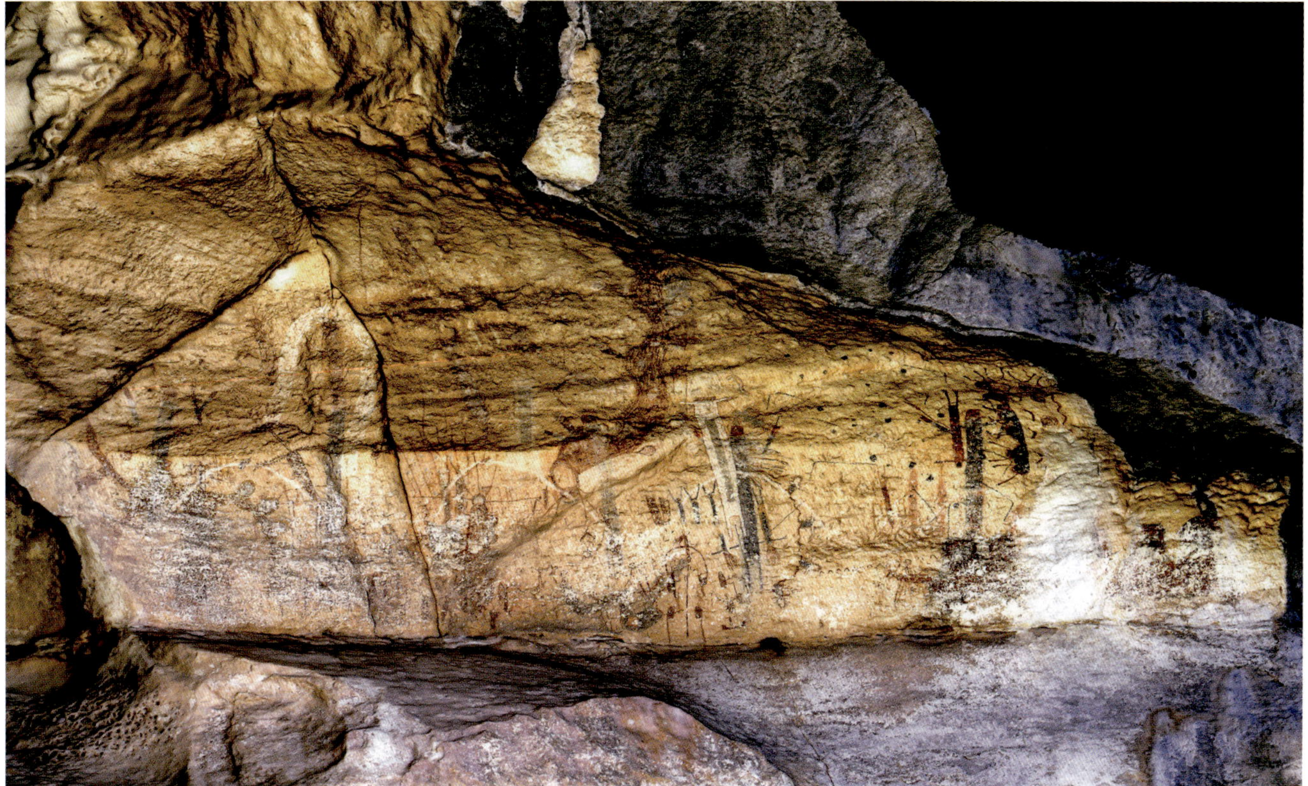

Figure 3.2. Rendering of 3D model of the White Shaman site. Produced by Mark Willis. Courtesy of Shumla Archaeological Research and Education Center.

which the figure is referred to and cataloged. Needless to say, the name is far from flattering, but it works.

A very helpful tool used throughout the recording process was a camera with digital image enhancement capabilities. This technology, known as Dstretch, was developed by Jon Harman and allows for on-site enhancement of faint images virtually invisible to the naked eye (figure 3.3). As a result, we were able to catalog figures never before documented and capture additional data for producing digital illustrations.

We used a total data station (TDS) to map the exact location of individual images. These data points were incorporated into the 3D model to visually represent the figure's location in the mural. The constellations of figure locations created using the TDS were then integrated into a spatially significant geographic information system (GIS) database. This database allows us to explore the density and ratios of figure concentrations within and among rock art sites.

Each figure was photographed with and without scale. In the lab, copies of each photograph were renamed and assigned a unique code, including the figure identification number. We digitally archived the original photographs; these remain untouched. We have cataloged thousands of photographs for White Shaman Shelter, and we still find it necessary to return for more. You can never take too many photographs.

Similarly, you can't illustrate the imagery too many times. Many people have tried to convince me that with the advent of super-high-resolution digital photography there is no longer a need for illustrations. I disagree; no manner of photographic documentation can replace illustrating the art, for "what I have not drawn I have never really seen" (Franck 1973:6). Like Kirkland (1937a:102), I don't create illustrations to serve as exact copies, reflecting all the spalls and flaking that have occurred through the years; photographs and 3D mapping fill that need. My goal is to reproduce the imagery as closely as possible to what it may have looked like when it was originally painted. Decisions of what to include in illustrations are based on existing data; nothing is arbitrarily added. The illustrations are stud-

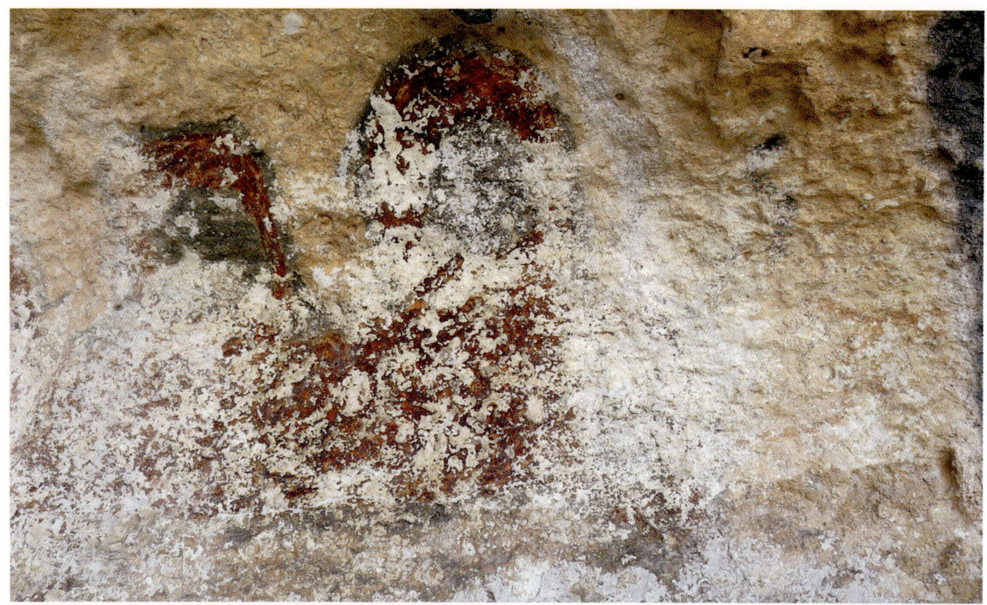

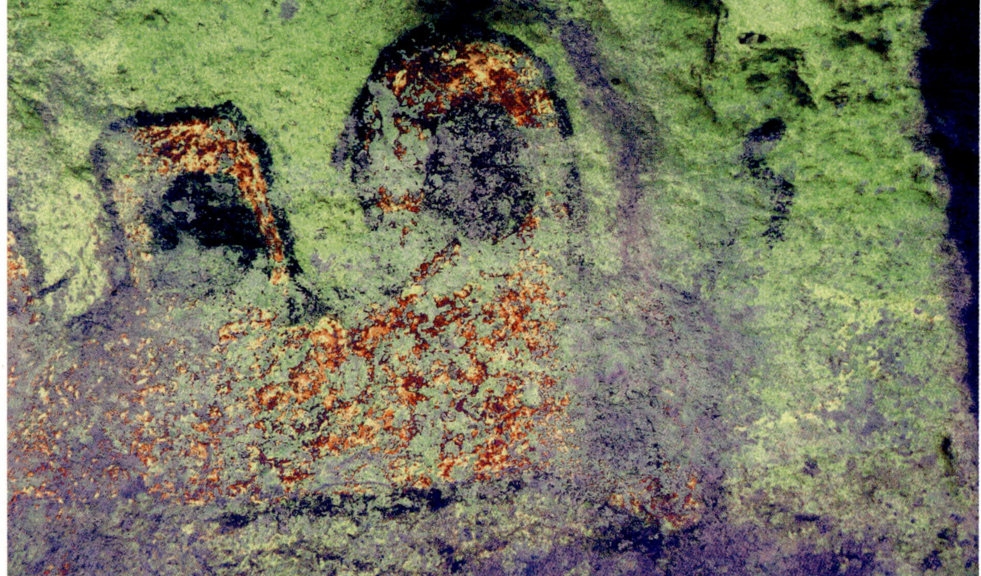

Figure 3.3. Dstretch image enhancement. (a) Photograph prior to image enhancement, with significant portions of the motif obscured by a white mineral skin. (b) Photograph after image enhancement. Note the additional lobe protruding from the right side of the figure.

ies through which we learn all that we can about the figure, such as what elements define it, in what order the artist applied the paint, what images overlay or are overlain by the figure, and so forth. Each study generates more information and an ever-increasing understanding of both the art and the artist.

Over the years I have illustrated the pictographs of White Shaman using several techniques, including on-site sketching, light-table tracing of photographs in the lab, and, most recently, digitally in Adobe Photoshop using a Wacom Cintiq Interactive Pen Display. This is by far the most efficient tool for illustrating. Using the paint function within Adobe Photoshop, I created digital, layered illustrations on the interactive pen display (figure 3.4). Photoshop layers are like sheets of clear acetate placed one on top of the other. For the background, or base layer, I used a high-resolution photograph of a figure. The next series of layers were digitally enhanced images of the background photograph. The Cintiq served as a drawing board. Using the interactive pen, I produced high-resolution illustrations directly on the screen displaying the figure photograph. I digitally applied the paint layer by layer, reproducing the painting sequence of the original artist. The layered composite, without the background photographs, represents the final illustration.

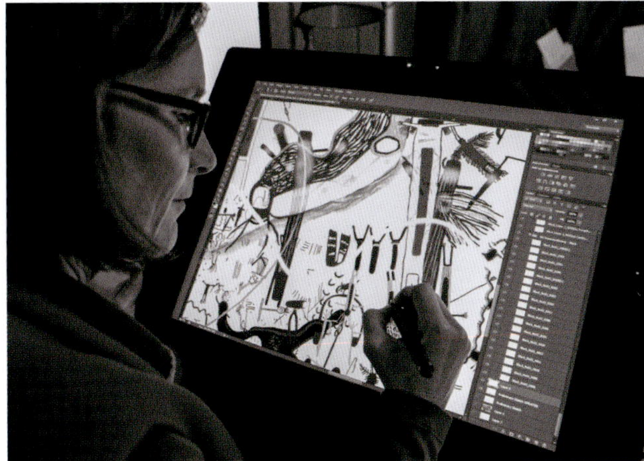

Figure 3.4. *(above)* Digital illustrations being produced on a Wacom Cintiq Interactive Pen Display using Adobe Photoshop.

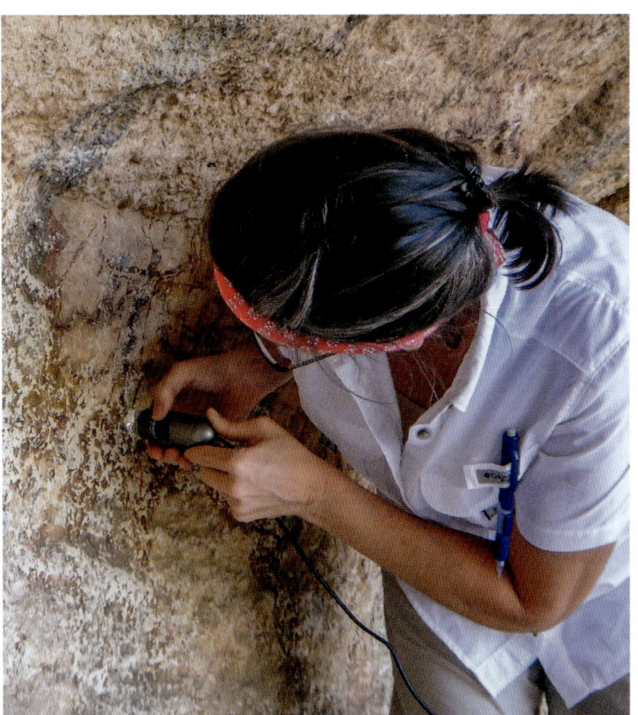

Figure 3.5. *(right)* Digital field microscopy: (a) The digital microscope is first carefully placed at the analysis location. (b) The microscope is connected via USB to a laptop where the microscopic imagery is viewed and photographs are captured.

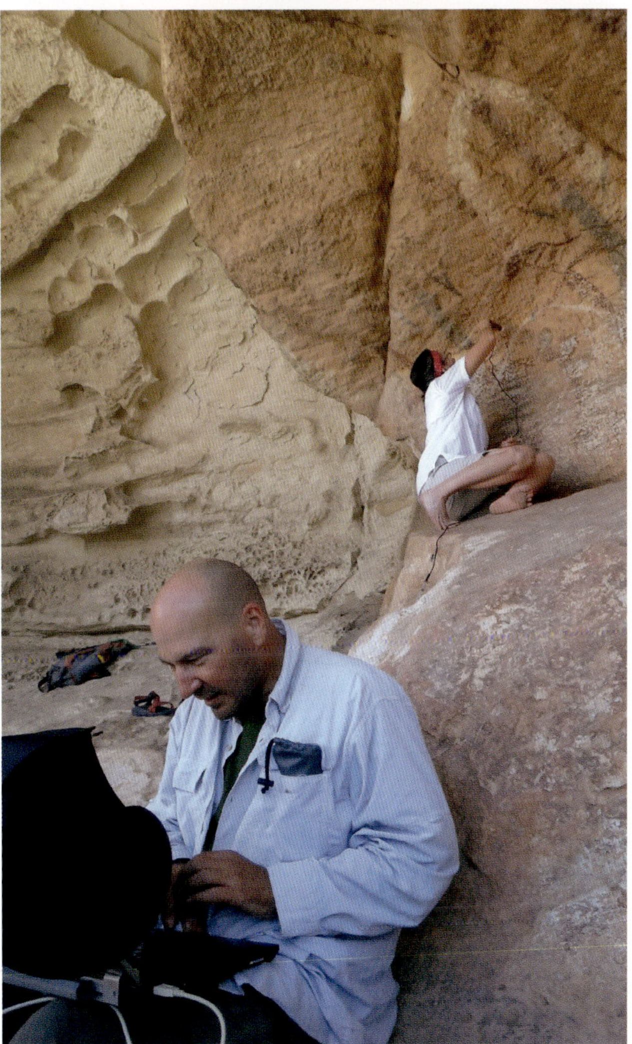

Identifying and Diagramming Mural Stratification

Determining painting sequence is critical to understanding the mechanics of the panel. The principle of superposition establishes that layers at an archaeological site are deposited in chronological order. For a rock art panel, this means that layers closest to the rock surface were painted prior to those overlying them. The span of time between painting sequences could be a matter of minutes or millennia.

Discovering the mural's stratigraphy was a seminal moment in the analysis of the White Shaman panel. As I was producing figure illustrations, I recognized two stratigraphic puzzles. The first involved the interweaving of figures—where a figure is simultaneously over and under another figure—and the second involved what seemed to be illogical, counterintuitive painting sequences. For instance, the red bodies of several upside-down anthropomorphic figures (A008, A011, and A012) and the body of a red deer (Z001) are decorated with black dots. As an artist, it seemed logical to me that the White Shaman muralist would have painted the figure's red form first and then added the black dots as decoration. With the naked eye, however, it appeared to be the other way around. To resolve this and other stratigraphic conundrums, I needed greater magnifica-

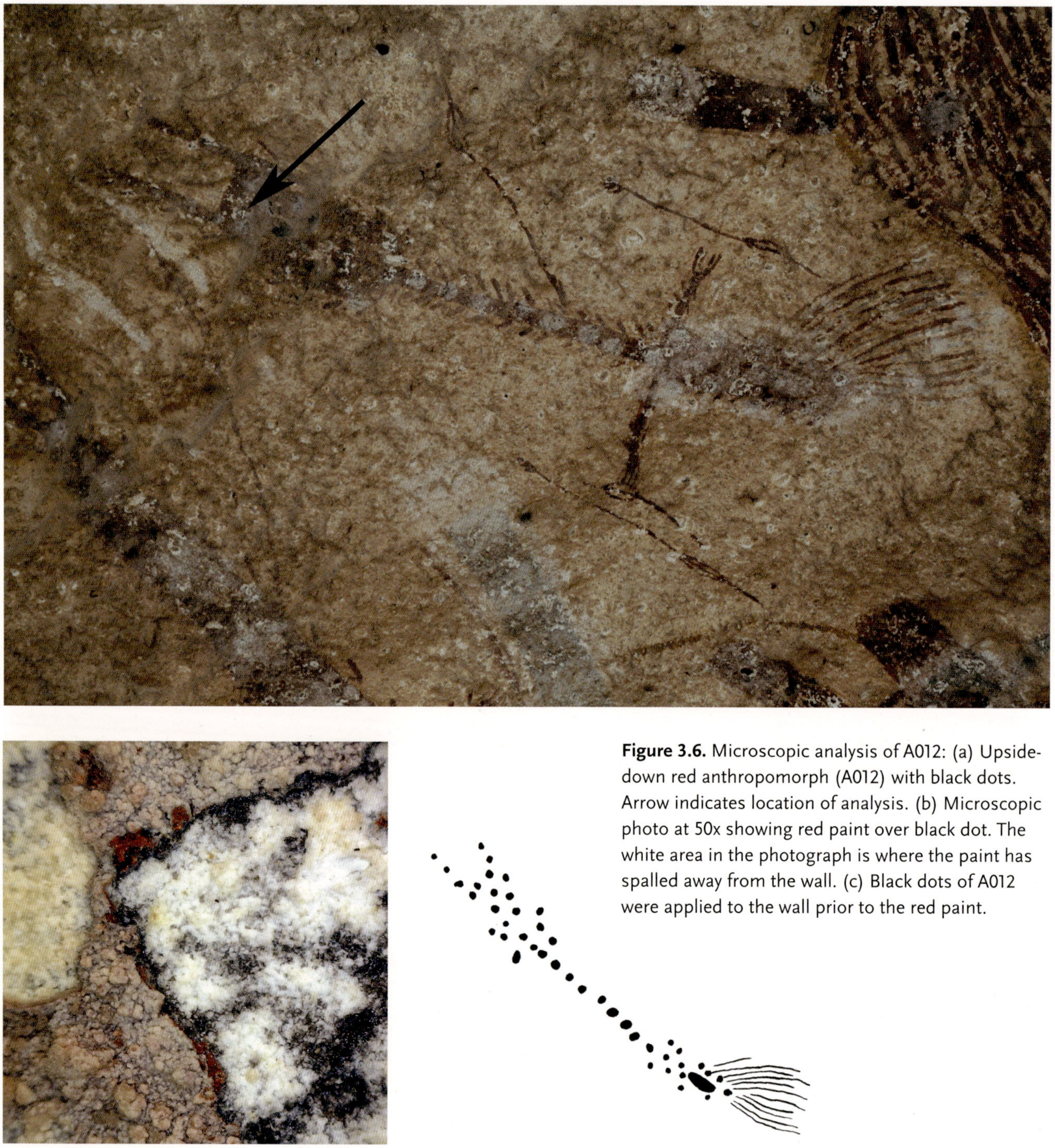

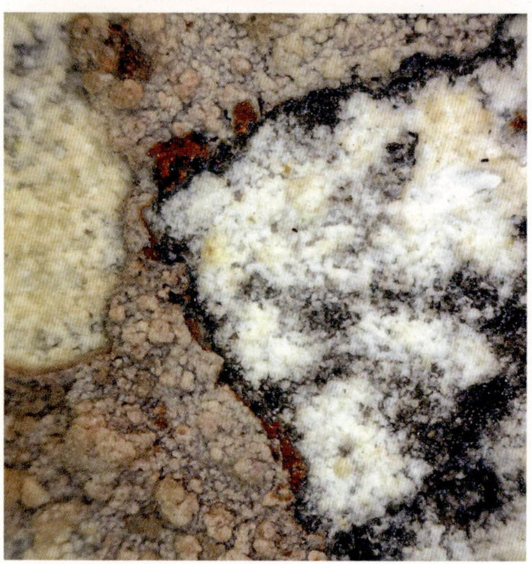

Figure 3.6. Microscopic analysis of A012: (a) Upside-down red anthropomorph (A012) with black dots. Arrow indicates location of analysis. (b) Microscopic photo at 50x showing red paint over black dot. The white area in the photograph is where the paint has spalled away from the wall. (c) Black dots of A012 were applied to the wall prior to the red paint.

tion and the ability to photograph what I was seeing at that level of magnification.

In 2010 I shared my frustration with Mark Willis, an archaeologist and rock art technology guru who has an uncanny ability to solve technological challenges economically. Sure enough, this was no exception. He introduced me to the Dino-Lite Pro, a handheld digital microscope with 20X to 220X variable magnification. We returned to the site with this tool to capture high-resolution digital images of microscopic areas within the mural (figure 3.5).

Our first targets were the red figures containing black dots. Using the digital microscope, we were able to confirm that the red paint overlays the dots (figure 3.6). In other words, the artist painted the black dots first and then proceeded to give form to the figure through the application of red paint. In some cases they painted around the black dots with minimal overlap. In other cases they applied red paint directly across the preexisting dot.

We proceeded to examine other locations in the mural where black and red intersect, including an antlered anthropomorph with black dots attached to its red antler tines (A006) (figure 3.7). I always assumed the tines were painted first and the dots added second; however, using the digital microscope, we determined the red tines were applied over the black dots. The dots were painted *first*.[6]

Further analysis of this antlered figure revealed that it is literally woven together with two other motifs, a serpentine line (E029) and a crenellated arch (E001) (figure 3.8). We analyzed several layers of paint. The first layer is black (figure 3.8a). This was followed by a layer of red forming the arch of E001 (figure 3.8b). It overlays the black serpentine line (E029) and the black central band of A006. The next layer of red forms the body of our antlered figure and his paraphernalia (figure 3.8c). These overlay the black of E001 and the black of E029. The red of A006 also overlays the red of E001. The next layer is the yellow of E001 (figure 3.8d), which overlays the antlered figure, sandwiching him into the crenellated arch. The white serpentine line was applied last and overlays A006 and E001 (figure 3.8e).

Harris Matrix Composer

We identified highly intricate stratigraphic relationships, such as described above, throughout the mural. Keeping track of these relationships proved challenging. In 1973 Edward Harris developed a system that allowed archaeologists to visually link complex stratified deposits across large-scale excavations. I adapted this system, which is known as the Harris Matrix, to manage and diagram the complex stratigraphic relationships identified in the White Shaman mural. To do this, I used a software program called Harris Matrix Composer. This software is designed to build up and graphically represent an archaeological stratification in the form of a sequential diagram.

Each node in a Harris Matrix represents a single unit of stratification. I determined the least inclusive unit

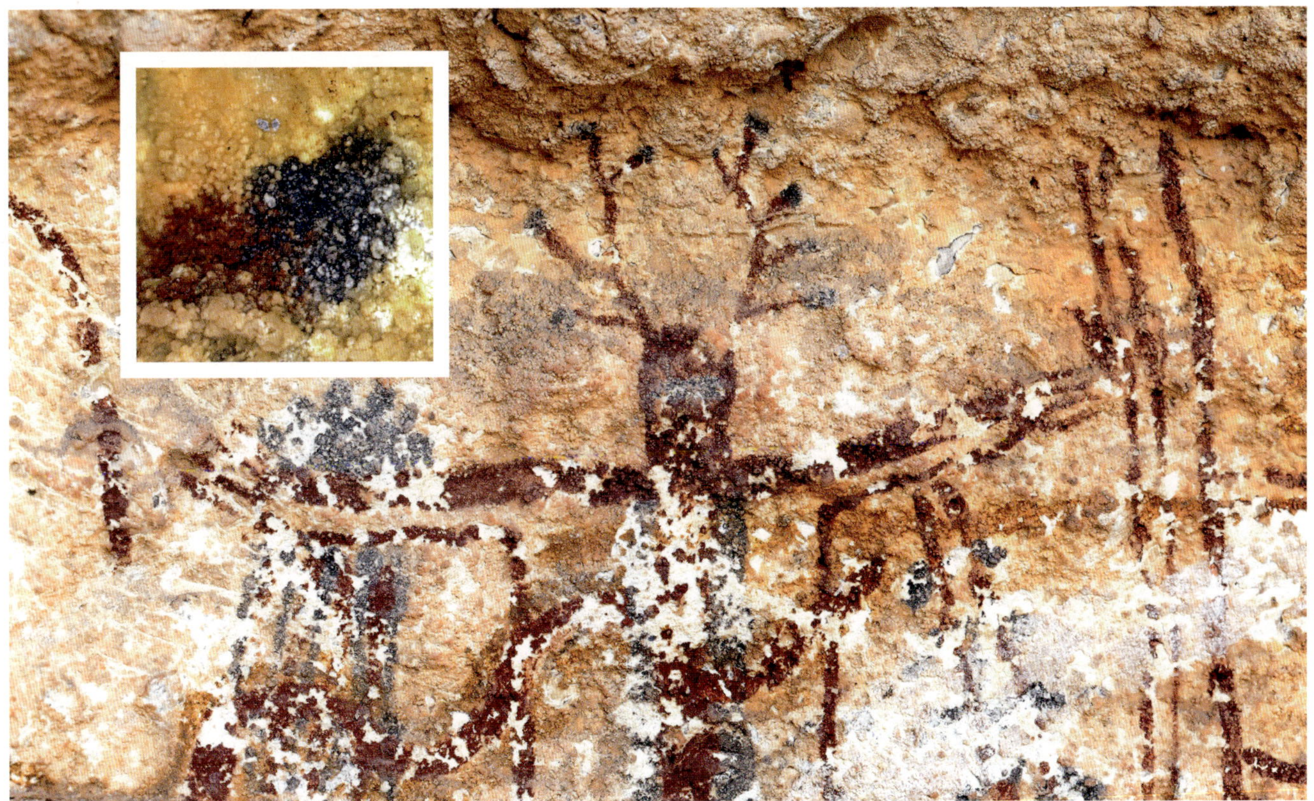

Figure 3.7. Microscopic analysis of A006: (a) antlered anthropomorph (A006) with black dots located at the end of each antler tine; (b) *(inset)* microscopic photo showing red antlers superimposing black dots.

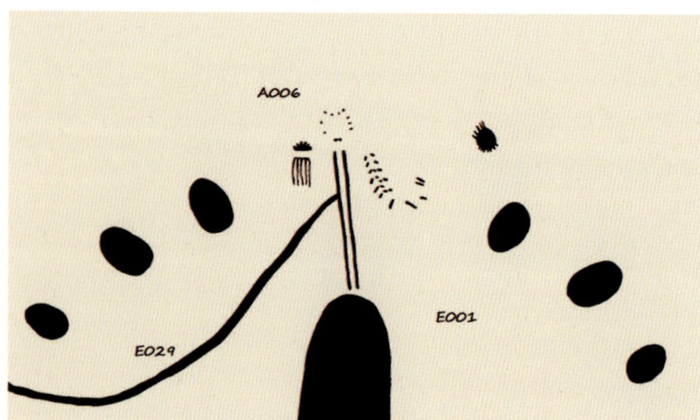

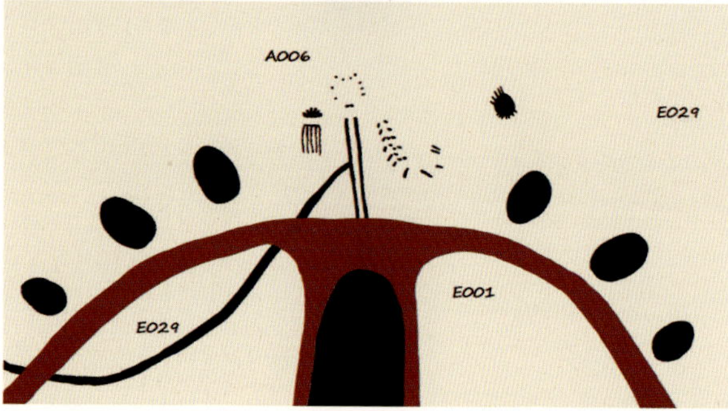

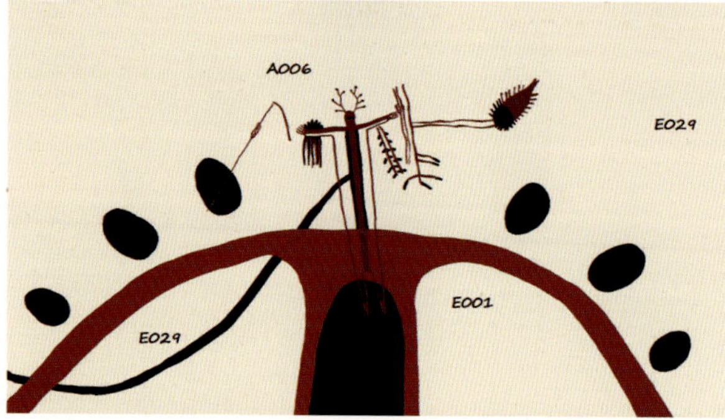

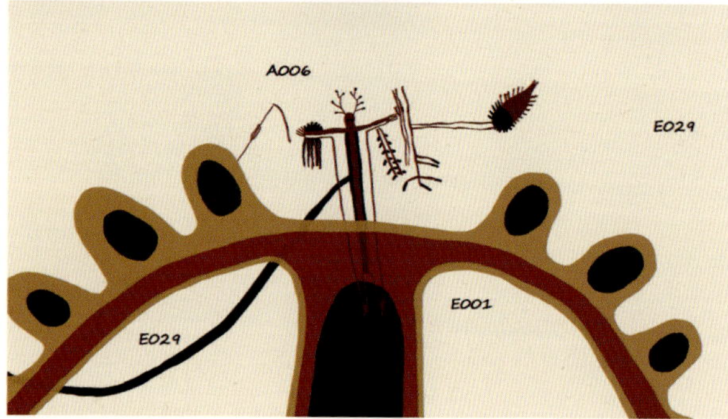

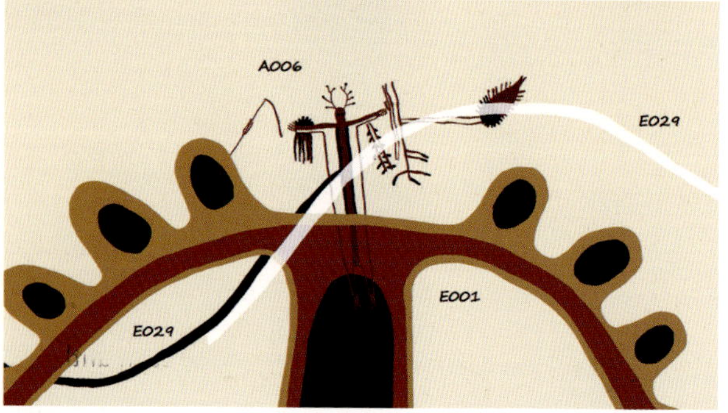

of stratification to be the individual layers of color that combine to form a single figure (figure 3.9). For example, if a figure is composed of three colors, it contains three units of stratification. If it is painted in two colors, it contains two units of stratification, and so forth. I built the matrix up from this narrowest level of analysis to the broadest level, which is the entire mural.

The top unit represents the interface of the topmost layer of paint with the atmosphere. The ground unit represents the interface of the bottom-most layer of paint with the shelter wall. Each arrow in the Harris Matrix diagram represents the stratigraphic relationships between paint layers and these two units. The unit labeled "Unexcavated" is a placeholder and represents all future units that will be added into the diagram. Once the matrix is complete, the placeholder is removed.

After inserting color units for a figure, we began adding units for figures it either superimposes or by which it is superimposed (figure 3.10). For example, A013 is composed of three colors: black, red, and yellow. The red of A013 superimposes the black body of A005, and the black body of A005 interfaces directly with the rock wall. The red legs of A013 also superimpose one of thirteen black L-shapes. Each L has a large black dot at its distal end. Arranged between the L-shapes with thirteen dots are nineteen additional black dots. One of the nineteen dots was likely converted by the artist into the black face or mask of A013. These congruent or morphologically similar figures are collectively referred to as E010. Two of the thirteen L-shapes and dots also superimpose the black body of A005, thus creating a second layer of black. The remainder of the L-shapes and dots, however, are not directly engaged in a stratigraphic relationship with either A005 or A013, but because they are congruent, they are considered contemporaneous with the L-shapes and are therefore included in the second layer of black.

Planned Composition

We continued this level of analysis throughout the mural, capturing 656 microscopic images of 42 locations requiring microanalysis and 1,635 macrophoto-

Figure 3.8. Color stratigraphy of A006: (a) Layer 1: black; (b) Layer 2: red; (c) Layer 3: dark red; (d) Layer 4: yellow; (e) Layer 5: white.

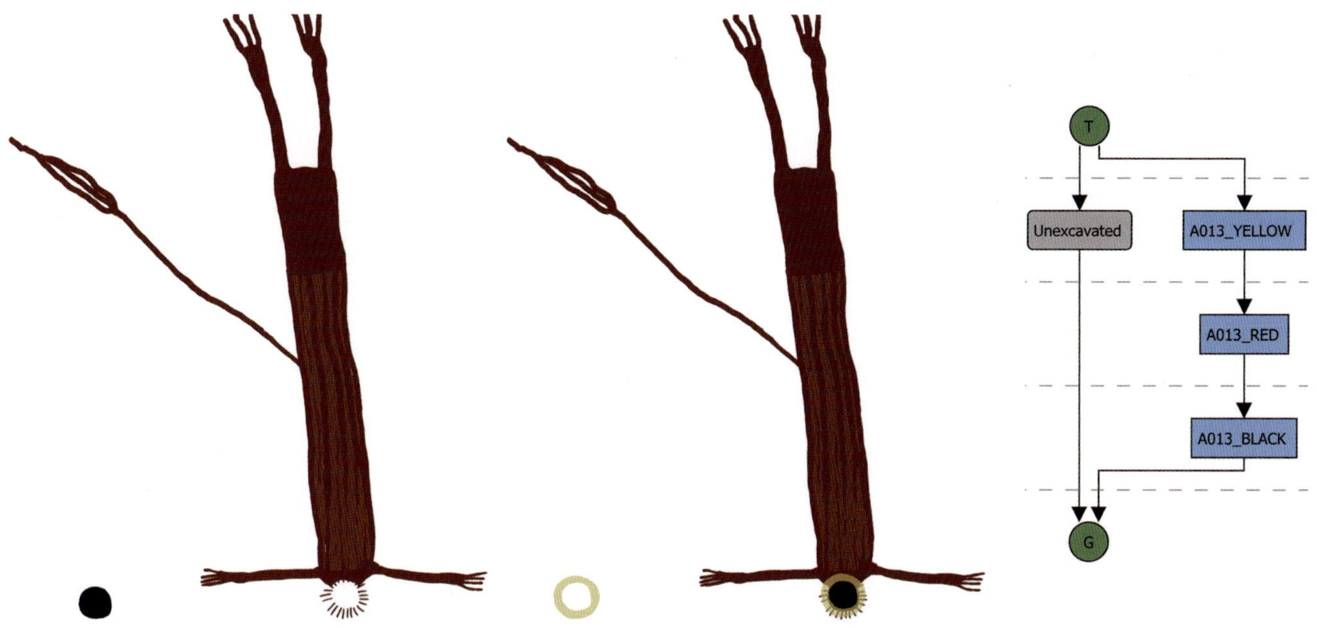

Figure 3.9. Managing and diagramming figure stratigraphy: (a) A013 is composed of three units of stratification representing three layers of paint applied to the wall in a specific sequence. (b) Harris Matrix for A013 diagramming the painting sequence. The black dot was applied first, followed by the red forming the figure's body. The final layer of paint applied was a yellow ring encircling the figure's head.

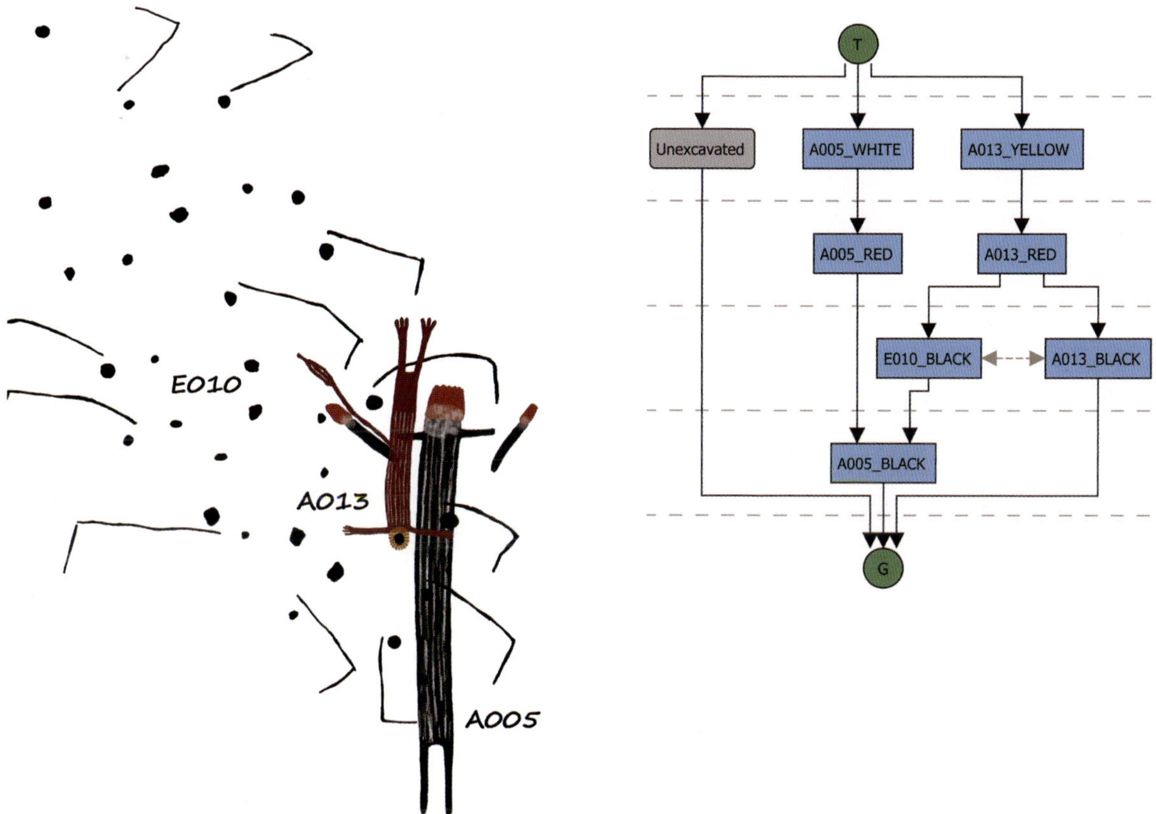

Figure 3.10. Managing and diagramming mural stratigraphy: (a) Composite illustration of A013, A005, and E010. (b) Harris Matrix diagramming stratigraphic relationships among units of stratification for multiple figures. The dashed gray arrow indicates contemporaneous units of stratification.

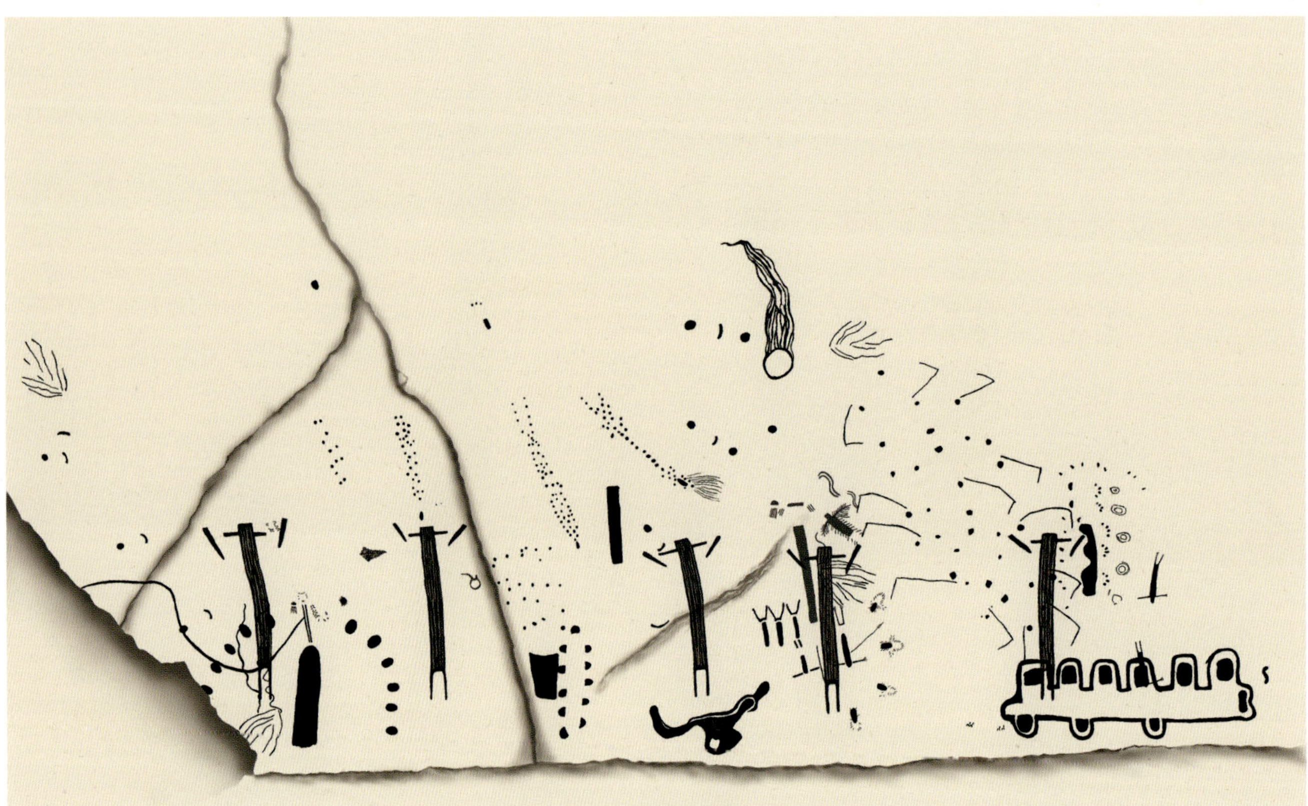

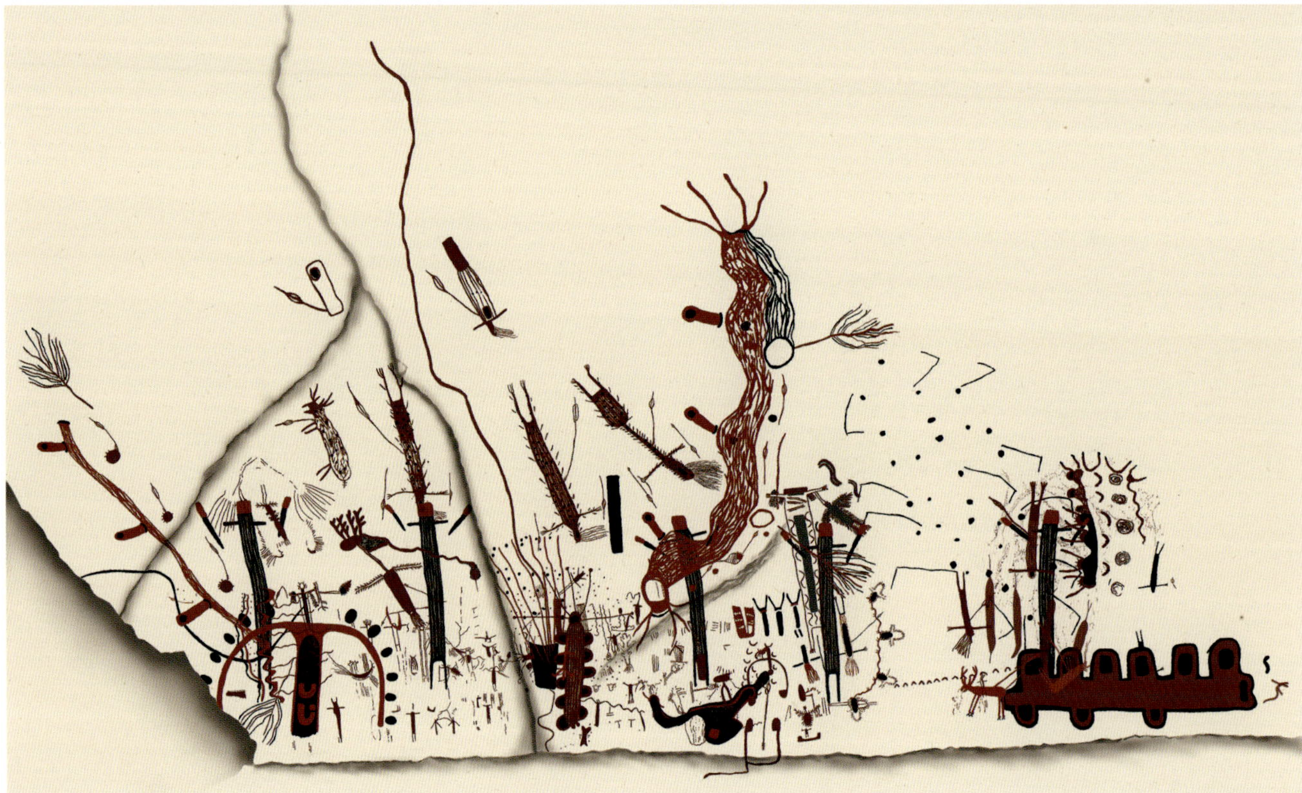

Figure 3.11. Painting sequence of the White Shaman mural: (a) Three layers of black paint consisting of 43 units of stratification form the first painting sequence. (b) Five layers of red paint consisting of 105 units of stratification form the second painting sequence.

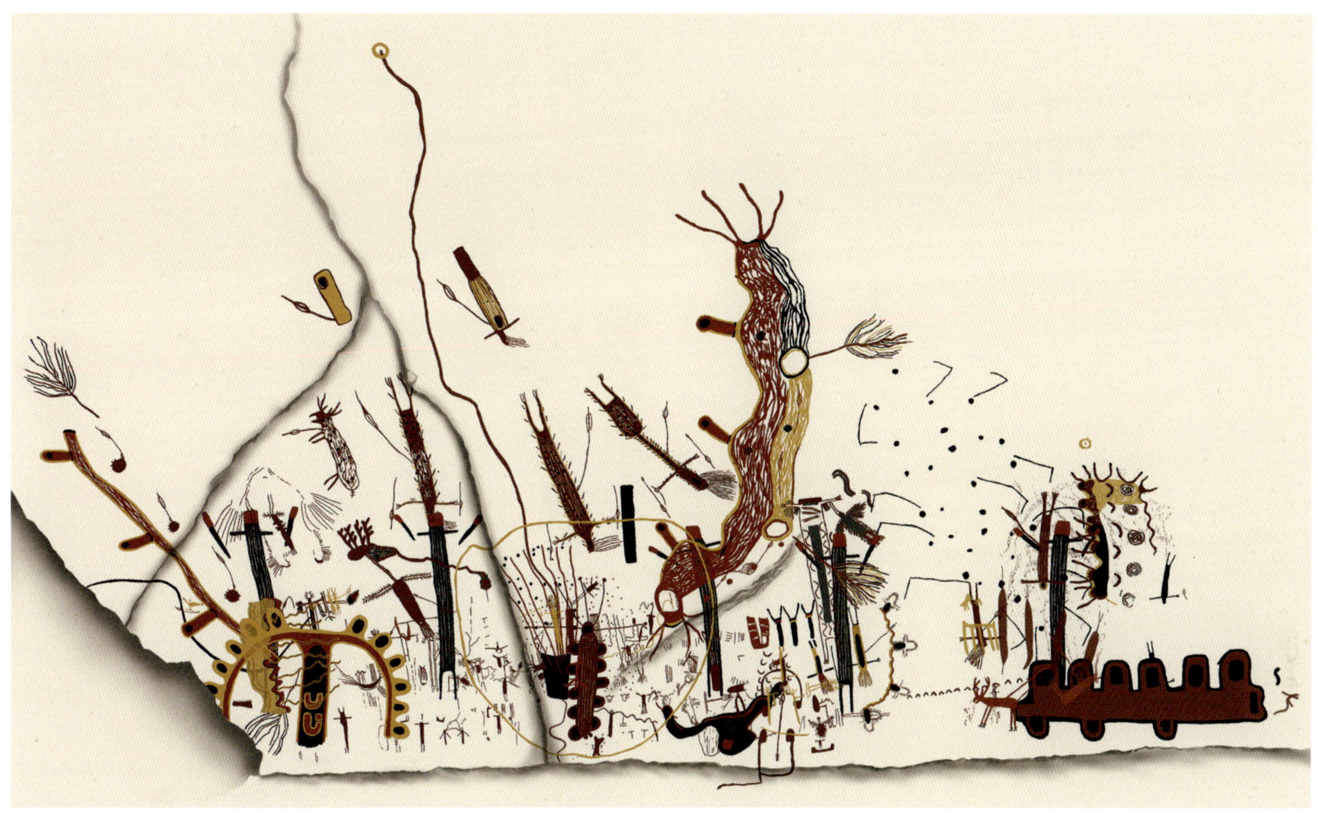

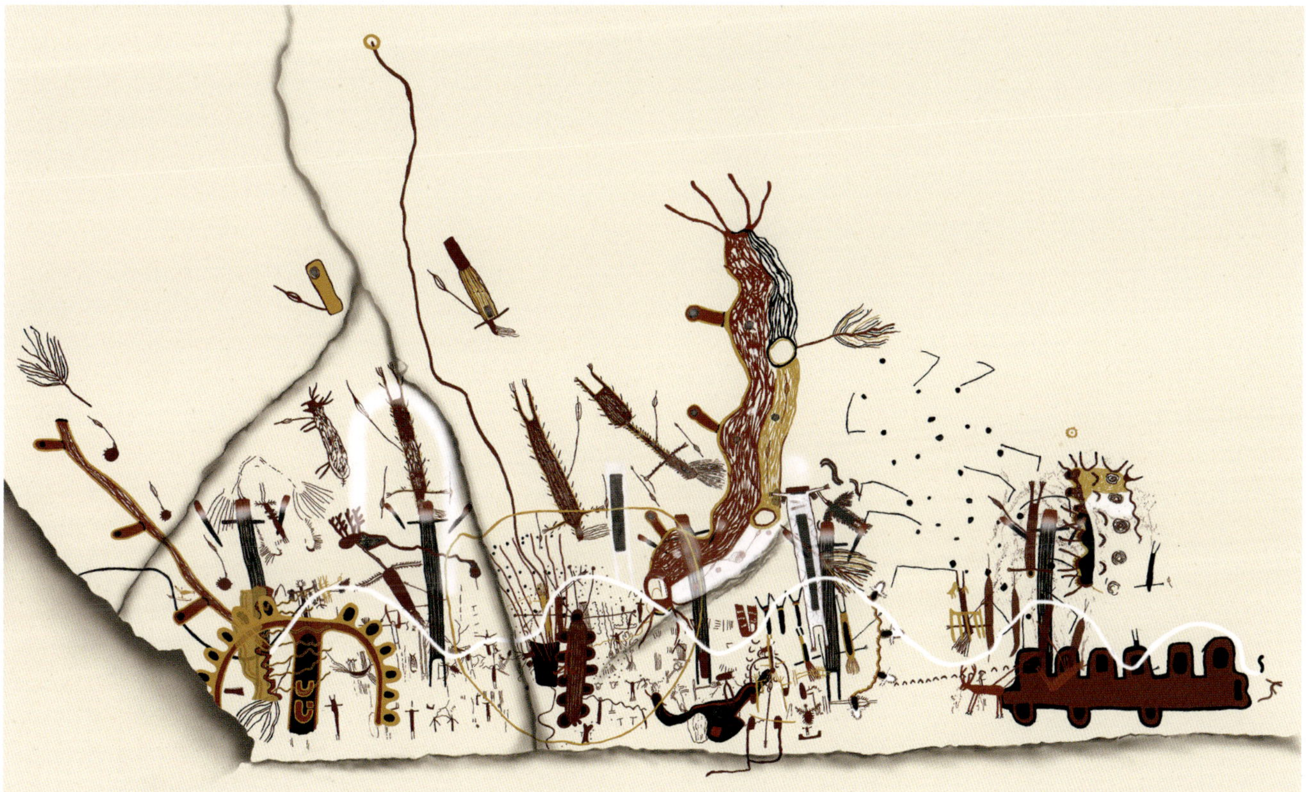

Figure 3.11. *(continued)* (c) Two layers of yellow paint consisting of 29 units of stratification form the third painting sequence. (d) Two layers of white paint consisting of 24 units of stratification finalize the painting sequence.

graphs. With this data we were able to complete the Harris Matrix not only for individual figures, but for virtually the entire mural. The results were startling. Strict rules governed the order in which the paint was applied. The artists of the mural painted all black imagery first, followed by red, then yellow, then white (figure 3.11).

Years ago, when I produced the first artistic rendering of the White Shaman mural, I instinctively knew the imagery was, by and large, produced by one artist as a single composition. When people asked how I knew this, all I could do was recite an analysis of the panel using artistic terminology, such as the artist's use of color and line, how the elements of the work interact and are configured along a visual plane, and the artistic devices used to move the eye across the mural. Identifying the order in which the artist applied paint, color by color, figure by figure, provided irrefutable evidence that the mural at White Shaman Shelter is a single composition: the planned arrangement of elements within a work of art to communicate an idea.

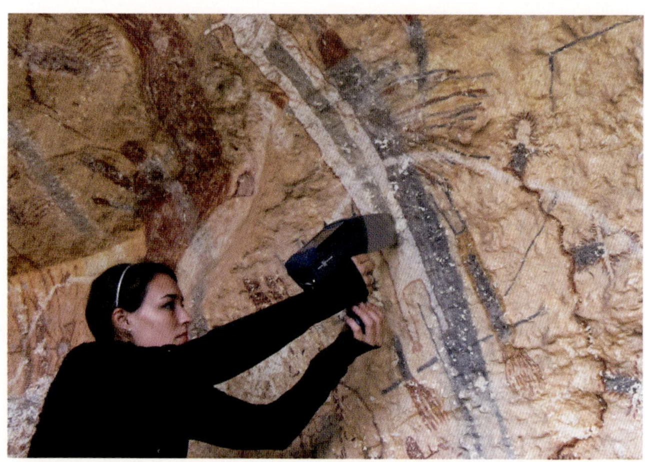

Figure 3.12. Shumla staff archaeologist Amanda Castañeda using pXRF to conduct an elemental analysis of the paintings.

Portable X-Ray Fluorescence

We conducted an elemental analysis of the painting using nondestructive portable X-ray fluorescence (pXRF) spectroscopy (figure 3.12) (Koenig et al. 2014). This type of spectroscopy is used to identify the specific chemical elements present in pigments.[7] We assayed thirty figures and obtained eighty-nine pXRF measurements from paintings in the main panel.[8] High concentrations of manganese were present in all black pigments, while red and yellow pigments contained significant levels of both iron and manganese.[9] Readings obtained for white paintings were inconclusive. Iron and manganese levels for these were comparable to unpainted background rock. We suspect that the white paint was produced using an aluminosilicate mineral such as kaolin clay. Interestingly, the smudges of dry-applied black pigment located around the corner and to the left of the mural did not contain manganese, suggesting charcoal was used in their production.

Figure Attribute Data

After figure illustrations were completed, we recorded their attribute data, which is information that can be classified, measured, and counted. For example, anthropomorph attribute data include physical attributes (such as size, color, and shape), paraphernalia (weaponry, staffs, and darts), and body adornments (feather hip-clusters, headdresses, and wrist and elbow adornments). According to Howells and Negreiros (2012:18), "By recognizing the attributes, we recognize the characters and the stories, and so help to crack the codes of much mythological and religious painting. The attribute isn't there because it is a casual part of the scene, but because it is deliberately included to indicate significance beyond its physical existence."

We collected an average of about 100 attributes for each of the 117 figures. In some cases, additional figure attribute data, now unavailable due to degradation of the art, was collected from legacy photographs dating back to the 1980s. These legacy photographs were compared to contemporary photographs to evaluate degradation of images and to identify possible agents of deterioration. After the illustrations and attribute data were field-checked, we entered the data into Shumla's searchable rock art database for analysis. As stated above, patterns are the clues to "making sense" of past human behavior. Analyzing attribute data through database queries reveals patterns needed to begin the process of interpretation.

Full Panel Rendering

Last, but far from least, I produced a digital rendering of the entire panel (see foldout insert). This was my second such endeavor; the first was created with pastels and Prismacolors on butcher paper, this one in Adobe Photoshop on the Cintiq pen display. I used the same method to produce the rendering as I did the individual illustrations. A super-high-resolution Gigapan image of the panel served as the background layer in Photoshop.[10] I traced the imagery to produce a line drawing of all figures in the panel and then gradually added color creating a new layer for each unit of stratification. In other words, each digital layer represented one layer of color for each figure in the mural.[11] This allowed me to view each layer independent of the other layers and to re-create, as best as possible, the painting sequence for the entire panel.

Written Inventories

Brief descriptions were written for each figure in the mural, as well as for the mural as a whole. These are formal analyses designed to describe through narrative the visual structure of the art. They are not interpretive, but instead simply document what the viewer sees, such as how pictographic elements are arranged and how they relate to other figures in the mural. The pre-iconographical description of *The Last Supper* provided earlier in this chapter is an example of this type of narrative. In chapters 5 and 6, I provide a brief pre-iconographical description for figures prior to entering into an iconographic analysis of the motifs.

Iconographic Analysis and Conventional Meaning

The method described above is a necessary prerequisite for interpreting visual texts. It provides objective data required for an iconographic analysis. It is at this stage that one begins to formulate hypotheses regarding the meaning and function of the art. Panofsky ([1939] 1972:6) says that this type of information can be apprehended when we "connect artistic *motifs* and combinations of *motifs* (*compositions*) with *themes* or *concepts*." The "motifs and combinations of motifs" are the attributes and patterns identified during the pre-iconographic analysis. The themes and concepts come from literary and artistic sources. For an example of how this works, let's return to our analysis of da Vinci's *The Last Supper*, this time informed by religious texts and cultural traditions.

> The serene central figure portrayed in *The Last Supper* represents Jesus. The twelve accompanying figures are his disciples. They are engaged in the Passover meal, their last supper before Jesus' crucifixion. Da Vinci depicts the disciples' devastation after Jesus informs them that one among them would betray him. The groupings of three and the triangle formed by Jesus' body represent the Holy Trinity. Judas, the betrayer, is holding a money bag and has knocked over the salt, a symbol of betrayal.

Howells and Negreiros (2012:25) write, "At this secondary or conventional level . . . we can tell the difference between a casual meal out and 'The Last Supper,' because we have brought our existing literary, artistic and cultural knowledge into play. We have progressed from the mere identification of motifs in level one to the interpretation of images in level two." When conducting an iconographic analysis of Pecos River style rock art, however, we lack religious texts and cultural traditions directly linked to the people who produced and consumed it.

It is true that direct information about the rock art is unavailable; the people who produced the images thousands of years ago are not here to explain it for themselves. But the myths, histories, and belief systems did not die with the people who produced the rock art. Peter Furst (1974), in a discussion on West Mexican art, writes:

> Explanations must be sought on a different plane if we are ever to move beyond seriation and description . . . But this requires something more than merely examining what seems obvious or logical within our ken. It requires knowledge of and insight into the shared symbolic world of the American Indian, prehistoric and contemporary, and more appreciation of the astonishing durability of this ancient ideological universe through time than some of us are evidently ready to grant. [Furst 1974:134]

López Austin (1997) sees this "shared symbolic world" as an archaic core, or hard nucleus, dating back thousands of years. This web of interrelated and intermeshed ideas forms a continuum still evident in Native American expressive culture. The actors and the details may change, but at the core, basic story lines and concepts are amazingly resilient to change. This allows contemporary ethnography and ethnohistoric accounts to be an effective bridge to the past. López Austin (2002:36) maintains that "the relationship between ancient and present myths is so evident that the comparison between the past and the present is highly enlightening."

If this is true, historical accounts and ethnographic observations of indigenous groups living in Mesoamerica should provide useful information for formulating hypotheses to explain patterning in the rock art of the Lower Pecos. As stated by López Austin (1993:310), although "one can never expect to find a total congruence, an unchanged tradition . . . One looks for clues. Finding the keys to indigenous thought allows the necessary hypotheses to be formulated." By comparing similarities between the understood concepts (ethnographic and ethnohistoric data) and new concepts (patterns in archaeological data), we formulated hypotheses that breathed life into images of the past. The shared patterns are the clues. They serve as an interpretative bridge between the past and the present.

Much of our research concentrated on the historical accounts and ethnographies of two principal groups, the Huichol and the Nahua. The Huichol were foremost for several reasons. They have, to some degree, successfully resisted acculturation into Mexican society and the Christian religion. They have maintained many of their old ways and beliefs, though admittedly more so in the earlier parts of the twentieth century than now.[12] But as Ángel Aedo (2003a:221) has pointed out, if you want to understand ancient Mesoamerican belief systems, you must begin with a thorough study of the Huichol.[13] So that is what we did. We expanded our existing knowledge about the Huichol through a reading of previously unexplored literature, much of it written in Spanish.

Three early ethnographers studied and wrote extensively about Huichol mythology and symbolism (Carl Lumholtz in the 1890s, Konrad Preuss in 1905–1907, and Robert Zingg in the 1930s). There is very little comparable early ethnography extant for the other Southern Uto-Aztecan-speaking groups of northern or western Mexico. Without the detailed observations of these early ethnographers, our work would have been far more difficult. An abundance of books and articles written by modern scholars describing the Huichol and their ancient practices and beliefs were also highly informative.

If the rock art is part of an Archaic core, then like all the rest of pre-Columbian Mesoamerican art, it should fit into the basic structure of that broader continuum, which means: (1) it must have inherent meaning, with nothing being random or arbitrary; (2) its inherent meaning is part of a larger structural meaning that directly relates to and arises out of an earlier culture and fits into the continuum that persists into later cultures;[14] (3) it works on several levels of interpretation;[15] and (4) it has functional equivalents in other mythologies, cosmologies, and iconographies.[16] To test this, we expanded our analysis to other indigenous groups living in Mesoamerica, most notably the Nahua (known by many as the Aztec).

An extensive body of literature exists for the Nahua. Early Spanish chroniclers more or less accurately recorded Nahua myths and rituals, and modern-day Mexican scholars have written extensively about their religion, symbolism, and cosmology. Thus, we are provided with a wealth of knowledge from which to draw. There is far more written about the sixteenth-century Nahua than any other Southern Uto-Aztecan-speaking group. However, there is always a caveat when dealing with the Nahua: we know they rewrote much of their history and at least part of their mythology. Grisel Gómez-Cano (2010) primarily attributes this to two factors: (1) sometime around the twelfth century AD they transitioned from a matriarchal hunter-gatherer society to a patriarchal agrarian city-state; and (2) the Nahua were an amalgamation of groups (Chichimec, Toltec, Teotihuacanos, and various conquered populations) with a concomitant amalgamated mythology. Félix Báez-Jorge (2000:19) says the Nahua borrowed several gods from conquered regions. Some gods kept their original characteristics, while others did not. But nothing in this line of historical or archaeological study is well-settled. Considerable debate continues regarding the identity of the Toltec and even the term *Chichimec,* which refers to a group of seminomadic people from northern Mexico who in reality were very diverse both culturally and linguistically. Some of these so-called Chichimec tribes spoke Southern Uto-Aztecan languages (including groups that later became the Huichol, Cora, Otomi, Yaqui, and others), and some of them ultimately became the Nahua. John Bierhorst (1984:5) claims that "After the fall of Tula, tribes from the north moved into the region the Toltecs had dominated, intermarried with the town dwellers already established there, and adopted the Toltec language, called Nahuatl." There is no universal agreement on this among anthropologists and historians; however, it seems that the language (and much of the mythology) can legitimately be traced back to northern Mexico sometime in the early to middle Mesoamerican Classic period.[17]

If the rock art is indeed a graphic manifestation of ancient interrelated and intermeshed Mesoamerican ideas, it should fit into the basic structure of this continuum and be "readable" using historical accounts and ethnographic observations of indigenous groups living in Mesoamerica beyond the Huichol. In other words, not only should we find shared patterns between Lower Pecos rock art and Nahua literature and iconography, but between the myths and beliefs of both the Nahua and Huichol. The results of this analysis are presented in the concluding chapter, where I reconstruct the narrative and propose a general myth and cosmology that informed production of the White Shaman mural.

Structural Analysis and Intrinsic Meaning

Through years of study I have come to realize that the meaning of Pecos River style rock art does not exist independent of its organizing structure. Our greatest challenge is not in deciphering what the rock art communicates; it is in recognizing the overriding principles that governed its production and provide the framework for understanding its message.

Panofsky ([1939] 1972:7) believed it was possible to apprehend this "intrinsic meaning" by determining the underlying principles that "reveal the basic attitude of a nation, a period, a class, a religious or philosophical persuasion—unconsciously qualified by one personality into one work." To do this, he argued, requires "synthetic intuition," a "familiarity with the essential tendencies of the human mind" (15).

Let's return to da Vinci's *The Last Supper* to help clarify the type of information we seek during this deepest level of analysis. At the first level we conducted a formal analysis and enumerated the painting's attributes. At the second level we connected the attributes to specific characters engaged in a specific event: the last supper. At the third level we seek to answer the bigger question of "Why?" Why is a spilled salt shaker a symbol for betrayal? Why does the Trinity define God as three divine persons? We are no longer concerning ourselves with identifying the narrative, but the underlying ideological assumptions of the society within which the visual narrative operated.

Chaîne Opératoire

In this step we transition from trying to understand *what* the visual text means to *how* it means: how meaning was communicated through the art, and how it formed part of the culture within which it was produced. To do this, we began by trying to understand the technical history of the White Shaman mural. What was the *chaîne opératoire* (operational sequence) of the art: How was it produced? Mesoamericanist Kay Read (1998) expresses the importance of this attention to detail most eloquently.

> Marking, as much as speaking, is a culturally defined act. All marking, whether it be expressly visual or referential, is both contextually based and a matter of choice because all discourse, visual or otherwise, is necessarily communal. All artists choose from a range of visual possibilities, a range constrained by both the subject matter and the particular style demanded by their cultural context. To analyze those constraints, one must "learn to see" the subject in a way similar to how the artist learned to see it in the first place. [Read 1998:19]

Fritz and Tosello (2007:78) assert that a "detailed analysis of the process of artistic creation in conjunction with a reconstruction of the techniques and chronology of parietal compositions clarify the cognitive behaviors which underlie the art." To do this, we documented stratigraphy, color sequences, and color combinations, and explored color choices for specific imagery. We considered the significance of incorporation, whereby imagery is strategically placed to incorporate natural features in the rock wall. We observed the interplay of light and shadow with the paintings at different times of the year. We considered morphology of the shelter, directionality, and possible astronomical correlations. This was a completely new paradigm for studying Pecos River style rock art. Essentially, it required nothing less than rewiring our minds, wiping the slate clean, and starting anew. Somehow we had to learn how to visualize the universe as the ancient artists saw it many centuries ago. Linguistics and semiotics provided insights into this level of analysis.

Linguistic and Semiotic Framework

The linguistic framework has to do with tracing the ideas and concepts of a people who spoke a parent language from some time in the past to the historical speakers of its daughter languages. Linguists try to reconstruct extinct languages and cultures by comparing the similarities among existing speakers of daughter languages and then projecting backward. This also applies to the worldview shaped by that language, which would also have been passed down to that protolanguage's linguistic progeny. For reasons that will be mentioned throughout but discussed at length in chapter 7, we believe that a possible explanation for the similarities we observe between Pecos River style rock art and Uto-Aztecan ethnographies is at least partially due to the shared symbolic world of peoples separated diachronically but who spoke related languages. Similar images, symbols, and metaphors not only followed the languages, but, as will be shown, may also have had linguistic components that were unique to those images, symbols, and metaphors.

The semiotic framework, on the other hand, is a bit more complicated.[18] Whereas scholars use linguistic connections to link groups and ideas diachronically, the linking of linguistically diverse groups synchronically through their shared symbology falls under the framework of semiotics.[19] Semiotics is the study of how signs acquire meaning and how they operate within a culture, as well as cross-culturally. On a very basic level it requires a signifier (i.e., a word, image, color, metaphor, or symbol) and a signified (an object or idea). The combination of the two is referred to as a "sign." In our analysis of the White Shaman panel, we consider figures and figure attributes to be signs. When seen (read) by the viewer, these images (signifiers) triggered a mental concept of an idea or an object (signified). Roland Barthes (1974) and Umberto Eco (1984) labeled the knowledge that allows individuals to read such signs in a consistent fashion as "codes." Codes are rule-driven systems directing the choice of signifiers (word, color, image, etc.) and their collocation (sequence of signifiers) to transmit the intended meanings in an effective way.

The term *cognitive codes* refers to systems operating within a specific language as well as cross-linguistically, or even outside of linguistics altogether, in order to communicate effectively. For example, most people would recognize and correctly interpret "No Smoking" signs and signs on bathrooms designating gender no matter which languages they speak or do not speak. These symbols operate cross-linguistically and cross-culturally. Among other things, semiotics deals with how people acquire these cognitive codes. People have to share the same codes in order to interpret the signifier in a uniform fashion and thereby communicate effectively.

Examining the patterns identified in Lower Pecos rock art and Uto-Aztecan ethnography within the framework of linguistics and semiotics provided remarkable insights into not just the symbology of the panel, but its inherent meaning. We began to grasp the framework of ideas and beliefs through which the culture interpreted and interacted with the world: their worldview. The results of this level of analysis are presented in the final chapter. In the next chapter, however, I provide an introduction to key concepts and terms used in the iconographic analysis of the White Shaman mural. It is a primer, of sorts, in which I discuss the Mesoamerican world vision and define core concepts of the shared symbolic world of Native America.

A PRIMER

ABIDING THEMES IN MESOAMERICAN THOUGHT

In spite of the differences in languages and people, Mesoamerican mythology is in fact fundamentally one and often tells the same story. Once that story is known, even if partially and imperfectly, it is easy to find . . .
MICHEL GRAULICH [1997:264]

This chapter is a primer. It provides an introduction to concepts that at one time permeated the belief systems of virtually every indigenous community in Mesoamerica. These concepts will be engaged throughout the remainder of the book. Some will be discussed when encountered within the text, but several require a somewhat more lengthy explanation.

Mesoamerican Core Concepts

In Mesoamerica there exists evidence for a deeply rooted and widely shared ideological and philosophical universe (Rice 2007:5). Numerous scholars have noted striking similarities in rituals, concepts of the cosmos, symbolism, and myths. Gary Gossen (1986:5–8) maintains that "symbol clusters" have persisted in Mesoamerican thought not only through time, but across cultural, political, linguistic, and ecological boundaries. These have shaped the Mesoamerican intellectual universe through the millennia. Five abiding themes identified by Gossen (1986:5–8) include:

1. *Cyclical time as a sacred entity.* Natural and cultural cycles are woven together with the daily and annual cycles of the sun "to create a cosmos that places humankind in an inherited, sacred, temporal order that demands human maintenance."
2. *Delimitation of the sky, earth, and underworld in the spatial layout of the cosmos, with mediation among these realms as a key intellectual, political, and religious activity.* Power, efficacy, and survival depend upon spatial mobility within the tripartite vertical cosmos and the related quadripartite horizontal cosmos.
3. *Supernatural and secular conflict as creative and life-sustaining forces.* Conflict, in Mesoamerican thought, was divinely ordained, and the parties engaged in a conflict often are dual aspects of the same supernatural being.
4. *Principle of complementary dualism.* The whole of existence is made up of substances existing in balanced and complementary opposition to one another.
5. *Spoken and written language (both pictographic and hieroglyphic) as an extraordinarily powerful symbolic entity in itself, beyond its neutral role as a means of communication.* Language is a sacred symbol allowing humans to share qualities with, as well as communicate with, the gods.

Prudence Rice (2007:5) adds to this list of key attributes the base count of twenty, which is referred to as vigesimal numeration, as well as complex calendrical and writing systems. She suggests that people may have begun developing these ideas "tens of thousands of years before entering the region to become Mesoamericans." Kent Flannery (2003:7) believes these and other basic cultural patterns endured across a vast area and likely persisted for more than eight thousand years.

López Austin (1997:5) similarly has argued for a shared symbolic world dating back thousands of years, deep into the Archaic. He demonstrated this through an extensive analysis of contemporary native religions in Mexico, including the Tzotzil Maya, Nahua, Otomi, Tepehua, Totonac, and Huichol. He noted these contemporary religions "are clearly not simply versions of pre-Hispanic thought and practices, but rather, despite strong Christian influence, they are part of ancient Mesoamerican traditions," and despite the presence of differing elements among these religions, there exists a "hard nucleus with components that were very resistant to historical change. They were almost unchangeable" (López Austin 1997:5).[1] He discusses these core components in his book *Tamoanchan Tlalocan* (1997). Although all are relevant to the analysis of the White Shaman mural, I will discuss only three here: the concept of replication, belief in souls, and a holistic division of the cosmos. Others requiring less explanation will be discussed in later chapters. This will be followed by a discussion of the importance of time in Mesoamerican belief systems and an introduction to the codices.

Replication

In Mesoamerican mythologies, each god contains "essences," which are distinct characteristics or "imperceptible forces" associated with that particular god (López Austin 1997:13). These essences can be shared with other gods or with sacred and mundane objects or symbols. This ability of the gods to reproduce them selves by transmitting their divine essences into other beings, objects, images, and so forth is referred to as "replication." López Austin describes the origin and sharing of essences as follows:

> The ancestors who died at the primordial sunrise formed the essence of everything in the world with their own essence. They made up the souls of everything that existed, not only plants, animals, and humans; they are the essence of springs, and even of things created by humans, such as the house and its hearth, objects that have personality.
>
> As examples of relationships of replication we can cite the ones that exist between a mythical place and its duplicate on earth, between a god and a human-god who is possessed by the god's essence, a god and his images, a town and a sacred mountain, a human being and his animal alter ego, the structure of the cosmos and that of a town or house, a god and his avatars and the list goes on. [López Austin 1997:151]

The identities of gods were fluid, often merging, overlapping, and folding into one another (Markman and Markman 1989:7). Contemporary Christians may recognize this concept in the replication of God the Father into God the Son and God the Holy Spirit. In Mesoamerican mythology, gods and goddesses frequently appear both as separate entities and as extensions of each other by way of their ability to replicate their essences. The transference and sharing of divine essences often makes it difficult to differentiate between gods and their divine derivations.

Take, for example, the supreme Nahua creator deity Ometeotl, which translates roughly as "Giver of Life." Ometeotl is a dual god consisting of a male and female aspect, Ometecuhtli and Omecíhuatl. The male aspect of this deity is replicated in the gods associated with fire, the sun, and the growth of corn. The female aspect of Ometeotl is replicated in deities associated with water, plants, and regeneration. Together they represent the divine creator couple (Carrasco 2008:47). In other words, the scores of Nahua gods are ultimately "manifestations of a single divine essence rather than having the wholly independent existence that the idea of a god often suggests" (Markman and Markman 1989: 138). The divine attributes of the deity are manifested in his/her names:

> He is the Lord and Lady of Duality (Ometecuhtli and Omecíhuatl)
> He is the Lord and Lady of our maintenance (Tonacatecuhtli and Tonacacíhuatl)
> He is mother and father of all the gods, the old god (Huehueteotl)
> He is at the same time the god of fire, who dwells in the navel of fire (Xiuhtecuhtli)
> He is the mirror of day and night (Tezcatlanextía and Tezcatlipoca)
> He is the star that illuminates all things, and he is the Lady of the shining skirt of stars (Citlallatóna and Citlalinicue)
> He is our mother, our father (*in Tonan* and *in Tota*)
> Above all, he is Ometeotl who dwells in the place of duality, Omeyocan. [León-Portilla 1990:90]

These gods, in turn, shared their essences with one or several other gods (a god and his avatars) to the extent that specific gods at times were almost reflections of each other. According to the Huichol, even the image of a god contains a part of the deity's essence (López Austin 1997:172). "Images are vessels . . . The gods and their images recognize each other. Like naturally goes to like, so portions of divine forces are poured into their divine receptacles" (López Austin 1993:137).

This sharing of essences is exemplified in Nahua naming conventions. All Uto-Aztecan languages are agglutinative, meaning they are characterized by polysynthesis, which is the construction of complex words through the use of what linguists call stems and affixes. This same rule applies to names. For example, the Nahua god Mixcoatl (the *x* is pronounced "sh") is a combination of *mixtli,* meaning "cloud," and *coatl,* meaning "serpent." The *-tli* is a singular noun ending that is dropped in the combination form. In Nahua mythology, Mixcoatl created the Milky Way, which is both cloud- and serpentlike, so it can be said that the Milky Way actually contains the essence of Mixcoatl. And the name for the Nahua moon goddess Coatlicue literally means "Serpent Skirt." She is often identified in the iconography by her skirt of snakes.[2] She is also frequently associated with rain, as are serpents.

According to the German philosopher Ernst Cassirer (1955:41), "The name of a god above all constitutes a real part of his essence and efficacy. It designates the sphere of energies within which each deity is and acts . . . In religious history we encounter the view that the true nature of the god, the power and diversity of his actions, is contained and, as it were, concentrated in his name." If one is to comprehend the message(s) in the White Shaman mural, understanding this concept is crucial.

The Souls

Another prevailing belief throughout pre-Columbian Mesoamerica was that the human body is the receptacle for two or more souls. The most common of these are the *tonalli* and the *yolia* (or *teyolia*). A third soul, the *ihiyotl,* is lodged in the liver and associated mainly with breath, wind, and the souls of the dead that become the wind (López Austin 1988:232, 323). Across Mesoamerica this soul is often conflated with the other two, so it will not be discussed separately.

The soul known as the *tonalli* is of solar origin and therefore related to heat and the sun. It was believed to be deposited by the creator deity into the head of a human embryo at the moment of conception and served to connect human beings with their gods (Carrasco 1998:68). This vital energy was thought to be responsible for the light energy transmitted through a person's eyes, their life force, temperament, and destiny (Chevalier and Sánchez Bain 2003:46; Megged 2010:111; Stuart 2011:120). *Tonalli* revealed itself as a person's breath and could be passed from generation to generation, appearing in the body as hair, fingernails, and blood (J. Furst 1995). Hair covering the head was believed to be a receptacle for *tonalli* and was responsible, in part, for preventing the soul from leaving the body (Carrasco 1998:69). Neurath (2001a:505) says that the Huichol *tukari* is equivalent to the Nahuatl concept of *tonalli.* It too is associated with the sun at the zenith, light, and solar energy.

The *yolia* (or *teyolia*) is the soul lodged in the heart. As opposed to the *tonalli,* the life force that dissipates upon death, the *yolia* is the ghost form of the soul that survives death and travels to the land of the dead (López Austin 1988:199; J. Furst 1995:22). *Yolia* was believed to animate the body and provide some portion of a person's character. It too could take the form of breath but was considered a "shadowy double of the body, and a precious gemstone" (J. Furst 1995:22). At death, a "heart-stone" was placed in the mouth of a corpse or in with a person's cremated ashes. This custom of placing small round stones in the mouths of deceased individuals was first recognized among the Olmec.[3] Modern ethnography tells us this was a way to capture the last breath (being the escaping *yolia* soul) of the individual (J. Furst 1995:54). Even recent ethnographers have reported a very similar practice among the Huichol, where small quartzite stones holding the souls of individuals are wrapped in sacred bundles and kept in sanctified places by their families. By giving a stone the identifying attributes of a particular god, the family enables the deceased person to merge with that god in the spiritual realm.

The Oppositional Schemes

The holistic division of the cosmos into oppositional pairs is one of the most distinctive components of Mesoamerican belief systems. A dual opposition of contrary elements operated within all things (López Austin 1997). In his 1962 treatise on mythology, *La pensée sauvage,* Claude Lévi-Strauss adapted and perfected this idea, arguing that the human brain thinks in structures, often defined by dichotomies.[4] Myths and cultural practices make sense only when understood as part of a system of differences and oppositions (Chandler 2007:102).

Across Mesoamerica the concept of a dual principle

establishing the universe permeated mental processes and established everything in a dichotomous nature (Markman and Markman 1989). In this classification system everything in the world has a counterpart, with the whole of existence consisting of substances in balanced opposition (López Austin 2002:32). Some of the dichotomies and their respective associations are listed in table 4.1 (cf. López Austin 1988:59).

Michel Graulich (1981) argues the daily course of the sun provided the basic metaphor for Mesoamerican myths. He writes that above all "is the obvious opposition between light and darkness and all the corresponding oppositions of the dualist Mesoamerican system: heaven (sun)-earth, fire-water, masculine-feminine, life-death" (Graulich 1981:45). Mesoamerican myths, he says, all have *the day* as their model: "The history told in the myths is that of the universe, of a people, an era, or a year, always compared to or equated with a day. The day provides a model for all of the oppositions because it encompasses both light and darkness" (Graulich 1997:265). The power of myth rests in the resolution of these opposites. And *the day* as conceived by Mesoamericans, with its cyclical alternation between light and dark, daytime and nighttime, resolves the oppositions (Graulich 1997:265).

In this dualist system day is equated with the color red and night with the color black. At the time of the conquest most Native American groups associated the cardinal directions with colors, as many of them still do. The most common association of colors in this scheme was red with the east and black with the west (DeBoer 2005; MacLaury 1997).[5] Everything else seems to fall into place under one of those two categories.

Another of the important dichotomies is that of hot and cold.[6] Almost all Mesoamerican belief systems held that every animate object (and most inanimate ones) is either hot, cold, or somewhere in between depending on the nature of its essence (Chevalier and Sánchez Bain 2003; Madsen 1955). Naturally, the day, sun, and fire are hot and equated with the color red and the world above. Night, the moon, the stars, and water are cold and equated with the color black and the world below—the underworld. Recognizing the hot/cold dichotomy in the colors assists in understanding the color scheme, which was critical to early ethnographers in deciphering the Mesoamerican codices, as it is for us today in deciphering the Pecos River style rock art.

Table 4.1.
Holistic division of the cosmos into oppositional pairs common to groups in Mesoamerica and the Southwest

DAY	NIGHT
Sun	Earth/Moon/Stars
Red	Black
Dry Season	Rainy Season
Morning Star	Evening Star
Hot	Cold
East	West
Male	Female
Father/Brother	Mother/Sister
Above World	Underworld
Desert	Water
Rain, Flowing Water, Blood	Large Bodies of Water, Pools
Beginning/Life	End/Death
Right Hand	Left Hand
Safety	Danger
Number 13	Number 9

Cycles of Time

In Mesoamerica everything was bound together and controlled by time. Every event, every thought, everything of any import was characterized and qualified by time as established in the pan-Mesoamerican calendrical system. In this system time both ordered and linked the present to the past and to the future (Boone 2007:13). These concepts of time, which were deeply integrated into Mesoamerican religions and philosophical texts, dominated Native lifeways (León-Portilla 2002a:65; see also, e.g., López Austin 1988). Timothy Knowlton (2010:19) writes, "Mathematics is employed to interpret all phenomena as interconnected at a single fundamental plane. This single fundamental plane is time. From movement in the heavens, meteorological events, treatment of illness, political fortunes, down to the quotidian activities of weaving, fishing, and carving, all had their effect within this single system."

In his book *Religions of Mesoamerica*, David Carrasco (1998:54) explains that in Mesoamerica time was believed to exist in three different but intersecting planes. The most ancient was primordial time: the time before creation, or the time before time. It is in this temporal realm the energies of the supreme creator deity (or deities) structured the universe. They created order out of chaos by organizing the universe into corresponding oppositions. This transcendent time of the gods is eternal and is located high in the celestial realms.

The next temporal realm is the time of myth. Mythological time is marked by the creation of supernatural beings who undergo "struggles, abductions, broken honor, death, and dismemberment" (Carrasco 1998:54). This cycle of time continues and exists in the sky and the underworld. It touches and is intimately engaged with the next temporal realm, that of human time, which is ordered and directed by a yearly calendar. Human time was created by the gods and exists on the earthly level. And as with the other two, it is touched by primordial time and mythological time. Carrasco (1998:54) imagines the relationship between cycles of time as a "wheel within a larger wheel within a larger wheel." Every day and every hour of every day is linked to primordial time and mythic time. Human time and space, therefore, are imbued with supernatural forces and divine beings.

In addition to these three temporal realms, all concepts of time were tied back into the solar, lunar, and seasonal cycles. In every prehistoric society these natural cycles produced cosmologies related to the sun, the moon, the planets, and the stars. Concepts of time essentially governed the way people viewed themselves and their world. And this view was expressed in their art. In fact, several authors have argued that perhaps most, if not all, prehistoric art in Mesoamerica is related to cosmogonic myths, those related to actual events taking place in a changing day and night sky.[7]

The expression of time in the artwork of pre-Columbian Mesoamerica is similar to that in the pictorial codices. Often it interweaves past, present, mythological, and cosmogonic time. "Viewing the world in such a manner and applying this conceptualization of time allows for entirely different periods to be placed side by side together in the same space" (Megged 2010:82). This concept of expressing multiple time periods together in the artwork is foreign to modern scholars not well versed in its Mesoamerican applications. Yet again, an understanding of these concepts of time is fundamental to understanding the artwork.

The Mesoamerican Codices

The few prehistoric and early historic books of the Mixtec, Zapotec, Maya, and Nahua that are extant today are all referred to as "codices"—manuscripts of ancient texts "whose content is significantly pictorial and painted in the native tradition, whether that manuscript is fully pictorial and executed in a screenfold strip of hide . . . or only partially pictorial and executed on European paper and bound as a European book" (Boone 2007:12). Twenty or so of these codices were created at or before the Conquest. All are composed of beautifully illustrated graphic writing. Much of what we know about the belief systems, religious ideology, and cosmology of the Nahua, Mixtec, and their neighbors is contained in these few codices (Boone 2007:6). Hundreds of other texts—ancient manuscripts that carried knowledge extending back over two thousand years (Carrasco 1998:14)—were tragically destroyed by the Spanish.

In 1562, Fray Diego de Landa, Spanish bishop of the Roman Catholic Archdiocese of Yucatán, ordered the burning of the great library at Mayapán. It is said that as many as a thousand codices were destroyed in the flames. What we know today of the pre-Hispanic beliefs of the Maya is contained largely in five books that were initially saved as souvenirs. The hieroglyphic form of the widely read *Popol Vuh*, the creation story of the Quiche Maya, was also burned for being a work of the devil, but around 1556 it was rewritten in a Latin-based alphabet by mission-educated Mayas. Between 1701 and 1703 the Dominican Fray Francisco Ximénez at Chichicastenango transcribed and then translated into Spanish the earliest existing copy of this codex (Brotherston 1992:215). It is today the most widely read, by far, of all the remaining codices.

Alternative Literacy

At the time of the Conquest (early sixteenth century) the system of symbolic representation (i.e., writing) used by indigenous Mesoamericans was significantly different than what most of us today identify as writing. The closest parallels to our view of writing were the Maya and Zapotec hieroglyphs. The surviving prehistoric and early historic codices of the Mixtec and Nahua, however, were mostly written in a graphic vocabulary, whereby the story was told solely with painted pictures. The pictures were the text: there was no distinction between word and image (Boone 1994:20). Fray Alonso de Molina's sixteenth-century dictionary of the Nahua language defines the Nahuatl word *tlacuiloliztli* to mean both "to write" and "to paint." But does this system of communication really qualify as "writing"? Were the authors of these ancient manuscripts "literate"? It all depends on how one defines those terms.

Boone and Mignolo (1994) tackled this controversial question head-on through a collection of important essays in *Writing without Words*. They and their collaborators argue persuasively that definitions we traditionally embrace for *writing* and *literacy* have Old World origins and are therefore prejudiced toward Western European culture. These definitions are simply inadequate when applied to areas where much graphic writing had no phonetic referent. Boone (1994:15) suggests a more inclusive definition for writing: "the communication of relatively specific ideas in a conventional manner by means of permanent, visible marks." This broader definition embraces the three different forms of representation through which meaning was communicated in the codices: pictorial representations, ideograms, and phonetic referents.

- **Pictorial representations:** iconography resembling what it actually represents (Boone 2000:33). Pictorial representations are pictograms and schematic drawings of objects "conceived to exhibit the images of what is to be communicated" (León-Portilla 1980:31–32). For instance, a picture of the hero god Quetzalcoatl meant that Quetzalcoatl was present in the action.
- **Ideograms:** single images communicating "larger or unportrayable ideas, concepts, or things" (Boone 2000:33). Ideograms are the symbolic representation of ideas that could be an "arbitrary (as far as we know) referent to a thing, idea or happening" (Boone 2000:35). For example, a picture of Quetzalcoatl could represent the deity, but as an ideogram it could also refer to the forces of wind, the ninth hour of the day, rulership, or one of the appearances of the planet Venus. Its meaning is context-dependent. The same is true of flower imagery. A picture of a flower could represent a certain type of plant, but depending on context, it could also represent a poem or sacrificial blood.
- **Phonetic referents:** graphic vocabulary and phonetic writing in which hieroglyphs represented sounds. Most were syllabic but also were used to symbolize single-letter sounds (León-Portilla 1980:32). For example, the letters *a*, *e*, and *o* were represented by "stylized pictographs for *a-tl* (water), *e-tl* (beans), and *o-tli* (road)" (León-Portilla 1980:32).

The symbols used in Nahua pictorial writing can be read superficially, but they usually are multivalent, having deep and multiple meanings (Boone 2007:61).[8] The meanings were conveyed through visual associations made by the reader, as well as by associations created through a graphic vocabulary. The pronunciation of the symbols conveyed messages through the lexicon, fashioning visual metaphors that "are like arbitrarily assigned ideographs in that they bear no immediate resemblance to what they mean" (Boone 2000:35). The most famous of the Nahua double entendres is the name *Quetzalcoatl*, which popularly means "plumed serpent" but in the lexicon can also mean "sacred twin."

The challenge to reading the codices and, as I will demonstrate, the rock art is being able to recognize the myriad of embedded meanings and associations behind the deities, actions, and symbols. Colas (2011:22) argues that to fully understand these types of writing systems, one must also know "all relevant contexts, such as persons, circumstances, culture, writing surface, and writing instruments."

In the ancient codices the placement of symbols within the context of other pictures and symbols on the page was extremely important in conveying meaning. Geoffrey Sampson (1985) called these types of writing systems "semasiographic."[9] These systems "function independently of language, although they operate on the same logical level as spoken language and can parallel it. These are the systems that the broader definition of writing embraces" (Boone 2000:30). They are governed by their own rules and "can be understood outside of language once one understands the logical system (a system comparable to a grammar) that drives and orders them" (Boone 1994:16).

For the most part, writings of the Mixtec and Nahua formed a composite system that was able to function across linguistic boundaries (Boone 2000:32). To be able to read these writing systems, it was not so much necessary to understand the language in which they were written as it was to understand the grammar. This grammar not only used pictograms, ideograms, and a graphic vocabulary, it could also "employ space, proximity, adjacency, sequence, and the properties of inclusion and exclusion to convey meaning" (Boone 2007:68). The reading order of these images, however, was not precisely set. This fluidity allowed for different readings of the same text. As a result, most of these pictorial writing systems "are far more flexible and efficient than the partisans of alphabets would recognize" (Houston 1994:34).

Orality and Reading Visual Narratives

In her discussion about the graphic images of the Nahua, Kay Read (1998:16) said that these types of works are not visual backdrops but instead tell a story and are actually intended to be "read." After all, "visual communication, like verbal communication, is discourse . . . Skillful seers . . . mark such things as its colors, lines, shapes, textures, and composition just as skillful listeners hear things such as a speaker's tone of voice, volume, accent, rhythm of speech, and placement of emphasis" (Read 1998:16, 18). Many of the Mesoamerican codices are visual narratives that combined images with other narrative devices, such as sound, music, and dialogue (Monaghan 1994; Navarrete 2000:37). In fact, they were not thought of as passive documents but as active devices that "speak" or "sing" through oration and performance (Houston et al. 2006:138). The artist, or *tlacuilo,* of the codices used pictorial conventions reflecting the existence of a highly developed visual narrative tradition in Mesoamerica (Navarrete 2000:31).[10] These ancient visual texts were not only intended to be read, but to be read aloud.

The few surviving pre-Hispanic codices contain cosmogonies, which are creation stories that invariably relate to the cosmos. I will demonstrate in subsequent chapters that the graphic images on the limestone wall of White Shaman Shelter functioned similarly in form and content to the pictorial-iconic presentations in Nahua pre-Columbian codices. They functioned to record cosmogonic ideas through permanent visible marks. These ideas were collective social memory that could be returned to over and over again, generation upon generation, for consideration and inspection. And the images could be read by people other than the artist who painted the mural. It is as close as one can get to a written text created by a people who did not have a written language.

Incarnated Images

There is one important distinction that must be made between the written word and the painted image. In Diana Magaloni Kerpel's (2014) essay on the artists and materials of the *Florentine Codex,* she illuminates yet another level of meaning communicated through the process of creating painted codices.

Nahua artists produced paint from both organic and inorganic ingredients. Plants and insects were used to create colorants or dyes, and earth minerals were used to produce pigments. Magaloni Kerpel's (2014) chemical analysis of the paintings revealed that the artists used both of these materials to produce the *same* color. She states that "their use in images was not directly related to their tone but rather to their materiality and provenance, implying that colors had a specific significance based on their raw material and their natural state" (Magaloni Kerpel 2014:35). For example, when portraying an image related to the upper world, Nahua artists selected organic colorants. If painting an image related to the underworld, they used pigments mined from below the earth's surface. And if the image was of a deity or concept related to both the upper and lower realms, the "painters blended mineral pigments and organic colorants in a ritual action similar to what was carried out by the gods at the origin of time . . . Together the substances form a complete and powerful being" (Magaloni Kerpel 2014:38).

Through the careful selection of colorants and the painting of attributes specific to a deity, the artist was not simply illustrating them, but making them incarnate—giving them life (Magaloni Kerpel 2014:18). As will be demonstrated in the chapters that follow, a similar practice appears to have been employed by the White Shaman muralist(s).

PILGRIMAGE TO CREATION

A READING OF THE WHITE SHAMAN MURAL INFORMED BY HUICHOL MYTHOLOGY

The Huichol are a Native American people living in western Mexico. In their Uto-Aztecan language, which is closely related to that spoken by the ancient Nahua, they refer to themselves as Wixárika (Wixáritari).[1] Due to their remote location high in the Sierra Madre Occidental of Mexico, they have resisted, to a large degree, acculturation and assimilation into Mexican society and the Christian religion; however, their culture, like any other, has not remained static. While holding fast to their own worldview, rich cosmology, and ceremonial cycle, the Huichol have reformulated and incorporated components of the Christian-Catholic faith. These components have been added but have not replaced the traditional Huichol religious schema (Fikes 2011:10; Sittón 1996).

It is estimated that there are about forty thousand Huichol living today. Approximately half of the population has moved outside the Sierra into cities such as Tepic and Guadalajara, and as far away as the United States. Those remaining in the Sierra live with their extended families in small, widely separated *rancherías*. The Huichol manage livestock and practice slash-and-burn agriculture, growing just enough crops to feed themselves and their families. Using digging sticks, they plant corn, beans, and squash along the steep, rocky slopes surrounding the *rancherías*. Deer hunting and gathering wild plant foods continue to be highly valued activities (Powell and Grady 2010).

There is, as yet, no consensus on where the Huichol originated. Some scholars argue they are descendants of a socially complex west Mexican culture that settled along the Pacific coast around 400 BC–AD 500. Those who adhere to this theory suggest the Huichol have been living in their current location, within what is now the Mexican states of Jalisco and Nayarit, since AD 200 (Fikes et al. 2004). Others convincingly argue the Huichol are related, at least in part, to an ancient hunting and gathering group from northern Mexico known as the Chichimec Guachichil (P. Furst 2006; Grady and Furst 2011). Recent genetic studies certainly support this idea (Páez-Riberos et al. 2006). The Guachichiles are believed to have migrated into the Sierra from their arid homeland in north-central Mexico around the time of the Spanish conquest. The Huichol encountered by the conquistadors in the Sierra were an amalgamation of various neighboring cultures that fled into the mountains in advance of the Spanish (Weigand 1978:101).

Early ethnographers studied and wrote extensively about Huichol mythology and symbolism. Among these were the Norwegian explorer Carl Lumholtz and French scholar Léon Diguet, both of whom studied the Huichol during the 1890s. Lumholtz's books *Symbolism of the Huichol Indians* (1900) and *Unknown Mexico* (1902) provided the first documentation of Huichol life and customs, including the famous peyote pilgrimage. Soon after, in 1906, German anthropologist Konrad Theodore Preuss arrived on the scene. Preuss devoted decades to studying the cultures of the Gran Nayar, a region home to the Huichol and also the Cora, Tepehuano, Tepecano, and Mexicanero Nahua. He was convinced that the myths and rituals of these indigenous groups held the key to unraveling the ancient Mexica religion. Even today scholars acknowledge the Huichol as the starting point for understanding pre-Hispanic Mesoamerican belief systems (Aedo 2003a:221). Sadly, much of Preuss's written accounts were destroyed in Germany during World War II. Those that remain provide valuable insights into the cosmovision and rituals of the Huichol. Inspired by the work of his predecessors, American anthropologist Robert M. Zingg traveled to the Gran Nayar in 1934 to live among the Huichol. His book *The Huichols: Primitive Artists* ([1938] 1977) remains one of the most significant contributions to Huichol ethnography. The importance of the detailed observations made by these early ethnographers of Huichol social and religious life cannot be overstated.

Whether reading the works of Lumholtz, Diguet, Preuss, or Zingg, one encounters a common theme: duality. As it was for other Mesoamerican groups, the universe of the Huichol has a dual structure (Neurath 2001a:503). In this universe the dark, feminine forces of the rainy season and underworld are engaged in a constant battle with the light, masculine forces of the dry season and the world above (Gutiérrez 2002:35). Huichol myths seek to explain the origin of this duality and inform the rituals required to maintain equilibrium between opposing forces. Balancing the opposites is not only the theme of Huichol art and ritual, it is their function (Kindl 2001:4).

Huichol art carries on the Mesoamerican tradition of pictorial codices (Neurath 2005a:71). Preuss referred to their elaborate graphic expressions as the nonverbal dramatization of myth (Orellana 2007:73). Beliefs are "written" as imagery into gourd bowls, yarn paintings, beadwork, and weavings (Kindl 2000:53). Art is a tool by which the Huichol sustain the existence of the gods and cycles of the world. It is produced not only as a way to communicate with the gods, but to make them manifest. Contemporary scholars maintain this view as well. Neurath (2005a:72) writes, "The figures that appear in each work are gods in the full sense of the word, not their 'images' . . . Each figure is a powerful being with a will of its own. These are gods engaged in creating the universe at the very moment they appear in a work of art." And when an artist captures a vision and places it on a flat surface or forms it into a sculpture, he or she is ensuring the continued existence of the cosmos (Neurath 2005a:72).

The Huichol pantheon is populated with ancestral deities referred to in kinship terms, such as Great-Grandmother, Grandfather, Father, or Brother. These are the Ancestors, who through supernatural feats put the world into order and continue to give life and sustenance to the Huichol today. Their ethics and religion are based on living a life according to the traditional ways, which includes invoking the ancestral deities and reenacting their achievements through ritual. Negrín (1975:6) writes, "The traditional way draws past and future together in an unbound present that is a never ending process of creation."

One of the most famous rituals performed as part of the complex Huichol ceremonial cycle is the peyote hunt, a ritual reenactment of creation. Carl Lumholtz (1900, 1902) was the first to describe the hunt for peyote, although he never participated directly in the pilgrimage. Peyote (*Lophophora williamsii*) is a spineless cactus possessing medicinal properties and containing hallucinogenic alkaloids.[2] It is not native to where the Huichol live today in western Mexico. To hunt peyote, they journey east to Wirikuta, their sacred homeland in the Mexican state of San Luis Potosí.[3] The pilgrimage documented by Lumholtz was, and continues to be, a 600-mile round-trip governed by strict rules of protocol. The Huichols travel most of the distance today by motorized vehicles, but in the 1890s it was a forty-day trip made strictly by foot.

Peyote is collected annually in Wirikuta and brought home to the rest of the community for use in religious ceremonies and as medicine. But it is far more than that. Peyote is integral to life. Stacy Schaefer (1996a:165), who has been conducting ethnographic research among the Huichol since 1985, was told by one of her consultants, "Peyote is the crossing of our souls, it is everything that is. Without it nothing would exist." And the pilgrimage is conducted more than simply to collect peyote; it is central to their religion, something the Huichol must do to maintain equilibrium in the universe.

As mentioned in chapter 1, in the 1990s I put forth the idea that certain elements of the White Shaman mural match up closely to the peyote pilgrimage. I proposed the mural functioned as a prescription for an ancient peyote ritual. My focus at that time was on analysis of the ritual itself, not on the myths informing it. In 2007 I began reading the works of Mexican ethnographers Johannes Neurath and Arturo Gutiérrez, among others, where I quickly realized I needed to shift my focus from ritual to myth. This proved immediately fruitful. With each passing year of study, it has become more evident that the mural contains elements strikingly similar to not only Huichol creation stories, but to those of other Southern Uto-Aztecan-speaking peoples—including the concepts of replication, complementary dualism, a primordial mountain in the east from which all life emerged, and of supernatural and secular conflict as being creative, life-sustaining forces. While one might argue that each element, individually, could be coincidental, in the aggregate they are hard to deny.

The remainder of this chapter is organized as follows. I begin by providing an abbreviated synthesis of two important Huichol creation stories: the Birth of the Sun and the Birth of Peyote. I then describe the peyote pilgrimage and hunt—a ritual performed to reenact the myths. The next section is an iconographic analysis of the mural, connecting artistic motifs identified during the pre-iconographic analysis with themes and concepts identified in Huichol myth and ritual. This information will be used to formulate hypotheses regarding the meaning and function of Lower Pecos art.

Stories of Creation

There are several versions of creation myths in Huichol lore. This situation gave the early ethnographers a certain amount of consternation but doesn't seem to have bothered the Huichol, who consider all of the stories to be equally true (P. Furst 2006:58).[4] Among those stories the basic themes and core elements are fixed (Furst and Anguiano 1976:113). Gutiérrez (2011:100) identifies the fundamental mythemes in Huichol creation stories:[5]

1. An aquatic world existing without form and without humans, where everything is in total darkness
2. The darkness being divided by the emergence of fire and the first pilgrims
3. An act of self-sacrifice that leads to the dawn of time, the birth of the sun, and, with this, light, humans, law, and time.

The two main Huichol myths relevant to the White Shaman mural are the Birth of the Sun and the Birth of Peyote. In some versions, such as those reported by Zingg (2004) and Neurath (2005a), these two acts of creation occur simultaneously and are conflated into one myth. In other accounts, because peyote is associated with the Morning Star, which precedes the sun in both nature and myth, the origins of peyote are recounted first (Neurath 2005c:96 fn25). The creation of peyote marks the beginning of social order, separating those who are initiated from those who are not. Parallel to the creation of peyote is the birth of the sun, marking the beginning of time. These two events put an end to the perpetual chaos and disorder of *la vida nocturna* "life of nighttime." The Huichol refer to this as *tikari* or *t+kari*. It is primordial time: time before time. It is obscurity, the underworld, femininity, and the western half of the cosmos. The birth of the sun ushered in *la vida solar*, "the life of day." It is called *tukari* and is light, the world above, masculinity, and the eastern half of the cosmos. Equilibrium is established through the alternation of these opposites (Neurath 2001b:478).[6] Presented below are abbreviated versions of both myths—the origins of peyote and the sun—drawn from several key sources.[7]

Birth of Peyote

In the beginning, before the dawn of time, the Ancestors lived below in the watery underworld of the west. The world was in a state of chaos and total darkness; only the moon illuminated the eternal night sky. The first Ancestors were not humans but wolves and serpents and other types of animals. The world was in total darkness, and they could not see, so they had to communicate telepathically. It was decided they should journey east in search of the mountain where the sun would rise. Their destination was the other side of the cosmos, Wirikuta, the arid semidesert "above in the east" where they could acquire *nierika* (the gift of sight) and they could find *taiyari* (their heart). These pilgrims formed the first group of *jicareros*—ancestral wolf-people who had not yet become deities. They were also the first deer hunters.

A deer, Tamatsi Parietsika, armed with bow and arrow, led the pilgrims on a five-day underworld journey to the east.[8] He was in pursuit of his spiritual being, in pursuit of himself. He was both the leader of the hunt and the prey.[9] Kawi, the caterpillar, marked the trail for the deer to follow. Kawi's path began in the west and followed the path of the sun along the ecliptic to the east, terminating at the peak of Dawn Mountain. Tatewari (Grandfather Fire) provided the pilgrims with fire to light the path and to protect them from dangerous animals during their journey. More important, when they arrived in the east, they would need his essence, his fire, to help Father Sun (Tayau) rise for the first time.

When Tamatsi Parietsika reached the end of Kawi's path, he found his prey: his spiritual being. Feeling pity for the hunters who had pursued him through the underworld, he shot the deer, who was at the same time himself.[10] Because of this act of self-sacrifice, his heart (*iyari*) was transformed into *hikuli*, the sacred peyote cactus. At the same time, a young boy threw himself into a fire in the west and then rose through a cave door at the top of Dawn Mountain in the east as the solar deity. The two events, the origin of peyote and the first dawn, not only happened at the same place, but at the same moment—precisely at the end of the caterpillar's path.

When the Ancestors ate the meat of the deer, they experienced the effects of peyote for the very first time. At that moment they too went through a transformation. They became deities; they became peyote; they became deer; they became stars. And, at the same time, their essence was transmitted into and created all the elements of nature that their descendants—the humans—would need to survive. Through autosacrifice the first Ancestors acquired *nierika* (sight) and *iyari* (heart). With the birth of the sun came a dualistic division of the cosmos: day versus night, hot versus cold, rainy season versus dry season. The constellations were set in the heavens, and the deities were born. Everything was put into place. It was the end of the primordial age and the beginning of time as we know it today.

Birth of the Sun

Before the dawn of time people lived in total darkness for there was no sun. This was an era before time, a time marked by chaos. The primordial ancestors lived in the waters of the underworld to the west. They asked Nakawé (Grandmother Growth) what they should do so that the sun could be born. It was decided that one among them should transform himself into the Sun Father through autosacrifice. Four volunteers tried, but each failed. Finally, a fifth volunteer stepped forward. A young, crippled, fatherless boy decided he would perform the sacrifice required so that his people could have light.[11] He flung himself into the fire (or into the western sea) and descended through five levels of the underworld where he battled dangerous animals seeking to devour him, including a double-headed serpent that surrounded the earth.

Nakawé and Tatewari (Grandfather Fire) told the animal people to follow the boy through the underworld and to attend to his birth in the east. After five days, when they reached the peak of Paritek+a (Dawn Mountain), the child burst forth through a cave door as the Sun Father.[12] But exhausted from his long journey through the underworld, the sun began to sink. He was unable to move. His intense heat threatened to melt everything that existed. So Tatewari gave the Ancestors fire to help the Sun Father rise high in the sky. Candles were placed at each corner of the universe and at the center to keep the sun at its proper height.[13] And so it was that time as we know it—with its rhythmic alternations between night and day, rainy season and dry season—began.

The Ritual Peyote Hunt

The Huichol peyote pilgrimage has been observed and described in detail by several individuals, some qualified as anthropologists and some not.[14] Perhaps the most well-known accounts of the pilgrimage were presented by anthropologist Peter Furst in his 1969 film *To Find Our Life: The Peyote Hunt of the Huichols of Mexico*, and by a colleague of Furst's, Barbara Myerhoff, in her book *The Peyote Hunt: The Sacred Journey of the Huichol Indians* (1974). Furst and Myerhoff were the first anthropologists to actually observe the ritual. Ethnographer Stacy Schaefer has shared her knowledge of Huichol cosmology and the peyote hunt in three publications: *People of the Peyote* (1996), which she coedited with Peter Furst; *To Think with a Good Heart* (2002); and *Huichol Women, Weavers, and Shamans* (2015). All three are invaluable resources. Fernando Benítez, a Mexican journalist, participated in the pilgrimage in 1967 and published an account of his experience in the popular book *En la tierra mágica del peyote* (1968), which was later translated into English (*In the Magic Land of Peyote* [1975]). Less well known, but of inestimable value to this discussion, is the comprehensive analysis of the ritual provided by Mexican anthropologist Arturo Gutiérrez in *La peregrinación a Wirikuta* (2002). Numerous other scholars have provided tremendous insight into the peyote pilgrimage, perhaps most notably Johannes Neurath, who has published extensively on Huichol myth and ritual.

Like the myths related above, no two accounts of the pilgrimage are identical, but as with the myths, one can readily identify common elements. The summary presented below is admittedly abbreviated. It synthesizes descriptions of the ritual provided by both the early explorers to the region and contemporary authors. I relate only elements of the ritual identified in two or more sources.

The first peyote hunt conducted by the Ancestors gave birth to creation and established balance in the universe. Each year the Huichol reenact this primordial event through the peyote pilgrimage. This is not simply a copy of the First Hunt; it is the original event. The pilgrims enter into mythical time and become the major gods/Ancestors responsible for creation (Schaefer 2002:188). Neurath (2005a:74) writes, "The myth of the ancestors is not a thing of the past—it is more like an event that always happens for the first time." Huichol pilgrims are balancing the world and ensuring the continuation of the cosmos. When they hunt the sacred peyote in Wirikuta, the flowered desert in the east, they are engaged in creation.[15]

At some point between the end of the rainy season in October or November and early spring, a Huichol shaman (*mara'akáme*) leads the peyote pilgrimage to Wirikuta.[16] He is accompanied by several individuals from his community. These peyote pilgrims (*jicareros*) become Ancestors journeying back to their home in the east. The first five become the principal deities and represent the primordial ancestors who participated in the First Hunt. It is the responsibility of the shaman to assist in the transformation and to assign a new name to each pilgrim.

The shaman who leads the group becomes the principal deity Tatewari, Grandfather Fire.[17] He carries the *muwieris*, which are the antlers of Kauyumari, Elder Brother Deer. Kauyumari is the intermediary between the shaman and the deities, and serves as the guide and protector of the pilgrims along the journey. As one would expect, he is envisaged in the form of a deer or as a human figure wearing antlers. The Huichol believe that when the sacred deer descended from heaven, he brought peyote on his antlers to the homeland in Wirikuta, leaving the divine peyote cactus behind in his tracks. He revealed himself to the Ancestors during the First Hunt and continues to do so during subsequent hunts if the *jicareros* are all of one heart. They must enter the sacred homeland as one.

Unity of the pilgrims is accomplished through a rite of purification, during which the pilgrims seek to be released from their human condition in order to become "pure." The ritual also involves confession of sexual misdeeds.[18] Each *peyotero*, including those remaining behind, publicly declares his or her transgressions before the group. Failure to confess puts the entire pilgrimage at risk. The shaman makes a knot in a short fiber cord for each transgression mentioned. After all of the pilgrims have confessed, the assistant to Grandfather Fire, Tatutsi Maxakwaxi (Great-Grandfather Deer Tail), burns the knotted cords in the fire. By this action, transgressions are cleansed by the flames, and the pilgrims undergo a metamorphosis. They are changed from adults into children, and ultimately into divine beings. They are no longer considered mortal. To signify unity among the pilgrims, the shaman removes from his pouch a long white cord which each pilgrim is instructed to grasp. They pass the cord behind themselves in a clockwise direction to represent the journey to Wirikuta, and then counterclockwise in front to represent the journey home.

Through performance of these rituals, pilgrims are not only transformed into Ancestors, but transported into the darkness of primordial time. As Ancestors, they begin their journey out of the embryonic waters and, through self-sacrifice, into the act of creation. The pilgrims embark upon the journey in single file. The shaman-leader goes first, carrying the bow and arrows with which he will slay the peyote-deer in Wirikuta. Strict attention is given to preserving the order of the pilgrims. They walk in single file, maintaining proper order no matter how awkward or inconvenient.

At designated points along the journey, and at sacred waterholes, the pilgrims display offerings they have brought to the ancestral deities. Each stands before his or her offerings and raises candles toward the ascending sun. The flames of Grandfather Fire fuel the sunrise, and the candles hold the sun and the sky in place.

Upon reaching the permanent waterhole of Tatei Manieri (Our Mother), *jicareros* collect "living water" to take back to the Sierra for use in rain ceremonies.[19] They have crossed over into the sacred homeland. This is the place where the sky divides and light begins. It is the gateway into Wirikuta. Here the shaman uses the antlers of Elder Brother Deer to hold the portal open for pilgrims to pass through.

They continue their journey eastward until they reach a hill at the center of Wirikuta. This is the home of Kauyumari (Elder Brother Deer). But before they can begin collecting the peyote, they must hunt for five of the cacti exhibiting specific characteristics equated with the Ancestors. When they find the peyote that is the deer who gave his life so that the sun could be born (Tamatsi Parietsika), they take aim and shoot him with arrows. This is a very solemn time. That evening, as the sun begins to set, the shaman conducts blessings, peyote is eaten, and the story of the First Hunt and creation is told.

At the first light of dawn, after a night filled with ceremony, the *jicareros* paint their faces with yellow designs representing the Ancestors, the deer, the sun, and peyote; in essence, they are all one in the same. During some pilgrimages, *jicareros* are called to climb Cerro Quemado or Reu'unar to leave offerings in a cave at Paritek+a. This is where Father Sun arose from the underworld at the dawn of time, and where the gentle, fertile rains from the east originate. The pilgrims carry these rains, as well as peyote, back to the Sierra. After a sufficient quantity of peyote has been collected, it is sorted, cleaned, and packed, and the long journey home begins.

Iconographic Analysis of the White Shaman Mural

In the following pages I connect elements of Huichol myth and ritual with artistic motifs in the White Shaman mural. I begin by providing a detailed description of the motifs under investigation. The analysis of each motif is numbered sequentially according to the order in which it is addressed. I will refer to the motifs engaged in the analysis according to their identification codes. For example, the first motif analysis focuses on five anthropomorphic figures holding black objects with red tips. The identification codes for the figures in the motif array are A001 through A005; however, once the figures have been linked with characters, events, or objects in Huichol ethnography, I refer to them by that name rather than their figure identification number. This makes the text more readable, but there are inherent drawbacks. It is easy to fall into the misconception that the muralists used these same names to refer to figures portrayed in the art. They did not. The artists were not Huichol. Further, the identifiers are not intended as one-to-one correspondences; they simply serve as semiotic analogs. For example, if I draw an analogy between a figure in the panel and the Huichol fire god, Tatewari, I am not identifying the figure as the Huichol deity, but proposing it represents a prototypical fire god existing at the time the mural was produced. It is a semiotic ancestor, if you will, to the present deity. Analogies such as this will be used to formulate hypothetical meanings for motifs, but as discussed in chapter 3, I am not looking for completely congruent, one-to-one relationships. Instead I am looking for patterns that can offer clues about indigenous thought from which hypothetical meanings for motifs can be formulated.

Motif Analysis I: Primordial Ancestors and Cosmic Pillars

A row of five similarly executed humanlike figures with rectangular black bodies and red heads are placed close to equidistant apart from one end of the panel to the other (figure 5.1). The black was applied as broad stripes lengthwise down their bodies. They stand erect along an imaginary plane with long, narrow bodies. Their arms and legs are disproportionately short. They have no hands, no feet, and their solid red heads lack facial features. They are each approximately 3.5 feet tall and 1 foot wide. A thin layer of white paint slightly obscures the region where the red head intersects with the black body. The black bodies of four of the figures (A001, A002, A003, and A005) interface directly with the limestone canvas. They overlay no other color and no other figures. The right arm of A004, however, overlays the gray-black central band of a headless white anthropomorph (A015). The red heads on all five figures overlay the black bodies. Each of the five anthropomorphs is portrayed with two narrow, black objects tipped in red, one to the right and the other to the left of the figure (figure 5.2). These objects closely resemble the figures wielding them. The red tips are tilted slightly away from the figure's body. And as with the anthropomorphs, the black portion was painted prior to the red, and a thin layer of white paint was applied to the location where the red and black intersect.

Formulating Hypotheses

An analysis of the White Shaman mural must begin with these five anthropomorphs and the objects they are holding. I previously identified these figures as pilgrims carrying torches as they travel single-file to the land where peyote grows (Boyd 2003:76–77). Because their black bodies are not centrastyled, I identified them as mortal pilgrims prior to transformation into ancestral deities.[20] Informed by Huichol creation sto-

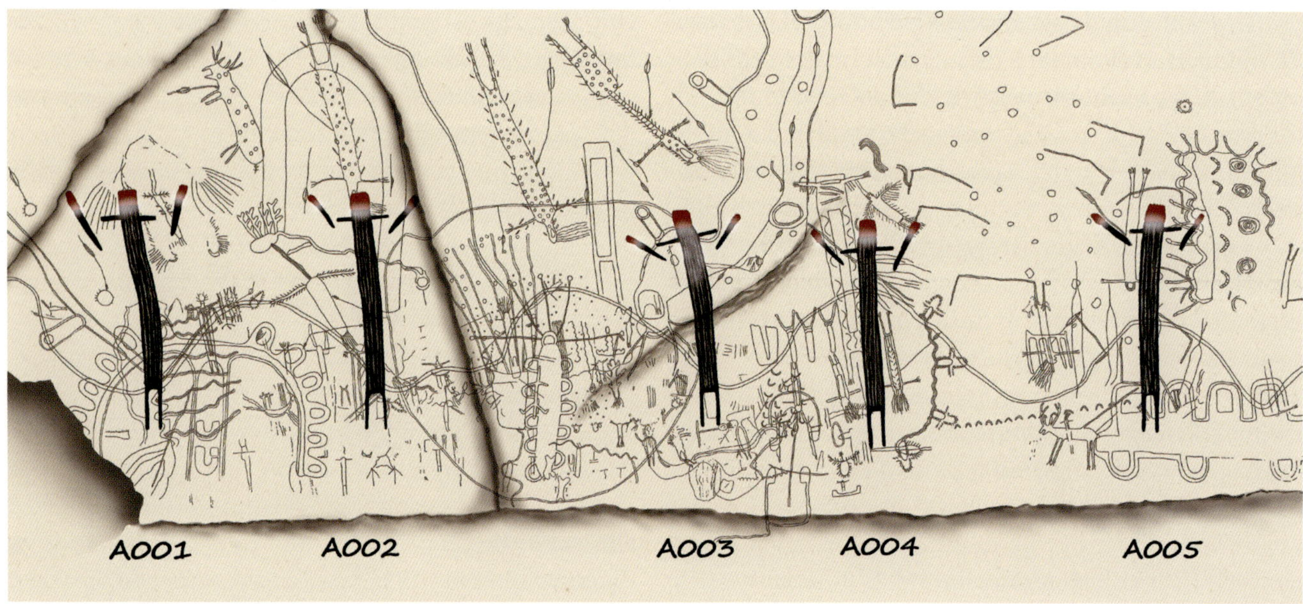

Figure 5.1. Motif I (A001–A005): Pilgrims, primordial ancestors, and cosmic pillars.

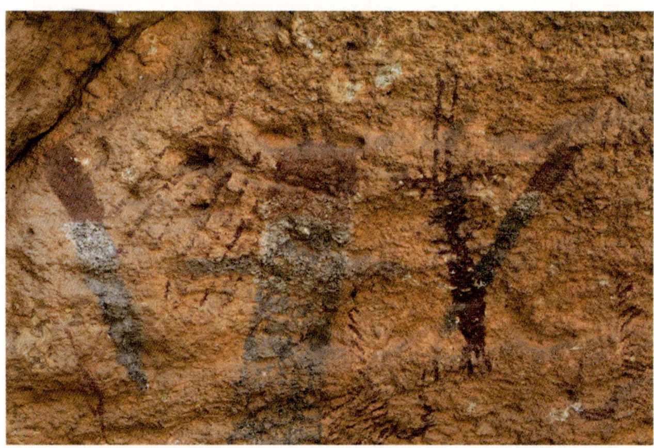

Figure 5.2. Black objects with red tips representing fiery torches used to fuel the birth of the sun.

ries and Mesoamerican core concepts, I now recognize this represents only one possible layer of meaning for these five figures.

Primordial ancestors. When the pilgrimage is conducted today, Huichol *jicareros* enter into mythic time to reenact the journey made by their primordial ancestors. The five *jicareros* represent not only these ancestors, but also five mythical hunters pursuing the deer through the underworld to the world above. They are the *awatamete,* the "antlered ones"—the original mythical deer hunters. And at still another level of meaning, they collectively represent the planet Venus as Morning Star (Neurath 2000a:82, 92, 2005a:74, 2005c:90).

The peyote pilgrimage is a metaphor for astronomical events witnessed in the heavens each night and throughout the year (Neurath 2005c:88). The primordial ancestors, and thereby contemporary *jicareros,* are stars journeying through the underworld with the sun to initiate the first dawn. "According to myth, the sun, with the help of its auxiliary troops, the *jicareros,* killed the stars at dawn. And in keeping with Huichol thought, the pilgrims are also the stars who sacrifice themselves to become the sun" (Neurath 2005a:74).

The five *jicareros* are placed in charge of the five directions (Neurath 2000b:68). The Huichol universe, like those of the Aztec and Maya, has a *quincunx* structure. This special division of the cosmos signifies the four cardinal points and the center. The number five represents perfection and completion, and is the most significant number among the Huichol (Gutiérrez 2000:112; Neurath 2000a:82). Five candles or, in some accounts, trees are placed at each corner of the universe, including the center, to uphold the sky (Gutiérrez 2002:104–106). The pilgrims in charge of the five directions represent the stars who, through autosacrifice, sustain the sky (Neurath 2001a:512).

The colors of the five figures in the mural are also significant. According to the Huichol, "[C]olors are words, and at the same time they are songs"; color is the language of the gods (MacLean 2001:309). As discussed previously, in the Mesoamerican dualist system, black or dark colors are associated with primordial beginnings. These colors are equated with stars and the dark, wet underworld of the west, for in the beginning, before the universe was structured into oppositional pairs, the world was in chaos and perpetual darkness.

In Huichol religion, as in numerous other Mesoamerican belief systems, people are envisioned as being born wet and cold, just like the primordial ancestors (Neurath 2001a:507). This early stage in human development is further associated with femininity, darkness, disorder, and chaos. The term used for peyote pilgrims, *jicareros,* identifies the pilgrims with these feminine, primordial elements. It is derived from the Spanish word for bowl, *jícara,* which is a ceremonial gourd bowl made by women to communicate with the gods.[21] They are visual metaphors for the womb and are associated with female deities and other feminine elements such as the underworld, the sea, and the west (P. Furst 2007:27; Kindl 2001:3).

The color black also is linked to penance and self-sacrifice (Olivier 2003:187). And the *jicareros* are quintessentially manifestations of both. It is only appropriate, then, that the five figures representing primordial ancestors should be painted black. But the five figures are not only black: they have red heads. This likely relates back to the oppositional scheme and concepts of soul.

The Huichol maintain that humans have two souls: *kupuri* and *iyari. Kupuri* is comparable to *tonalli;* it is an energy or life force that was made when the first rains came and humans were born (Fikes 2011:125). At that time the gods transmitted *kupuri* to humans. The Huichol say that without *kupuri* a person would be irrational and crazy. This crucial life force is transmitted by the gods into their heads through an invisible silky thread. Throughout life they acquire increasing amounts of *kupuri,* gradually filling up their *iyari,* which is their heart-soul (MacLean 2012:206-213). *Iyari* is primordial and was present before time began, before the first rainy season that created *kupuri.* In Hope MacLean's (2000:86) interview with a Huichol shaman/artist, she quotes him as equating the *iyari* (heart) to a glass and to *kupuri* as the water filling the glass. Indeed, *kupuri* is believed to be the living or everlasting water of the Ancestors (Fikes 2011:117).

Infants begin life with the *kupuri* placed in their heads while in the womb. As they grow in spiritual knowledge and wisdom, the heat of *kupuri* spreads from the head to the rest of the body. They are transformed from cold, wet beings associated with the world below (black) to hot, dry beings associated with the world above (red). Pilgrimages, laden with responsibility and self-sacrifice, are essential for this transformation (López Austin 1997; Neurath 2000b:63).

Given this, the black bodies of the five figures represent the pilgrims who have returned to their primordial state, which is equated with the color black. Their black bodies are the "bowls" or "wombs" that will be filled with *kupuri,* the divine energy and life force of the gods. Their red heads are repositories of the hot *kupuri* soul placed in them by the gods while still in the womb.[22] But why are they faceless? For the Huichol, the face and eyes are closely linked to a concept known as *nierika* (MacLean 2012:56). *Nierika* is the gift of sight, the ability to see the "hidden reality or true being of a thing" (Neurath 2000a:83). It is a magical force obtained through initiation and reactualization of the cosmogonic sacrifices that the Ancestors suffered in the beginning.[23] The original Ancestors were not yet divine and did not have *nierika.* They went east to *encontrar taiyari* (to find their heart) and to gain *nierika* (the ability to see). To look for *iyari* and to acquire *nierika* means to become involved in the world of the Ancestors, to bring to life the original community of the gods, and to facilitate the continuance of the natural cycles (Neurath 2001a:503).

The anthropomorphs lack faces because, like the original Ancestors, they lack *nierika.* They have not yet been transformed into divine beings. Their hearts must be transformed. During the contemporary peyote hunt, *jicareros* who enter the sacred homeland are bathed in the rays of the rising sun. To portray this union with the sun's essence, pilgrims paint their faces with yellow designs. Their yellow-painted faces are reflections of the gods and of peyote; they are *nierikas* (Faba Zuleta 2003). Painting their faces in the peyote ritual literally converts them into the deities they represent.[24] It is like wearing a mask, and for the Huichol, masks are not simply images of gods; they *are* the gods (Neurath 2005d:24).[25]

The five pilgrims in the panel exist in a time prior to the acquisition of their true identities—those by which the people of the Lower Pecos would have recognized them. Neurath (2001a:498) says the original ancestral pilgrims were not yet divine and went to the east to find their hearts and to gain *nierika*. In the panel they present themselves in subrogation to the creator god(s), who are the source of what is uniquely human. The fact that the pilgrims have black bodies and lack facial features demonstrates they lack spiritual maturity. They stand before the creator god(s) offering themselves in sacrifice and petition to acquire the essence of life for themselves and their progeny. By donning the images of the gods, participants in the ritual became capable of understanding the transcendent realities of what was taking place. They were to transform into the face and the heart of the deities they represented. Up until that time, the pilgrims would have no face.

Sacrificial fire and the union of opposites. Each of the black primordial ancestors is portrayed holding two black objects with red tips (see figures 5.1 and 5.2). In 2003 I proposed that these objects are analogous to candles used in present-day peyote ceremonies, but their meaning is far more multifaceted and metaphorical. During pilgrimages *jicareros* stand before their offerings while holding candles toward the ascending sun. This ritual reenacts the use of fire to light the Ancestors' path through the underworld and, most important, to help the sun rise in the east.[26]

Fire is the axis mundi: the point of intersection between the celestial realm and the underworld (Gutiérrez 2008:295). It existed before the dawn of time and gave birth to the sun (Lumholtz 1900:26). Because of this, it facilitates conversion or transformation and serves an instrumental role in the metamorphosis of the five pilgrims (or their souls) into a sacred state.[27] López Austin (1993:41) suggests that "at some time in the past fire was considered to be the implicit transforming element of the gods in the process of creation." Fire was used as a cleansing and transforming tool in the peyote complex documented by Carl Lumholtz and Robert Zingg in the early twentieth century and continues to be in the modern Native American peyote religion (Stewart 1987:41).

Candles are indispensable offerings in Huichol ritual. Flames consuming candles are equated with sacrifice. The body of the candle is equated with water, the center of the earth, and humans (Gutiérrez 2002:104,106), all of which in the hot/cold dichotomy are quintessentially cold and therefore black. And fire, which is of course hot, is the source of the color red (MacLean 2001:316). Tsakaimuka, god of the setting sun and assistant to Father Sun, demands ten candles as an offering (Zingg [1938] 1977:316). In the mural the ten black objects held by the primordial ancestors are analogous to fire being carried through the underworld to fuel the sunrise, but metaphorically they represent the pilgrims themselves.

In Huichol mythology five candles were placed at the four corners and center of the universe to sustain the sky and newly born sun (Neurath 2001a:499, 512). As discussed above, *jicareros* also serve as sky pillars. They are candles whose bodies are consumed by the flames. They are surrogate sacrifices of the child who was thrown into the fire at creation, whose sacrifice gave birth to the sun. Grandfather Fire therefore demands five candles as an offering (Zingg [1938] 1977:316). These five candles represent the pillars and the sacrifice made at the dawn of time.

The establishment of posts to uphold the sky is a Mesoamerican core concept (López Austin 1997:15). These posts functioned as hollow trunks through which the gods' essences could flow. The essences associated with *tukari*, the sky above, were hot and masculine, in contrast to the cold and feminine essences associated with *tikari*, the underworld. They were opposing essences, but through their union time was born. And the continued cycling of divine essences between the world above (*tukari*) and the world below (*tikari*) perpetuates time (López Austin 1997:16).

This union is expressed in the White Shaman mural. The black bodies of the five figures, like the black portion of the torches they carry, are analogous to the cold, wet, feminine essence of earth and water. Their red heads are analogous to the hot, dry, masculine essence of fire, sun, and sky. Their black bodies were painted before the red heads because black is equated with primordial time—before the dualist system of opposing essences. The application of red therefore signifies not only the union of the two opposing essences, but establishment of the division that led to creation.

Motif Analysis II: Path of the Sun and Cosmic Umbilicus

In striking contrast to the vertical bodies of the pilgrims is a sinuous horizontal line moving rhythmically across the panel (E029) (figure 5.3). The left end of the line is solid black. Moving toward the viewer's right, the black line crosses the legs of the first pilgrim (A001). Here the black line is joined by a white line. The two lines travel

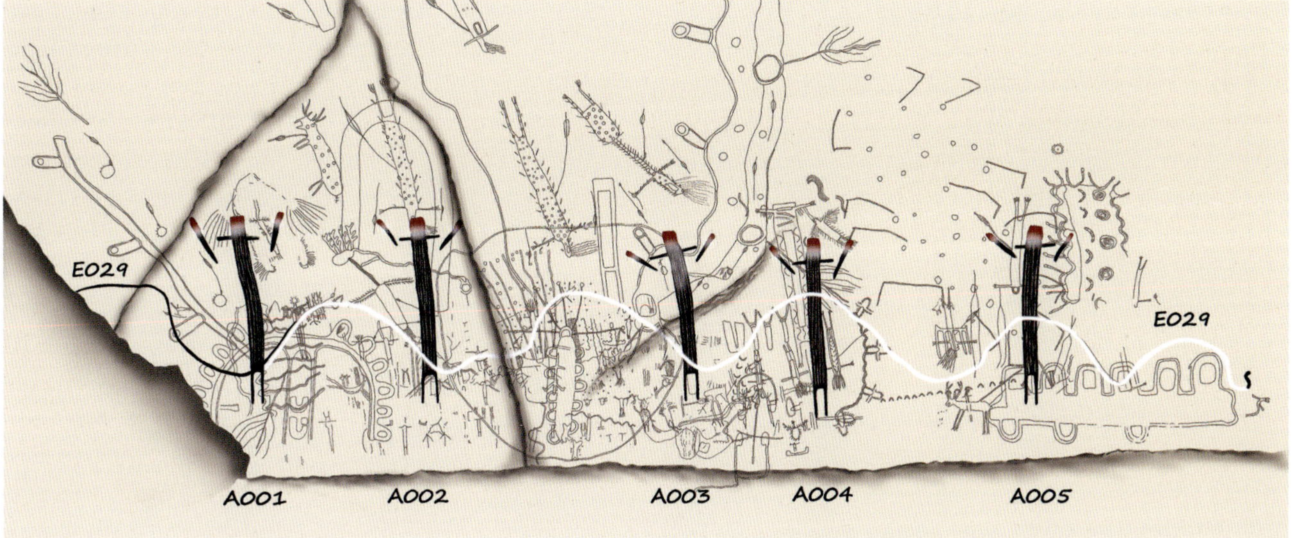

Figure 5.3. Motif II (E029): Path of the sun, cosmic umbilicus, and the cord uniting the pilgrims.

side by side until reaching a small, antlered, humanlike form (A006) (figure 5.4). The black line runs under the body of this small figure and then stops abruptly at its chest area. The white line crosses over the body of the antlered figure and continues its sinuous path to the right. It carries the viewer's eye along the path, stopping momentarily as it crosses each of the four remaining pilgrims. At the far right end of the panel, the white line changes back to black for a short distance before terminating.

The white portion of the line superimposes all figures with which it comes into contact. No figures in the mural overlay the white line. On the left side of the panel, however, the black line is superimposed by the antlered figure, as well as enigmatic imagery discussed under Motif Analysis III. The only figure superimposed by the black portion of the line appears to be the black body of the first pilgrim. (This section of the mural is badly damaged, making it difficult to be sure of paint layering.)

Formulating Hypotheses

I previously proposed that the sinuous line is analogous to the cord used to bind pilgrims together during rites of purification (Boyd 2003:77). As with the torches, this interpretation was simplistic and missed its broader symbolic significance. The cord is a metaphorical umbilical cord binding the pilgrims together (cf. P. Furst 2006:73). It unites them as one. Other analogies for the cord are afforded to us through a reading of Huichol mythology.

According to myth, Kawi (the caterpillar) marked the path to Dawn Mountain. It began below in the watery underworld of the west and traveled east to the desert above, the place of the sunrise. The white cord binding pilgrims in the modern-day pilgrimage represents the ancestral path marked by Kawi (Negrín 1977:16).[28] The word *kawitu*, which is related to *kawi*, means "myth" or "history." Thus, to travel Kawi's path is to read the myths written upon the landscape (Neurath 2000b:65). The path the pilgrims traverse is Kawi's path, but also the path of the sun—the ecliptic (Schaefer 2002:193–194). Today, when *jicareros* reach sacred points along the journey, they replicate the path of the sun by making serpentine movements as they metaphorically weave themselves together with its rays (Schaefer 2002:194).

As the path of the sun, the white line is also analogous to the Mesoamerican concept of the Flower Road, part of a complex system of spirituality centered on metaphors of flowers. Although this ancient concept is most pronounced among Southern Uto-Aztecan-speaking peoples, it was also part of the cultural repertoire for many prehistoric peoples in the American Southwest and Mesoamerica (Hill 1992:117).[29]

The Flower Road is perceived as a celestial floral pathway along which the sun, the gods, and the Ancestors travel (Hill 1992:125; Taube 2010a, 2010b). It is the road leading to Flower Mountain, the place where the sun is reborn and the rains originate. In Mesoamerican iconography, the road is often portrayed as a serpentine form (Mathiowetz 2011:305). Neurath (2005c:91–92) has argued that the Flower World concept is deeply entrenched in Huichol beliefs and practices. He suggests the pilgrims' path is the Flower Road to Wirikuta, "a 'flowered desert' in the east . . . where they climb the Mountain of Dawn, the place where the sun is born, to dream about cloud serpents (the first rains) . . ." (Neurath 2005c:92). Wirikuta is described by the Huichol as a desert covered with "flowers of brilliant colors," flowers being a metaphor for peyote (P. Furst 2006:82). Pilgrimages along the Flower Road to Wirikuta involve a language of reversals. That which is ugly is called beautiful, the dry desert becomes a flowering garden, and peyote is called a flower (Myerhoff 1974).

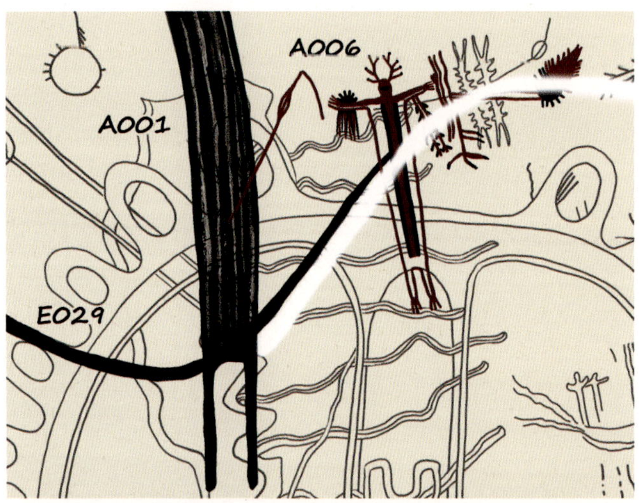

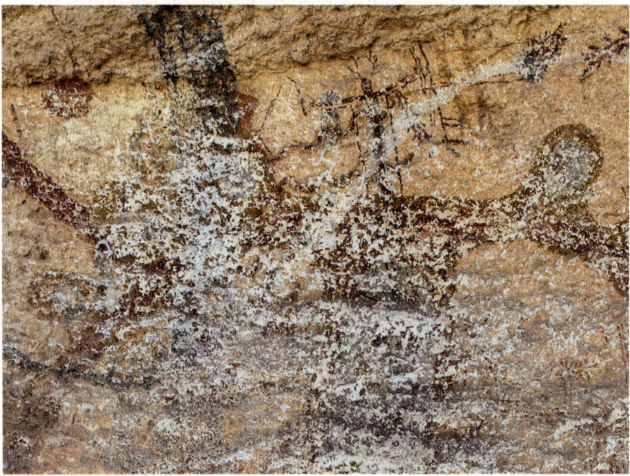

Figure 5.4. The sinuous black and white lines run parallel to each other only between A001 and A006, thereby linking the first Ancestor (A001) to the antlered anthropomorph (A006).

At yet another dimension, the cord represents a serpent. In Huichol beliefs, two serpents surround the world. As a result, the undulating horizon is perceived as the serpent's body demarcating the world above from the world below. One of the serpents is equated with the dry season and light, the other with the rainy season and darkness (Magriñá 2001). Together they symbolize the interrelationship of the two seasons. Stacy Schaefer (2010:58) notes that in Huichol double-cloth weaving "the light-colored warp threads symbolize the dry season and the rays of the sun; the dark-colored threads represent the wet season and falling rain. Interwoven they create a textile that meshes like two snakes, with dark and light threads, along with their symbolism for wet and dry cycles." The pilgrims, symbolically woven together with the cord, are collectively transformed into an ancestral cloud serpent bringing the gentle eastern rains (Gutiérrez 2002:115).

When the pilgrims reach Dawn Mountain, rain serpents appear to them in their dreams. Like the sun born from the death of the stars, rain too is born from the sacrifice of the pilgrims. Through their sacrifice they initiate the change from the dry season to the rainy season. The sun, which is low in the sky during the dry season, is raised to its zenith, and the summer rains begin to fall. When the *jicareros* return from the pilgrimage, they return as an astral deity (Venus) and as the cloud serpent (*haiku*) bringing peyote and the gentle rains from the east (Gutiérrez 2002:115,167; Neurath 2001a:511).

The cord, therefore, is a polyvalent symbol. It is not only analogous to the unity cord used in contemporary rituals, but also to the path of the pilgrims (stars), the path of the sun (ecliptic), the Flower Road, and a serpent. In the mural each pilgrim is attached to the other via the white portion of this line. Like an umbilical cord, it is the conduit through which their essences flow, transforming them into one entity—one star, one sacrifice, one serpent, and one path. It is a cosmic umbilicus or spiritual lifeline uniting mortal to divine.[30]

The black portion of the line may be analogous to the serpent associated with the rainy season. Its location in the mural is telling. According to Huichol myth, Kawi's path stopped at the top of Dawn Mountain. And it is at Dawn Mountain that the pilgrims dream of and become the rain serpent. At the left end of the mural the sinuous white line terminates at a crenellated arch. If the white line represents the path of the sun, the

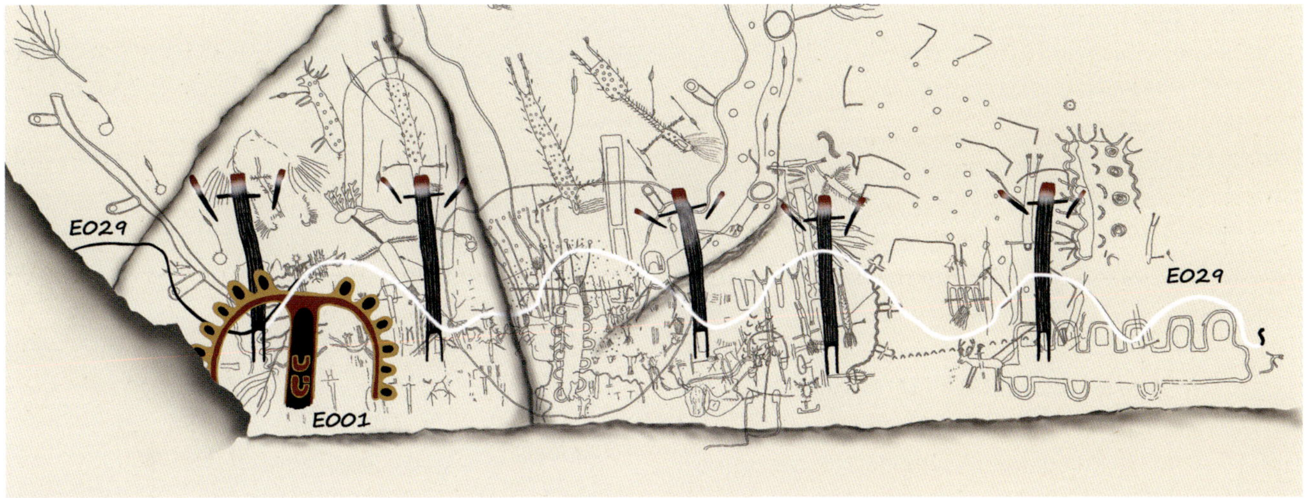

Figure 5.5. Motif III (E001): Solar steps, birthplace of the sun, and Dawn Mountain in the east.

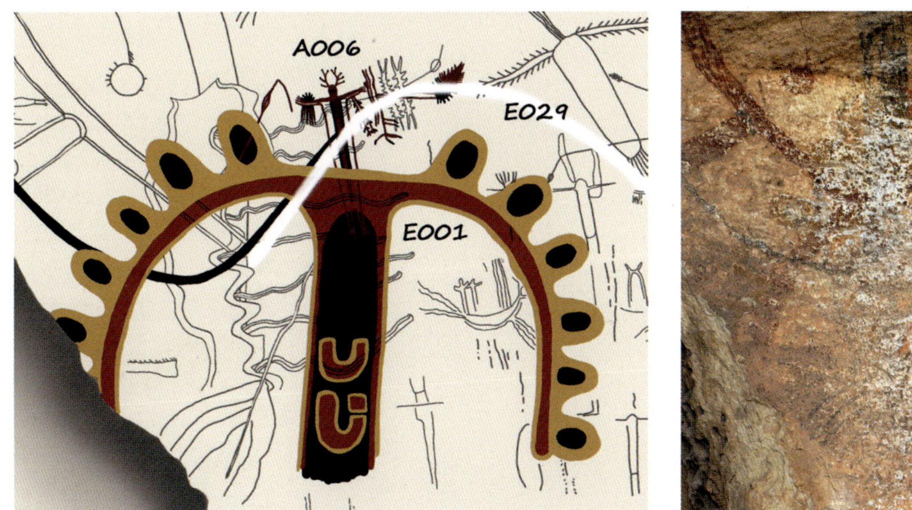

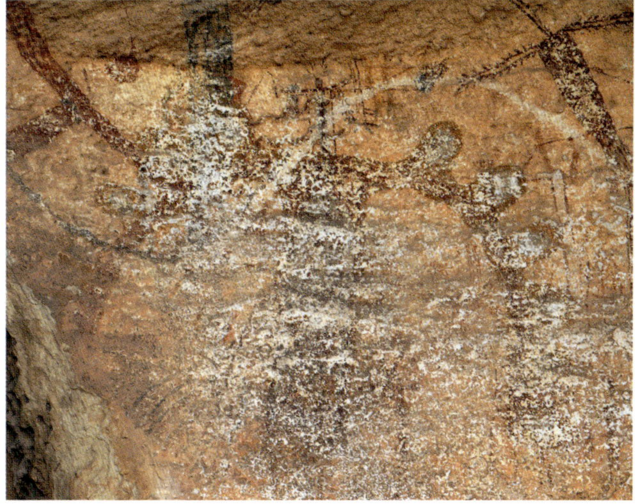

Figure 5.6. All color layers of Dawn Mountain (E001) are sandwiched between the white and black portions of the cord (E029). The antlered anthropomorph (A006) emerging from the underworld at Dawn Mountain is not only wrapped in the black and white portions of the cord, but is also sandwiched between the yellow, red, and black layers forming the crenellated arch. (See the caption for figure 3.8 for more detail on stratigraphy.)

pilgrims, and the dry-season serpent, then the crenellated arch, as will be discussed below, is analogous to the Mountain of Dawn. For according to myth, the two events, the origin of peyote and the first dawn, occurred at the same time in the same place—precisely at the end of Kawi's path (Neurath 2005a:73).

Motif Analysis III: Solar Steps and Birthplace of the Sun

At the left end of the serpentine line (E029) discussed above is a red, black, and yellow crenellated arch (E001) (figure 5.5). It is sandwiched between the black and white portions of the line. The arch has six lobes along the right side and only five remaining on the left; a probable sixth lobe may have been lost to damage. Running down the center of the arch is a vertical black band resembling the throat of a volcano. The black interior of the throat and the black centers of each lobe were painted first. This was followed by red and then yellow. Yellow dominates this motif, forming the lobes and outlining the entire image. Because of the order in which the artist applied the paint, figures associated with the arch are sandwiched between layers of color. This is exemplified most clearly with the small antlered figure (A006) whose red legs superimpose the black throat of the arch, but whose body is overlain by yellow paint (figure 5.6).

Formulating Hypotheses

In 1996 I proposed that the arch represents a gateway serpent and portal into the upperworld and underworld. Similar examples of this motif are found at several sites in the Lower Pecos (Boyd 1996, 2003) (figure 5.7). When considered within the context of other imagery in the mural and informed by Huichol myth and ritual, further analogies can be drawn.

In the Huichol creation story the Ancestors accompanied the child-sacrifice through the underworld. When they reached *tukari* (world above) at the summit of Dawn Mountain, the child emerged from a cave as Father Sun. According to the Huichol, the sun climbs a ladder or stairway out of the underworld into the sky each day, just as it did for the first sunrise. In the sacred landscape of Wirikuta, this birthplace is equated with a hill referred to as Cerro Quemado (Burned Mountain) or Cerro del Amanacer (Dawn Mountain). Here, too, are caves representing the birthplace of the sun and humanity. According to *jicareros* interviewed by Gutiérrez (2002:200), these caves are the location from which everything emerged and everything returns.[31] This event and location on the landscape are manifested in Huichol material culture, as well as in the architecture and spatial orientation of ceremonial centers.

During Carl Lumholtz's exploration of the Sierra Madre Occidental in the 1890s he found a small block of sandstone into which six steps had been carved. He referred to this object as an ancient "staircase of the gods" (Lumholtz 1900:62). His Huichol informants said the staircase represents travel, with each step representing one stage of the peyote journey. "It signifies especially the travels of Grandfather Fire and Great-grandfather Deer-Tail from the coast to the country of the *hi'kuli* [peyote]" (Lumholtz 1900:62). Zingg ([1938] 1977:594–596) also encountered one of these objects. He was told it represents the ladder used by "Sun-Father" to climb out of the sea when he was born. Effigies of the staircase are "hung on prayer arrows and carried by the peyote hunters . . . so that they can climb that long trail or 'ladder' that leads to the sacred country" (Zingg [1938] 1977:595).

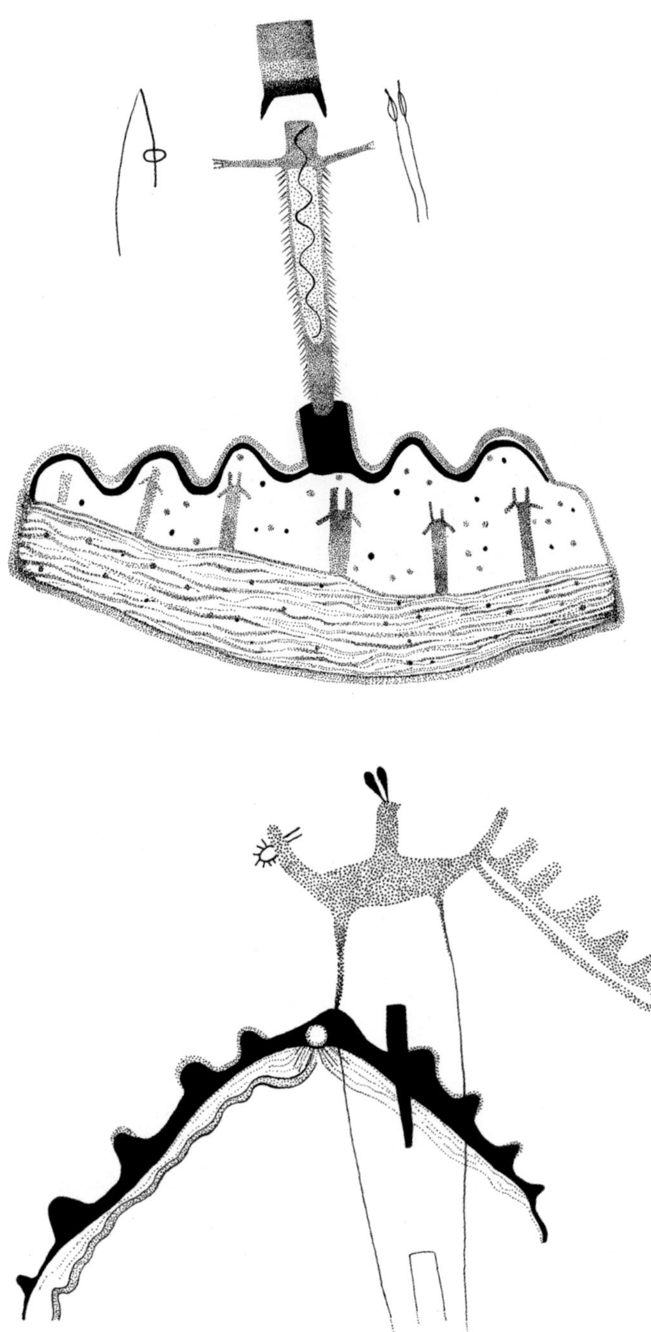

Figure 5.7. Gateway serpent motifs in Pecos River style at (a) Mystic Shelter (41VV612) and (b) Rattlesnake Canyon (41VV180).

Stacy Schaefer (1996b:342) describes an altar at San Andrés temple as a stepped pyramid. According to her consultant, it "is the stairway that the sun climbs on its journey across the sky." Wooden stepped pyramids with five and, in at least one case, six steps serve as replicas of Dawn Mountain (Neurath 2005b:594–595) (figure 5.8). Neurath (2000a:102) notes that two small altars in the form of pyramids are placed on the east side of the ceremonial center. The larger of the two is dedicated to the deer god Tamatsi Kauyumari and represents Dawn Mountain. The other altar, which is slightly smaller, is a pyramid for Father Sun (Tayau). Both represent the easternmost edge of the universe.

Symbolic hills or mountains of origin are a recurring concept in Mesoamerica. Indeed, it is one of the core concepts of Mesoamerican religions. And, as discussed above, symbolic mountains filled with life-giving sustenance are one of the fundamental traits of the Flower World complex. Flower Mountains are mythical places of emergence associated with the east and function as reservoirs of the divine essences of the gods, which are spirits of the seeds of life (López Austin 1997:153; Taube 2004:88-90). Among the Huichol, Wirikuta is described with elaborate chromatic symbolism and represents the Flower World (Hill 1992:128). Dawn Mountain has been equated with Flower Mountain, the location where the sun is born and rain originates (Neurath 2005c:91).

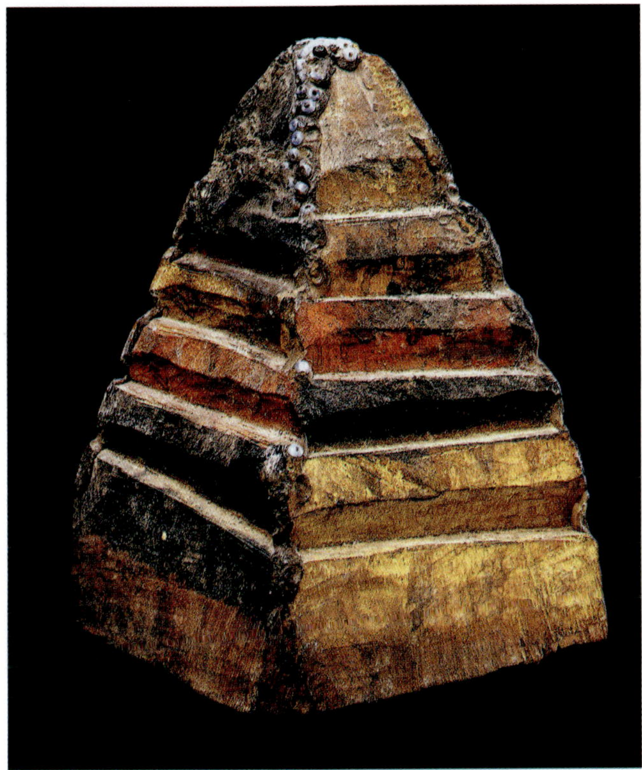

Figure 5.8. Huichol effigy of solar steps and the primordial mountain in the east. Photo by Martin Franken. Courtesy of Staatliche Museen zu Berlin, Stiftung Preußischer Kulturbesitz, Ethnologisches Museum. Inv.-Nr. IV Ca 34932.

Caves, which are viewed as the mouths of giant serpents, serve as subterranean conduits through which spirit seeds and rain are emitted from Flower Mountain. The Huichol perceive the earth to be surrounded by a giant two-headed serpent or two serpents facing each other. At sunset the solar deity plunges into the serpent's mouth and, with proper ritual performance, emerges from the cave—the jaws of the serpent—at sunrise.

The crenellated arch in the White Shaman mural bears a striking resemblance to "the hill in the east" and its replicates in Huichol art and architecture. The yellow crenellations are comparable to solar steps and undulations of the serpent surrounding the world. The black throat of the arch is analogous to the cave or serpent's mouth through which Father Sun and the Ancestors emerged after reaching Dawn Mountain. According to Huichol beliefs, the precise place from which the sun arose was a cave at the summit of the mountain. And in some accounts, Dawn Mountain was a volcano, and the cave, a volcanic crater (Neurath 2001b:481).

The color symbolism and painting sequence are also relevant to this discussion. The motif was painted in black, red, and yellow—in that order. Among the Huichol, yellow is associated with dawn and is symbolic of the sun's rays. Preuss (1996:127) writes that "the rising of the sun is formally celebrated and extolled in a chant that tells how the sun god called forth the yellow rattlesnake (dawn), how he loosed his arrow among the deer (the stars) . . ." The Huichol refer to Dawn Mountain as the place where "the Ancestors paint our faces with yellow designs." The color yellow is obtained from the root of a plant (*uxa*) collected during the pilgrimage.[32] According to Neurath (2005d:39), the yellow face paint of the *jicareros* is considered a reflection of solar light on the pilgrims' faces. The light of the sun transforms the hearts of the *jicareros* (Zingg [1938] 1977:585). The yellow paint enveloping the crenellated arch and accompanying figures is analogous to the sun's illumination at dawn.

The crenellated arch is a prototypical primordial mountain, the location from which all life emerged. In Huichol myth it is analogous to Dawn Mountain, the flowered destination of the pilgrims as they pursue the deer through the underworld. It is the place where the

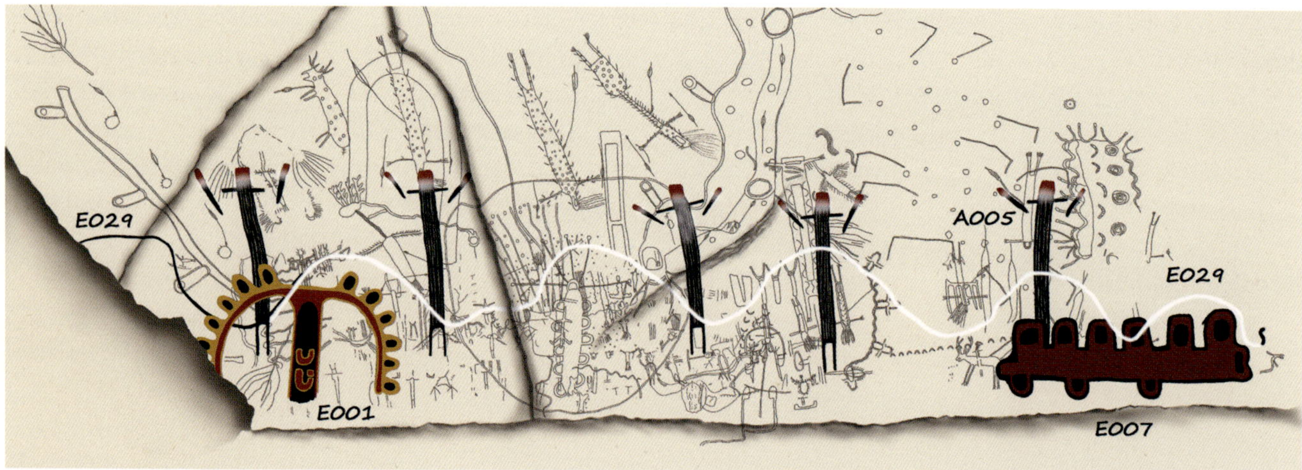

Figure 5.9. Motif IV (E007): Western entrance into the underworld, the primordial origin of the Ancestors, where darkness overcomes light.

Ancestors emerged and the deer committed autosacrifice so that the sun could be born.[33] It is the birthplace of the sun and peyote, and the source of the gentle rains from the east.[34]

Motif Analysis IV: Dark Waters of the Underworld

At the opposite end of the white cord (E029) is a crenellated horizontal band painted red and outlined in black (E007) (figure 5.9). Six large lobes are arranged across the top of the band, and across the bottom there are three. Each lobe is red with a black center. Water seeping out of the wall has left a white mineral skin obscuring the imagery (figure 5.10). Photographic enhancements allowed us to identify the top six lobes and bottom three. It is here that the white line and paintings end—or perhaps begin.

Formulating Hypotheses

If the crenellated arch (E001) represents the eastern edge of the cosmos, then the opposite end of the mural represents the western edge. As mentioned previously, the ocean is a metaphor for the underworld and is the most ancient place in the universe. It is equated with the west, female rain deities, serpents, the rainy season, and the color black. It is the place of darkness, called *t+kari* (the place of midnight) or *y+wita* (where it is dark/black) (Neurath 2005b:588). The Huichol perceive the ocean as a giant serpent encircling the world. It is artistically portrayed on votive bowls as a crenellated band around the rim or as a horizontal band with crenellations along the top (Lumholtz 1900).

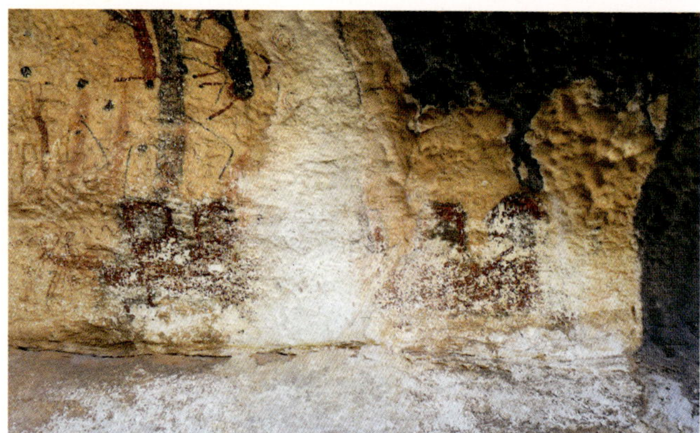

Figure 5.10. Water seep obscuring E007.

The crenellated band in the mural is analogous to the western entrance into the underworld.[35] Its crenellated lobes are similar to the undulations of a giant serpent, which is also the sea (and the underworld).[36] It is painted black and red: it was the union of the black feminine forces of the underworld and the red, masculine forces equated with life that gave birth to the sun. According to some versions of the Huichol sun myth, when the crippled young boy sacrificially threw himself into the sea (or fire), the dark waters turned red with his blood (Schaefer and Furst 1996:14).[37] In contrast to the crenellated arch (Dawn Mountain) on the opposite end of the panel, which is outlined in yellow, this motif is outlined in black. Darkness has overcome light.[38] It is the place where the sun dies each day, but it is also the primordial origin of the Ancestors and the deer who guided the pilgrims through the nether regions before rising as the new sun at dawn.

Motif Analysis V: Celestial Deer and Astral Heroes

Two deer (Z002 and Z006) are located at the right end of the mural, and another (Z001) is located at the opposite end, above the Dawn Mountain motif (E001) (figure 5.11). Z001 is impaled in its chest by an atlatl dart (figure 5.12). The dart tip is stylized with short, vertically intersecting lines. Twelve large black dots fill the deer's body. As noted above, the dots were applied to the limestone canvas first, followed by strokes of red paint to create the form of the deer. A thin wash of white paint was applied over the red paint at each location where red overlays black. The deer has bifurcated antlers and either brow tines or ears. It has no hooves and no dewclaws.

The second and third deer (Z002 and Z006) are on the right end of the mural below the white line (figure 5.11). Z002 is located immediately left of E007 and is facing "east" toward Dawn Mountain. Unlike the first deer, it has black hooves and black dewclaws (figure 5.13), which were painted prior to the deer's red body. Its bifurcated antler rack and possible ears or brow tines are similar to those of Z001. Stylistically, however, there are differences. Z001 has short legs and its body is formed from strokes of paint, leaving negative space between strokes. Z002 is completely filled in and its legs are long. Red splatter paint appears to be coming out of its mouth. Two red lines connect the back of Z002 to the crenellated horizontal band (E007). It is unclear whether or not either of these two lines represents a dart; no fletching is visible. Superimposing this deer is a small red anthropomorph with hair standing straight up from the top of its head (A021).

The third deer (Z006), upside down and with a dart impaling its chest, is virtually lost to mineral accretion and paint-flaking. It is similar in style to Z002, completely in-filled with red paint and possessing long legs. Interestingly, this deer has black hooves on its front legs but red hooves on its back legs. Preservation is too poor to determine the presence or absence of antlers. As will be discussed below, these three deer are analogous to the celestial deer of Huichol mythology.

Formulating Hypotheses

Konrad T. Preuss, who lived among the Huichol and other groups of the Gran Nayar during the early 1900s, was a proponent of the astral school of myth. He was the first to suggest that the peyote pilgrimage is not a retelling of a historical migration, but a metaphorical reenactment of astronomical events witnessed in the heavens (Neurath 2002:156). In the Huichol creation story five mythical hunters pursue the deer along Kawi's path through the underworld. Astronomically, Kawi's path refers to the ecliptic, and the deer to Venus. Venus is one deity with two contrasting aspects: Morn-

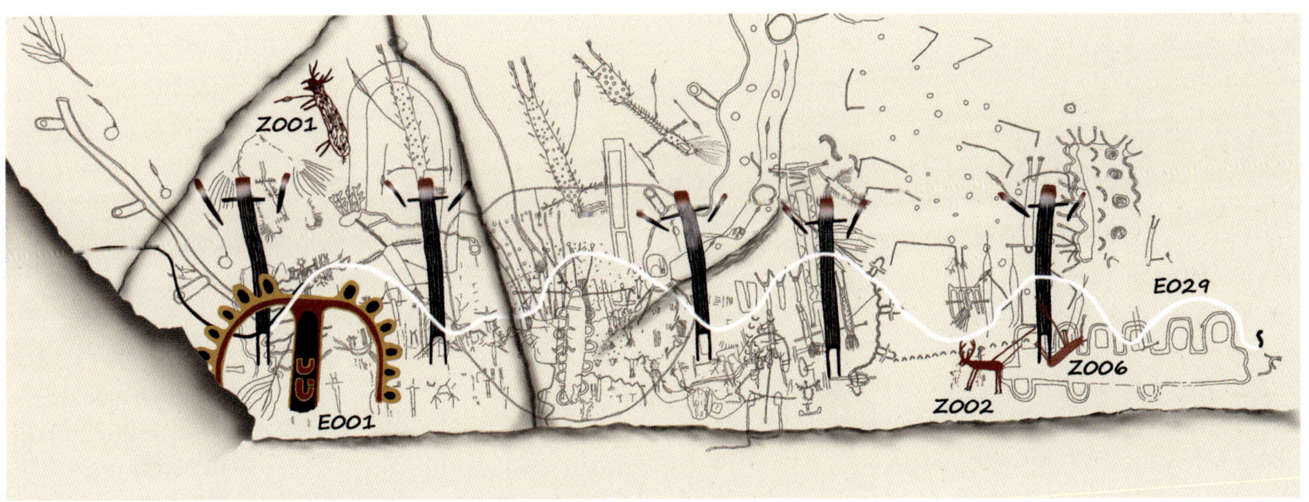

Figure 5.11. Motif V (Z001, Z002, Z006): Celestial deer, Ancestors, and Venusian heroes.

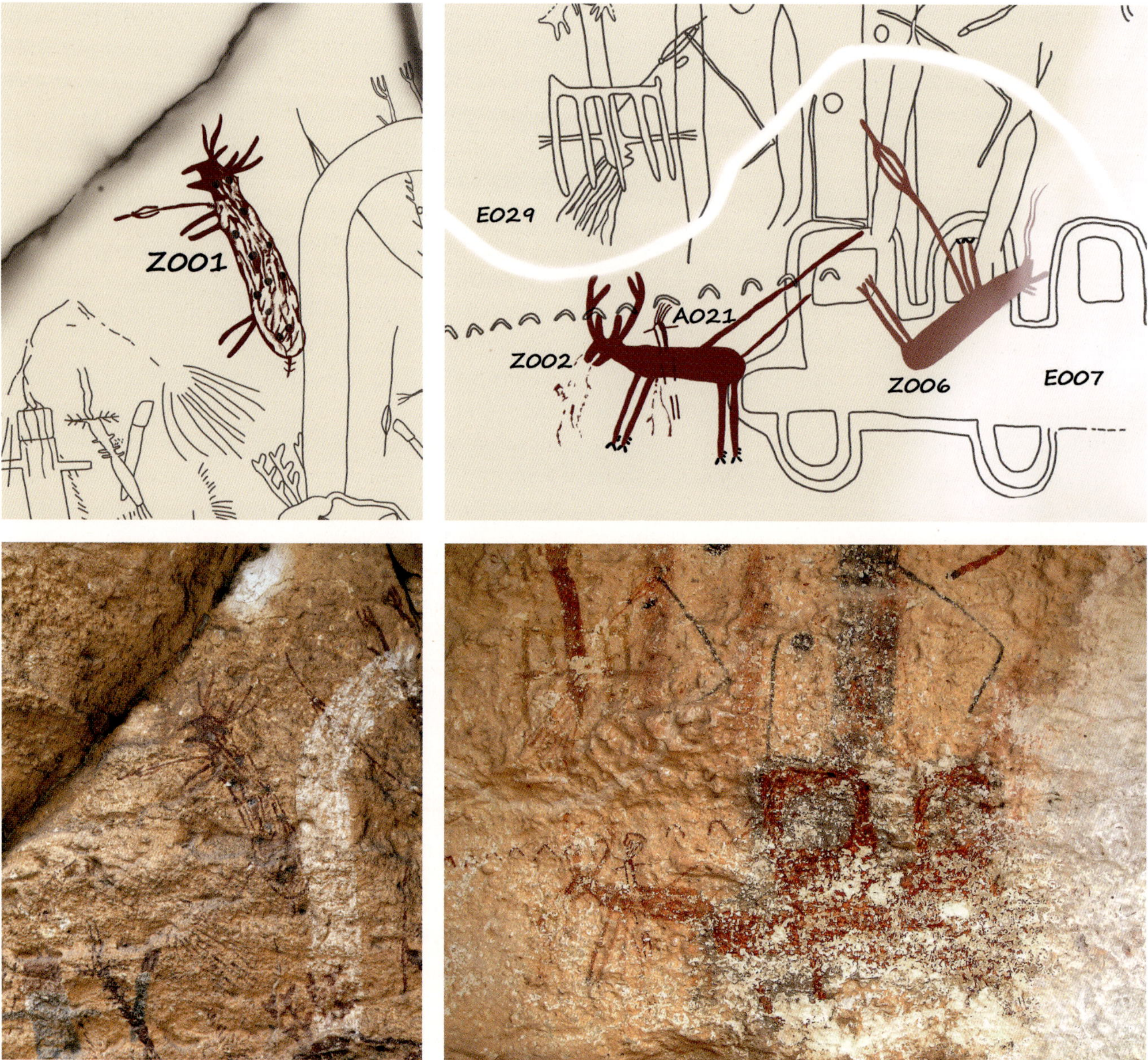

Figure 5.12. Slain deer (Z001) representing the Venusian hero whose autosacrifice gave birth to the sun and whose heart was transformed into peyote.

Figure 5.13. The death of the Evening Star (Z006) gives birth to the Morning Star (Z002), who travels east through the underworld with the future sun (A021).

ing Star and Evening Star. This planetary hero possesses incredible transformative abilities, changing himself into his alter ego on a cyclical basis. According to Neurath (2005c:75), the most significant characteristic of Venus symbolism in Gran Nayar mythology is "its dynamic ambivalence, based on the planet's coming and going between east and west."[39]

The foundational basis for this "dynamic ambivalence" relates to the planet's dual nature. As Morning Star, Venus is visible in the eastern sky at dawn until subsumed by the rays of the sun. As Evening Star, it is visible in the western sky at dusk until it joins the sun in the waters of the underworld (Neurath 2002:158). The sun, like Venus, is also an ambivalent character. It rises in the east after defeating the forces of the underworld, only to be defeated by its enemies in the west at dusk. The rising sun is the Day Sun, reigning from sunrise to noon, and his alter ego is the Night Sun, reigning from midday to sunset. As a result, Venus mythology and accompanying rituals are enmeshed with the solar calendar. The Morning Star and Day Sun are conflated, as are the Evening Star and Night Sun.

Annual ritual cycles reenact a full round of creation and destruction of the cosmos. A ritual year represents one day and, at the same time, an entire "sun," or era (Neurath 2002:158). Neurath (2005c) writes:

> The contrasting aspects of life are complementary in a processual way. During the rainy season, which is the "night of the year," the dark forces of the underworld defeat Sun Father, who has to die to allow the forces of fertility to be released. This explains why transgression and "sin" are *also* necessary in order to obtain life and growth.
>
> Venus mythology is especially appropriate to express this process of cyclical transformations. Generally speaking, Morning Star is associated with Wirikuta, the desert "above in the east," . . . Evening Star is associated with the sinister underworld "down below in the west" . . . Venus as Morning Star and Evening Star periodically changes from one extreme to the other. [Neurath 2005c:86]

The deer guiding the primordial ancestors to Wirikuta was Tamatsi Parietsika (Elder Brother of Dawn).[40] He is Master of the Hunt, shooter of arrows, and owner of the game (Negrín 1975:50). He is also Venus as the Morning Star (Neurath 2005c:81).[41] His arrows are rays of light with powerful transformative capabilities.[42] Upon reaching Dawn Mountain, this celestial master of the hunt shoots the deer, who is at the same time himself (Preuss 1996:130).[43] In his role as hunter, he is the Morning Star, and as prey, he is the Evening Star.[44] He is both sacrificer and the sacrificed, predator and prey, hunter and hunted. Once slain, he transforms into his alter ego, and as a result of this act of self-sacrifice, the heart (*iyari*) of the deer (Evening Star) is transformed into peyote, which is Morning Star and the sun. Morning Star and Evening Star are frequently identified one with the other in Huichol mythology (Preuss 1998b:324, 1998c).

The impaled red deer located above the Dawn Mountain motif is analogous to this Venusian hero. When the artist painted this image, he or she began by applying a constellation of twelve black dots. The black dots are analogous to *iyari*, the heart of the deer, which is also the seat of the soul. It is a nocturnal entity, traveling about at night and leaving the body permanently at death (Perrin 1996:406). Through self-sacrifice "above in the east," the deer's *iyari* is transformed into peyote, the sun, and the Morning Star. The artist may have applied the black dots first because the stars and *iyari* were first, and they came from the west, from primordial time. To apply the black over red would reverse the order of events and communicate a very different story.

In Huichol thought, deer (stars and Ancestors) originated in the fertile underworld of the west (Preuss 1996:129). Two of the three deer in this analysis are located in association with the motif (E007) identified as the western waters of the underworld. One is upright and facing east (Z002); the other is upside down and impaled in the chest (Z006). The impaled deer is analogous to the Evening Star falling at sunset into the underworld, where it transforms into its alter ego. According to myth, the death of the Evening Star gives birth to the Morning Star, who travels through the nether regions with the sun until reaching Wirikuta (Neurath 2005c). The upright deer with black hooves is analogous to the Morning Star. The small, red, humanlike figure overlaying him may be analogous to the sun or, rather, the sacrificient who will be transformed into the sun deity. But what is the significance of the black hooves on these two deer? I have documented only one other deer in the region with this distinctive attribute (figure 5.14).

According to the Huichol, wherever the deer steps, peyote grows in its tracks. In some cases, peyote *is* a deer track (Schaefer 1996a:146, 2002:200; Zingg [1938] 1977:528). In Mesoamerica, deer hooves are also symbolic of female genitalia and equated with fecundity (Stross 2007a:417, 2007b:13), and black is the color associated with femininity and fertility. Stacy Schaefer (2002:215) writes that hunting peyote is infused with

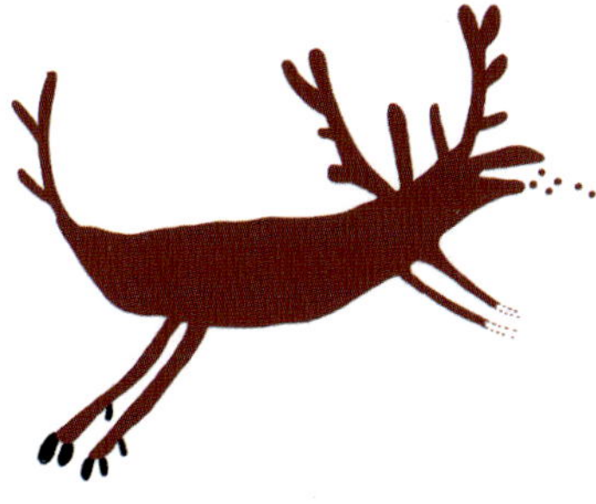

Figure 5.14. Deer with black hooves from Delicado Shelter (41VV1284).

"sexual and procreative imagery. Peyote plants are considered to be female, and symbolically they represent the fertility of a woman's womb."[45] Deer, and deer hooves specifically, were also important in the creation of terra firma. They brought form to the amorphousness of the cosmos by stirring the earth with their hooves (Bernal-Garcia 2007:101; Neurath 2001a:505). The black hooves, therefore, may be analogous to the "womb" that will be filled with *kupuri*—the life force and divine energy of the ancestral deities—when slain in the east. And, as a womb to be filled with *kupuri*, it is also an expression of *iyari*. Footprints and tracks metaphorically represent one's walk on earth, which are equated with one's *iyari*. Upon death a person's footprints must be erased so that the *iyari* can merge with Sun Father (Fikes 2011:76–77).

This may partly explain variations in hoof portrayal in the mural. The upside-down, impaled deer in the west (Z006), with only his front hooves portrayed in black, is going through a metamorphosis. He is dying as Evening Star and separating from Father Sun, leaving his celestial journey to be reborn in the underworld as Morning Star (Z002). Fertility is released through the star's death, making life, growth, and the next sunrise possible in the east. As Morning Star, the deer (Z002) transports the anthropomorphized sun (A021), peyote, and fertility through the underworld to Dawn Mountain. His *iyari* is manifested in his black hooves, which represent his footprints, his tracks through the underworld. The impaled deer in the east (Z001), representing Venus as both Morning and Evening Star, however, lacks hooves of any kind. The absence of hooves could communicate that the peyote brought from the west was left behind in the tracks of the deer at Dawn Mountain. At a deeper level, it may relate to the liberation of the deer's *iyari* from where it walked on earth. By erasing the deer's "footprints," his *iyari* is released from its earthly attachments and is able to return to the Sun Father (Fikes 2011:76-77).[46] And this is exactly what occurs in Huichol myth when, upon his death, the Morning Star merges with the sun. When *jicareros* complete the pilgrimage, they too must erase their footprints from the sacred homeland—a way of saying good-bye to all the places they visited and all the activities they engaged in during the hunt. This act, in turn, releases them from the onerous taboos required of them during pilgrimage. And because *jicareros* embody the Ancestors, stars, and deer, this act metaphorically merges all three with the sun, fueling its ascension and the onset of rain. They dance to erase their footprints, stirring up "much dust in order for it to begin raining" (Fikes 2011:136).

Motif Analysis VI: Stars and Cloud Serpents

Numerous black dots are located throughout the mural. Many are incorporated into figures (e.g., A008, A011, A012), including those inside the body of the deer (Z001) discussed above. Other dots are free-floating, such as a constellation of thirty-two large black dots (E010) clustered at the right end of the mural (figure 5.15). In all of these examples, the black dots were applied before any other color of paint.

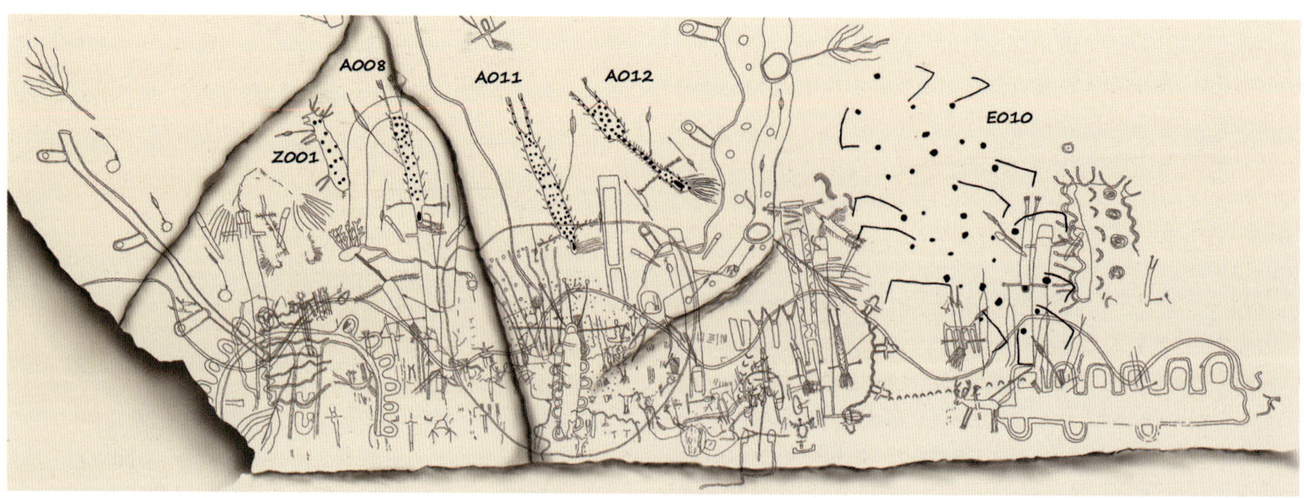

Figure 5.15. Motif VI (Z001, A008, A011, A012, E010): Black dots representing stars, heart-souls of the Ancestors, and water.

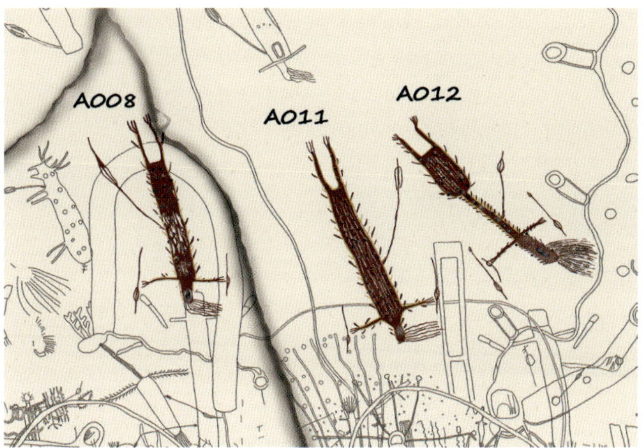

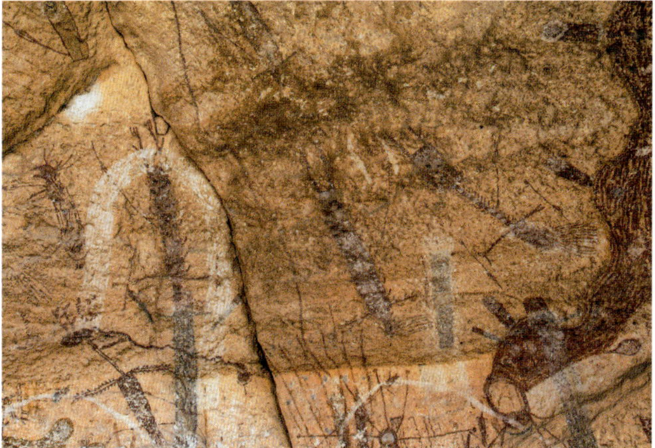

Figure 5.16. Stellar Ancestors (A008, A011, A012) returning to the west, where they descend to earth bringing fertile rains from the east.

Formulating Hypotheses

The black dots (E010) on the right end of the mural are analogous to stars and *iyari* souls of the Ancestors. In Huichol mythology the planetary hero and his stellar companions journey back to the west, where they descend to earth bringing fertility and rain (Neurath 2005c:79). In contemporary pilgrimages *jicareros* returning from Wirikuta collectively represent a great cloud of stellar Ancestors, a cloud serpent, bringing the fertile rains to the Sierra. The upside-down, impaled figures whose bodies are filled with black dots (A008, A011, A012) may be analogous to the Ancestors, who are stars returning to the west in the form of a cloud serpent (figure 5.16). This heralds the approaching rains of the summer solstice and a transition into the "night time" of the year (*tikari*), when the world is without form, without humans, and devoid of law and order. The right side of the White Shaman mural is analogous to *tikari*. It is the time and the place from which the Ancestors, deer, and stars began and ultimately return.

Motif Analysis VII: Birth of Peyote

In some cases dots on the mural are impaled—but only red ones. Three large red dots (E002) are located on the far left edge of the mural, immediately above and to the left of the crenellated arch (E001) and directly above the black portion of the serpentine line (E029) (figure 5.17). Each is pierced by a fletched dart. The stylized dart tip is similar to the one piercing the body of the deer (Z001), whose body is filled with black dots. Each of the three red dots is also slightly rayed, resembling a pincushion.

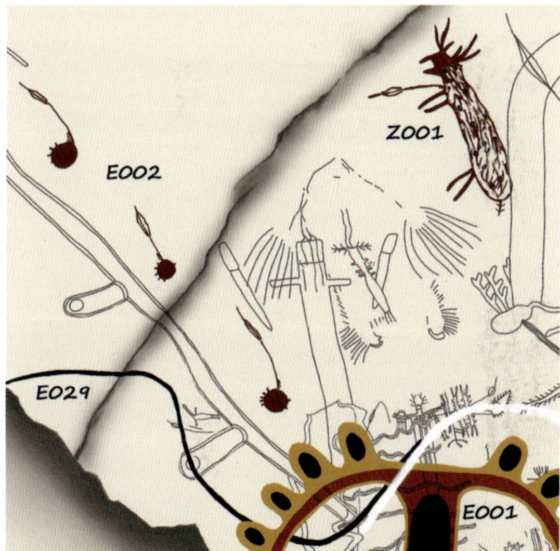

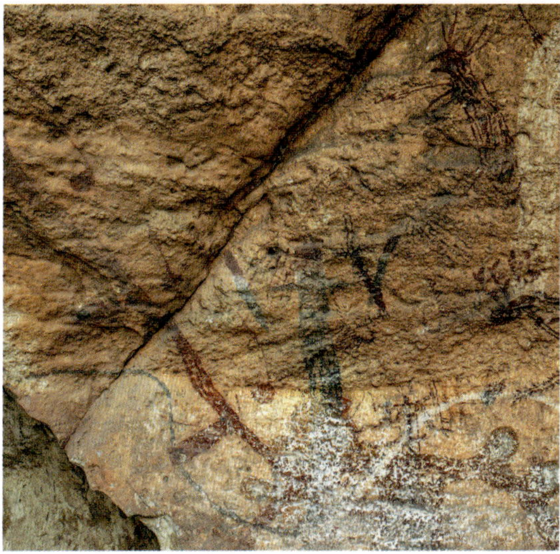

Figure 5.17. Motif VII (E002): The heart of the deer filled with red-hot life force through the arrows/rays of the sun as the Morning Star, which transform it into peyote.

Formulating Hypotheses

Impaled red dots are a recurring motif in Pecos River style rock art. They are commonly found in association with representations of deer, such as Z001 discussed above, and antlered anthropomorphic figures with dots attached to their antler tines (figure 5.18). In previous publications I related this motif to peyotism and the symbolic association of deer and peyote (Boyd 1996; 2003; 2012). I interpreted the impaled dots of this motif, including those described here, as representations of slain peyote.

When Huichol pilgrims reach Dawn Mountain during contemporary peyote pilgrimages, they begin hunting the sacred peyote-deer. Once found, it is shot with an arrow. This is a ritual reenactment of the first pilgrimage, when the deer sacrificed himself to the hunters and his heart (*iyari*) was transformed into peyote (*hikuli*). This relationship between deer and peyote is graphically portrayed in Huichol iconography. Large dots representing peyote decorate the bodies of deer or are attached to their antler tines (figure 5.19). In Huichol yarn paintings, characters from creation stories are represented shooting the peyote and the deer.

As discussed above, the black dots within the body of Z001 are analogous to the deer's heart, his *iyari*. They represent that which will be transformed through autosacrifice into peyote, into a flower in the floral desert of Wirikuta. Arrows are considered to be transforming rays of the Morning Star and Father Sun. According to myth, Evening Star is pursued by Morning Star through the underworld. When they reach Dawn Mountain, the predator identifies with the prey and slays himself. Evening Star is transformed into Morning Star at the moment of sacrifice. The black *iyari* heart of Evening Star is filled with the red, hot *kupuri* life-force transmitted through the arrow of the sun and Morning Star. The *iyari* of the deer is transformed into peyote, irradiated by the *kupuri*.[47] The three impaled red dots are analogous to this transformation. Pierced with the transforming rays of the Morning Star, they represent a heart filled with the essence of the sun through autosacrifice.

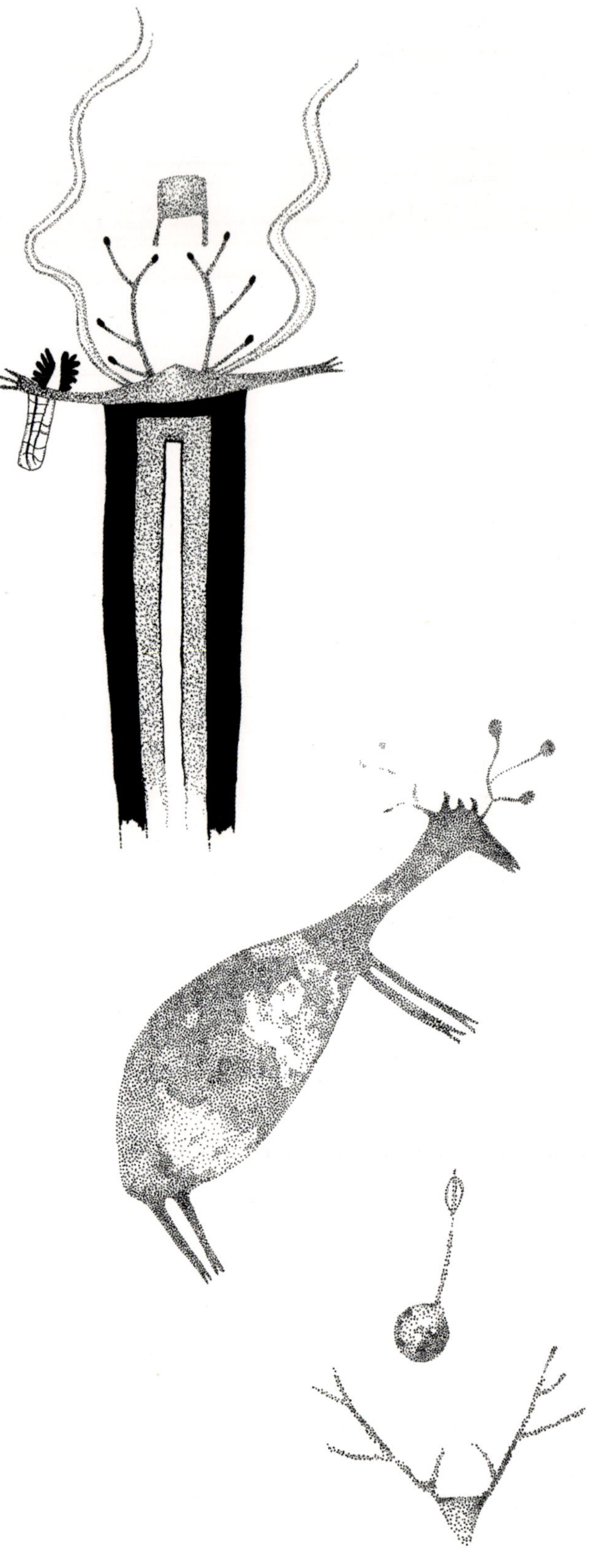

Figure 5.18. Pictographs, patterns, and peyote in Pecos River style: (a) antlered anthropomorph with dots attached to the end of each tine (41VV696); (b) red deer with red dots attached to its antlers (41VV696); (c) impaled dot associated with deer antlers (41VV74).

Motif Analysis VIII: Fire, Sun, and Morning Star

The first *jicarero* (A001) is coupled with a small, antlered human figure (A006) emerging out of the motif interpreted as Dawn Mountain (E001) (figure 5.20). Black dots appear at the tip of each antler tine; however,

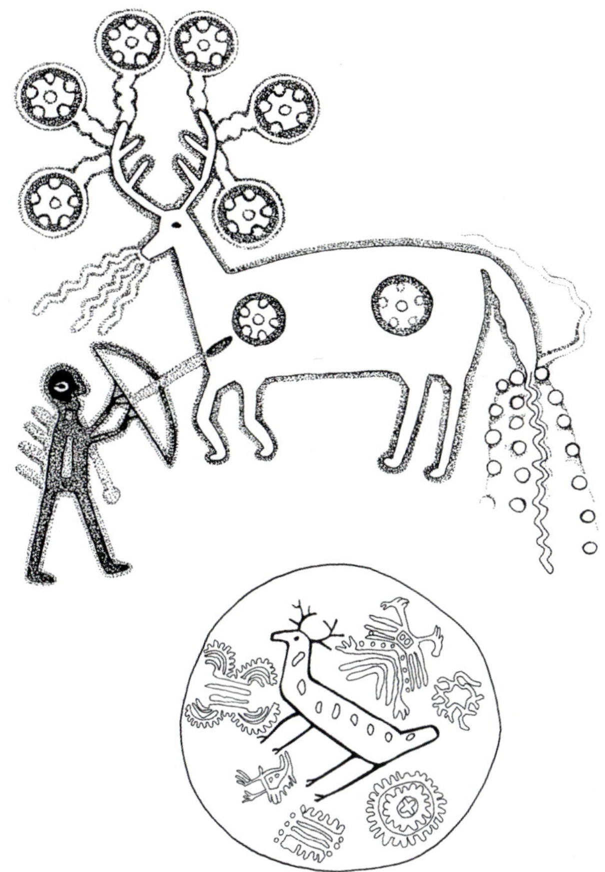

Figure 5.19. Peyote-deer in Huichol visual culture: (a) Huichol yarn painting by Chavelo Gonzalez illustrating the transformation of the sacred deer into peyote. Partial rendering of yarn painting redrawn from Furst 2006. (b) Huichol god disk of the sacred deer with peyote. Redrawn from Lumholtz 1900:32.

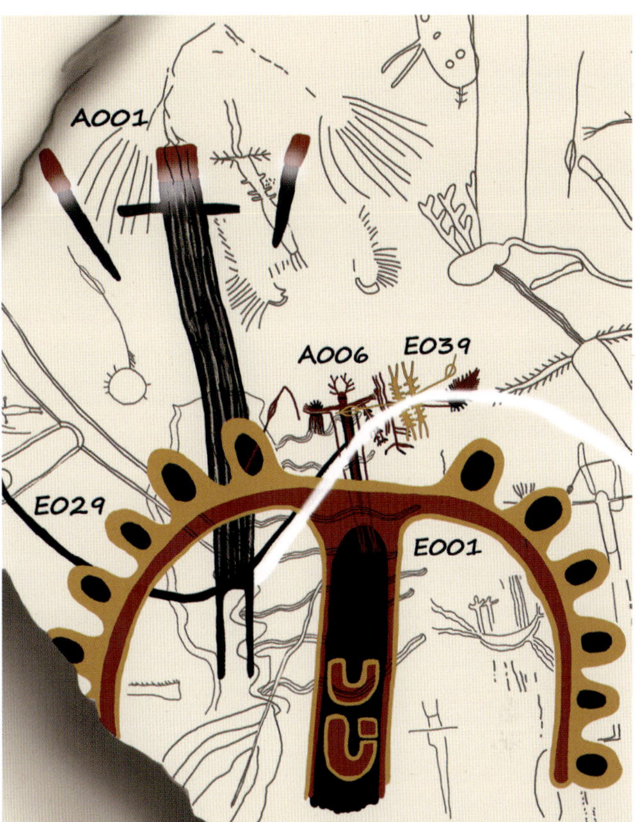

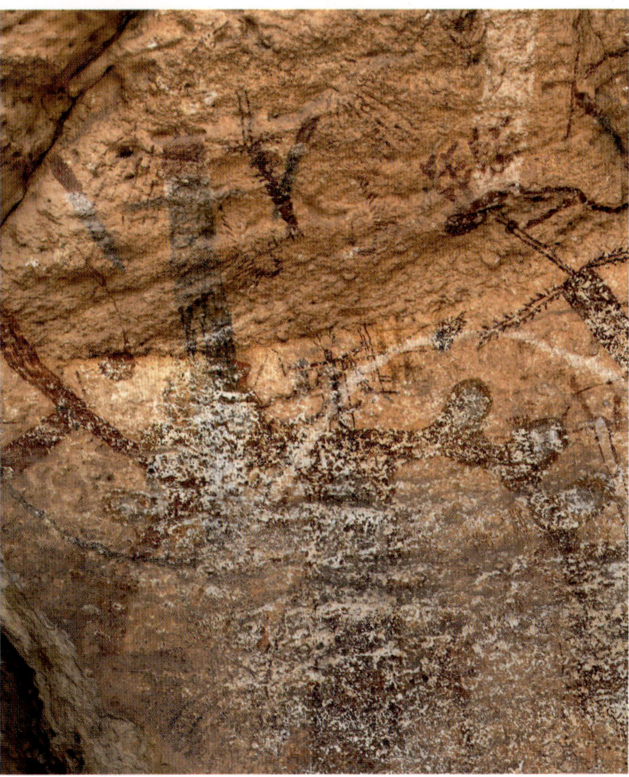

Figure 5.20. Motif VIII (A001, A006): The first Ancestor (A001) being transformed into the Fire-Sun God (A001). As the embodiment of the sacred deer he leads the ancestral pilgrims out of the underworld and represents multiple deities simultaneously: the god of fire, the sun, and the Morning Star.

the dots were applied before the tines. Using the digital microscope, we determined the red antlers overlay the black dots.[48] This small figure has fingers and toes, as well as a black band across its face resembling eyes or a mask (figures 5.21 and 5.22). It is holding an atlatl loaded with a dart in its right hand. In its left hand are extra darts and an upside-down staff. At the distal end of two lines running perpendicular to the staff is a spiny ovoid shape painted black and red. Overlaying and perpendicular to the two lines are two impaled yellow figures resembling centipedes (E039) (figure 5.22). An elaborate black and red wrist adornment is attached to the antlered figure's right arm, and an elbow adornment hangs from its left arm. All black paint associated with the figure was painted first, followed by red.

The antlered figure is sandwiched into Dawn Mountain through a very complex painting sequence. The

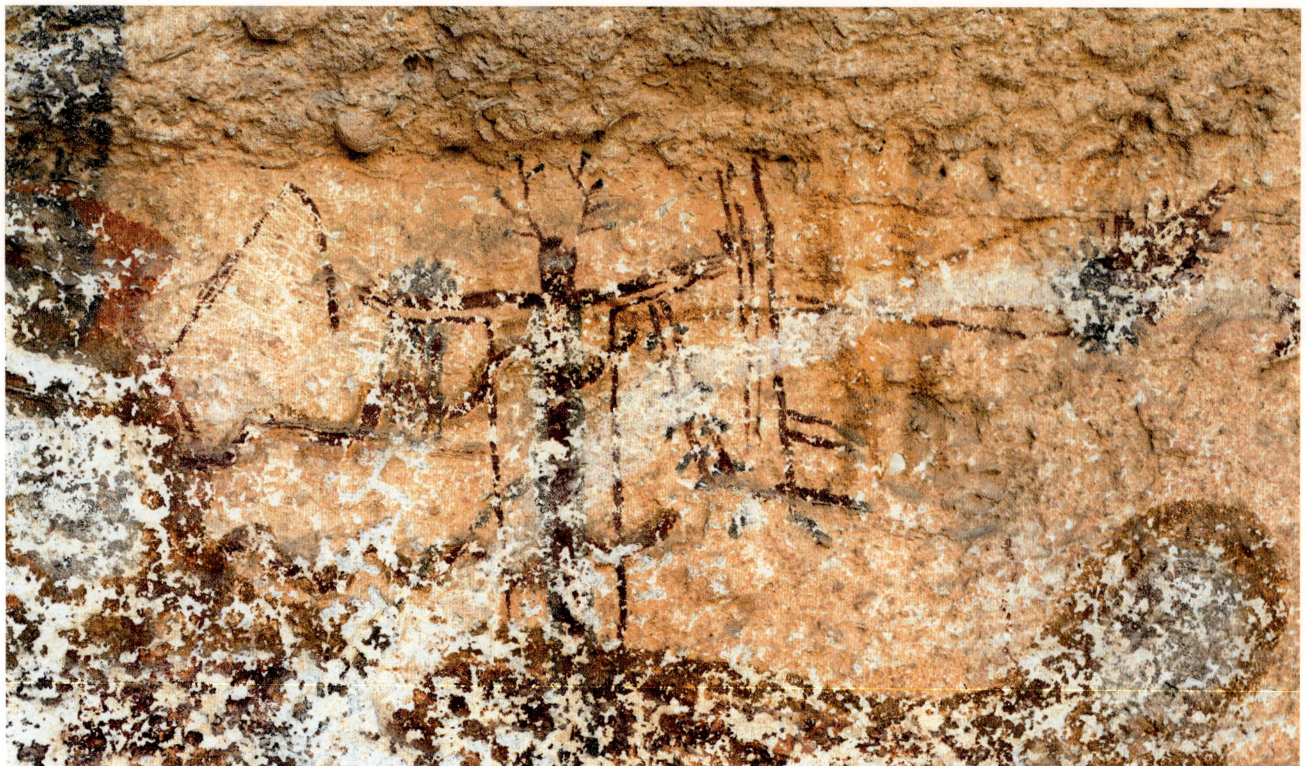

Figure 5.21. The antlered Fire-Sun God (A006) with the heart-souls of the Ancestors attached to his antler tines.

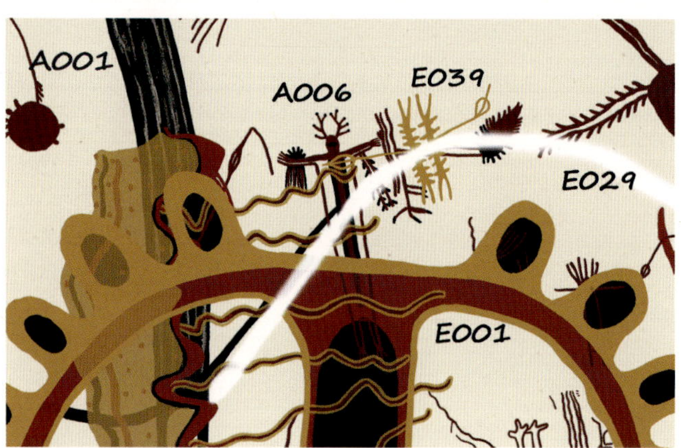

Figure 5.22. Impaled yellow, centipede-like motifs (E039) are associated with the left hand of the antlered Fire-Sun God (A006). The centipede is an insect associated with the arrival of rain, the emergence of the Ancestors from the underworld, and the birth of the sun.

black paint of Dawn Mountain and the black band running down the center of the antlered figure's body were painted first. The next layer, as best as can be determined, is the red paint of the crenellated arch. This layer overlays the black central band of the antlered figure. The next layer of red gave form to the anthropomorph. Its legs and toes were painted over the black of the arch, and its lower torso over the red. The final paint layer applied was the yellow of Dawn Mountain, which overlays the antlered figure at its waist. Thus, the antlered figure is incorporated into all three levels of the crenellated arch.[49]

The anthropomorph is also sandwiched between the white and black sinuous line (E029), interpreted above as the ecliptic path of the sun and cosmic umbilicus. The black portion of the line begins at the left end of the panel, crosses over the black body of the first *jicarero*, then proceeds underneath the antlered figure.[50] At the black central band of the antlered figure, the black line stops. The white line begins at the first *jicarero* and runs parallel to the black line for a short distance before crossing over the body of the antlered figure. The white and black lines run parallel only between A001 and A006—the first *jicarero* and his antlered avatar. Thus the two are united.

Formulating Hypotheses

Juan Negrín (1975:38) identified the principal Ancestors who participated in the First Hunt and who must be represented during all subsequent hunts as "Tamatsi

Kauyumarie (Our Elder Brother Deer Spirit), Tamatsi Maxikuaxi (Our Elder Brother Deer Tail), Tacutsi (the Wisest, who was to become Our Great Grandmother Growth), Tatei Yurianaka (Our Mother Moist Earth), and Tatewari, who had discovered the only source of light on earth, *tai*, the fire, and his is the name of Grandfather Fire." Zingg ([1938] 1977:316) includes Tsakaimuka (Setting Sun and assistant to Father Sun) among the list of original Ancestors.[51] Neurath (2000a:94) includes all of the above plus several more, including Tayau (Our Father Sun) and Tamatsi Parietsika (Our Elder Brother Sunrise).[52] Through the course of the pilgrimage *jicareros* are emptied of their human existence, plunged into primordial time, and filled with the divine essence of these ancestral deities.

In previous publications (Boyd 2003, 2010), I proposed that the transformation from *jicarero* to deified Ancestor is portrayed in the White Shaman mural. The black figures with red heads (A001–A005) identified as *jicareros* are coupled with complex anthropomorphic and enigmatic figures. Using various artistic conventions, such as described above, each pilgrim is connected to a corresponding deity-identity. In the first peyote pilgrimage the primordial ancestors became deified through participation in the sacrifice that gave birth to the sun. Today *jicareros* must be transformed into the ancestral deities in order to reenter the sacred homeland and engage in this cosmic event (Myerhoff 1974). The semiotic analogues for each of the gods who participated in the First Hunt are portrayed in the White Shaman mural.

I begin with the first *jicarero* (A001) and its corresponding deity avatar (A006). This *jicarero* is embodied by multiple deities simultaneously or, perhaps more accurately, multiple derivations of the same deity. This relates back to the concept of shared essences discussed in chapter 4, whereby gods and goddesses appear both as separate entities and as extensions of each other by way of their ability to replicate their essences. The small antlered figure (A006) associated with A001 was described by Zintgraff and Turpin (1991:40) as one of the minor figures accompanying the white shaman in his ascendancy. True, it is diminutive in scale compared to other figures bearing a more commanding presence, but its size is not an indication of its importance. This antlered figure is analogous to a deity with multiple avatars, each integral to the birth of the sun and peyote. Three of these avatars will be discussed below, beginning with the oldest of all Huichol deities, Grandfather Fire.

God of fire. All Huichol male deities are avatars of the ancient fire god, Tatewari.[53] Grandfather Fire dwells at the center of the world and uniquely exists in all three realms: the upper-, middle-, and underworlds. He unites all that is above with all that is below: he is thus an *axis mundi*, or the location where the world above connects with the world below and all four directions meet. He is the fifth direction (Neurath 2000a:99). That aspect of him that is aboveground is associated with the sun of daytime, and that which is belowground is associated with the sun journeying through the underworld. In both manifestations he has power over and gives birth to the sun (Lumholtz 1900:25). In a creation story collected by Zingg (2004:34), Tatewari actually becomes the sun.

The primordial ancestors carried Tatewari's fiery essence with them to direct their path through the blackness of the underworld.[54] When they reached their eastern destination, the essence of Grandfather Fire strengthened Father Sun so that he could emerge from the cave at Dawn Mountain. But when Father Sun rose, he remained too low in the sky, and everything began to melt from his burning heat. The Ancestors placed candles at each of the five directions, and the flames of Grandfather Fire fueled Father Sun so that he could climb the ladder up to the zenith. The antlers of Kauyumari, who is called Elder Brother, are considered the chair of Grandfather Fire (Lumholtz 1900:70). They are the ceremonial candles—the flames fueling the sun and holding the sky in place (Fikes 2011:150). During contemporary peyote pilgrimages, the shaman who

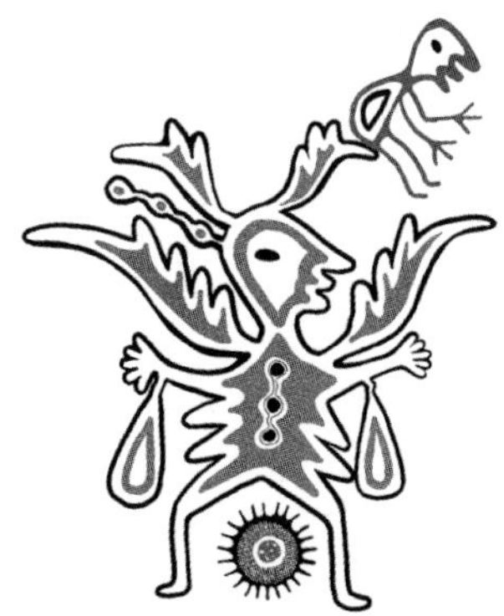

Figure 5.23. Huichol yarn painting of the fire god Tatewari. Yarn painting by José Benítez Sánchez. Redrawn from Benítez Sánchez 2005a:83.

leads the *jicareros* on the hunt embodies Grandfather Fire. He carries the antlers of the sacred deer, Kauyumari (Lumholtz 1900; Neurath 2000a). In Huichol iconography Grandfather Fire is portrayed as a deer or as a person wearing antlers, which are his flames (figure 5.23). There is no difference between fire and Tatewari; they are the same thing.

The figure emerging from the Dawn Mountain motif shares several attributes with this ancient Huichol deity; he is a prototypical fire god. The antlers of the divine deer, which are the flames of the fire god, rest upon his head. He is situated at the center of the world: the hill in the east from which everything emerges and everything returns. And he is the *axis mundi*. Half of the figure's body is above the crenellated arch, and the other half below. The lower half remains in the underworld as the sun of night, while his upper torso emerges as the sun of day. But the artist(s) went beyond the simple graphic portrayal of the figure emerging from the Dawn Mountain motif to illustrate his centrality. Through the painting process and the ordering of paint layers, he was placed at the center of the world. The black underworld layer of the Dawn Mountain motif was applied first, followed by the red body of the fire god and the red of Dawn Mountain. The red legs of the fire god overlay the black of the underworld. The final layer applied was the yellow paint encasing Dawn Mountain, and superimposing the antlered figure at his waist, sandwiching him between the black and the yellow of Dawn Mountain, between the dark of the underworld and the light of the sun.

Sun god. The sun god is a new impersonation of the fire god (Lumholtz 1900:26). The divine essence of Grandfather Fire, carried out of the underworld by the primordial ancestors, was infused into the sun. This conflation of deities is an example of replication in which the substance of a god—its essence—is transferred into the formation of a new divine being that becomes an avatar of the source deity (López Austin 1997). At the break of day the sun releases his arrows into the deer, who are, at the same time, the stars and the Ancestors (Preuss 1996:128). It is through their sacrifice that the sun is born. Neurath (2005c:92) provides an eloquent description of this cosmic event: "Sunrise is an event of violence and beauty. It is a sublime vision, as the Sun and rain snakes are born as an effect of the pilgrim's vision quest, but at the same time, mythology explains that the pilgrims are the ones who were violently killed by the Sun. Through their vision quest, pilgrims transform themselves into violent sacrificers of themselves."

This event is reenacted during each contemporary peyote hunt. After reaching Dawn Mountain, the leader of the pilgrims stalks the peyote, which is simultaneously the deer, the stars, the Ancestors and, metaphorically, themselves. He is armed with *tocari uruyari*, Father Sun's arrow, which is considered the most important arrow in the universe, signifying the rainy season and life (Fikes 2011:127). Once the peyote-deer is located, he shoots it with the arrow of the sun.

The pilgrim's sacrifice produces not only the birth of the sun, but rain. Father Sun is the one who establishes the rainy season (Fikes 2011:128). Prior to the birth of the sun, there was no rain, only the perpetual waters of the underworld. Deer are equated with the dry season and drought; therefore, they must be slain to release the rain. Their blood must be offered in sacrifice. Rain serpents manifested in the visions of *jicareros* are believed to be either tears of joy at the birth of the sun or tears of sorrow over the sacrifices begetting his birth (Neurath 2005a:74). The sun is therefore regarded as the principal bringer of rain. Preuss (1996) explains it as follows:

> Without catching deer . . . there will be no rain . . . But the real explanation for how such ideas came about is that the deer are seen as the embodiment of the stars which the Sun, or his assistant the Morning Star, slays or chases off each day, but especially in the spring, at the time when the sun really does win out over the night. Then, toward the end of June and the summer solstice, it actually does begin to rain. [Preuss 1996:129]

The antlered figure in the mural is not only a semiotic analogue of the fire god, but of the sun god as well. He is portrayed emerging from Dawn Mountain armed with his rays of light to usher in the first dawn and the first rains. He carries a red atlatl loaded with a red dart in his right hand.[55] He is one of only three characters in the mural brandishing the weapon.[56] In this context it is analogous to Father Sun's arrow, beckoning the transition to the rainy season. Directly above him is the deer, who is the star slain at sunrise. The deer is pierced in its chest with a red dart bearing a stylized tip. To the right of Father Sun's loaded atlatl are the red dots, each pierced by a red dart exhibiting a stylized tip similar to the dart impaling the deer. The impaled dots are the heart of the deer transformed into peyote by the rays of the sun god. But there is yet another attribute linking the antlered figure to the sun, one that further identifies him as the principal bringer of rain.

Jicareros journey to Dawn Mountain in order to hunt the peyote-deer so that the sun will rise and the rains will come. Once the hunt meets with success and the peyote-deer has been slain, the pilgrims are bathed in the rays of the rising sun. They paint their faces with yellow designs to portray this union with Father Sun and their success in capturing the peyote-deer.[57] Interestingly, one of the yellow facial designs painted on pilgrims' faces is a centipede (figure 5.24a). Because it comes up from the underworld, the centipede is intimately associated with the arrival of rain.[58] It is also associated with the emergence of the primordial ancestors and Father Sun. In Huichol ethnographer Paulina Faba Zuleta's (2004:59) comparison of face paintings with petroglyphs of the Sierra, she writes that images of centipedes are directly linked "con los mitos de la emergencia de los antepasados y el nacimiento del sol" (with the myths about the emergence of the ancestors and the birth of the sun). Painted at the left hand of the sun god are two yellow, impaled centipede-like figures (figure 5.22 and 5.24b). These figures are virtually identical to the centipede facial designs documented by Faba Zuleta (2003:87).

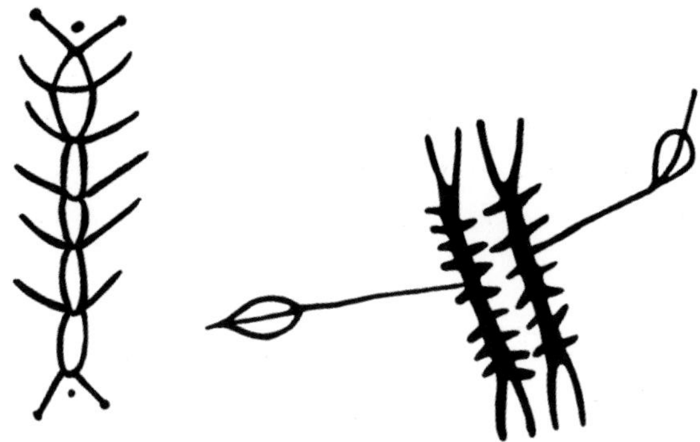

Figure 5.24. Huichol centipede face-painting designs: (a) Centipede design painted on the faces of Huichol pilgrims to portray their union with the sun. Redrawn from Faba Zuleta 2003:87. (b) Centipede-like design (E039) associated with the antlered anthropomorph identified as the Fire-Sun God (A006) emerging from the underworld.

Deer god. Perhaps the most striking parallels between the antlered figure in the rock art and Huichol creation stories are found in the deer god, Kauyumari, who is one of the principal actors in the Huichol story of the birth of the sun and creation (Preuss 1996; Zingg 2004). He is referred to by a variety of other names, such as Tamatsi, Maxa Kwaxi, Parikuta Muyeka (He Who Walks at Dawn) and Tamatsi Parietsika (Elder Brother of Dawn) (Fikes 2011; Neurath 2005c; Preuss 1996). Kauyumari and all his derivations are, however, like the sun god, avatars of Grandfather Fire.

One of the attributes unique to the antlered figure in the White Shaman mural is the portrayal of eyes or a mask resembling eyes.[59] Among the Huichol, the eye is a symbol of power—of being able to see and know things hidden from others. In myth, Kauyumari is credited with being the first to make use of the eye. He possesses the unique ability to see into the earth and everything above it. With this power he battles the forces of the underworld in order to "put the world into shape" (Lumholtz 1900:154–155).[60]

Perhaps the most compelling analogies between the rock art motif and the deer god are related to his antlers and the black dots at the tip of each tine.[61] The leader of the pilgrims, who embodies the fire god, carries the antlers of Kauyumari to communicate with the Ancestors and to open the portal into the sacred homeland (P. Furst 1972; Lumholtz 1900). According to the Huichol, "We call him *Kauyumarí*, we call him *Maxa Kwaxí*. It is all one. *Kauyumarí* aids Grand-father Fire. He aids Father Sun. He guides the *mara'akame* in what must be done. So that the peyote can be hunted. So that the *mara'akame* can take the peyote from the horns of the deer, there in *Wirikúta*" (Myerhoff 1974:87). In previous publications I argued that the black dots attached to the antler tines represent peyote brought to the Ancestors by the sacred deer, but this interpretation, as explained below, is an oversimplification.

Kauyumari is an anthropomorphic representation of the deer and the stars, including the arrow-shooting Morning Star (Preuss 1996:108, 122). He is perceived as a deer or as a person wearing deer antlers. Antlers are a "summarizing symbol" among the Huichol, meaning they are imbued with multiple layers of meaning, collectively exemplifying "what is essential to being Huichol" (Fikes 2011:1).[62] According to myth, when the fire god, Tatewari, placed two ceremonial arrows on

Kauyumari's head, they were transformed into antlers. Ceremonial arrows transport messages between men and gods; therefore, Kauyumari's antlers become a vehicle through which communication with the Ancestors is possible. He is considered "master of the words" or the word itself; "he links us to Our Ancestors and creates bonds between them and their creatures" (Negrín 1975:16). Words, which are messages from the Ancestors, are transported inside ceremonial arrows and inside Kauyumari's antlers (Fikes 2011:163; Myerhoff 1974:203–204).

In addition to words, water and rain are inextricably associated with Kauyumari and his antlers (Fikes 2011:1). Like Father Sun, he is considered an agent of water (Negrín 1975:17). The Huichol believe all water originates from the sea and is carried through the underworld by aquatic serpents. Water embodies the ancestral deities who control the rain, which is the original source of *kupuri*.[63] According to the Huichol, *kupuri* is "the living water we need to survive"; it never evaporates; it is the Ancestors (Fikes 2011:1, 117, 144). All rain originates from a cave at the top of Dawn Mountain from which the sun god emerged after the deer, who was himself the sun, committed autosacrifice (Gutiérrez 2011:108). The emergence of the sun marked the triumph of light over darkness and over the aquatic serpents of the underworld. Father Sun heated the waters of the primordial world, and the earth began to dry. The moisture taken from the wet earth rose to the heavens as giant clouds and ushered in the first rainy season (Neurath 2001a:508)—and with the first rains came life—*kupuri*.[64]

This pivotal event is reenacted during contemporary peyote hunts. *Jicareros* collect water from sacred springs in Wirikuta. These permanent waterholes are wombs of the female Ancestors who did not dry up completely when the sun rose at creation. Before the *jicareros* take water from the sacred spring, they make offerings of deer blood and antlers.[65] This *kupuri*-containing water is sprinkled into the air by the pilgrims' leader. Holding the sun's rainy-season arrow and Kauyumari's antlers, the leader, as the god of fire, asks Father Sun and the Rain Mothers to release the rains.[66]

Through autosacrifice the divine deer facilitates the sun's birth and, thereby, the rainy season. With the first rains came the creation of *kupuri*, the life-force placed by the gods into the first humans and into every child since conceived. And with *kupuri*, the *iyari* heart is moved to act in accordance with the world established by the Ancestors through their sacrifices. Peyote, too, was born through the sacrifice committed by the deer, whose own *iyari* was transformed into peyote, an important source of *kupuri*. When the Ancestors ate the flesh of the slain deer, they too went through a transformation. They became deities; they became peyote; they became deer; and they became stars. And at the same time, their essences created and were transmitted into all the elements of nature their descendants would need to survive.

The Huichol still believe peyote is borne in the antlers of the deer. As noted by Denis Lemaistre (1996:311), "The entire mythology confirms it for us: the deer (which at that time was also a man) carried the peyote inside its horns." In Huichol myth and art the divine deer is portrayed with peyote attached to his antlers. Eating peyote, the heart of Kauyumari, in ritual contexts and participating in the sacrifices of the Ancestors allows the Huichol to see into the heart and mind of the sacred deer.

The black dots on the tines of the small antlered anthropomorph, however, are not peyote. Instead, they are analogous to that which was transformed into peyote and into the sun. Kauyumari offered his heart as a sacrifice, which is the *iyari* soul of all the Ancestors and, by extension, water. According to the Huichol, ancient water from the great beyond "is the life of our gods" and embodies the Ancestors (Fikes 2011:119). The small black dots therefore represent the heart of the deer *prior* to transformation into peyote. They are black because they are primordial; they are the souls of the Ancestors, water brought up from the underworld at the dawn of time. Placing them at the tips of the antler tines, which are the flames of the fire god, is analogous to placing them on a sacrificial pyre. Through their sacrifice, they were transformed into the sun and into peyote—the flowers of Wirikuta. And they were transformed into rain, the life-giving source of *kupuri*.

This small antlered figure was a key player in the creation of time as we know it today. He is analogous to the fire god who dwells at the center of the world and whose flames consumed the sacrifice freely given by the Ancestors: their heart-soul. He is analogous to the deer, the Morning Star, who through a violent sacrifice gave his life so that the sun would rise, and with his eyes he shaped the world. Finally, he is analogous to the sun god, who with his sacred arrow calls forth the *kupuri*-containing rains of life.

Motif Analysis IX: Principal Deer God and Master of the Deer

Located immediately to the right of the antlered anthropomorph (A006) is another antlered figure (A007) (figure 5.25). This complex figure has attributes of a bird, deer, and human. It has arms or wings, tail feathers, and not one, but two sets of antler racks. Its head is connected to its body by a long, thin neck. The back of its head is tethered by an enigmatic red and black serpentine shape to a large red dot terminating in a sharp needlelike point (E049). The body of A007 is pierced just under its left arm by a dart with a stylized tip. Its right arm and tail feathers rest on the white line (E029).

A broad white band (E032) shoots up from the head of this antlered, birdlike creature, brushing up against the hind quarters of the impaled deer (Z001). It then arcs across A008, one of the upside-down, impaled figures interpreted in Motif Analysis VI as a *jicarero* returning to the west after transformation into a stellar deity. The head of A008 and the head of A002 appear to be interwoven. Although it is difficult to determine with a high degree of confidence, the red head of A002 appears to be sandwiched between the black mask and red head of A008.[67] After crossing A008, the broad white band plummets downward until it rests gently alongside the second black and red anthropomorph (A002), whose body is the same width as the white band.

Formulating Hypotheses

One of the most important of all Huichol deities is Tatutsi Maxa Kwaxi, or Great-Grandfather Deer Tail (Ne-

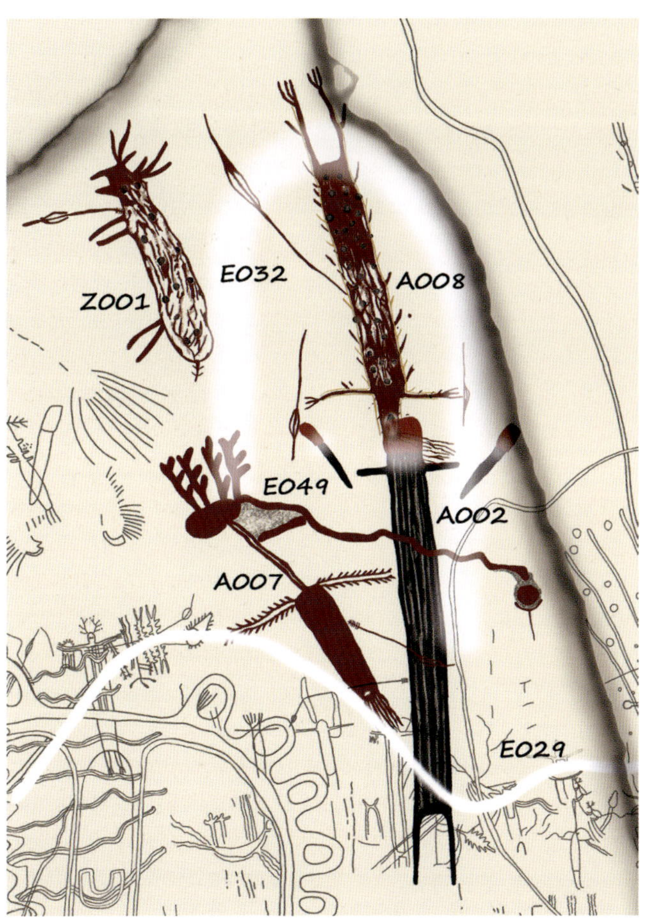

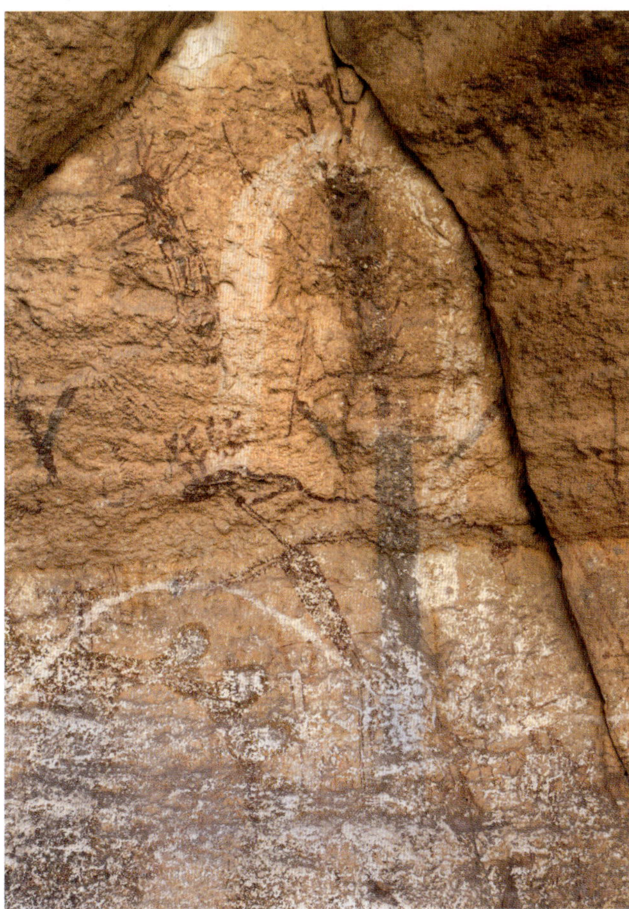

Figure 5.25. Motif IX (A002 and A007): The second Ancestor (A002) transforming into the second fire god and principal deer god (A007).

grín 1975:38; Myerhoff 1974:85). He was one of the principal Ancestors who participated in the primordial peyote hunt. Like the deer god, Kauyumari (discussed above), Maxa Kwaxi guides the pilgrims on the journey through the underworld. The two gods, Maxa Kwaxi and Kauyumari, are often perceived as the same entity. Lemaistre (1996:319) distinguishes them as follows: "Kauyumári is perhaps above all the word, or rather what has emerged from all the paradigms of the word, namely song. More than anyone else Maxa Kwaxí, Kauyumári's active double, knew how to turn the word into action, and then into ritual" (Lemaistre 1996:319). Myerhoff (1974:84) suggests that whereas Kauyumari serves as a mediator between the shaman and the fire god, Maxa Kwaxi represents the Guardian of the Deer. Maxa Kwaxi is closely associated with the white-tailed hawk (figure 5.26a) and is represented literally and figuratively by pairs of antler racks (figure 5.26b). The four antlers on his head are a distinct identifying feature of both Maxa Kwaxi and Kauyumari (see Kindl 2005:99; Benítez Sánchez 2005b:98–99; Myerhoff 1974:86). They are both avatars of the fire god, Tatewari.

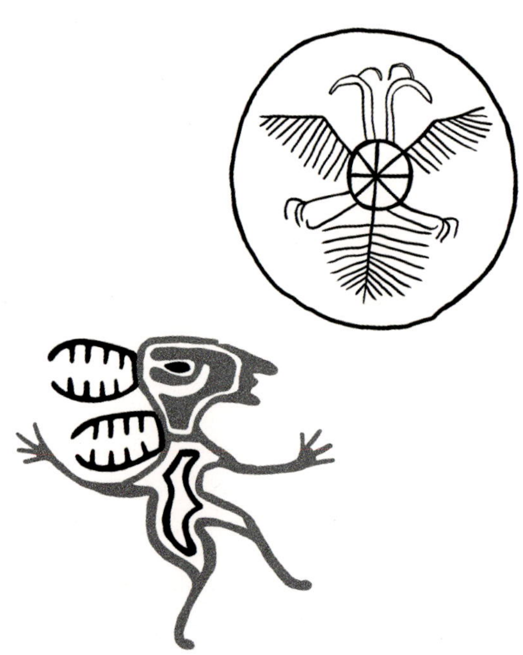

Figure 5.26. In Huichol visual culture Great-Grandfather Deer Tail possesses attributes of a white-tailed hawk and but is also portrayed with two sets of antler racks: (a) Huichol god disk of Great-Grandfather Deer Tail. Redrawn from Lumholtz 1900:36. (b) Huichol yarn painting by José Benítez Sánchez portraying Great-Grandfather Deer Tail with dual antler racks. Redrawn from Benítez Sánchez 2005b:98.

Great-Grandfather Deer Tail assists Grandfather Fire. He is the second fire god but the chief deer god (Lumholtz 1900:10). In myth, and as reenacted during contemporary peyote hunts, Maxa Kwaxi walks directly behind Tatewari when in single file or to his left during ceremonies. He is the "confessor" in charge of burning the knotted cords representing transgressions confessed during purification rites (Neurath 2000a:91). The Huichol describe Tatutsi Maxa Kwaxi as "the path that emerges from the earth, from his chest and from his antlers in the east" (Negrín 2005:80). His emergence is accompanied by Tatewari, Grandfather Fire, who is predecessor of the sun (Negrín 2005:80).

In the White Shaman mural the second *jicarero* (A002) and his deity avatar (A007) share attributes with this Huichol deity. Placement of these figures in relation to the fire god and Dawn Mountain is significant and corresponds to the positioning of these principal deities in myth and ritual. The second *jicarero* is located to the left or, if viewed as walking in single file, immediately behind the fire god. A broad white band connects the *jicarero* to an unusual figure with two sets of antlers and distinctive tail feathers, both attributes related to Maxa Kwaxi. The broad white band emerging from his antlers not only unites him with the *jicarero*, but also with the impaled deer previously identified as Venus. While Arturo Gutiérrez (2008:295) identifies Maxa Kwaxi with Venus as Evening Star, Konrad Preuss (1998b:324) suggests that the Morning and Evening Star are often conflated.[68] Either way, the identification of this figure with Venus is reinforced by its placement on the panel. It is sweeping along the white line—the ecliptic—in the direction of the sun.

Motif Analysis X: Earth Mother

To the right of the second *jicarero* is one of the most striking figures in this pictorial narrative: a large catfish-serpent-like figure (Z003) superimposing the right arm and upper torso of the third black and red anthropomorph (A003) (figure 5.27). This huge creature appears to be two-headed, with whiskers at each end of its undulating body.[69] Its head rests on the white ecliptic line (E029), and its body reaches upward more than twice the height of the *jicarero* it superimposes. The figure not only divides the mural vertically into halves, its body is also vertically divided. The "back" of the creature is painted red, while the "underbelly" is separat-

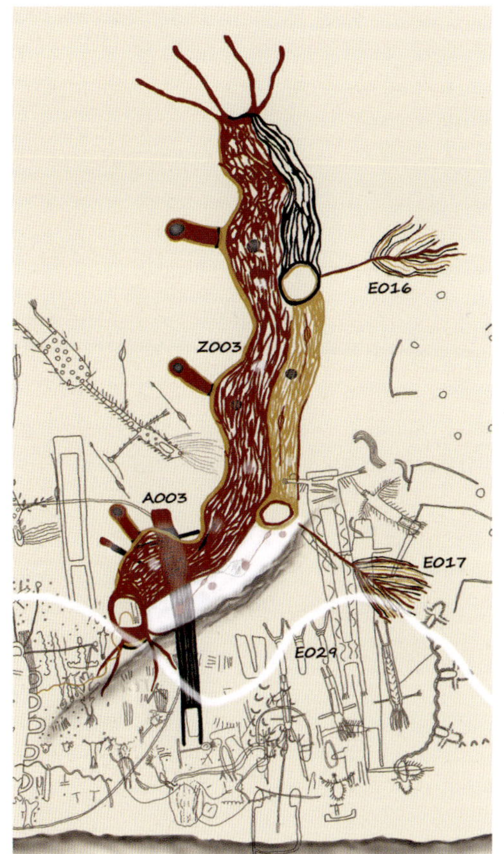

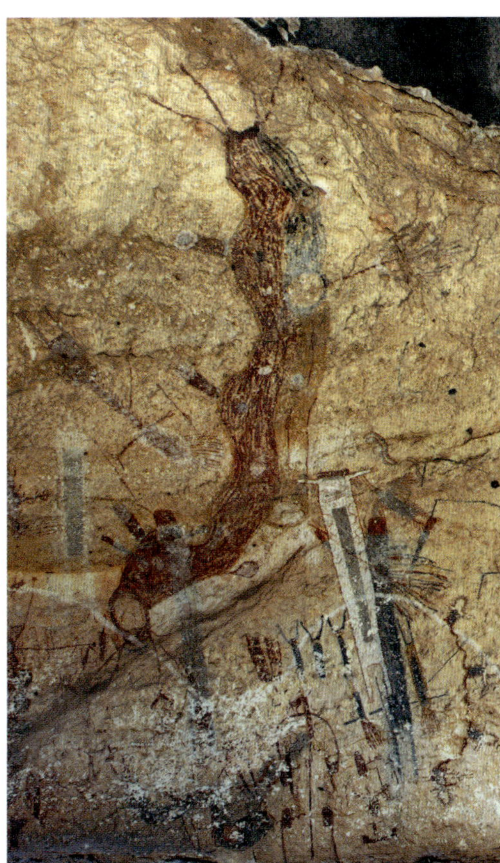

Figure 5.27. Motif X (A003 and Z003): The third Ancestor (A003) transforming into Earth Mother (Z003), mother of all the gods, who possesses the attributes of both a serpent and a catfish, and is associated with the colors of the four directions. Photo by Jean Clottes. Courtesy of Shumla Archaeological Research and Education Center.

ed horizontally into three segments: black, yellow, and white. A plume of red, yellow, and black lines emerges from circles that divide each segment (E016 and E017). Black and white dots are painted inside each segment except the white one. Hidden within this region are red dots, two of which are impaled. The back of the creature's body is outlined in yellow, as are the three stubby red appendages attached to it.

As with the other figures discussed thus far, all black paint in this section of the mural was applied first. This was followed by the application of red, yellow, and then white. The black paint of the *jicarero*'s body interfaces directly with the wall, as does the black of the torches it carries and the black dots within the body of the creature. The red of the creature's body, as well as an impaled red dot within its white underbelly, superimpose the *jicarero* and its torches. The yellow outlining the creatures back and appendages superimpose the red. A thin white wash was added to each black dot, and solid white dots were applied along the creature's red back. The white serpentine line (E029) superimposes both the pilgrim and the creature. A natural concavity in the wall was incorporated into the image. The creature's white underbelly rests within and follows this natural feature.

Formulating Hypotheses

Just as Grandfather Fire, Tatewari, shares his essence with all male deities, Great-Grandmother Growth, Takutsi Nakawé, shares her essence with all female deities.[70] She is the most ancient of the Huichol gods, and all female deities are united under her (Schaefer 2002:50). Whereas the sun rules during the dry season, Takutsi rules the cosmos during the rainy season. She is both goddess of the earth and the moon (Preuss 1996:118). As Earth Mother she is called Yurianaka and Utuanaka, and demands offerings of an image of herself, which is a catfish perceived as a snake (figure 5.28).[71] She is the prototype of the goddess equated with the rain serpent, Nia'ariwame (Preuss 1996:124).[72] Earth Mother is described as taking the form of a fish and was the first ancestor to have carried out the pilgrimage to the desert. Gourd bowls dedicated to her are painted black with designs in the shape of fish, specifically catfish, on the inside (Kindl 2000:41–42). In keeping with other Mesoamerican earth deities, the body of the Huichol goddess is perceived to have been dismembered, and from each part of her body emerged the plants and animals needed to sustain life (Negrín 1975:92). All vegetation, therefore, is her product (Lumholtz 1900:13). In her chest she keeps the "principal" of maize, which is peyote (Lemaistre 1996:321).[73] She also holds as her possession all mineral colors; thus her idols are covered with spots made from these colors—red, black, yellow, and white (Lumholtz 1900:24, 43).

As with all female deities sharing her essence, Grandmother Growth is associated with the underworld, night, rain, and serpents. Lumholtz (1900:81) says Grandmother Growth is perceived as a giant, all-devouring serpent with two heads, between which the sun must pass when setting.[74] She shares her essence with the eastern rain serpent, Nia'ariwame, which is closely associated with peyote and the summer solstice (Magriñá 2001; Neurath 2005c:91).[75] A key moment during the peyote pilgrimage is when she appears to the *jicareros* in their visions as the great Cloud Serpent. The *jicareros* collectively become this goddess, embodying her essence and carrying her back to the Sierra with them to ensure rain. Nia'ariwame's body is divided into five aspects, each associated with one of the four directions plus the center. The *jicareros*, who are at the same time Ancestral deities, represent these five aspects of Nia'ariwame and collectively represent the cloud serpent. They return home as the rain serpent from the east (Neurath 2001a:515, 519).

In Mesoamerica the four cardinal directions of the earth are almost always associated with colors. In fact, the practice is so pervasive in the Americas, as well as in eastern Siberia, that it might well have been included in the "cultural baggage" brought across the Bering Strait by the first immigrants (Marcus et al. 2003:38–39). The most common of these color schemes, and apparently the earliest known, is red/east, black/west, white/north, and yellow/south (DeBoer 2005:74; MacLaury 1997). According to DeBoer (2005:82), this was most likely the original color scheme of the ancient Uto-Aztecans.

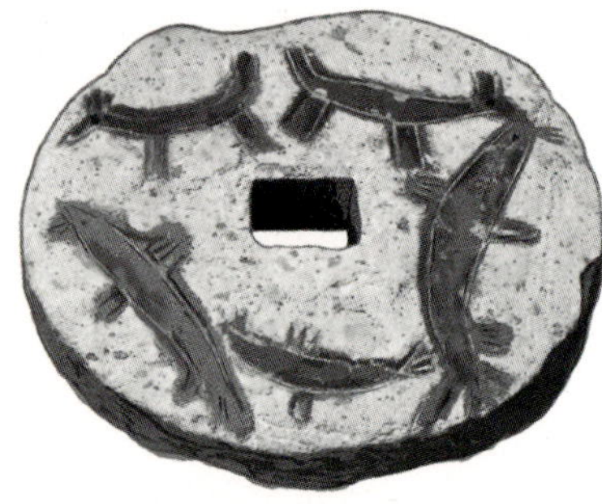

Figure 5.28. Huichol god disk dedicated to Grandmother Growth. Redrawn from MacLean 2005:22.

The catfish-serpent-like creature in the White Shaman mural shares several attributes with this Huichol earth goddess. She possesses characteristics of a snake (possibly two-headed) and a fish, the long, whiskerlike tendrils suggesting a catfish. Her sinuous body is painted in four segments, each representing one of the colors associated with the four directions; however, as the eastern rain serpent she is predominantly associated with the east, and therefore the color red, which is her dominant color. Inside her white underbelly are two impaled red dots symbolizing life-giving sustenance in the form of peyote, for from the dismembered body of the earth goddess all vegetation was born.

Motif Analysis XI: Moon Goddess

Superimposing the yellow segment of Earth Mother's underbelly is the arm of a striking white, humanlike figure (A015) (figure 5.29)—the one for which the panel was named. In contrast to the undulations of the figure it superimposes, this captivating image is angular, its body a long rectangle tilted slightly off vertical. Although the white body sets it apart from other images in the panel, it isn't painted only in white. A precise red line outlines the figure, and a row of red S-shapes runs vertically down each side of its body. Between the two rows is a long, dark gray, rectangular band. The figure has no head. A slender band of red paint caps the top of the figure. Its arms and legs, like those of the pilgrims, are disproportionately short. Unlike them, this figure has fingers and toes. The headless anthropomorph wields in its left hand two gray and red S-shaped objects. In its right hand, although obscured by the Earth Mother's body, is another red S-shape. Attached to its right arm is a wrist adornment very similar to the one on the antlered figure we identified as a fire and sun god. Attached to the white anthropomorph's left arm by fine red lines is a dark gray, human-bird conflation with red eyes, its entire body adorned with long red and gray feathers. Two S-shaped objects identical to those asso-

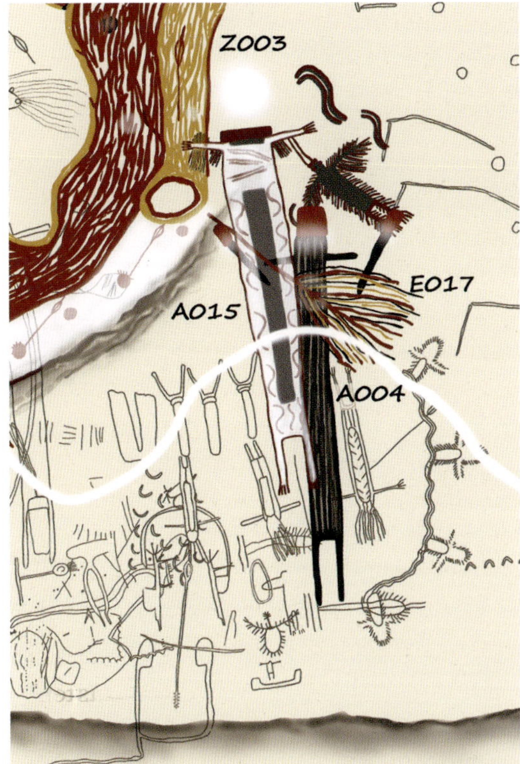

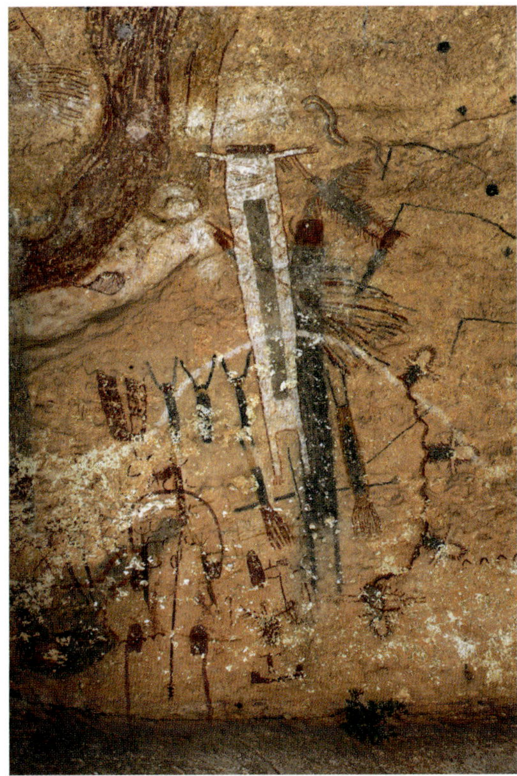

Figure 5.29. Motif XI (A004 and A015): The fourth Ancestor (A004) transforming into the Moon Goddess (A015), who provided light to the pilgrims before the first sunrise. She is associated with rain, serpents, and the color white. Photo by Jean Clottes. Courtesy of Shumla Archaeological Research and Education Center.

ciated with A015 are wielded in its left "hand," and one in its right. Because the painting sequence of superimposed figures in this section of the panel is extremely complex, I will discuss this section color by color.

Before any other color was applied to the mural, the artist painted the dark gray central band running down the body of the white figure (A015).[76] This color interfaces directly with the rock wall and does not superimpose any other imagery. Given similarity in color, it is likely that the wrist adornment, winged figure, and S-shaped paraphernalia were painted from the same paint pot. The black arm of the fourth *jicarero* (A004) and the black portion of its torch superimpose the gray band within the white anthropomorph. Thus, the black body of A004 and its torches represent the second paint layer. The black plumes of E017 overlay the pilgrim's black body and were the third layer of paint added.

The next color applied to this section of the panel is red. No black superimposes red. The first layer is the red outline of the white figure, as well as the S-shaped designs within its body. The black arm of A004 is overlain by the red outline, thus sandwiching the arm between the two colors of A015. Likely associated with this layer of red paint are the red lines within A015's right wrist adornment and the red feathers of the winged figure attached to its left arm. The second layer of red includes the pilgrim's head, the torch tips, and a line running along the yellow underbelly of the earth creature's body. The red head and torch tips superimpose the red feathers of the winged figure. The red line running along the creature's underbelly superimposes the red outline of A015's right arm and wrist adornment. The final layer of red is the feather plume (E017). This enigmatic figure superimposes the red torch tip, the S-shaped lines decorating A015's body, and the pilgrim's black body.

There is one layer of yellow paint. The yellow underbelly of Z003 superimposes the black and red of A015's wrist adornment and right arm. The yellow plumes of E017 superimpose the red plumes and the pilgrim's body. The only color that superimposes the yellow paint is white, which was the final color applied.

There are two layers of white. The white body of A015 was filled in after all the other colors had been applied. The white overlays the red designs within its body and superimposes the black torch and black right arm of the pilgrim, further integrating A004 into A015. The two figures are interwoven. The same is true for the white anthropomorph and the figure identified as

Earth Mother (Z003). Her yellow underbelly superimposes the red and black portion of A015's arm and paraphernalia, but the white portion of A015's right arm overlays the yellow underbelly. A thin layer of white paint was applied to the neck area of both the pilgrim and the torches. Above the white anthropomorph is a circular area of what appears to be white paint, but it is very faint. The final layer of paint produced the white ecliptic line. It overlays the yellow, red, and black, as well as the white body of A015.

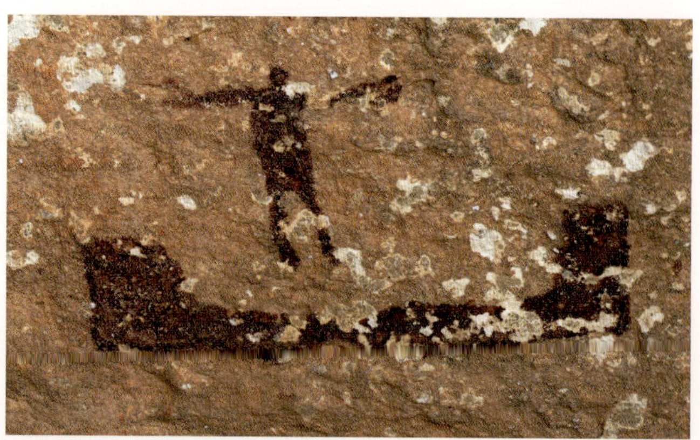

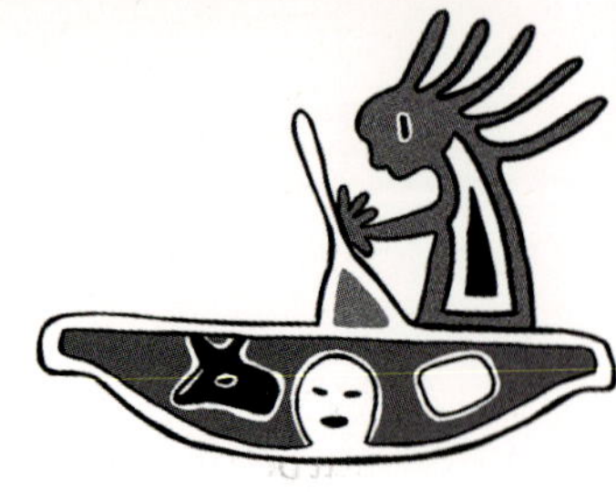

Figure 5.31. In Huichol mythology the moon goddess saved a single man, Watakame, by placing him in a canoe to avoid the Great Flood: (a) A small anthropomorph (A016) associated with a canoe-like motif (E047) located directly below the Moon Goddess (A015). (b) Huichol yarn painting of Watakame escaping the rising waters. Redrawn from Love 1999:34.

Formulating Hypotheses

As discussed above, Great-Grandmother Growth (Takutsi Nakawé) shares her essence with all female deities, including the goddess of the moon (Schaefer 2002:50).[77] Whereas Takutsi's earth aspect is associated with the rain serpent of the east, the summer solstice, and peyote, her moon aspect is associated with the rain serpent of the west, the winter solstice, and the dangerous hallucinogenic plant *kieri* (solandra and datura) (Magriñá 2001). This western rain serpent is called Kiewimuka, which is etymologically related to *kieri*.[78] Kiewimuka is in direct conflict with the rain serpent of the east. And by virtue of her name, she is equated with the color white. According to Lumholtz (1900:24), white is produced from a mineral called *tata'mi* or Kyewimo'ka (an alternative spelling for Kiewimuka).

In Huichol myth and art the moon goddess is portrayed as dressed in white and wearing a gray mask with a necklace made of shells. Lumholtz (1900:46–47, 49) reports that serpents are the arrows of Takutsi Nakawé, which are represented in Huichol art as S-shaped lines.[79] She is portrayed carrying serpent staffs in both hands, and on her back she carries her child, who will become the goddess of the earth (Neurath 2001a:513).

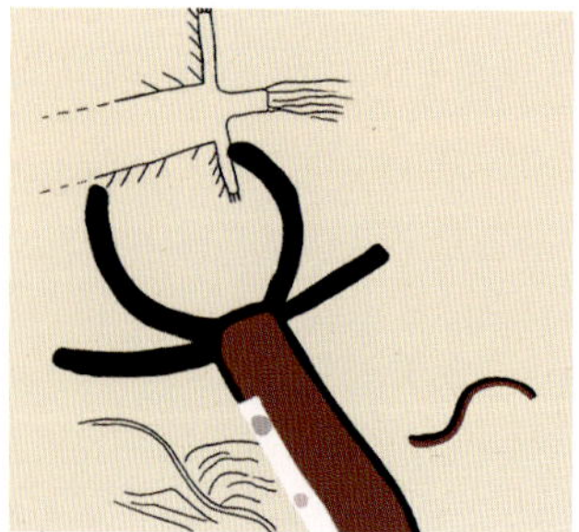

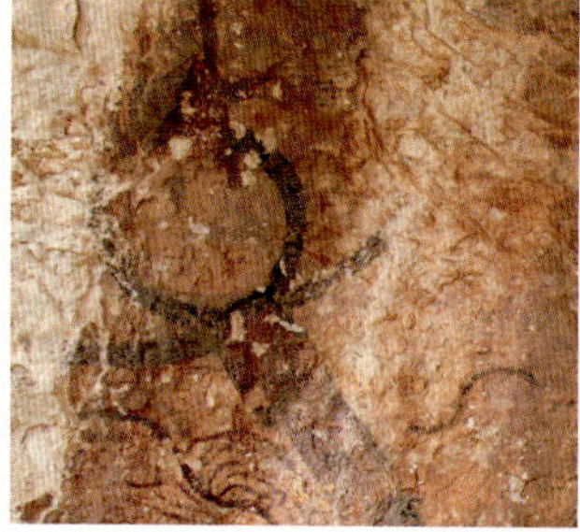

Figure 5.30. A horned serpent at Mystic Shelter (41VV612) associated with an S-shaped motif identical to the staffs held by the Moon Goddess (A015).

Likely due to her changing nature, the Moon is generally distrusted (Aedo 2003b:194). On the first peyote pilgrimage, however, the moon goddess provided light to the pilgrims prior to the first sunrise.[80] And in the Huichol flood myth, it was Takutsi who helped Watakame escape the rising waters and begin human life again in the new world. She instructed him to make a canoe out of a tree and then navigated his small vessel across the dark waters of the night sky (Preuss 1998b). The journey made by Watakame, who has Venus-sun related traits, refers to the sun's nocturnal journey through the underworld (Neurath 2005c:97 fn34; Preuss 1998b). As a result of this pivotal role, Takutsi Nakawé demands as offerings images of the ark in which the only man survived the flood (Preuss 1996:124).

The famous white anthropomorphic figure (A015), previously referred to as the White Shaman, is analogous to the moon goddess. She is dressed in white with S-shaped serpent arrows or, in this case, staffs or darts in both hands and S-shaped lines painted vertically down the interior of her body. She and the figure attached to her left arm are the only ones in the mural portrayed with the S-shaped paraphernalia. An identical S-shaped motif, however, is found in association with a giant horned serpent at another site in the region (figure 5.30).

Perhaps the most intriguing correlation between A015 and the moon goddess appears directly below the figure: a very distinctive image of a human form (A016) standing in a canoe-like motif (E047) (figure 5.31). This is analogous to the survivor of the great flood and, at the same time, the Venus-sun journeying to the east across the waters of the underworld.

Motif Analysis XII: Setting Sun and Snarer of the Deer

The fifth and final *jicarero* (A005) and its deity avatar (A013) are located on the far right end of the panel (figure 5.32). A005 is surrounded by thirty-two large black dots and thirteen enigmatic L-shapes (E010). The black dots and L-shapes were applied after the black body of A005, but before the red body of A013. One of the thirty-two black dots was converted into the face of a brick red anthropomorph (A013) (figure 5.33). This human-like figure is upside-down and impaled with a dart in its left side. Surrounding the black mask is a vibrant yellow disk divided by fine red lines radiating outward like spokes on a wheel (figure 5.34). The body of this inverted figure superimposes the torch and right arm of the fifth *jicarero*. The legs of the fifth figure are completely obscured by the horizontal band painted red and outlined in black (E007), which I interpreted above as the western entrance into the dark waters of the underworld. Located above the head of A005 is a small yellow circle resembling a wheel cog (E043) (figure 5.32). The tendrils of E009 superimpose A005's left arm and torch.

There are three layers of black paint in this section of the panel. The first layer includes A005's body and torches. These interface directly with the wall. The second layer is the black of the horizontal band and its crenellations (E007). This band overlays the legs of A005. Included in the second layer is the black dot located at the end of the red tendril superimposing A005's arm. The third layer is the black L-shapes and dots of E010. Two of the L-shapes and two of the dots overlay the black body of A005. A third L-shape appears to overlay the first lobe of E007.

After the black paint was applied to the wall, layers of red were applied. The first includes the red of the upside-down figure with the rayed disk surrounding its

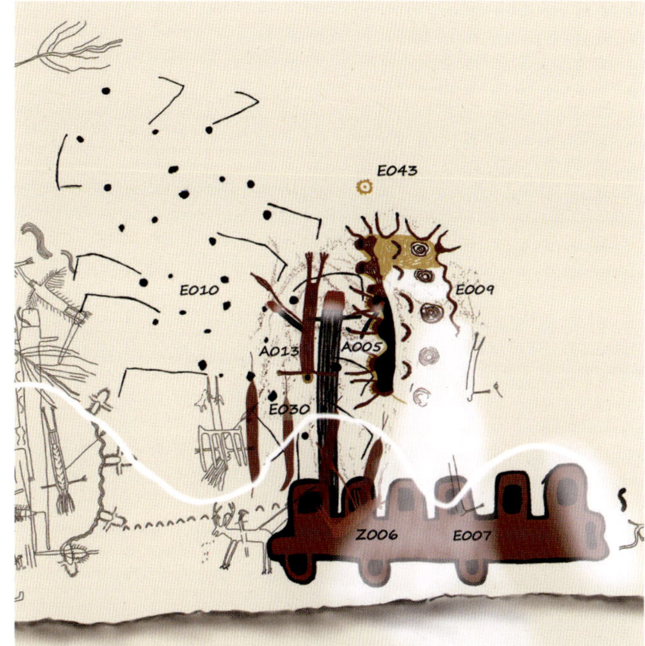

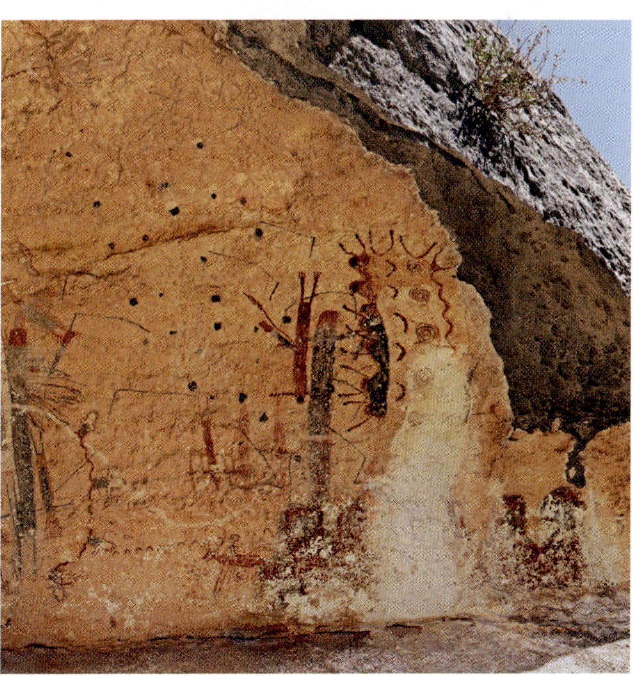

Figure 5.32. Motif XII (A005, A013): The fifth Ancestor (A005) being transformed into the western solar deer deity: Setting Sun, Snarer of the Deer (A013).

black mask (A013), the red of E009, and the red portion of the horizontal band (E007). These either overlay black paint or interface directly with the wall. The red head and torch tips of A005 were painted as part of the second layer. This was established based on the relationship between A005 and the enigmatic figure (E009) overlaying its left arm and torch, which will be

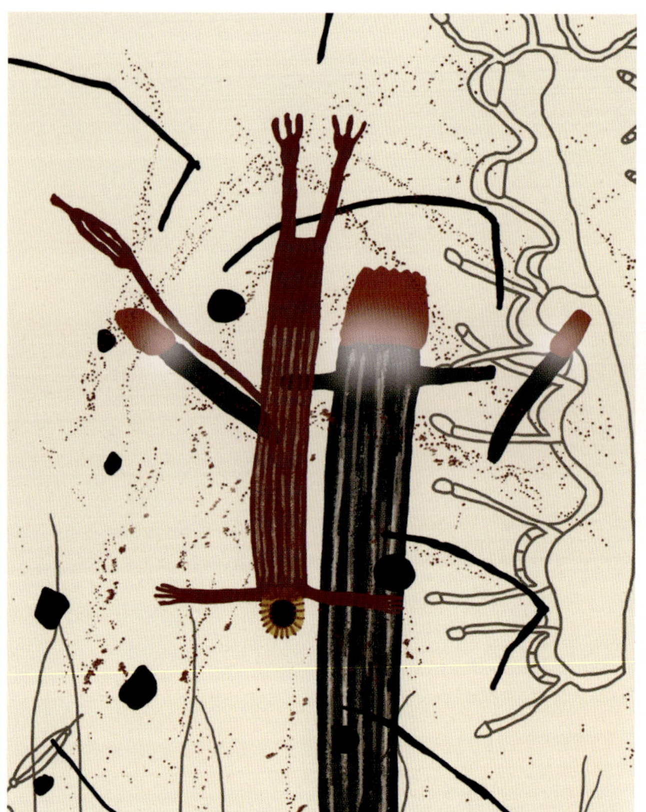

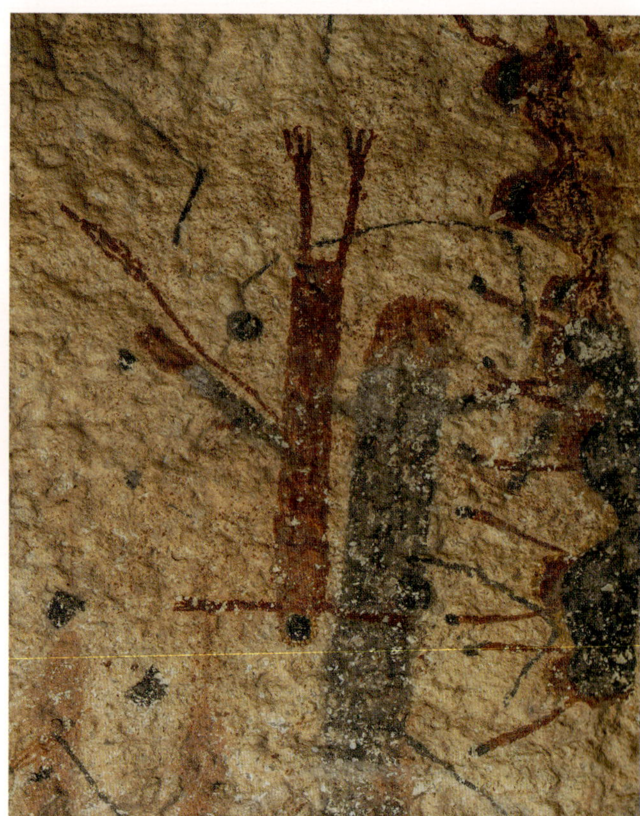

Figure 5.33. The western solar deity (A013) descending in the west, surrounded by a splatter of sacrificial blood erupting from the sacrifices made to give birth to the sun.

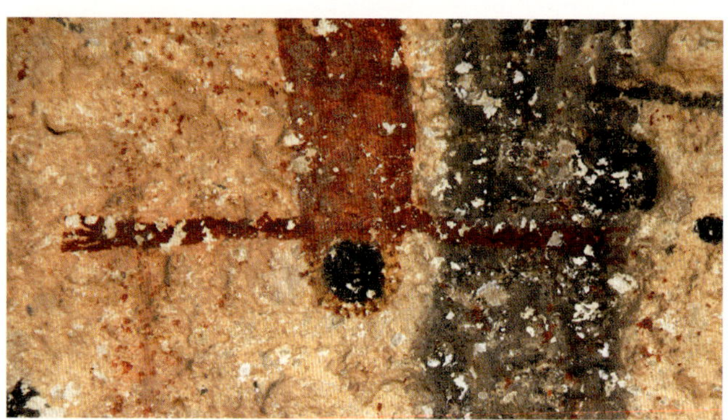

Figure 5.34. Encircling the head of the Setting Sun (A013) is a yellow, rayed solar disk. It is the snare used to capture the deer (Morning Star) who will travel with the sun through the underworld.

discussed under Motif Analysis XIV. One in a series of four, light-red cattail-like figures (E030) superimposes the lower portion of A005's body, as does the red dart impaling Z006 (figure 5.32). We were unable to determine the stratigraphic relationship between E030 and Z006. The last red applied to this section of the mural appears to be splatter paint covering A013, A005, and E009.

A single layer of yellow interfaces directly with the wall, and may possibly overlay red imagery. Even with the microscope we were unable to confirm that the red lines within the rayed disk are overpainted by yellow. It appears that the yellow was painted between the radiating red lines. There is also only one layer of white. A fine wash of white was applied to the neck area of the pilgrim (A005) and its torches. And finally, the end of the white ecliptic line (E029) was added. The line overlays the fifth pilgrim.

Formulating Hypotheses

As with the small antlered figure (A006) identified as the fire god, through replication the figure (A013) associated with this fifth pilgrim has multiple divine derivations. In contrast to A006, however, the divine derivations for A013 are all associated with the west and the underworld. According to the Huichol, after the sun rises in the east and shoots his arrows (rays) among the deer (stars), he travels across the sky to be received by (or transformed into) Tsakaimuka, a western solar deer deity (Preuss 1996:128).[81] He is god of the setting sun and patron deity of the deer hunt. Myerhoff (1974:88) refers to him as "Snarer of the Deer." He was one of the Ancestors who participated in the First Hunt and, as assistant to Father Sun, demands ten candles as an offering to help the sun to rise (Zingg [1938] 1977:316). As with Kiewimuka, the rain serpent of the west, Tsakaimuka is associated with the west and the location where Kawi, the caterpillar, came out of the sea.

Lumholtz (1900) describes a Huichol god disk dedicated to this setting sun deity and the characteristics attributed to him. On the disk he notes the presence of an unusual yellow circle around the head of Tsakaimuka (figure 5.35). Lumholtz (1900:41) writes that the "peculiar ring over its head is meant to represent a snare for catching deer," and deer snares are considered a particularly meaningful form of *nierika*. As discussed earlier, to obtain *nierika* is to gain the ability to see hidden realities. It is a visionary ability: the ability to see clearly that which before was obscured. *Nierika* is gained through, among other things, self-sacrifice and participation in pilgrimages. As offerings, *nierikas* are instruments for seeing and can be expressed visually as a circle with radiating spokes. God disks, rock art images, yarn paintings, and tiny round, netted deer snares are all *nierikas*. Some have a mirror embedded in the center of the image (MacLean 2012:42–49). They are sometimes referred to as "the face of the sun" (Zingg [1938] 1977:620). Lumholtz (1900:41) also described numerous *nierika* designs resembling yellow wheel cogs. The Huichol told Lumholtz that these designs represent votive bowls and that Tsakaimuka "owns" gourd votive bowls painted black or yellow. As with deer snares, votive bowls are another referent for *nierika*.

The upside-down, impaled figure (A013) overlaying the right arm of the fifth *jicarero* shares attributes with this western solar deity. He is portrayed with a rayed disk surrounding a black mask. This disk is analogous to the *nierika* and face of Father Sun, but it is also the snare used to catch the deer (Venus) that will travel with the sun through the underworld. Located above A013 is a yellow design (E043) reminiscent of the yellow *nierika* and votive bowl design that the Huichol attribute to Tsakaimuka (figure 5.32 and 5.36). It is similar both in color and shape to designs on Tsakaimuka's god disk. He is portrayed falling headfirst toward the motif interpreted as the ocean or the western entrance into the underworld (E007). According to the Huichol, it is into the ocean that "the sparks of Our Great-Grandfather the Setting-Sun, *Tatutsi Sakaimuka*, disappear as he enters one of his subterranean aquatic canals, and one waits for Our Father [Sun], *Tayau*, . . . to reappear on the other side, in the sacred desert of the east, *Wirikuta*" (Negrín 2006:2).

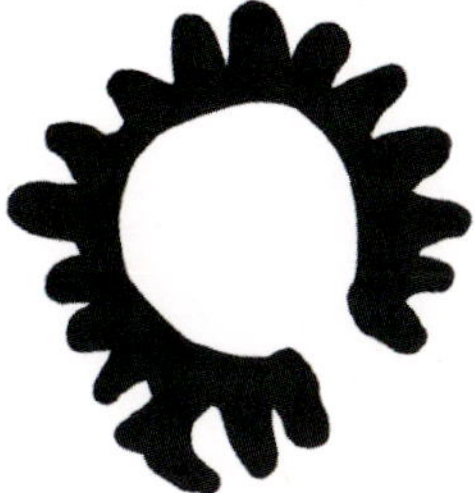

Figure 5.35. Tsakaimuka's yellow deer snare. Redrawn from Lumholtz 1900: plate II.

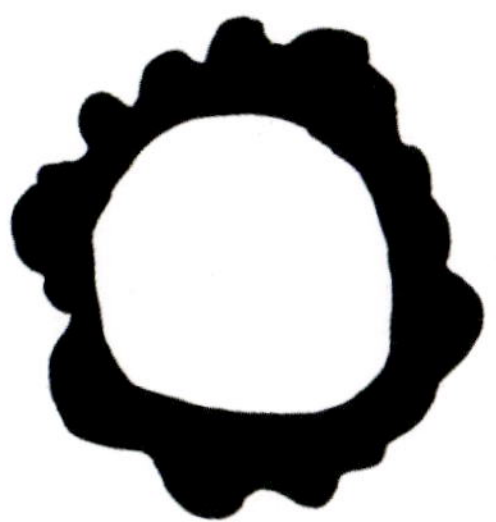

Figure 5.36. Yellow crenellated circle (E043) resembling Huichol *nierika* and votive bowl designs associated with the western solar deity.

A substantial amount of red paint-splatter is isolated to this section of the panel. It crosses the body of both the setting sun deity and the fifth *jicarero*. Gutiérrez (2000:116) writes that "daytime comes after a huge eruption that stains everything with sacrificial blood, and it is through a repeated self-sacrifice that the day disappears into the night (and the dry season turns into the rains)." Blood sacrifice is a key feature in most Huichol ceremonies and is performed, in part, to recapture a state of unity with the gods (Gutiérrez 2000:112). By offering blood sacrifices, the Huichol identify with the deities who in the past made their own difficult sacrifices so that the sun could be born.[82] In the mural the red paint splattering the body of the Setting Sun and the *jicarero* may represent not only the initial sacrifice that led to the birth of the sun, but the sacrifice that is repeated at dusk each day and at the changing of the seasons each year. It is death that brings life in the form of *kupuri*-containing rain.

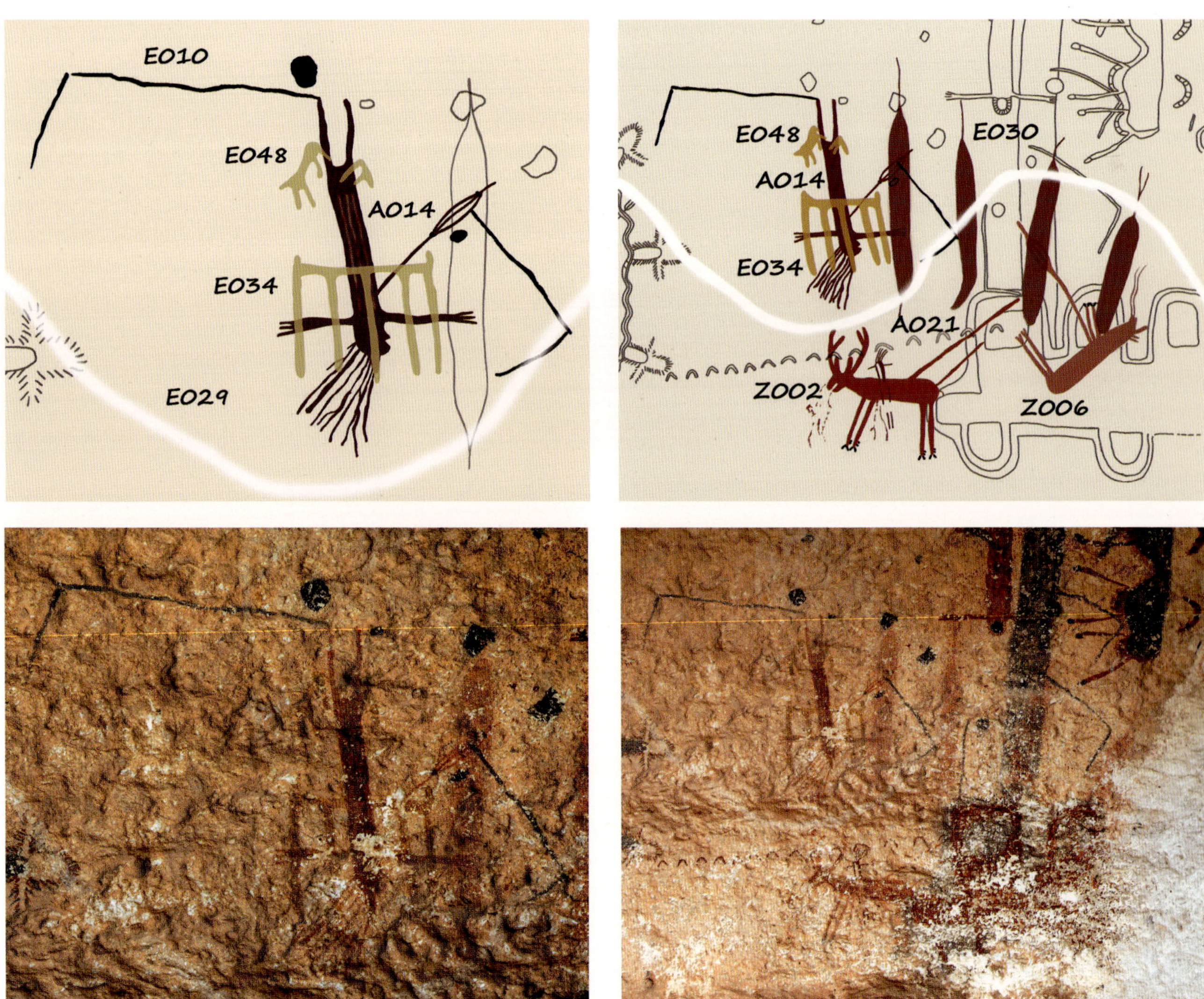

Figure 5.37. Motif XIII (A014, E034): Evening Star (A014) being sacrificed in the west and descending into the underworld. The five-pronged comb (E034) signifies completion and perfection.

Figure 5.38. The transformation of the Evening Star (E030, Z006) into the Morning Star (Z002).

Motif Analysis XIII: Evening Star

Below the figure interpreted as the Setting Sun (A013) is another upside-down anthropomorph (A014) (figure 5.37). This figure has long, flowing hair and what appears to be a pointed head. Overlaying the torso of A014 is a yellow, five-pronged comb shape (E034). Two yellow enigmatic shapes (E048), one of which may be a quadruped, superimpose the figure's legs. A fletched dart is impaling the anthropomorph's right side, and its footless left-leg is touching one of the 13 L-shapes (E010). Falling away from this figure, like a series of images in a flip book, are four enigmatic shapes resembling cattails (E030) (figure 5.38). The final in this series of cattail figures connects with the upside-down deer (Z006) identified above as Evening Star. The painting sequence here follows what we identified throughout the mural. All black imagery was painted first, followed by red, yellow, and white.

Formulating Hypotheses

The upside-down figure (A014) is analogous to the anthropomorphized Venus as Evening Star sacrificed in the west and descending into the underworld. He (or she) is overlain by a five-pronged comb shape. The number five, according to the Huichol, represents perfection and completion. Its appearance here may indicate completion of the cycle and the perfect sacrifice required for continuation of the cosmos. Venus, who is both Morning and Evening Star, is not only anthropomorphized by the Huichol, but also perceived as a deer who travels with the sun through the underworld (Neurath 2005c:84). The cattail-like figures (E030) and the impaled deer with black hooves on its front legs (Z006) illustrate the transformation of the anthropomorphized Evening Star (A014) into the deer who, as Morning Star (Z002), travels with the anthropomorphized sun (A021) through the underworld. At sunrise the astral deity commits autosacrifice, and the sun and peyote are born and the rains begin. Just as the Morning Star and Rising Sun are equated with peyote, the Evening Star and Night Sun are equated with a powerful plant; this one, however, is the dangerous kieri.

Motif Analysis XIV: Datura Hawk Moths and Transformations

The left arm and torch of the *jicarero* identified with the Setting Sun (A005) are overlain by an enigmatic caterpillar-like figure (E009) (figure 5.39). It is painted in black, red, yellow, and white. Water seeping out of the wall has left a white mineral skin obscuring portions of this figure; however, it is still possible to identify five sets of concentric red and black circles running the length of this enigmatic figure. Five short red bars, each bearing four black dots, are paired with the concentric circles. Eight sets of two red, tendril-like shapes extend off the figure. Each is tipped with a black dot.

We identified the same painting sequence in this motif as elsewhere in the mural: black first, followed by red, yellow, and white. There are two layers of black. The first is the body of A005. Overlaying its left arm is one of the black dots attached to the tendrils of E009. The most unusual stratigraphic relationship we identified was between the torch of A005 and the body of the caterpillar-like figure.

A close relationship between the *jicarero* and E009 was communicated by intricately weaving the two images together. While the black "wooden" portion of the torch held by the pilgrim is overlain by the red tendrils, the red torch tip overlays the black body of the caterpillar, and the yellow of the caterpillar overlays the red of the torch. The final color applied was a wash of white within the body of E009. It is confined to the area of the second concentric circle at the top of the figure.

Formulating Hypotheses

The caterpillar-like figure located in the western section of the mural and associated with the figures identified as the Setting Sun (A013) and the Evening Star

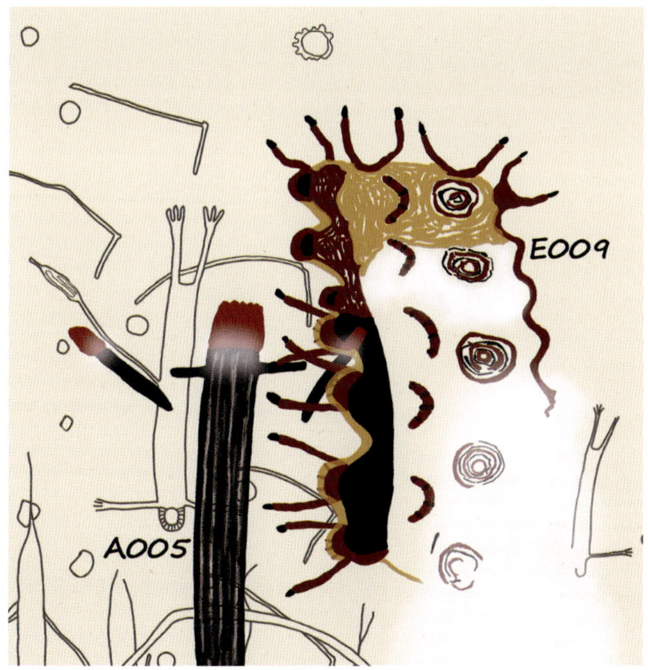

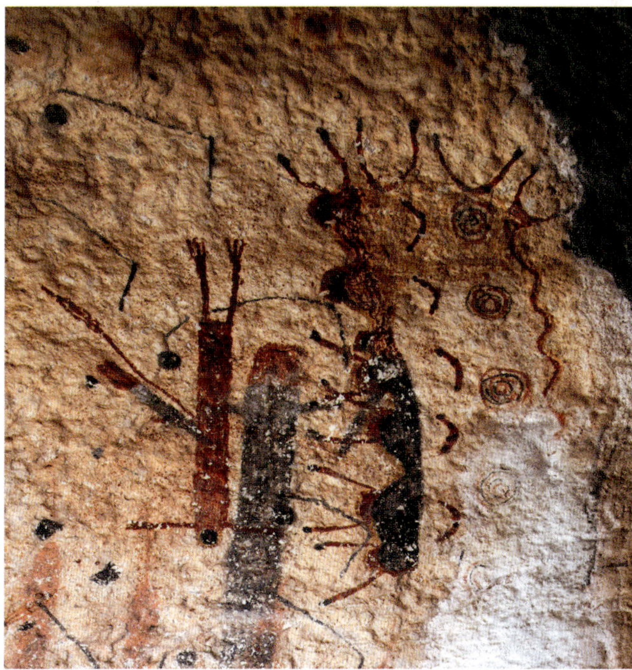

Figure 5.39. Motif XIV (E009 and A005): The fifth Ancestor (A005) and his avatar, Setting Sun/Night Sun (A013), are equated with the kieri complex and the hawk moth caterpillar (E009).

(A014) may be analogous to the hawk moth caterpillar identified with the kieri complex. Kieri, who in some versions of the Huichol creation story was one of the original pilgrims, is a radical nocturnal figure associated with death and the forces of darkness. In Huichol cosmovision, at nightfall and every summer solstice the sun transforms himself into his alter ego, the Night Sun, a dark deity who is identified with the dangerous psychotropic plant kieri and with Venus as the Evening Star (Neurath 2005c:87). Whereas Morning Star is associated with the east, peyote, red, daytime, and the Day Sun, Evening Star is associated with the west, *kieri*, black, nighttime, and the Night Sun. Venus transforms from one extreme into the other. Myths recounting battles between Morning Star and Evening Star underscore the hierarchical dualism of the universe and the opposition between peyote and *kieri* (Aedo 2001:133, 142–143).

Angel Aedo (2003a:229) has argued for the existence of an ancient and widespread kieri complex spanning Mesoamerica and the American Southwest. He identified the plants operating within the complex as *toloache* (datura), *kieri* (solandra and datura), and *ololiuhqui* (morning glory). These plants were symbolically interchangeable for the ancient Nahua and continue to be for modern Huichol (Aedo 2003a:233). Datura grows in abundance in the Lower Pecos and, in fact, today grows just below the White Shaman Shelter. Seeds from this toxic plant were recovered from archaeological deposits in the region dating to between 3,400 and 4,900 years ago, and images of datura seed pods are represented in the art (Boyd and Dering 1996).

Hawk moths are the principal pollinators of the night-blooming flowers comprising the kieri complex, including datura. Their caterpillars are the only known creatures capable of eating datura with impunity. Aedo (2003a, 2003b) has argued that because of the shared characteristics between the insect and the plant, the hawk moth is an expression of kieri. The kieri complex is intimately equated with the Night Sun, chaos, disorder, sexual transgression, madness, and all things associated with the underworld. The association of *kieri* with these underworld activities is founded on more than simply the fact that the plant is a night-bloomer. The physiological effects of intoxication by datura, as well as other plants of the kieri complex, include extreme pupil dilation (resulting in the ability to see clearly in the dark), photophobia, aggressive behavior, and sexual arousal, among many other things. It can also lead to madness and to death.

In the Huichol creation story Kawi the caterpillar establishes the path for the Ancestors. At the end of its path the caterpillar emerges with Father Sun as a butterfly. Although we do not know which type of caterpillar is referred to in the Huichol myth, perhaps the caterpillar the artist of the White Shaman panel had in mind was the larva of the hawk moth, an expression of datura. Hawk moths lay their eggs on datura plants, and after an average of five days or so caterpillars emerge to begin feeding on the plant's broad leaves. They have eight pairs of legs: five sets of prolegs and three sets of thoracic legs. Over the course of a few weeks larvae pass through five stages of development (instars). When they reach maturity in the fall, they drop to the soil where they burrow underground to pupate and remain throughout the winter. In the spring they emerge as enormous moths with wingspans of 4 to 5 inches (Capinera 2001:504).

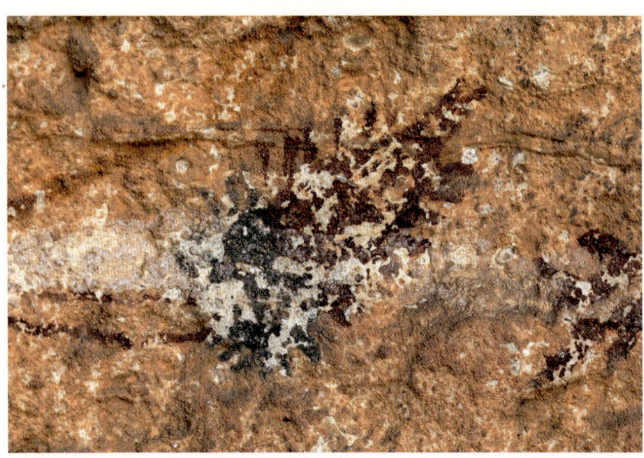

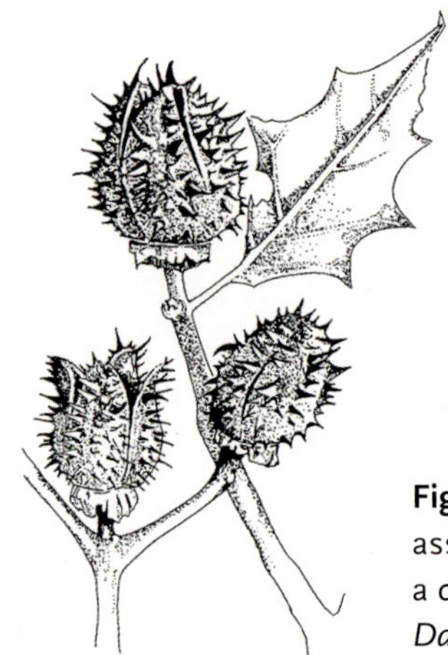

Figure 5.40. Datura: (a) motif associated with A006 resembling a datura seed pod; (b) sketch of *Datura stramonium* seed pods.

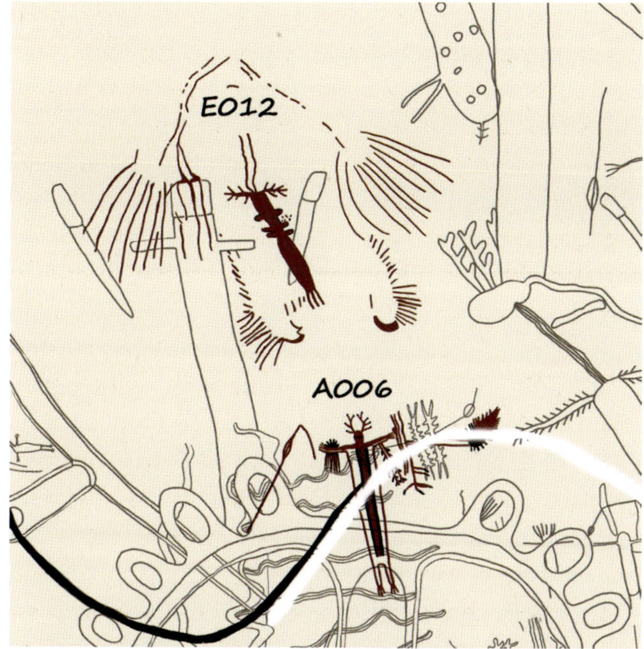

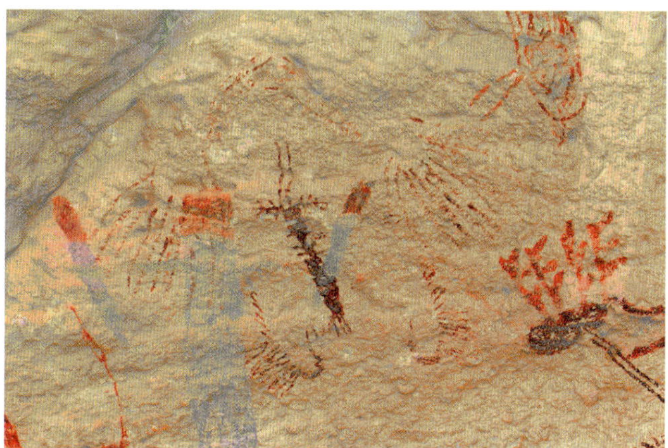

Figure 5.41. Kawi emerges as a butterfly (or moth) with the sun at dawn in the east: (a) E012 as a butterfly or hawk moth; (b) digitally enhanced photograph of E012.

The figure in the mural is portrayed with eight sets of paired tendrils, perhaps indicating the number of prolegs and thoracic legs of the caterpillar. The five concentric circles running vertically down the creature's body may relate it specifically to the diagnostic attributes of the Five-spotted Hawk Moth (*Manduca quinquemaculata*) or perhaps to the five developmental stages of the caterpillar.[83]

The five circles also may relate back to Huichol mythology, which refers to five holes serving as passages into the underworld, where Kawi dwells. Zingg ([1938] 1977:327, 2004:24) identified radiating circles as the location from which the stars emerged as balls from the sea. The black dots located in this section of the mural were interpreted above as stars.[84] Because the watery underworld was filled with dangerous snakes, Grandmother Growth enlisted the help of the stars to destroy them. As shooting stars they attacked the snakes, creating ripples in the water where they fell from the sky. But the snakes always won and came out five at a time. The moon, too, was believed to have emerged from the underworld through five holes (Zingg [1938] 1977:514).

As noted above, the hawk moth caterpillar enters the ground (indicated by E007—the western entrance into the underworld) in the fall and emerges as a moth in the spring. In myth, Kawi marks the path for the Ancestors through the underworld during the dry season (fall and winter) and rises as a "butterfly" with Father Sun at Dawn Mountain to initiate the beginning of the spring and summer rains. In the Proto-Corachol-Aztecan language the phrase for a flower's blooming, a butterfly emerging, and something bursting into flames was likely the same phrase (see Maxwell and Hanson 1992:141). According to Jane Hill (1992:131), "The metaphoric association of flowers and flames is very widespread in Uto-Aztecan languages. The metaphor of the blooming flower as 'bursting into flame' can be reconstructed as a lexical item meaning 'blos-

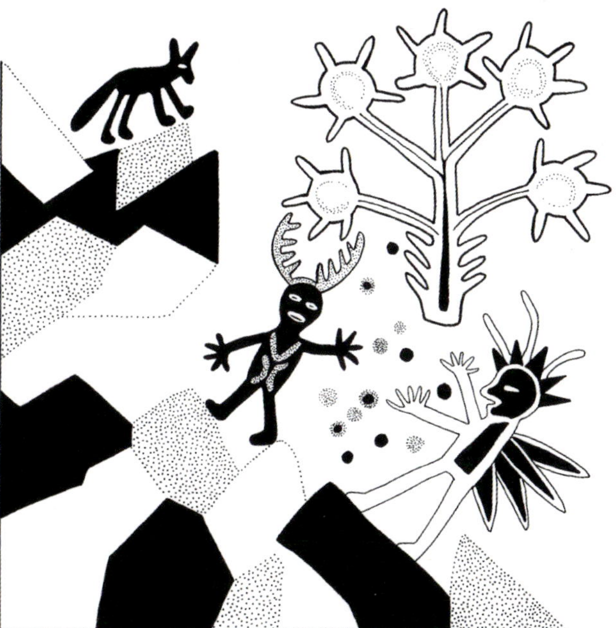

Figure 5.42. Huichol yarn painting of the battle between Kieri and Kauyumari. Yarn painting by Ramón Medina. Redrawn from Furst and Myerhoff 1966.

som, bloom' for proto-southern-Uto-Aztecan." There is a clear association between the blooming flower, emerging butterflies, the sun (which follows the Flower Road), and fire, or bursting into flames. The sinuous white line (E029) identified as the path of the caterpillar terminates at the antlered figure emerging from Dawn Mountain. This emerging figure (A006) represents the rising sun god and the sacred deer whose antlers are the flames of the fire god. In its left hand is a pictorial element that Phil Dering and I (Boyd and Dering 1996) have suggested resembles the seed pod of datura (figure 5.40). Located directly above the rising sun deity and overlaying the torch of A001 is a winged figure (E012) possibly representing the emerging hawk moth (figure 5.41).

The spinescent seed pod held by the sun deity is painted half red and half black, divided in half by the white path of the caterpillar.[85] The black portion, which was painted first, is below the white line, and the red portion is above. The duality expressed in this motif may relate to the ambivalent nature of Venus and Huichol conceptions of the human body. According to Huichol myth, in ancient times the sacred deer, Kauyumari (Morning Star), and the evil Kieri (Evening Star) were antagonistic brothers; Kauyumari was the "light deer" of the day, and Kieri the "dark deer" of the night (P. Furst 2006:117). In reality, though, they are two aspects of the same person or, perhaps more appropriately, the same planet, Venus, which transforms itself into its alter ego according to context (Neurath 2005c:75). Zingg (2004:18) collected a myth recounting a mighty battle between the two astral deities (figure 5.42). Ultimately, the good singing of Kauyumari (peyote) counteracts the bad singing of the evil Kieri (datura). Thus, Kieri is killed, with his stone heart, his *iyari*, all that remained. Father Sun, however, does not allow Kieri to remain dead. He changes his heart, and therefore his color, so that he was only half bad.[86] In this context the bicolored, spinescent seed pod wielded by the emerging sun may reflect the dual nature of Venus.

This cosmic duality is incorporated not only into the Huichol worldview, but also into conceptions of themselves. On the horizontal plane the Huichol divide the human body into two parts. The lower part is equated with *t+kari*, "life of midnight," which is related to the uncontrolled, brute forces of the underworld, the west, Evening Star, and Kieri. The upper portion of the body is equated with *tukari*, "life of midday," which is produced through the practice of austerity, the east, Morning Star, and peyote (Aedo 2003a:238). The human body, like Venus, is one entity composed of two complementary opposites.

Through sacrifice the Night Sun and Evening Star (datura) are transformed into the Rising Sun and Morning Star (peyote), and through the practice of austerity the Huichol are transformed. But these beliefs are not just about real-world cosmological events or what is manifested in cycles of nature, such as the transformation from caterpillar to majestic moth. As Neurath (2005c:75) so keenly observed, the ambivalent and dynamic character of Venus and the myths of Morning Star and Evening Star vividly articulate through ritual the ongoing transformations of every person throughout the course of their lives.

Summary

The White Shaman mural documents with extraordinary similarity the basic components of the Huichol creation story, as well as the rituals conducted to reenact and manifest that cosmological event. It also expresses the shared symbolic language of ancient Mesoamerican traditions, such as the replication of divine essence, complementary dualism, and cyclical time, to name a few. If the rock art is indeed a graphic manifestation of these ancient, interrelated, and intermeshed Mesoamerican ideas, it should fit into the basic structure of that broader continuum and be "readable" using historical accounts and ethnographic observations of indigenous groups living in Mesoamerica. Although the actors and details may change, we should also find strong similarities between the basic story line of the Huichol creation narrative and those told by others who are part of this ideological universe. In the next chapter I test this hypothesis by attempting to "read" the narrative using historical accounts and ethnographic observations of other Native American groups—in particular, the Nahuatl-speaking people of central Mexico.

RETURN TO CREATION

A READING OF THE WHITE SHAMAN MURAL INFORMED BY NAHUA MYTHOLOGY

When the Spanish entered the Basin of Mexico in the early 1500s, they encountered a vast empire of people who spoke "Aztecan" languages. These people referred to their own language as Nahuatl, which roughly translates to "clear speech" (Launey 2011:xvii).[1] The consensus among Mexican scholars is that the people encountered by the Spanish had migrated into the Basin of Mexico from northern Mexico and the American Southwest between AD 500 and 800. These migrants were the *chichimeca* (Chichimecs), groups of nomadic hunters and gatherers who claimed Chicomoztoc (Place of Seven Caves) as their place of origin and creation.[2]

The *Mapa de Cuauhtinchan No. 2*, produced only two decades after the conquest, illustrates the story of the Chichimecs' emergence from their cave birthplace and their ensuing pilgrimage in search of paradise.[3] Seven tribes emerged from the caves; among these were the Nahuatl-speaking Mexica, who founded the great city of Tenochtitlan in AD 1325. Even before the establishment of this great city, however, other urban civilizations had influenced vast reaches of Mexico—the Olmec (ca. 1800–300 BC), the Classic Maya (ca. 250–850 AD), and the Teotihuacanos (ca. 150 BC–750 AD)—but all three collapsed prior to the Spaniards' arrival.[4] Those with whom Hernán Cortés waged his war of conquest between 1519 and 1521 were the Mexica of Tenochtitlan.

The more familiar name, Aztec, that most of us know them by is a slang term and not the name preferred by modern historians and anthropologists. By the time of the conquest, it is more likely the Nahuatl speakers inhabiting Tenochtitlan referred to themselves as the Mexica or Mexica-Tenochca (Read 1998:203). The greater group of Aztecan speakers generally are referred to as "the Nahua," meaning speakers of a Nahuatl language. Therefore, when we refer generally to the speakers of Nahuatl languages, we use the term *Nahua*.

The Spanish conquest of the Mexica and other Nahuatl-speaking people was greatly facilitated by the introduction of Old World diseases such as smallpox (Diamond 1997). Although the Spanish had developed a certain amount of immunity to these diseases, the occupants of the New World had none. It is estimated that in the early part of the sixteenth century Mesoamerican populations were reduced by between 80 and 93 percent. An estimated five to eight million people are believed to have perished from disease between 1519 and 1520 in central Mexico alone, with millions more to follow in the highlands later in the century (Acuña-Soto et al. 2002:289, 2005:405).

The Sources

If the ancient Nahua were decimated by disease and conquest, how do we know what we know about them today? How can we reconstruct their history, cosmology, and worldview? First, it is important to understand that although the ancient Nahua are no longer available to interview, their descendants are. It is estimated that over a million Nahuatl speakers live in communities in and around the Basin of Mexico. These descendants carry on many pre-Hispanic beliefs and practices, and have knowledge of indigenous ways of healing, speaking, praying, drawing, and telling stories that have been known for thousands of years (Carrasco 2008:19).

The past can also be partially reconstructed from the rich archaeological record left by the ancient Nahua. Mexican archaeology, considered "one of the most productive scientific research traditions in the world today" (Carrasco 2008:13), has unearthed a wealth of information through excavation of vast ceremonial centers, pyramids, temples, sculptures, and human and animal remains. These discoveries are continually revising our view of ancient Mexico, its history, and its people.

For this study, however, the primary sources are interpretations and analyses of the few remaining pictorial manuscripts, or codices, as well as sixteenth-century written accounts produced by Europeans and descendants of the ancient Nahua. In 1535 Spanish bishop Juan de Zumárraga ordered the destruction of a collection of Nahua codices. These ancient texts contained vast knowledge about such things as astronomy, medicine, history, and nature. They also carried knowledge of pictographic symbols communicating both literal and metaphoric meaning extending back as far as two thousand years (Carrasco 2008:14). Thankfully, not all were destroyed. Included among the surviving pictorial manuscripts are seven codices referred to as the Borgia Group, most of which were produced prior to conquest and all of which were referenced for this study.[5] These manuscripts illustrate ancient Nahua concepts of the cosmos, calendrical systems, and ritual protocols. Each is beautifully illustrated in red, black, yellow, and white paint on parchment made from deerskin and folded accordion-style. Although not included within the Borgia Group, the *Codex Borbonicus* is another significant resource. It is considered the "great masterpiece of Aztec painting" (Boone 2007:6) and was produced just before or just after the conquest. In contrast to the Borgia Group, this codex was painted on a long sheet of *amate,* a type of paper made from the bark of the sacred ficus tree. *Codex Borbonicus* contains one of the most elaborate and comprehensive portrayals of the ancient 260-day ritual and astronomical calendar referred to as the *tonalpohualli.* With this calendar, priests created horoscopes and divined the future. It also documents the 52-year cycle and its attendant rituals and ceremonies, most notably the New Fire Ceremony.

Other valuable resources were written in Nahuatl, Spanish, and French during the sixteenth century. These important texts illuminate Nahua cosmovision, myth, ritual, and history. The sources referred to most frequently for this analysis are the creation epics *Leyenda de los soles* (Legend of the suns) (Bierhorst 1992), *Historia de los mexicanos por sus pinturas* (History of the Mexicans as Told by Their Paintings) (Phillips 1884), and *Histoyre du Méchique* (History of the Mexica) (Johghe 1905), as well as examinations and interpretations of these texts by modern scholars. Equally important is the twelve-volume *Florentine Codex,* an ethnographic encyclopedia compiled in the 1500s by Franciscan friar Bernardino de Sahagún and two groups of indigenous collaborators, Nahua students (grammarians) and Nahua elders (*principales*). Sahagún posed questions to the elders about a wide range of topics, including their culture, religion, history, astronomy, and the natural world. The elders painted pictures to answer his inquiries, for this was the form of writing they used prior to conquest. Grammarians, who were Nahua students able to read and write three languages—Nahuatl, Spanish, and Latin—listened intently as the elders "read" the painted books and then transcribed the elders' interpretations in Nahuatl below the paintings (Magaloni Kerpel 2011:49). In Sahagún's words, "They gave me all the matters we discussed in pictures, for that was the writing they employed in ancient times. And the grammarians explained them in their language, writing the explanation at the bottom of the painting" (Sahagún 1950–1982, "Introduction and Indices," p. 54).[6] Without these remaining resources, our reading of the White Shaman mural would have been significantly limited.

As with the Huichol, we discovered numerous components in the White Shaman mural relating to the structure of Nahua myths and ceremonies documented in these various sources. At the mythological core they incorporate similar patterns, reveal similar actions and symbols, and share a common function. Numerous authors, most notably ethnographer Konrad Preuss, have identified striking similarities between Huichol and Nahua myths and deities associated with creation.[7] Furst and Anguiano (1976:116–117) state, "It is possible that both the central Mexican solar myths and that of the Huichols derive ultimately from common roots and that the basic elements of the story of the birth of the sun, as recorded in the sixteenth century in central Mexico and more recently among the Huichols, were already present in an older Uto-Aztecan substratum ancestral to both the Aztecs [Nahua] and far-flung linguistic cousins." Carrasco (2008:230, 235) and López Austin (1997:248) observe that even the Huichol peyote hunt shares many symbols and ritual meanings with the

Nahua world. The most notable similarities with White Shaman iconography can be found in Nahua myths recounting the birth of the sun and rituals reenacting this cosmic event, such as the New Fire Ceremony.

Legend of the Suns

According to Nahua mythology, before the birth of the fifth sun there were four previous suns or ages.[8] Each sun was ruled over by a specific deity and corresponded to one of the four elements: earth, wind, fire, and water. The demise of each sun and its inhabitants was dictated by its ruling element and was driven by a cosmic battle between the gods Quetzalcoatl and Tezcatlipoca.[9] Quetzalcoatl is associated with the east and dawn, light, life, breath, and the celestial realms. His complementary opposite, Tezcatlipoca, is associated with sunset, darkness, conflict, and the earth. It was out of destruction that the next sun, a more perfect age, was born.

Tezcatlipoca ruled the first sun, which was called the Jaguar or Earth Sun. Quetzalcoatl defeated Tezcatlipoca by throwing him into the sea, but he did not die. He transformed into a jaguar and devoured the giants inhabiting the land, thus ending the first sun. The victorious Quetzalcoatl ruled over the second sun, called the Wind Sun. Tezcatlipoca, however, returned to earth, defeating Quetzalcoatl and destroying the second sun with a mighty wind. Tlaloc ruled the third sun, which was the Fire-Rain Sun. Quetzalcoatl returned to destroy the third sun, this time with fire that rained down from the sky. Tlaloc's sister, Chalchiuhtlicue, ruled over the fourth sun. This was the Water Sun, and it was destroyed by a devastating flood. The only ones to survive were a husband and wife called Tata and Nene. Tezcatlipoca instructed the couple to hollow out a tree and get inside it to save themselves from the rising waters.

After the terrible deluge ended the fourth sun, the waters eventually subsided and the heavens were lifted back into place by Tezcatlipoca and Quetzalcoatl. Tezcatlipoca transformed into the Venusian deity Mixcoatl to drill a new fire (the origins of the New Fire Ceremony), and Quetzalcoatl set out to repopulate the earth. He descended into the land of the dead to fetch the bones of the Ancestors. After a mighty battle with the lords of the underworld, he retrieved the bones and brought them to Cihuacoatl (Snake Woman), a mother goddess who represents the creative powers of the earth. She ground them up and placed them in a bowl, and Quetzalcoatl bled sacrificially upon them from his penis. From their bones and the sacrifice of Quetzalcoatl, a new race of humans was created. The world, however, was still in total darkness, so the gods gathered to plan the creation of the fifth sun, the Sun of Movement (León-Portilla 1995:454). This is the story of its creation.

At midnight the gods, each associated with one of the cardinal directions, took their place around the divine fire hearth. Their task was significant. They needed to bring into being the fifth sun to put an end to darkness and chaos, and to establish the divisions of time. This would require a supreme act of self-sacrifice, but none of the four was willing. The gods summoned Nanahuatzin and Tecuiçiztecatl, who offered themselves as sacrifice.[10]

Nanahuatzin was a god of ancient lineage, but his body was deformed and covered with oozing sores. The others decided he wasn't a suitable sacrifice, so they called upon Tecuiçiztecatl. Four times he tried to throw himself into the blazing fire drilled by Tezcatlipoca-Mixcoatl, but Tecuiçiztecatl was too afraid. The gods then called forth Nanahuatzin and told him that he must become the sacrifice. Nanahuatzin pierced his body with spines, and after four days of penance the gods feathered him and smeared his body with white chalk.[11] He then bravely fell into the fire, the divine hearth, to be consumed by the flames and transformed into Tonatiuh—the fifth sun. Not to be outdone by Nanahuatzin, Tecuiçiztecatl then threw himself into the smoldering fire. He became covered in ashes and black soot, and was transformed into the moon.

Suddenly the red light of dawn surrounded the gods. Disoriented, they debated where the sun would rise but soon learned that he refused to move. This angered Tlahuizcalpantecuhtli (Venus, lord of dawn). He shot arrows at the sun but failed to slay him. Ultimately, the sun proved to be a better warrior and shot the star with arrows, which were rays of light with shafts like flames. Tlahuizcalpantecuhtli was defeated and fell into the underworld. The gods, who were also stars, then sacrificed themselves and offered the sun their hearts and blood as sustenance to help him move along his path.[12] And so it was that the sun of 4 Movement appeared, and there was the first day and the first night. The year was 13 Reed (approximately 751 AD) (Bierhorst 1992:26). To ensure the sun's continued movement and thereby the maintenance of life, humans had to be sacrificed to appease Tonatiuh, giving thanks for his initial sacrifice that gave birth to the sun.

A myriad of cosmic beliefs and rituals documented in the 1500s revolved around this solar myth, leading to the Nahua becoming known as "the people of the sun." Their creation story was reenacted in the performance of the New Fire Ceremony and numerous other rituals related to the birth of the sun and the continuance of time. It was through these sacrificial rituals that the renewal and movement of the sun was ensured.[13]

The New Fire Ceremony

In the *Florentine Codex,* Sahagún was the first non-Native to document the New Fire Ceremony, also called Binding of the Years. In its original form (at least the earliest recorded one) the New Fire Ceremony was conducted every 52 years to renew the cosmos. This 52-year time cycle was based on the interconnection of the 365-day solar calendar and the 260-day divinatory calendar, whereby the same dates would only coincide on both calendars every 52 solar years (52 x 365 = 73 x 260). The end of each cycle is a dangerous period of transition. The New Fire Ceremony, which included the sacrifice of human hearts and the drilling of a new fire, was performed to ensure a safe transition into the next temporal period. Just as Nanahuatzin's heart and body had been burned for creation of the fifth sun, the sacrificial victim would be burned as fuel for a new temporal period.

The ceremony took place at the beginning of the dry season, when the Pleiades are at their zenith and moving contrary to the sun, which is at its nadir. In readiness, all the fires in the kingdom were ritually extinguished, and all household idols, which were regarded as the gods themselves, were thrown into the water. People discarded cooking utensils and fire implements, and swept their houses clean of rubbish. On the night of the ceremony they climbed to their rooftops to watch the events unfold. Children wore masks of maguey fiber and were kept awake; otherwise, they might be transformed into mice. Pregnant women also wore masks and were hidden in granaries for safekeeping. If the new fire was not sparked, they would become female star demons, which were monstrous, cannibalistic beasts called Tzitzimime.

In Sahagún's account of a New Fire Ceremony conducted in 1507 at Tenochtitlan, a procession of priests slowly made their way in total darkness to a temple at the top of a mountain called Hill of the Star.[14] Each was a priest of the fire god Xiuhtecuhtli, and all "were arranged in order, arrayed in and wearing the garb of the gods. Each one represented and was the likeness of perhaps Quetzalcoatl, or Tlaloc, etc., or whichever one he went representing. Very deliberately, very stately, they proceeded" (Sahagún 1950–1982, bk. 7:27). Once atop the mountain the priests carefully watched the movement of the Pleiades in the night sky.[15] When they reached their meridian, signaling the heavens had not ceased moving, a highly skilled fire priest attempted to drill a small fire directly on the chest of the sacrificial victim. The cosmos hung in the balance. If he failed, darkness and chaos would follow, the dreaded star demons would descend to earth, and the light of the fifth sun would shine no more. "When a little fire fell, then speedily the priests slashed open the breast with a flint knife, seized the heart, and thrust it into the fire. In the open chest a new fire was drawn and people could see it from everywhere" (Sahagún 1950–1982, bk. 7:26). Onlookers who watched anxiously from their rooftops participated in the sacrifice by cutting their ears and the ears of their children, and flicking their blood toward the mountain, where the fire consumed their sacrifice.

The heart sacrifice fueled the new temporal period and the next dawn: the cosmos would continue. Torches were lit from the new fire and carried by the fire priests, whose bodies were painted black in penance, to the top of the pyramid temple of the sun and fire god, Huitzilopochtli. Here the new fire was given its first home and placed in the fire holder at the statue of the sun god. From the top of this cosmic mountain, the fire was carried down the steps to the homes of the priests and then throughout the Mexica empire.

Iconographic Analysis of the White Shaman Mural

In chapter 5 I identified patterns between motifs in the White Shaman mural and Huichol cosmology and creation stories. A hypothetical meaning was proposed for each motif in accordance with these patterns. In this chapter I examine ancient cosmological concepts expressed in Nahua myth and ritual in search of patterns

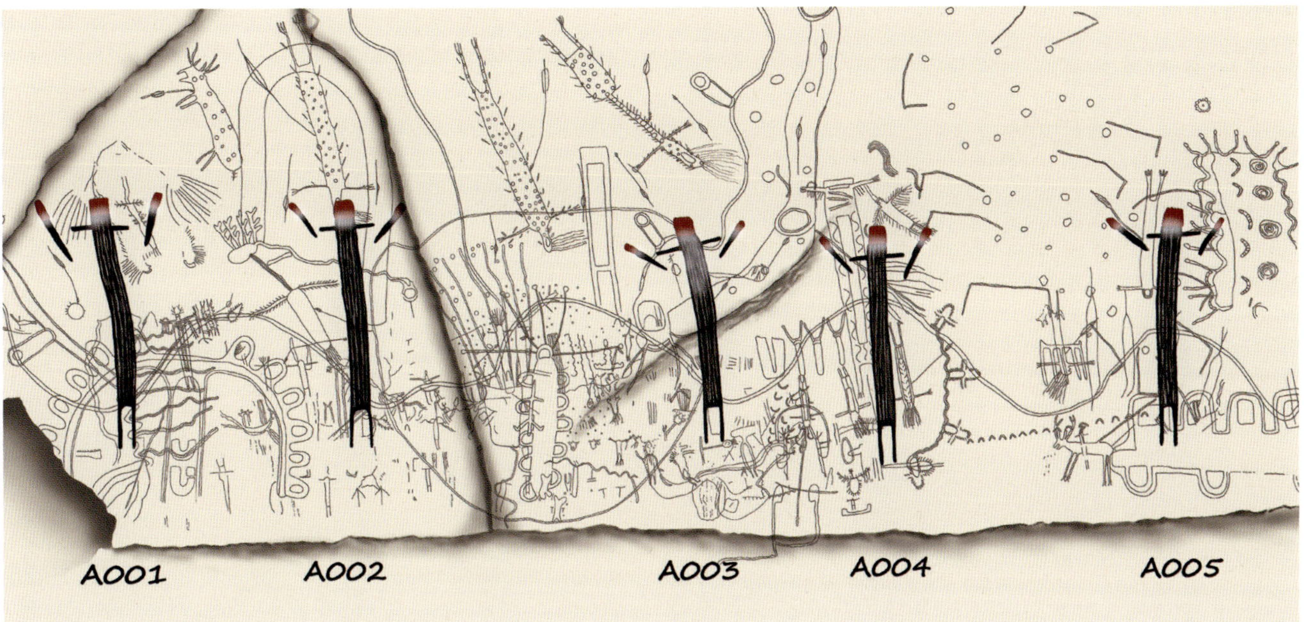

Figure 6.1. Motif I (A001–A005): Primordial ancestors and fiery sky-bearers.

shared with these same rock art motifs. The resulting patterns are then compared with the hypothetical meanings offered in the previous chapter. If Pecos River style rock art is a graphic manifestation of ancient, interrelated, and intermeshed Mesoamerican ideas, it should fit into the basic structure of that broader continuum and be "readable" using historical accounts and ethnographic observations of indigenous groups living in Mesoamerica, beyond the Huichol. At the end of each motif analysis I offer a narrative reconstruction engaging the motifs under investigation.

Motif Analysis I: Primordial Ancestors and Sky-Bearers

Five virtually identical black anthropomorphic figures with red heads and outstretched arms (A001–A005) are portrayed in a horizontal line across the mural at the White Shaman Shelter (figure 6.1). They lack faces, hands, and feet. A thin layer of white paint overlays the area where the red heads join the black bodies. Each of the five anthropomorphs is portrayed with two narrow black objects tipped in red, one to its right and the other to its left. These objects closely resemble the figures holding them. The red tips are tilted slightly away from each figure's body. As with the anthropomorphs, the black portion was painted prior to the red, and then a thin layer of white paint was applied where the red and black intersect.

Formulating Hypotheses

Each hypothetical meaning proposed in chapter 5 for the black and red anthropomorphs (A001–A005), as well as the objects held by these figures, has a corollary in Nahua myth and ritual (table 6.1). At the core, the parallels between Huichol and Nahua accounts of creation and their ritual reenactment of this event are strikingly similar; however, Nahua myth and ritual provide information from which additional hypotheses can be formulated.

Primordial ancestors. In both Huichol and Nahua cosmology Venus represents the human soul and is at the center of the cosmic drama. In the Huichol account of creation the Ancestors gather to decide what they should do to put an end to eternal darkness. It was decided that one among them would have to commit autosacrifice so that the sun could be born. Four of them tried but failed. A deformed boy, who is identified with Venus, steps forward, throws himself into the fire, and is transformed into the sun. But then the sun refused to move, requiring the sacrifice of all the gods (stars) to

Table 6.1.
Motif Analysis I: Five anthropomorphs (A001–A005) carrying torchlike objects

HUICHOL	NAHUA	HYPOTHETICAL MEANINGS
X	X	Rituals are conducted to "reenact" creation; those participating in the rituals become Ancestors (A001–A005) engaged in the creation and maintenance of the sun.
X	X	Number of Ancestors (five) represents completion.
X	X	Number 5 relates to the five directions of a quincunxial universe.
X	X	Ancestors (A001–A005) carry fire to the east to facilitate the dawning of time and birth of the sun.
X	X	Black objects with red tips held by the Ancestors are burning torches equated with sacrifices fueling the first sun.
X	X	Ancestors are fiery pillars erected at the four cardinal directions and center to uphold the sky.
	X	White at the intersection of red and black on the bodies of the Ancestors and the torches they carry denotes the location of transformation or change of condition through sacrifice.
X	X	Ancestors are stellar beings equated with Venus who travel through the underworld with the sun.
X	X	Black bodies and lack of faces denote the Ancestors' cold, wet primordial state as well as their role as penitents and sacrificients.
X	X	Red heads denote the presence of a hot solar life force and the knowledge of the Ancestors.
	X	Lack of hands and feet (digits) denotes lack of ability to perform supernatural actions.

begin its journey across the sky. During peyote pilgrimages reenacting this event, each pilgrim becomes one of the stellar deities who is ultimately sacrificed in this act of creation.

Similarly, in the Nahua myth of the fifth sun, the ancestral deities gathered around the divine fire hearth to plan the creation of the sun. They knew it would require a sacrifice, but none were willing to throw themselves into the fire. The brave but disfigured Venusian deity, Nanahuatzin, stepped forward and leapt into the flames and was transformed into the sun. But the sun would not move until all the stellar gods were sacrificed. This mythic event was reenacted during the New Fire Ceremony. Four fire priests impersonating the gods would hold down the sacrificial victim while a fifth priest ripped out the victim's heart and threw it into the fire. Each of the four priests represented one of the cardinal directions but also were considered manifestations of the gods who participated in the birth of the fifth sun.

As with the Huichol, the Nahua universe had a quincunxial structure. The earth's surface was divided into four quadrants, each associated with a specific deity. And, as with the Huichol, the fifth cardinal point, the center, was attributed by the Nahua to the fire god, Xiuhtecuhtli. Brundage (1983:5) states the four deities representing the four directions were "in quadruplicate the very person of the fire god." And, as with the Huichol, these deities represent fiery sky-bearers who prevent the heavens from falling upon the earth (Phillips 1884:621).

In the *Codex Borbonicus* the fire priests who engage in the New Fire Ceremony are painted black, the color of penance. The blackening of the body was historically documented in Mesoamerica, where priests were painted with a "black pitch, mixed with ground poisonous insects and certain herbs [that] protected them from danger, especially from wild animals, made them invisible in the night, and gave them power to communicate with the divinity" (Heyden 1988:222). By painting their bodies black, the penitents demonstrated an act of faith and prepared themselves for divine confrontation (Olivier 2003:187, 188). Aedo (2003a:247) has noted a similar practice among contemporary Huichol, who paint their bodies black to convert themselves into vicars of darkness. The five black-bodied figures in the mural are analogous to the fire priests painted black in penance who, through sacrifice, became gods themselves and served as sky-bearers upholding the heavens.

But the bodies of the five figures in the mural are not only black; they have red heads and a thin wash of white paint slightly obscuring the point of intersection between the red and the black. A possible explanation for the application of white paint may be found in the primordial sun myth and Nahua ceremonial practices. In the myth, after Nanahuatzin serves his penance, the gods prepare his body for sacrifice by smearing it with white chalk. Sacrificial victims were customarily chalked with white earth, and white feathers were pasted to their heads, arms, and legs. This was done to symbolize that they would pay their debt to the gods through sacrifice (Sahagún 1950–1982, bk. 2:47–48). They were called "the sun, white earth, the feather" (Broda 1970:204). But the sacrificial victims also represented deities, who in turn represented celestial entities (Aguilar-Moreno 2006:154). The five black-bodied figures in the mural are not only analogous to the fire priests painted black in penance, but to sacrificial victims who are celestial deities, chalked white for sacrifice. For through Nanahuatzin's sacrifice the sun was born, but it was through the sacrifice of the gods that the sun was put into motion.

On yet another level, the black bodies and red heads of the Ancestors fit into the Mesoamerican core concept of oppositional schemes and the hot/cold dichotomy.[16] The ancient Nahua, like contemporary Nahua and Huichol, believed children were born wet, cold, and feminine—characteristics associated with the color black. Also like the Huichol, the Nahua creator deity was believed to have deposited a soul of solar origin into the head of an infant at the moment of conception (Carrasco 1998:68).[17] Called *tonalli,* it is comparable to the Huichol soul, referred to as *kupuri. Tonalli* was a vital energy—a life force determining a person's temperament and shaping their destiny. It is knowledge of and a connection with ancestral deities.

In contrast to the cold, wet bodies of newborn children, *tonalli,* which is collected and stored in the head, is considered hot and equated with the color red.[18] The word *tonalli* is derived from *tona,* which means "to irradiate or make warm with sun" (Carrasco 1998:68). Solar heat animates life and resides in the *tonalli* soul. This was beautifully expressed through the ritual placement of newborns near the fire and, as soon as possible, exposing them to the sun to increase their *tonalli.* Through the rays of the sun, a person's *tonalli* spreads from the head to the rest of the body, transforming them from wet, cold beings to hot, dry beings.[19] The black bodies of the anthropomorphs in the White Shaman mural represent the cold, wet beings of primordial time, before there was a sun to irradiate their bodies and increase their *tonalli.* The heads of these anthropomorphic figures in the White Shaman mural may have been painted red to indicate them as "hot" repositories of knowledge—the *tonalli* soul of the Ancestors.

As discussed in chapter 4, hair and digits are indices of *tonalli* (J. Furst 1995:126).[20] Unlike virtually all other anthropomorphs in the mural, the five black figures with red heads have no hair, and the absence of digits indicates they have no hands or feet. We have learned that everything in the panel carries meaning; nothing is random or arbitrary, including the presence or absence of hair and the number of digits. The fact that the five figures were not given hair and digits suggests the absence of a fully developed *tonalli.* They are in their primordial infancy. López Austin (1997:238) suggests that in Mesoamerican iconography the portrayal of feet communicates a god's transition into the world of humans, and hands, their ability to perform supernatural actions. In contrast, the five black-bodied figures in the mural are transitioning from the world of humans to that of gods, and at this stage in their development they lack the ability to perform supernatural actions. A major theme of the mural is development of the *tonalli* soul through penance and sacrifice. How one develops *tonalli,* and thereby acquires knowledge of the Ancestors, is important to the story of the White Shaman mural and the ceremonies that likely took place here.

The five figures also lack faces. Not having a face is, to some degree, like not having hands and feet. The face is similar to the *yolia* soul—the soul lodged in the heart that animates the body and contributes to a person's character. In Horacio Carochi's seventeenth-century *Grammar of the Mexican Language,* the Nahuatl word *ixtli* can be translated as "face" but sometimes refers to the eye (Lockhart 2001:222). It is a locus for perception (Read 1998:110). The Nahuatl couplet *in ixtli in yollotl* literally means "a face a heart," but the combination of two words, ideas, symbols, or metaphors in Nahuatl frequently conveys a third idea that can be somewhat unrelated to its component parts. This linguistic technique was called a *difrasismo* by Nahuatl scholar Ángel María Garibay K. (León-Portilla 1990:75).[21] Linguists call these couplets diphrastic kennings, couplet metaphors, or metonyms (Knowlton 2010:22). They were a common stylistic device in Nahuatl literature (Knowlton 2002:9).

According to Markman and Markman (1989:150), the couplet "face and heart" in Nahuatl texts "carries a complex metaphoric meaning based on the conception of the beating heart . . . as the symbol of the dynamic center of the person, and the face . . . as expressive of his being in the deepest sense." It describes what is uniquely human (León-Portilla [1956] 2006:191) and refers to an individual's character or personality (Maxwell and Hanson 1992:37). A person's physical face (outward appearance) metaphorically signified one's true face (inner, spiritual being) (Markman and Markman 1989:150).

The Nahuatl word for heart (*yollotl*) is derived from the same root as both the word for motion (*ollin*) and the name of the *yolia* soul, which is lodged in the heart. The Nahuatl combination of the face with the heart is a metaphor for the human ability to know or to understand (Kusch 2010:179). These are the unique characteristics of human beings: the identity of self, the ability to take action, and the capability of understanding. You cannot see the ability to take action, the capability of understanding, or the *yolia* soul, but you can see the face of the individual, and a true face reflects a deified heart. "It is no wonder, then, that an important goal of Aztec education was to teach a person to create such a 'deified heart,' thus enabling him to develop his innate spiritual potential by becoming 'one who divines things with his heart,' one who infuses ordinary experience with spiritual energy" (Markman and Markman 1989:150).

Similarly, the Huichol pilgrims travel east to "encontrar taiyari" (to find their heart) and to gain *nierika* (ability to see), to acquire a face (*ixtle*). To look for *taiyari* and to acquire *nierika* allows the pilgrims to become involved in the world of the Ancestors, to bring to life the original community of the gods, and to facilitate the continuance of the natural cycles (Neurath 2001a:503). After arriving at the Hill in the East, the Huichol pilgrims painted their faces with images of their deity avatars. And the mask is a metaphor converting the human face into a visual symbol of an inner spiritual reality—a face expressive of the "deified heart" within (Markman and Markman 1989:63).

The five black and red figures in the mural may have been painted without faces to symbolize their primordial nature. They have no identity—at least in the Nahuatl sense. Just as children are born cold, wet, and feminine, they are also born without a face (*ixtli*), but through courage and self-discipline they gradually acquire a face and develop a good reputation (Trigger 2003:530). A person who "lacks a face" is ignorant, drifting, and unable to find meaning in life or themselves. But a person who is educated has developed a face and can discover a reality transcending *tlaltícpac* (that which is on the surface of the earth) (León-Portilla [1956] 2006, 1990). The active participants in the White Shaman mural are the five black figures with red heads: the Ancestors, penitents, and sacrificial victims. They are the players in the ceremony, the actors in this cosmic drama. The events of the panel engage their actions and their experiences. The ceremony, among other things, was a process by which initiates acquired their identities—that is, the transformation of their faces from the earthly to the spiritual.

New fire of the sun. The five ancestral figures are portrayed holding two narrow black objects whose red tips are tilted slightly away from their bodies. As with the ancestral figures, the black portion was painted prior to the red, and a thin layer of white paint was applied to where the red and black connect. We have identified a strikingly similar motif at Jaguar Shelter (41VV584), located upriver from the White Shaman site (figure 6.2).

I suggested earlier that the black objects with red tips are analogous to the torches carried by primordial ancestors to fuel the first sunrise. In the Huichol account of creation, and reenacted in ritual, fire is carried by the pilgrims to Dawn Mountain, birthplace of the sun. This concept is mirrored in Nahua myth and ritual.

In *Historia de los mexicanos por sus pinturas* (see Phillips 1884:621), we learn that the heavens collapsed upon the earth at the destruction of the fourth sun. Once the gods saw what had occurred, they dug four holes penetrating the earth to its center in order to raise the celestial vault back into place. They also created four men to serve as assistants in this monumental task. Tezcatlipoca and Quetzalcoatl then transformed themselves into enormous trees. The gods, the men, and the trees raised the heavens, dividing the watery heav-

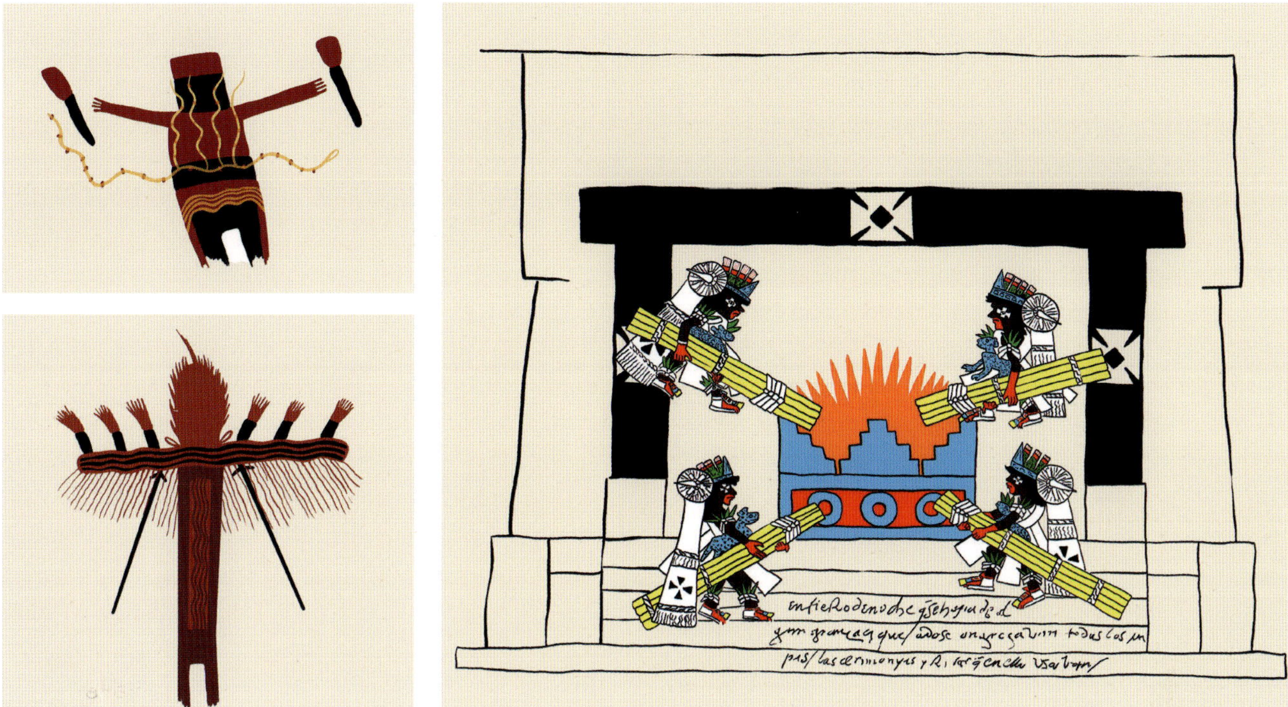

Figure 6.2. *(left, top and bottom)* Torches in Pecos River style at Jaguar Shelter (41VV584): (a) Anthropomorph with a red-capped head, holding a torchlike object in each hand. Redrawn from Kirkland and Newcomb 1967:55 and photographs and field sketches. (b) Anthropomorph with six torchlike objects attached to the top of outstretched wings. Its head resembles flames, and two protrusions at the base of the "flames" resemble deer ears. Redrawn from Kirkland and Newcomb 1967:55 and photographs and field sketches.

Figure 6.3. *(right)* The New Fire Ceremony. Redrawn from *Codex Borbonicus* 34.

ens from the earth. In the pictorial manuscripts *Codex Fejérváry-Mayer* and *Codex Borgia*, there are five supports installed to hold up the heavens: one at each of the four corners and the fifth at the center (Graulich 1997:60–61). After the firmament was reestablished, Tezcatlipoca drilled the first fire, and the gods brought forth out of the flames a new sun to light the world. Thus was the origin of the New Fire Ceremony.

On the night of the Nahua New Fire Ceremony reenacting this event, fire priests climbed to the top of the Hill of the Star, where a new fire was drilled directly on the chest of a sacrificial victim. Torches were lit from this new fire and carried by priests, whose bodies were painted black in penance, from the Hill of the Star to the Temple of the sun (figure 6.3). This was done to assure the next sunrise and continuation of the cosmic order (Clendinnen 1995). Fire was believed to be the *axis mundi* at the heart of the cosmos: the mother and father of all deities, the creator of all things. The god of fire, Huehueteotl-Xiuhtecuhtli, was a god of duality: both male and female, black and red, night and day.[22] Fire alone existed in and connected all three regions of the universe: the upperworld, the earthly realm, and the underworld. Stone sculptures of this deity portray him with a fire brazier on top of his head, sometimes holding fire sticks in each hand (figure 6.4).

In the White Shaman mural the black objects with red tips are analogous to the torches carried by fire priests to the Temple of the sun in the east. They are black and red to signify the duality of fire and the joining of oppositional forces; out of this union of opposites—fire (red) and matter (black)—the sun is born. The white paint applied at the point of union between the two colors may indicate transformation or change from one state of being to another, at that specific location, through sacrifice. As noted previously, the Huichol equate the body of a candle with the human body and water (feminine, black). The flames (masculine, red) consuming the candles are equated with sacrifices fueling the sun (Gutiérrez 2002:104, 106).

The five black and red anthropomorphs mimic the torches they are holding. I suggested in the preceding chapter that these five figures are analogous not only to primordial pilgrims, but also to candles (fire) holding the sky in place. In Huichol mythology, candles or, in some accounts, trees are placed at each corner of the universe and center to hold up the sky (Neurath 2001a:512). In Michel Graulich's (1983:579) analysis of the Nahua myth discussed above, the men created by the gods to serve as sky-bearers are firelike characters whose names are directly related to fire. He suggests this relationship between the deities holding up the heavens and fire can easily be understood because fire is "the tool that restores the waters to their place and fastens up the sky" (Graulich 1983:579). Fire sustains the gap between heaven and earth. The five black and red figures, therefore, are analogous to primordial ancestors, penitents, sacrificial victims, and fiery sky-bearers.

As repositories of knowledge passed down from the Ancestors, the black and red anthropomorphs carrying fire to fuel the sun also are akin to *tlamatini*, the wise man. Elderly native informants reported to Sahagún that "the wise man is writing and wisdom," he is *Tlilli Tlapalli*, which literally means that the wise man is "black ink, red ink." He is the painter and keeper of the illustrated manuscripts, the codices. He is "a light, a torch, a stout torch" illuminating the path of truth; he is "handed-down wisdom" (León-Portilla 1990:10). The black and red figures are like the *tlamatini* in color—black and red; in form—the shape of the torches they carry; and in function—repositories of Ancestral knowledge inscribed in black and red ink by the *tlamatini*.

In the preceding chapter I was unable to offer a hypothesis for the white paint applied to the neck area of both the Ancestral figures and the torches they bear. The Nahua practice of painting white those who are marked for sacrifice provides information from which a hypothesis can be proposed. If the black and red anthropomorphs are analogous to Ancestors who give their lives to fuel the sun, then the white paint may indicate that they are marked for this sacrifice. Perhaps more accurately, the white paint placed at the intersection of the black and red may indicate the location at which oppositional forces (hot and cold, masculine and feminine) are joined, and the resulting sacrifice produces a third state.[23] For example, the Huichol equate the body of a candle or torch with the human body and with water. The flames transform the body/water into a third state—vapor (smoke), which circulated through the cosmos to initiate time. It also represented clouds filled with life-giving water. Throughout Mesoamerica, as well as the American Southwest, ancestors are conceived of as clouds who release the rains when the sun reaches its zenith around the summer solstice (Pohl 1998:197). As will be discussed below, the Ancestors are bound together and transformed through sacrifice into a great cloud serpent.

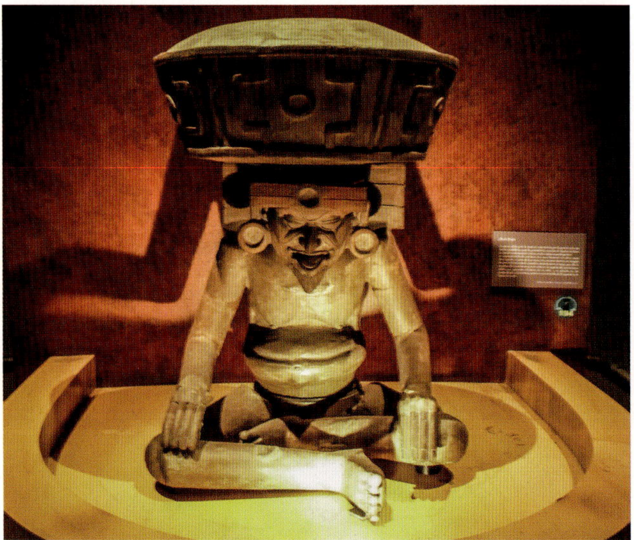

Figure 6.4. Sculpture of the old fire god, Huehueteotl, with a fire brazier on top of his head. Photo by Kim Cox.

Narrative Reconstruction

The five black and red anthropomorphs (A001–A005) represent Ancestors engaged in the creation and maintenance of the sun. They are primordial beings, stellar entities existing in a place and time marked by chaos and total darkness—before the dawning of the first day, before time begins. At this point in the narrative the Ancestors are cold, wet beings lacking fully developed souls of solar origin. There is as yet no sun to heat them up and dry them out, thereby increasing their life force through its irradiating rays. The Ancestors not only carry the fire that gives birth to the sun; through autosacrifice they are themselves the fuel. But it is not a one-time sacrifice: as fiery pillars they remain in place to hold up the sun of their quincunxial universe.

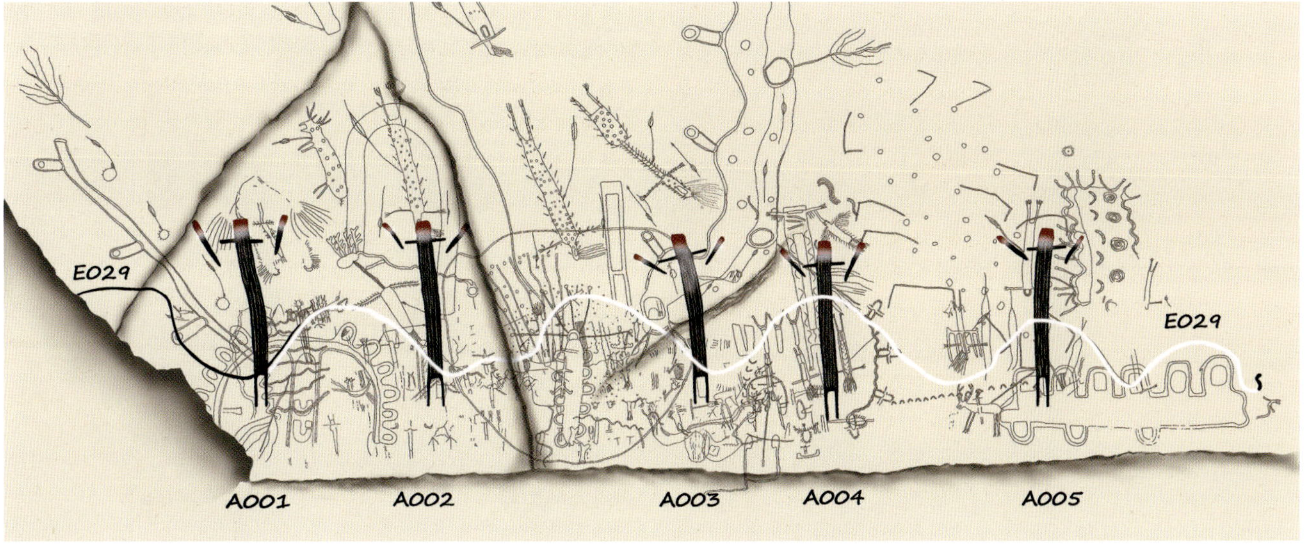

Figure 6.5. Motif II (E029): Cord of men, the Flower Road, the ecliptic, and conduit for transmission of blood and sustenance to the sun.

Motif Analysis II: The Cord of Men and the Flower Road

The five primordial ancestors (A001–A005) are connected to each other by a long, sinuous line (E029) (figure 6.5). The left end of the line is solid black. Reading from left to right, at the legs of the first Ancestor (A001), the black line is joined by a white line. The two travel side by side until reaching a small antlered human form (A006) (figure 6.6). The black line runs under the body of this small figure and then stops abruptly at its chest area. The white line continues to the right, crossing over the body of the antlered figure (A006) and across each of the four remaining Ancestors. At the far right end of the mural the white line overlaps a crenellated, black and red horizontal band (E007). Just beyond this crenellated band, the white line appears to change back to black (figure 6.7).

Formulating Hypotheses

The hypothetical meanings proposed in chapter 5 for E029 have corollaries in Nahua myth and ritual (table 6.2). At the core, Nahua and Huichol cord symbolism is strikingly similar. The Nahua believed people were bound by a metaphoric cord through kinship with a common ancestor. In Nahuatl this ancestral lineage was called *tlacamecayotl,* meaning a "rope of people" or "cord of men" (Megged 2010:136).[24] Ropes, therefore, were commonly used as a genealogical symbol, representing a metaphorical umbilical cord (Kellogg 1995:175). It communicated the blood link between parent and child, but also the interdependent relationship between people and their ancestral deities (Morán 2007:161).

The act of binding merges the past with the present, and one abode with another (Megged 2010:139). Amos Megged (2010:244-245) has observed that Nahua "cord symbolism may denote the context of 'future memory,' connecting otherworldly events of the remote past, with present and future reenactments, and with the manifestations of such foundations as they are recorded on paper and screenfolds, all for the sake of future generations." He further suggests that the knotting-in ceremony conducted by the Huichol during their annual pilgrimage reenacting the sun's birth "may be a remnant of a ritual akin to the ones we find in primordial titles and even in earlier Mesoamerican cultural heritage records and artifacts" (Megged 2012:186).

The cord as a link between past and present, mortal and divine, was clearly expressed in the gladiatorial sacrifice of the Tlacaxipehualiztli ceremony, the Nahua Festival of the Rising Sun. This ceremony was conducted just before the spring equinox as a ritual reenactment of the events following the sun's birth (Broda 1970). During this rite a captive called "the Son of the Sun" was sacrificed, and his heart and blood were offered to the sun as sustenance (Graulich 1989:48).[25] Ac-

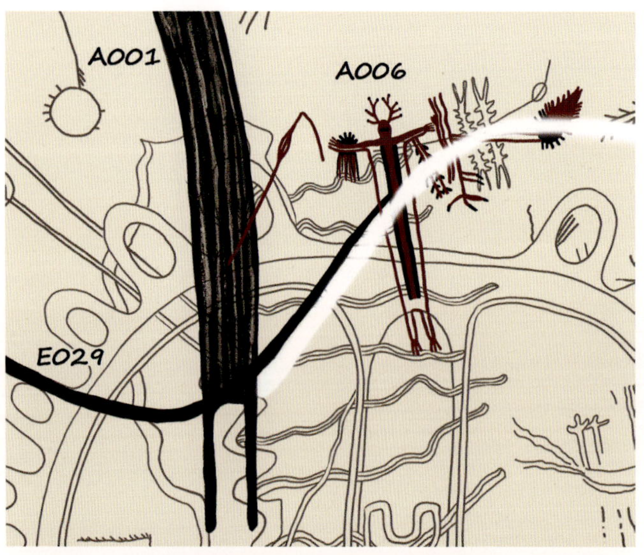

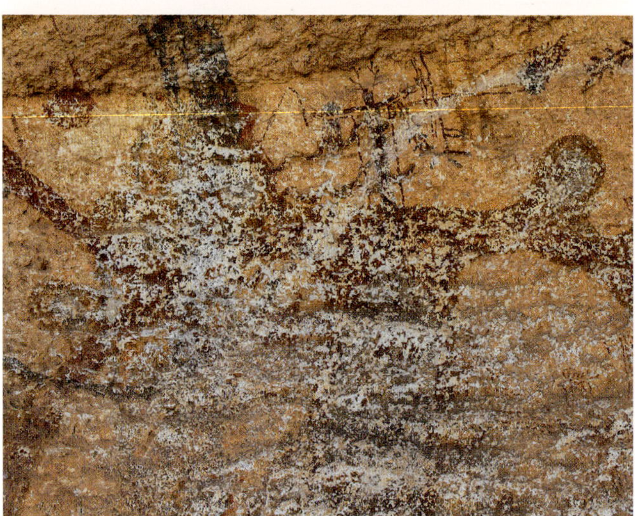

Figure 6.6. The sinuous black and white lines run parallel to each other only between A001 and A006, thereby linking the first Ancestor (A001) to the antlered anthropomorph (A006) and marking the transition from the rainy season to the dry season.

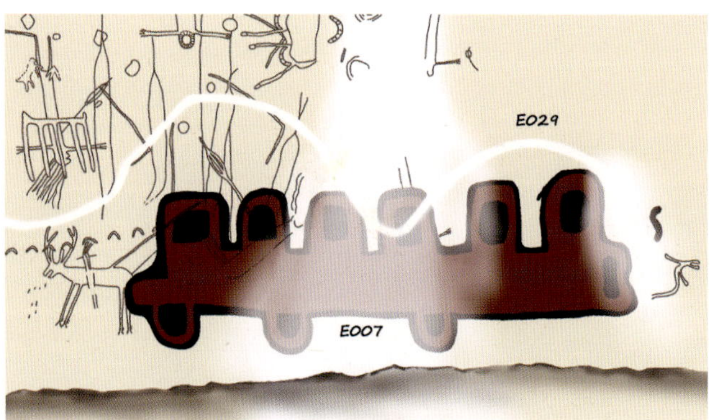

Figure 6.7. The sinuous line transitions from white to black (E029) at E007.

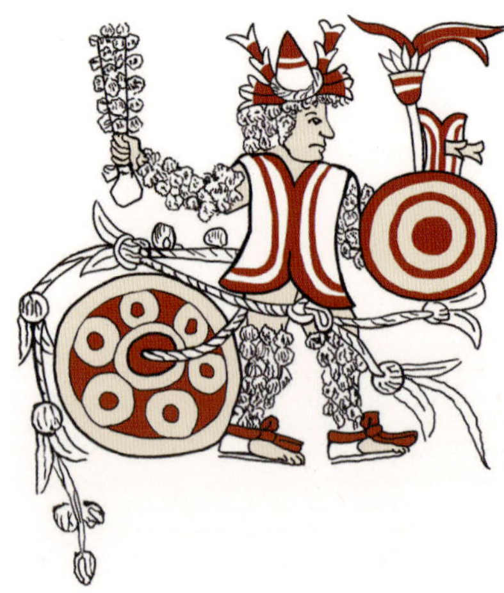

Figure 6.8. Sustenance rope. Redrawn from *Codex Magliabechiano* 30.

cording to Sahagún's sixteenth-century account, a "rope of sustenance" was tied around the waist of these sacrificial victims and then tethered to a "hole in the earth," which was located in the center of a round sun disk on top of the Temple of the sun (Graulich 1989:48) (figure 6.8). The "rope of sustenance" is a metaphor for the umbilical cord, and the "hole in the earth" metaphorically represents the womb. The sacrificial victim was linked to the deity for whom he was being sacrificed, the sun. The two are interdependent and united by the rope of sustenance.[26]

In the Mixtec *Bodley Codex* two adults are linked by an umbilical cord representing not only a relationship of descent, but also alliance between two related groups.[27] The umbilical cord metaphorically represents the road along which goods—like blood, and therefore sustenance—flowed between them. The causeway traveled by the procession of fire priests as they carried the new fire from the Hill of the Star to the Temple of the sun at Templo Mayor likewise can be viewed as a metaphorical umbilicus (Monaghan 1994:95). The Nahuatl word *ohtlatoca* translates as "to follow a road" and "to go along in life." It refers to the path of the sun and the moon along the ecliptic, but also the road traveled by traders bearing their goods (Read 1998:250 fn49). Among the Maya, *sakbehs,* or "white roads," reference the color and construction of ancient Mayan roads, as well as metaphorically a cosmic umbilicus and the Milky Way (Schele and Mathews 1999:114) (Monaghan 1994:95). They also represent the road of life and the passage of time (Keller 2011:156).

Table 6.2.
Motif Analysis II: Sinuous white and black line (E029)

HUICHOL	NAHUA	HYPOTHETICAL MEANINGS
X	X	The sinuous line (E029) represents a cord or rope binding the Ancestors to each other.
X	X	As a metaphorical umbilicus and spiritual life line, it denotes an interdependent relationship between people and their ancestral deities.
X	X	The ecliptic path of the sun
X	X	Road of life and the passage of time
X	X	A conduit for the transmission of blood and sustenance, including rain, between mortals and the divine
X	X	The Flower Road
X	X	Path traveled by the Ancestors
X	X	Rainy season and dry season serpent(s) surrounding the world
X	X	Horizon dividing the world above from the world below

> . . . the conflation of roads and time entails not only a linear path from there to here, but also multiple, interwoven cycles of time that form the fabric of life. The road of life is likened to the roads of the sun, moon, and stars that run in great circles around our everyday world forming transits in the sky and tunnels through the underworld. By walking along their roads, the Maya performed time. They displayed the passage of time, and the transition of temporal cycles as spatially rooted entities. [Keller 2011:156]

As with the Huichol, the earth was perceived to be surrounded by either two snakes or one snake with two heads. It divided the heavens from the underworld, and the sun, traveling its daily course across the sky, was consumed by this giant serpent when it set each day in the western horizon. The horizon, with its undulations, represented this reptilian beast. Serpentine motions and snake imagery, however, also evoke an association with the undulations of the ecliptic path (Milbrath 2013:128 fn60). Sinuous sky ropes, threads, and white cotton cords link heaven and earth, mortal and divine, past and present, throughout Mesoamerica (Milbrath 1999:74). As discussed in the previous chapter, they represent the ecliptic—a celestial floral pathway (Flower Road) traveled by the sun, the gods, and the Ancestors.

Pages 33 and 34 of the pre-Columbian *Codex Borgia* relate the story of the birth of the sun. On *Borgia* 33, a white cord descends from the top of a celestial temple (figure 6.9). This cord has been interpreted in different but complementary ways. Boone (2007:186) suggests it represents a white sacrificial cord bearing heaven-

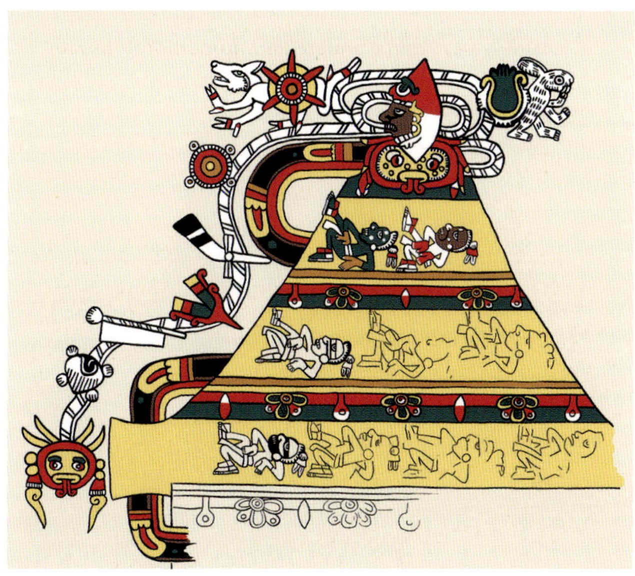

Figure 6.9. Sinuous sky rope/ecliptic. Redrawn from the *Codex Borgia* 33 (see Díaz and Rodgers 1993).

ly and religious elements. This is similar to the sustenance rope used in gladiatorial sacrifices. Milbrath (2013:81) interprets this white cord as the ecliptic; in Maya iconography the ecliptical cord is formed by intertwined serpents, arching serpents, or ropes (Schele and Mathews 1999:114).[28] In all of these examples, the ecliptic is the sun's path as well as the channel for feeding blood sacrifices to the sun.[29]

Narrative Reconstruction

The five Ancestors in the White Shaman mural are bound together by a rope of sustenance, a metaphoric umbilical cord through which they are not only united one to the other, but with Ancestors past, present, and future. This cord is the ecliptic path of the sun. It serves as a conduit for the transmission of blood and sustenance, including rain, between mortals and the divine. It is the rainy season/dry season serpent surrounding the world, binding both time and space. It is the horizon, the juncture between the world above and world below. The cord metaphorically represents the Flower Road, the path of life along which participants in the ritual reenactment of creation walk in the footsteps of their Ancestors.

Motif Analysis III: The Hill in the East

Large crenellated shapes anchor each end of the Flower Road (E029). On the left end of the mural, the white portion of the road superimposes a red, black, and yellow crenellated arch (E001) (figure 6.10). Each lobe of the crenellation is yellow with a black center. It has six lobes on the right side and only five remaining lobes on the left. A probable sixth lobe was lost to spalling. Running down the center of the arch is a vertical black band (figure 6.11).

Formulating Hypotheses

In Chapter 5 I hypothesized that the crenellated arch with its yellow solar steps represents the Hill in the East, birthplace of the sun and peyote, the flowery desert, and source of rain and the seeds of life (table 6.3). The concept of a sacred mountain as the birthplace of the sun and origin of life is woven throughout Nahua mythology and manifested in their art and architecture. Although peyote is not directly mentioned in Nahua mythology, we know the Nahua revered the cactus and conducted ritual hunts similar to those conducted by the Huichol today (Carrasco 2008:235). Its expression in Nahua mythology is likely metaphorical, such as in flower symbolism associated with the sacred mountain.

In Mesoamerican beliefs, a sacred hill or flowery mountain in the east contained the creator gods, ancestors, seeds of life, and life-giving water. These emerged from the mountain through sacred caves, which served as portals between the world above and world below (figure 6.12). This ancient concept continues to be deeply entrenched in Mesoamerican thought. According to García Garagarza (2012:195), ". . . the cult of sacred mountains lies at the heart of the Mesoamerican notion of the world, so that every effort to obliterate this form of worship has so far failed . . . There, during ritual pilgrimages to sacred peaks, the traditional shamans—the old *tlaziuhque*—still transmit the original memory of creation." The primordial mountain was a flowery paradise and location of the birth of the sun; all other hills were simply replications of this sacred place (López Austin 1997:191). It was a flower mountain, equated with abundance, filled with birds, butterflies, and flowers (Taube 2004:87). In Sahagún's *Historia general de las cosas de Nueva España* (1829:115) he writes that the god of fire dwells within the abyssal waters at the center of the earth among the flowers, which are *paredes almenadas* (crenellated walls) wrapped with rain clouds.

As previously discussed, the Huichol created small wooden stepped pyramids as replicas of this sacred place. On a much grander scale, the Nahua constructed massive stepped pyramids as re-creations of the primordial mountain (Heyden 1972). The pyramid steps represent the pan-Mesoamerican concept of thirteen divisions of daylight and thirteen levels of the heavens (Seler 1901:19). They were a stairway for the sun, with the top of the pyramid representing the zenith, noon, and the *axis mundi*—the place where the world above is connected with the world below.

Templo Mayor at Tenochtitlan was the *axis mundi* of the Nahua universe (López Austin and López Lujan 2009). It was a symbolic, human-made primordial mountain representing, among other things, the birthplace of the sun.[30] During the New Fire Ceremony, fire priests carried torches, blazing with the new fire drilled at the Hill of the Star, up the steps of Templo Mayor to the shrine of the sun god. This ancient concept of the Templo Mayor representing a stepped solar pathway is clearly expressed in Fray Diego Durán's sixteenth-

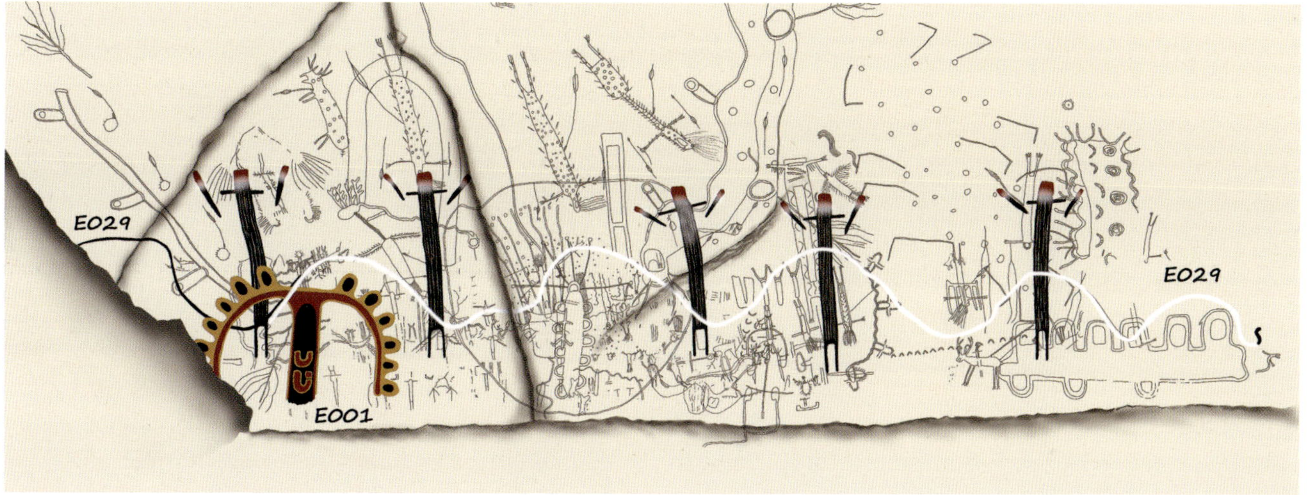

Figure 6.10. Motif III (E001): Hill in the East, solar steps, and the primordial mountain where the sun is born.

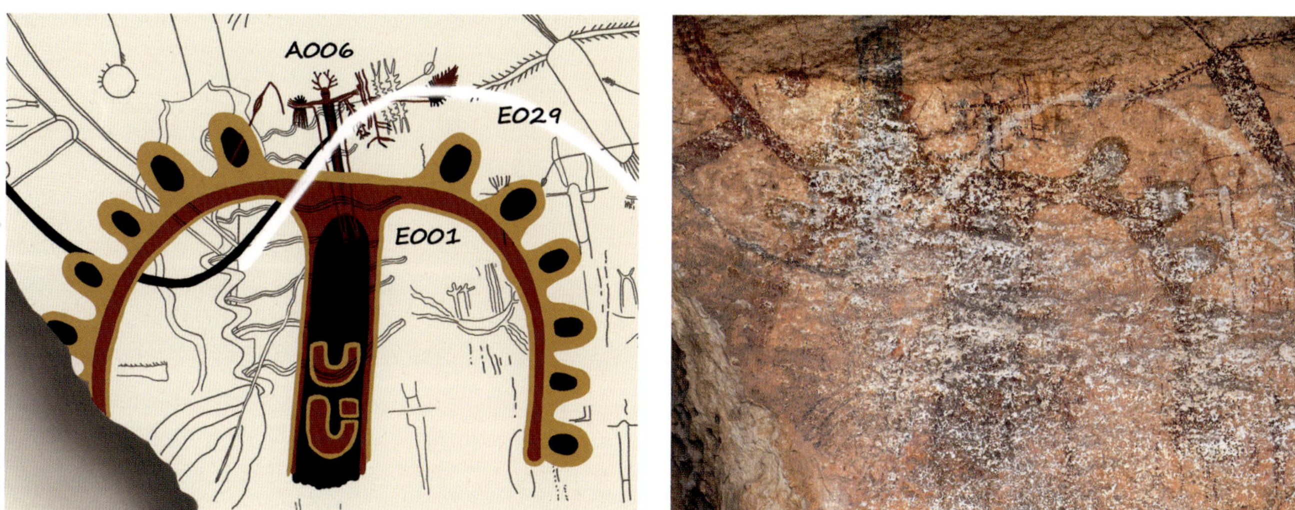

Figure 6.11. All color layers forming the Hill in the East (E001) are sandwiched between the white and black portions of the sinuous line (E029). The antlered anthropomorph (A006) emerging from the primordial mountain is not only wrapped in the black and white portions of the line, but is also sandwiched between the yellow, red, and black layers forming the crenellated arch. (See the caption for figure 3.8 for more detail on stratigraphy.)

century account of the Nahua Festival of the Sun. During this ceremony a sacrificial victim slowly climbed the temple, pausing at each step along the way to replicate the sun's course upon the earth. The victim was sacrificed at the top of the temple upon a stone disk engraved with symbols of the sun (Durán [1570] 1971:189).

The crenellated arch (E001) in the White Shaman mural is very similar to its Mesoamerican counterpart, which in some accounts has six steps ascending and six steps descending, with one at the top (zenith) for a total of thirteen (Thompson 1970:195).[31] In the mural the crenellated arch is portrayed with six yellow steps ascending and what at one time was likely six yellow steps descending. Sadly, a portion of the left side of the motif is missing, making it impossible to know for certain the number of descending steps. Just before sunset on the fall and spring equinoxes, this motif is illuminated in an arch of light (figure 6.13). The sun climbs the crenellations—step by step—while the rest of the mural remains in shadow until the arch is fully illuminated.

Among the Huichol the color yellow is equated with

the light of dawn and the sun's rays upon one's face. According to Ellen Baird (1985:140), the Nahua equated both red and yellow with the sun. She suggests that "red is the color of the sun at its zenith and yellow the color of the eastern sun on the horizon." Other scholars suggest yellow is the color of the sun-drenched earth or drought (Hernández Sánchez 2010:262; Woolley and Milbrath 2011:42), or even the sun god, Tonatiuh, himself (Soustelle [1979] 2012:160).

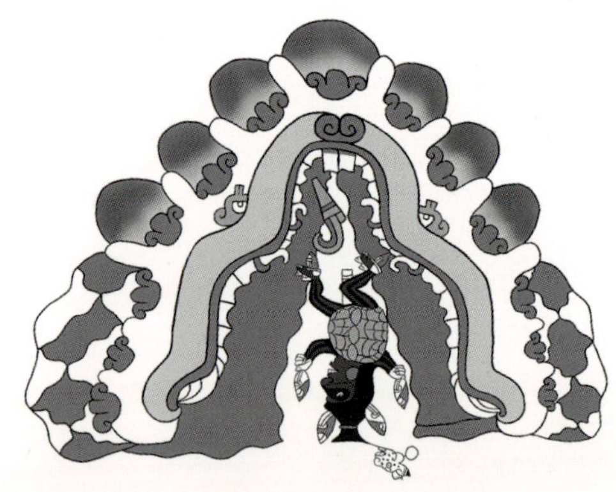

Figure 6.12. Cave birthplace within the primordial mountain. The dark lobes across the top of the motif represent the seven caves from which the Ancestors emerged after creation. Redrawn from *Codex Selden Roll* (see Wake 2007:224).

Narrative Reconstruction

Bound together by the rope of sustenance, the five Ancestors travel the Flower Road, the path of the sun, to the mountain of origins. Here, their fiery sacrifices cause the sun to climb the solar steps and emerge from the cave at the top of the mountain. The yellow light of dawn bathes the moist earth of primordial time. The Ancestors' sacrifice flows through the metaphorical umbilicus into the mountain to fuel the rising sun, and life-giving sustenance, the divine essence of the gods, flows back to them in a reciprocal relationship.

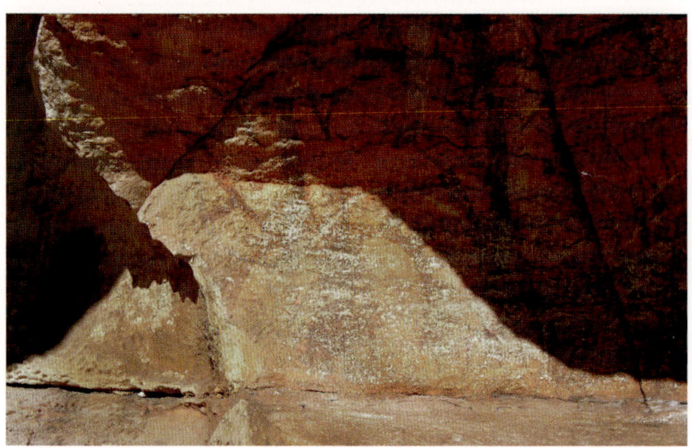

Figure 6.13. An arch of light illuminates the Hill in the East (E001) as the sun sets on the equinox.

Motif Analysis IV: Land of Black and Red

At the opposite end of the long, sinuous black and white line (E029) is a large, crenellated, horizontal band painted red and outlined in black (E007) (figure 6.14). This motif superimposes and completely obscures the

Table 6.3.
Motif Analysis III: Crenellated arch (E001)

HUICHOL	NAHUA	HYPOTHETICAL MEANINGS
X	X	The crenellated arch (E001) represents the sacred Hill in the East where the sun is born and the spirits of the seeds of life are stored.
X		Birthplace of peyote
X	X	Location where the primordial ancestors emerged from the underworld at the dawn of time
X	X	Crenellations along the arch represent the serpent(s) surrounding the world and also solar steps, a stairway for the sun to climb out of the underworld.
	X	Twelve solar "steps" plus the zenith at the top represent the thirteen divisions of daylight and the thirteen levels of the heavens.
X	X	Black throat of the crenellated arch represents an axis mundi and the cave from which the sun emerges.
X	X	Yellow encasing the Hill in the East denotes eastern solar light.

legs of A005. Water seeping out of the wall has deposited a thick white calcium carbonate skin over the top of the paintings in this section of the mural. Though still difficult to see, through photo enhancement we have identified six lobes across the top and three across the bottom (figure 6.15). An additional lobe appears to protrude from the right end of the band. Each lobe is red with a black center.

Formulating Hypotheses

In chapter 5, I hypothesized that E007 is analogous to the western entrance into the underworld and the most ancient place and time in the universe. Among both the Huichol and the Nahua, the west is equated with caves, primordial waters, female rain deities, and the color black. It is the place where, according to Huichol myth, the deformed child was thrown into the fire and began his journey through the nether regions before rising as the new sun at dawn. Likewise, in Nahua mythology, it is analogous to the location where the invalid Nanahuatzin threw himself into the first fire drilled by Tezcatlipoca-Mixcoatl so that the sun could be born (table 6.4).

In Nahua accounts of creation, Nanahuatzin throws himself into the fire created by Tezcatlipoca-Mixcoatl to be resurrected as the sun. This cosmic event was reenacted every fifty-two years through the New Fire Ceremony. In total darkness, a procession of fire priests arrayed in the garb of gods and painted black in penance would snake their way along the causeway, a metaphorical umbilicus, from the Templo Mayor to a temple atop the Hill of the Star. The temple was painted black to represent Tlillan, a place or house of blackness (Carrasco 1999a:100). It was the abode of the devouring serpent and moon goddess Cihuacoatl, associated with water and rainfall (Milbrath 1997:191,197).[32]

At Tlillan the fire priests drilled a new fire on the chest of their sacrificial victim, the surrogate Nanahuatzin. The survival of the fifth sun and the renewal of the cosmos depended on their success. The fire, which would burn the heart and body of the sacrifice, would also fuel a new temporal period. The new fire was then

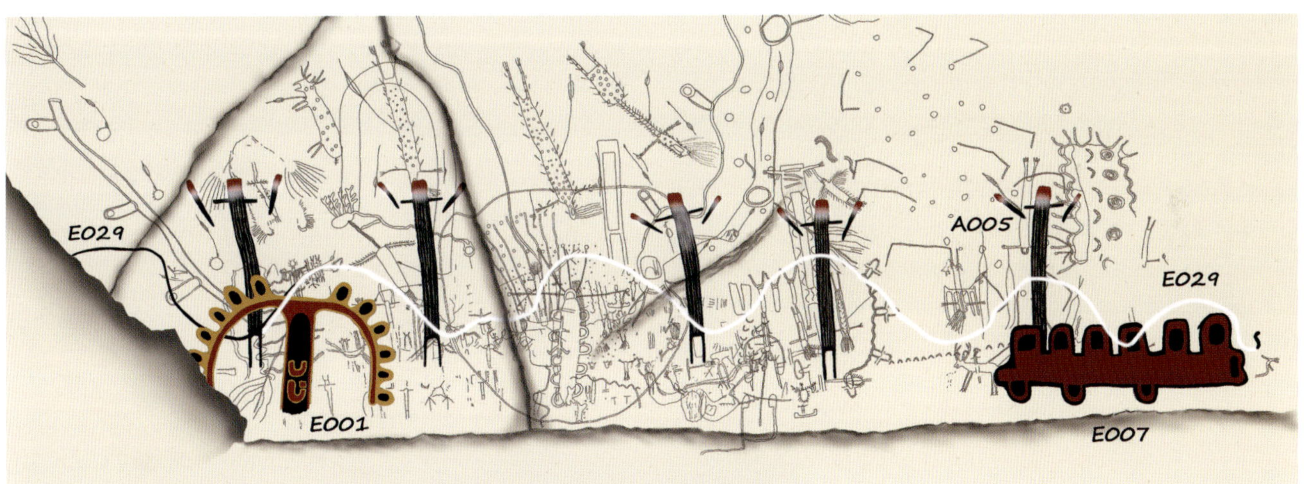

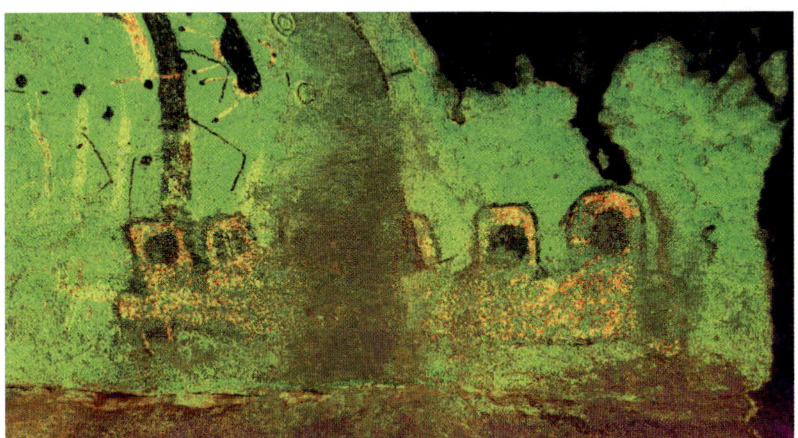

Figure 6.14. *(above)* Motif IV (E007): The Land of Black and Red, which serves as a cosmic portal into the underworld in the west. The eastern (E001) and western (E007) *axes mundi* are linked by the cosmic umbilicus (E029).

Figure 6.15. *(left)* Enhanced photo of the western *axis mundi* (E007).

Table 6.4.
Motif Analysis IV: Horizontal red and black crenellated band (E007)

HUICHOL	NAHUA	HYPOTHETICAL MEANINGS
X	X	The red and black crenellated band with nine lobes (E007) represents the westernmost edge of the cosmos where the sun plunges into the underworld.
X	X	Location where the sacrificient threw himself into the fire to be reborn in the east as the sun
X	X	Dwelling place of the earth-moon goddess
X	X	Most ancient time and place in the universe
X	X	Equated with feminine rain deities and primordial waters
X	X	Crenellations are undulations of serpent(s) surrounding the world.
X	X	The combination of red and black denotes the union of oppositional forces, fire and matter, masculine and feminine.
X	X	Black encasing motif denotes darkness overcoming light.

carried by the fire priests to the shrine of the sun god at the top of the Templo Mayor.[33]

Although this ceremony was conducted every fifty-two years, the sun's death and rebirth is witnessed on a daily basis. The Nahua considered the sun a mighty warrior who daily fights the forces of darkness, a battle lost each sunset when he falls into Tlillan Tlapallan, the Land of Black and Red (Caso 1988:25). *Tlillan* is equated with the land of darkness, night, and the color black; *Tlapallan* is the land of light, day, and the color red. In the west, where the blackness of night overcomes the red of the sun, these two places are united (Caso 1988:25). Tlillan Tlapallan is the point of intersection between the black of night and the red of day, between the world below and the world above, between the feminine and the masculine.

Narrative Reconstruction

The Hill in the East (E001) at the left end of the mural and the Land of Black and Red (E007) at the right end both represent the *axis mundi*. Respectively, they represent the east and west, sunrise and sunset, life and death. In the west, darkness envelopes the land in black. In the east, light overcomes darkness, bathing the primordial mountain with the yellow light of the sun. And, like the Templo Mayor and Hill of the Star, the two regions are connected by a causeway, the Flower Road (E029), representing the ecliptic along which the life-giving sustenance of sacrifice flows to the sun. The five Ancestors begin their journey during primordial time, leaving their cave birthplace in the west to travel through the underworld and emerge in the east with the rising sun. They follow its path, which serves as a cosmic umbilicus linking the two cosmic portals.

Motif Analysis V: Solar Deer/Stellar Deer

Overlaying the Land of Black and Red (E007) and below the Flower Road (E029) is an upside-down red deer (Z006) with a red atlatl dart impaled in its chest (figure 6.16). The hooves on its front legs are black, but those on its hind legs are red. Immediately left of Z006 is an upright red deer (Z002). It has black hooves on both front and hind legs, bifurcated antlers, and is facing the Hill in the East (E001). The black hooves of Z002 were painted before its red legs. Superimposing Z002 is a small red anthropomorph with raised ("ecstatic") hair (A021). On the opposite end of the mural, above the Hill in the East, is a red deer (Z001) with bifurcated antlers but no hooves (figures 6.17 and 6.18). Its chest is impaled by a red dart with a stylized tip, and within its body are twelve large black dots. The dots were applied

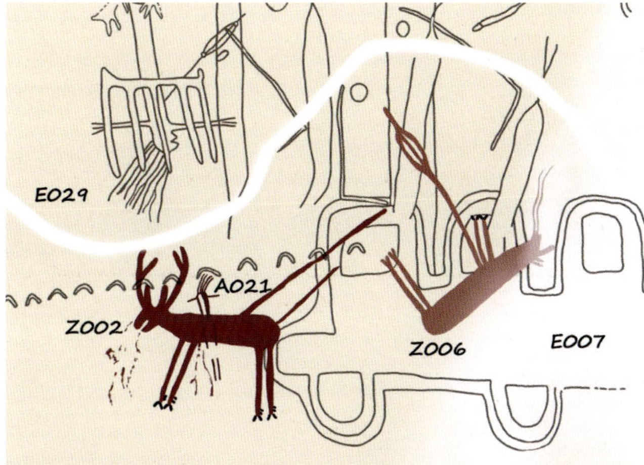

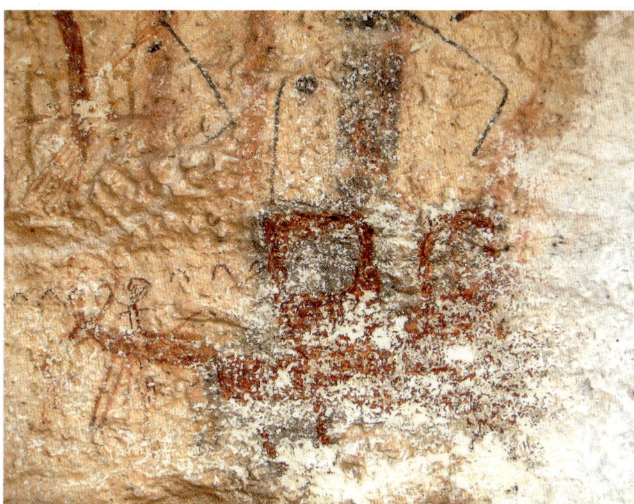

Figure 6.16. Night Sun (A021) travels through the underworld with Venus after transformation into a deer (Z006, Z002) portrayed with black hooves (obsidian sandals).

to the wall before the red paint that gave form to the deer's body.

Formulating Hypotheses

Drawing from Huichol mythology, I hypothesized in the previous chapter that the three deer portrayed in the mural (Z001, Z002, and Z006) symbolize Venus/Sun as either Morning Star/Day Sun or Evening Star/Night Sun. Although the iconographic and ethnographic correlations are strongest with Huichol creation stories, there also are notable parallels with Nahua mythology (table 6.5). In both mythologies deer are closely associated with the birth and death of the sun, as well as with Venus. In some myths deer are said to have been present since the beginning of time (Brundage 1983:38; Read and Gonzalez 2000:162). They were intimately involved in creation (Sachse 2008:141), securing safe transition for the sun through the underworld to the Hill in the East (Megged 2010:116). Deer are portrayed in Nahua mythology and iconography as solar bearers or guides. Page 33 of the *Codex Borgia* relates the story of primordial sacrifices that lead to the sun's birth. At the top of the page a deer bearing a solar disk is attached to a white ecliptic cord (Milbrath 2013:81) (figure 6.19). Milbrath (2013:139 fn45) suggests this solar deer may represent a seasonal construct in which the deer carries the sun swiftly across the sky during the dry season between the fall and spring equinoxes.[34]

Times of transition—such as moving from one human cycle to another, or from one seasonal cycle

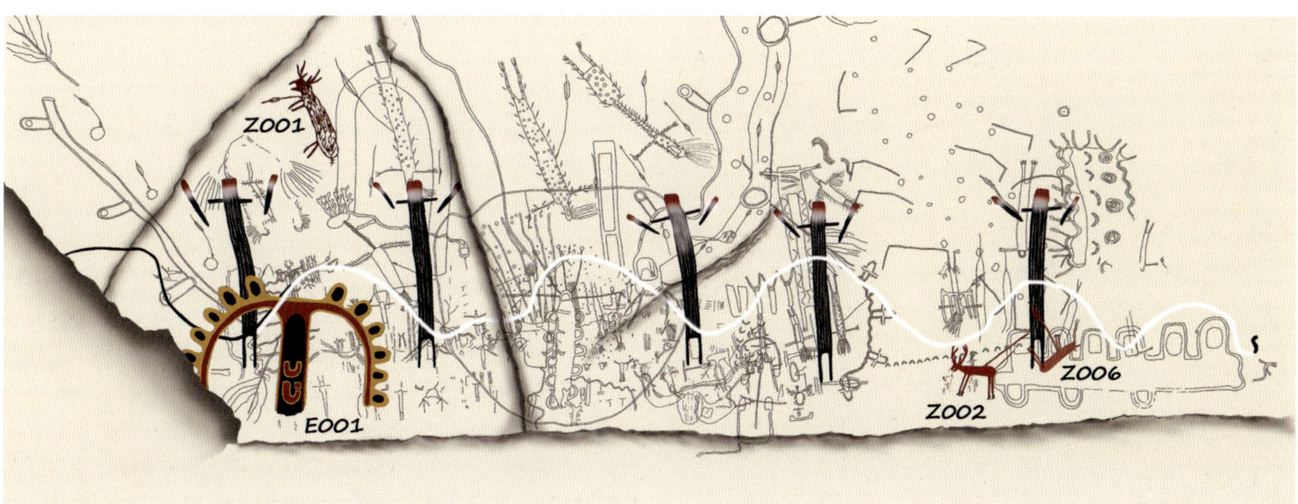

Figure 6.17. Motif V (Z001, Z002, Z006): Solar deer/stellar deer.

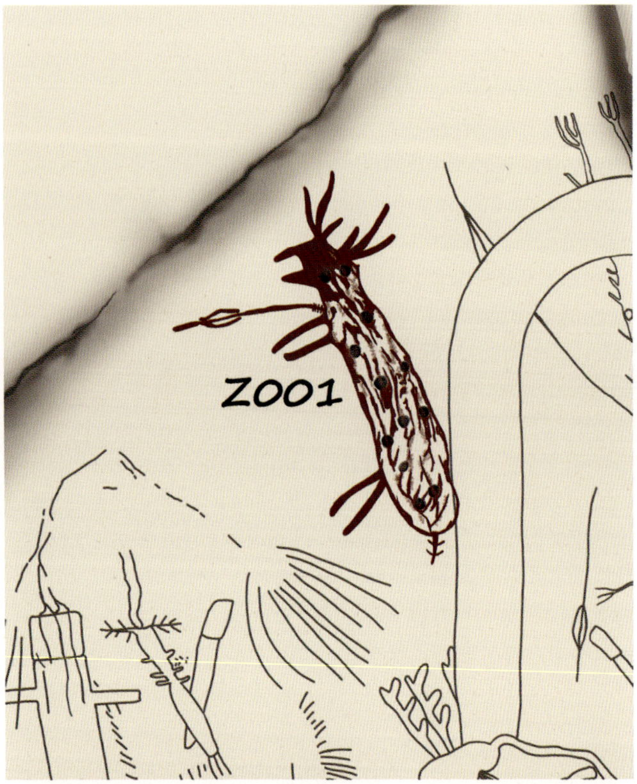

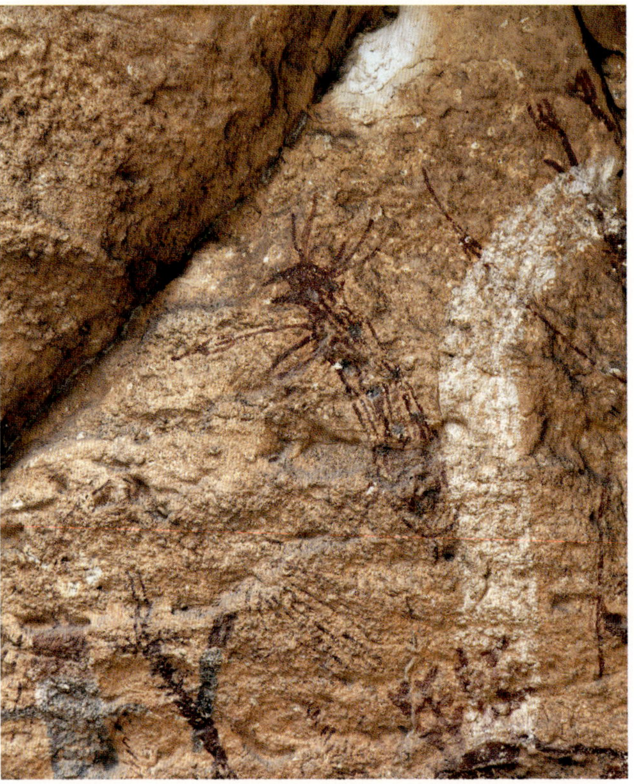

Figure 6.18. Venusian deer deity and leader of the primordial pilgrimage who was the first stellar warrior to die in the cosmic battle with the sun. The black dots in his body represent stars and heart sacrifices provided as nourishment to the sun.

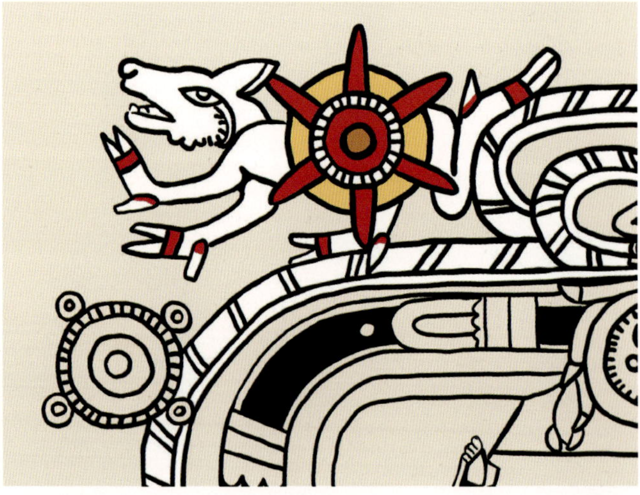

Figure 6.19. Deer as a solar bearer. Redrawn from *Codex Borgia* 33 (see Díaz and Rodgers 1993).

to another—were believed to be fraught with peril. They were periods subject to any manner of supernatural threat due to transgressions and sins committed by community members—or the community at large (Megged 2010:116). During such dangerous times the deer was considered the medium through which safe transition and transcendence were possible. For example, the nocturnal journey made by the sun through the underworld was a perilous and unpredictable time of transition, and the deer figures prominently in this transition (Megged 2010:114-116).

In Nahua mythology, as in the Huichol's, the sun and Venus are ambivalent characters who change into their alter egos on a cyclical basis. They are also often conflated, with the Morning Star fused with the day sun, and the Evening Star with the night sun.[35] As a result, Venus mythology and accompanying rituals are enmeshed in the solar calendar. At dusk the lunar or night sun transforms into Venus, who in turn transforms into a deer to guide or carry the sun through the underworld. Cohodas (1975:103) writes that the "sun descends in the form of a deer" and is swallowed by the earth in the west; this sacrificial death magically "transforms the sun into an underworld fertility deity."

The nocturnal counterpart of the sun is known by a variety of names, one of which is a magical name of the deer, Piltzintecuhtli (Noble Prince) (Ingham 1984:385; D. Kelley 1980:34–35), the young solar god who transformed himself into a deer (Venus) to travel through

Table 6.5.
Motif Analysis V: Impaled deer with black dots inside its body (Z001), red deer with black hooves (Z002) superimposed by an anthropomorph (A021), and an upside-down, impaled deer (Z006)

HUICHOL	NAHUA	HYPOTHETICAL MEANINGS
X	X	The impaled deer (Z001) represents Venus, who through autosacrifice becomes the sun.
X	X	Twelve black dots on Z001's body denote stars and the heart-souls of the Ancestors who died in sacrifice to the sun.
	X	Twelve dots on Z001's body denote association with the lord of dawn and/or patron of the twelfth day, the medicine lord who discovered peyote.
X	X	Z006 represents Night Sun/Evening Star transforming into a deer in the Land of Black and Red (E007) at the end of an astronomical cycle.
X	X	Z002 represents Venus carrying the sun (A021) through the underworld and leading the primordial pilgrimage to the east.
X	X	Black hooves of Z002 denote femininity, fecundity, and association with the underworld.

the night sky and woo the beautiful earth-moon goddess Xochiquetzal. He is associated with the earth, death, west, and darkness, and he travels through the underworld in the guise of a deer before rising at dawn as the sun god, Tonatiuh (Klein 1976:6). Through his union with the earth-moon goddess, the Morning Star is born. "Piltzintecuhtli" is also another name for Tezcatlipoca and Yohualtecuhtli, who are equated with the night sun (Olivier 2003:34).[36] The night sun is portrayed in iconography with a deer hoof tied to his right ankle to indicate swiftness and agility (Read and Gonzalez 2000:251) (figure 6.20).

In *Historia de los mexicanos por sus pinturas,* Tezcatlipoca transforms himself into the Venusian deity Mixcoatl (Cloud Deer Serpent) to drill the fire upon which the sun is sacrificed.[37] Mixcoatl is god of the hunt, shooter of arrows, and the mighty warrior who initiated the sacred war to capture hearts to feed to the sun and Earth. Those he waged war against were his very own creation: the four hundred Mimixcoa, who are equated with deer and stars (Gingerich 1988:216, 217). Ultimately, he became one of the four hundred; he was both hunter and hunted. Johanna Broda (1999:105) says Mixcoatl was "the prototype of the first warrior who died in warfare, the victim that sustains the universe; in this sense he was assimilated to the deer." He was the leader

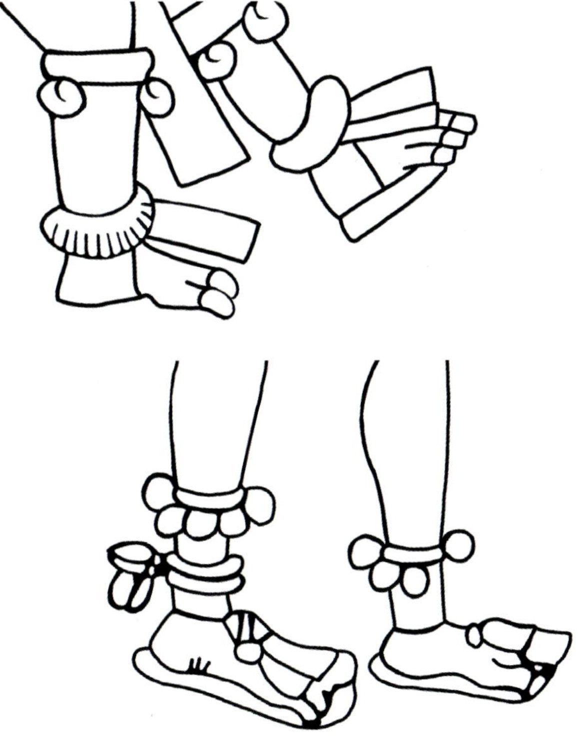

Figure 6.20. Deer hooves and Night Sun. (a) Representation of Tezcatlipoca with right foot portrayed as a deer hoof. Redrawn from Olivier 2003:283. (b) Representation of Tezcatlipoca with deer hoof attached to right ankle. Redrawn from Olivier 2003:282.

of the pilgrimages made during primordial times and embodied the souls of sacrificed warriors who were transformed into stars at death (Broda 1999:105).

Mixcoatl is equated with deer throughout Nahua mythology. In a myth similar to that of Piltzintecuhtli (an avatar of Tezcatlipoca-Mixcoatl), he is said to have sired Quetzalcoatl-Ce Acatl (sun and Morning Star) through a union with the earth-moon goddess Cihuacoatl. Called "the Deer of Culhuacan," Cihuacoatl lived in Tlillan (Graulich 1997:169–187). After Mixcoatl's death, Quetzalcoatl retrieved his father's bones, which were magically resurrected as a deer (Ingham 1984:390). And in *Leyenda de los soles*, Mixcoatl is reported to have lain with the deer and earth-moon goddess Chimalman. In Mesoamerican myth and iconography, married or copulating couples such as this often represent the male and female aspect of a singular deity (Klein 2001:186). Through the union of Mixcoatl (Evening Star/Night Sun) and Chimalman (earth-moon goddess), Ce Acatl, an avatar of Quetzalcoatl, was born. Chimalman, however, died giving birth to her son. As a consequence, she was masculinized by her inability to bear children and became the most dangerous star demon, Itzpapalotl (Obsidian Butterfly), and the first female warrior to die in warfare (childbirth). After her death, her son, Ce Acatl, was raised by another of her avatars, Cihuacoatl (Bierhorst 1992:153).

In Nahua myth and iconography, *itzcactli*, "obsidian sandals," are a diagnostic accoutrement of the night sun deities, as well as of Itzpapalotl and her avatars. *Itzcactli* are black, triangular-shaped motifs adorning the feet of these gods (figure 6.21). They are a powerful symbol of the underworld and night (García-Goyco 2007:382; Olivier 2007:294, 304), both of which are equated with femininity. As mentioned above, the night sun deity Tezcatlipoca is portrayed with a deer hoof attached to his right ankle. Black deer hooves may metaphorically represent obsidian sandals.

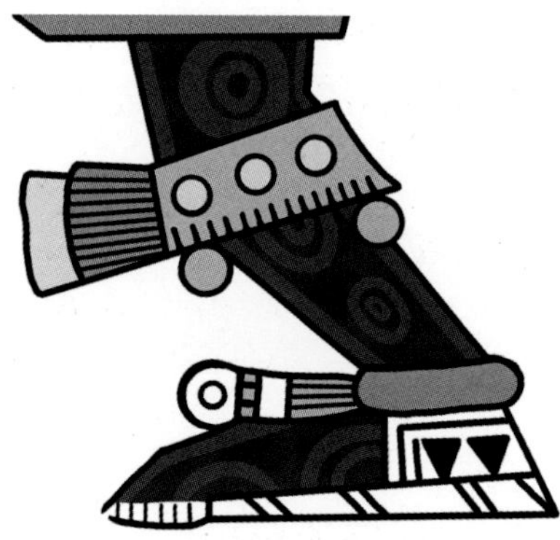

Figure 6.21. Night Sun's obsidian sandal. Redrawn from *Codex Borgia* 21 (see Díaz and Rodgers 1993).

In the mural the upside-down red deer (Z006) overlaying the crenellated black and red band (E007) has black hooves, possibly representing obsidian sandals, on its front legs (figure 6.16). It is analogous to the Evening Star/Night Sun falling into the Land of Black and Red. Here, in the home of the earth-moon goddess, it is transformed into the deer (Z002) to carry the Night Sun (A021) through the underworld. Z002 is portrayed with black hooves on both its front and back legs. As with the masculinized Itzpapalotl, this deer is dual gendered, both male and female. It is antlered, a male attribute, but wears the obsidian sandals associated with the night, underworld, and femininity. Cecilia Klein (2001:185) has argued gender ambiguity and duality was a powerful Nahua metaphor capable of facilitating much-needed change under the right conditions. These conditions arose during the Nahua calendar at strategic and dangerous occasions "marking the end of one important astronomical period or season and the need for a smooth transition to another" (Klein 2001:185). And, as stated above, deer were deemed the medium through which safe transition was possible.

On the opposite end of the panel, above the Hill in the East (E001), is another red deer (Z001) (figure 6.17 and 6.18). Its chest is impaled by a red dart, and its body is filled with twelve black dots. In the previous chapter I interpreted this deer as Venus, who, after guiding the future sun through the underworld, committed autosacrifice and was transformed into the sun he was transporting. The cosmic deer was both predator and prey, hunter and hunted. This is echoed in Nahua solar myths.

In *Historia de los mexicanos por sus pinturas*, it is the son of Quetzalcoatl (Venus) who is sacrificed in the fire (Phillips 1884:622). Brundage (1983:228 fn22) observes "this would imply that the god sacrificed to become the sun (elsewhere Nanahuatl) was really a form of Quetzalcoatl, the Morning Star. Ergo, Nanahuatl was himself a form of the Morning Star." In other accounts, it is Xolotl, the Evening Star and twin of Quetzalcoatl, who is sacrificed. Either way, Venus is transformed into the sun through an act of self-sacrifice.[38] And in Nahua myth, Venus is slain by the sun, who is none other than an aspect of himself. The same predator-prey relationship is embodied in Mixcoatl, who essentially wages war against himself to nourish the sun. Brundage (1982:170) writes, "In one curious sense a cast of actors does not exist at all in these dramas. There is only one actor, Mixcoatl, alone on the stage. He dons and doffs various masks as he moves about, miming the vicissitudes of the embattled light."

In the previous chapter I hypothesized that the black dots within the body of the deer (Z001) represent stars and the heart-souls of Ancestors that will be transformed into the sun, peyote, and the Morning Star. It is possible this meaning can be applied here as well. Mixcoatl, who was equated with both Venus and the deer, provided the hearts required to sustain the universe. The hearts were stellar Ancestors, all of whom were embodied in the Venusian deity Mixcoatl. The nourishment received from their sacrifice fueled the sun's movement across the sky. The impaled red deer with black dots is analogous to Mixcoatl, who was the leader of primordial pilgrimages and the prototype of the first warrior to die in the cosmic battle with the sun, a battle he waged against himself. Upon his death, he was transformed into the new sun of dawn. The black dots may represent stars and souls of Ancestors who died a sacrificial death.

The fact that there are exactly twelve black dots portrayed in this deer may also be of significance. The patron of the number 12 is none other than the dawn lord, Tlahuizcalpantecuhtli—an avatar of Quetzalcoatl (Boone 2007:41). The twelve dots might also denote an association with Patecatl, the twelfth lord of the twenty day-signs. Patecatl is the medicine lord or god of healing (Boone 2007:47) and is reported to be the discoverer of peyote (Alexander 1920:77).

Z001 lacks hooves: the deer's legs simply end as stumps. In chapter 5 I suggested that the black hooves of Z002 and Z006 denote footprints and are a feminine expression of the heart-soul of the deer, which will be transformed into peyote. According to Huichol myth, wherever the deer steps, peyote will grow in its tracks. Interestingly, in Nahuatl, the word *chocholli* translates as either "to walk/leap about" or "a deer's hoof." It is also a metaphor for inducing an altered state: to become "deer-hooved" is "to become drugged" (Maxwell and Hanson 1992:338).

The portrayal of Z001 without hooves may also have been intended to denote the liberation of the deer's heart-soul from the earth. When a person dies, the Huichol metaphorically erase their footprints so that their heart-souls can merge with Father Sun. In the same way, erasing the deer's hoofprints, would release its heart-soul from all earthly attachments and enable it to merge with the sun. In both Nahua and Huichol cosmology, the souls of the dead are liberated from their earthly condition, transformed, and united with the sun through the fire of sacrifice (Megged 2010:117–118; Séjourné 1978:108).

Narrative Reconstruction

In the bowels of the earth (E007), the Setting Sun transforms into a deer (Z006) to unite with the earth-moon goddess. Their union joins the hot (red) and cold (black) oppositional forces, giving birth to Venus (Z002), the stellar deer who carries the anthropomorphized Night Sun (A021) through the underworld. It is the deer who secures safe transition from the night to the day, and from one cosmic era to the next. Together they travel along the ecliptic (E029) to the Hill in the East (E001). At the primordial mountain this stellar deer (Z001) is pierced in his chest by the rays of the sun, who he would himself become at the dawn of time; in other words, he shoots himself with himself to become himself. He is both hunter and hunted, predator and prey. Upon his death, his heart-soul is transformed, and all earthly ties are erased as he merges with the sun.

Motif Analysis VI: Star Demons and Stellar Sacrifices

The artist (or artists) who created the White Shaman mural applied all black paint first. These first layers of black produced a mural filled with a multitude of ordered black dots spread across the upper portion of the limestone canvas. With the addition of the next color of paint, many of these dots became incorporated into figures, including A008, A011, and A012, as well as the deer (Z001) discussed above.

In the section of the mural representing the east, a group of anthropomorphs appear to be flying down from above (figure 6.22a). The three leading figures (A008, A011, A012) are upside-down and impaled by red darts with stylized tips. Each figure has long arms and spindly fingers and toes, and their elongated bodies are formed by a series of vertical red stripes. They are fringed in red and yellow; their faces are masked in black. A yellow line outlines their bodies and arms. They

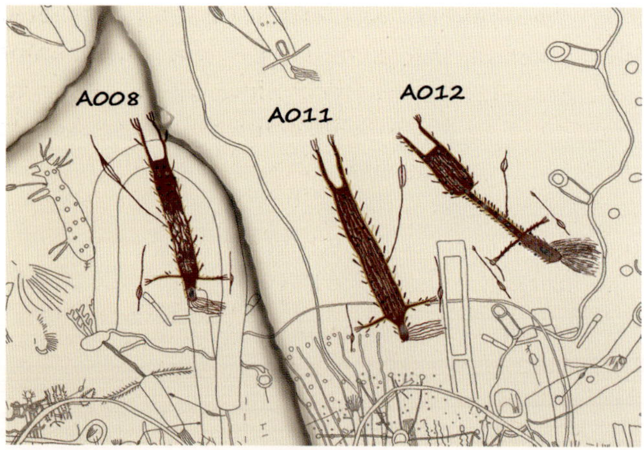

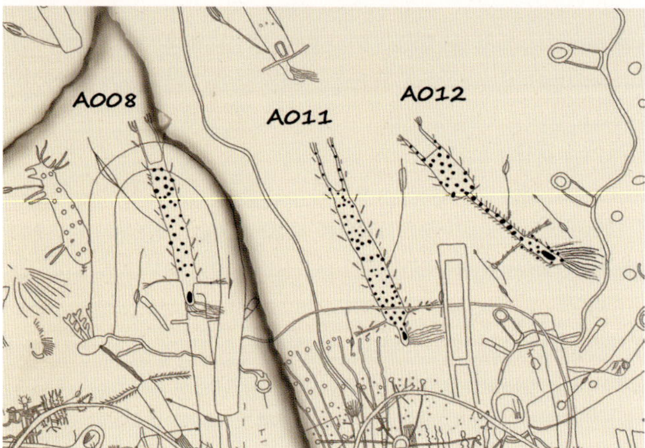

Figure 6.22. Motif VI (A008, A011, A012): Star demons and stellar sacrifices. (a) Ancestral figures resembling Nahua star demons. (b) Stars and heart-souls of the Ancestors.

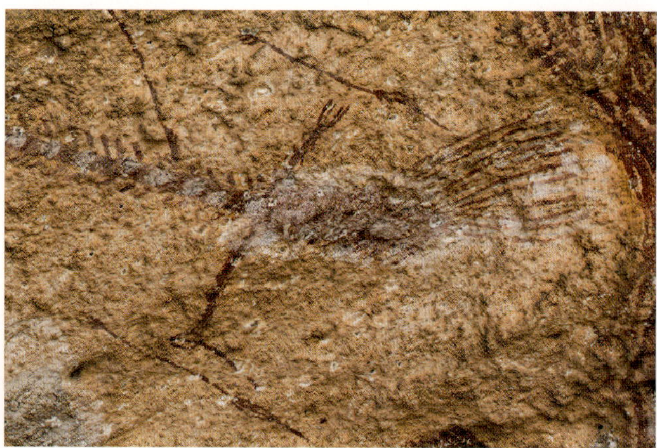

Figure 6.23. Skeletonized anthropomorph (A012) resembling Tzitzimime.

have long, flowing hair extending off the right side of their heads. Under their red bodies are numerous black dots (figure 6.22b). A thin layer of white paint overlays each black dot, thus sandwiching the red between the black and white. Each figure is holding a fletched spear or dart in their right and left hands. The torso of A012 resembles a spinal column stripped of its flesh (figure 6.23). This black-masked figure is holding additional paraphernalia in its left hand, possibly a finger-looped atlatl, and its hair is strewn with white dots.

Other dots are free-floating, such as a constellation of approximately thirty-two large black dots arranged in the western region, or right side, of the mural (figure 6.24a).[39] Thirteen black L-shapes encircle this grouping of dots, with a dot strategically placed at the distal-end of each L-shape (figure 6.24b). These dots and L-shapes are collectively referred to as E010. This motif is located directly above the Land of Black and Red (E007) and the two deer (Z002 and Z006). I will discuss E010 in considerable detail later in this chapter under Motif Analyses XII and XIII.

Formulating Hypotheses

In the previous chapter I proposed that the black dots throughout the mural represent stars: the heart-souls of Ancestors, which are associated with rain. I also proposed that the upside-down figures (A008, A011, A012), whose bodies are filled with black dots, are analogous to the stellar cloud serpent: pilgrims journeying back to the west with the gentle eastern rains. An examination of Nahua mythology not only supports this interpretation, it enhances it (table 6.6). As the Huichol also believe, the soul associated with the heart leaves the body upon death and becomes a cold, stellar entity. These souls travel with the sun across the skies from sunrise to sunset, bringing with them the rains from the east.

According to *Historia de los mexicanos por sus pinturas*, Mixcoatl drilled a multitude of fires to celebrate the gods after the heavens were separated from the earth. These fires provided the only light there was, for this was before the sun was born. In *Histoyre du Méchique* we learn the fires created by Mixcoatl are metaphors for stars (Graulich 1983:579). When we envision stars, we think of twinkling white lights. In Mesoamerican thought, however, water, night, the stars, and the underworld are cold and equated with the color black. Nuttall (1901:35) noted that as counterintuitive as it might seem, the most expressive sign for a shining star was a black dot. Collections of black dots represented star groups or constellations.[40]

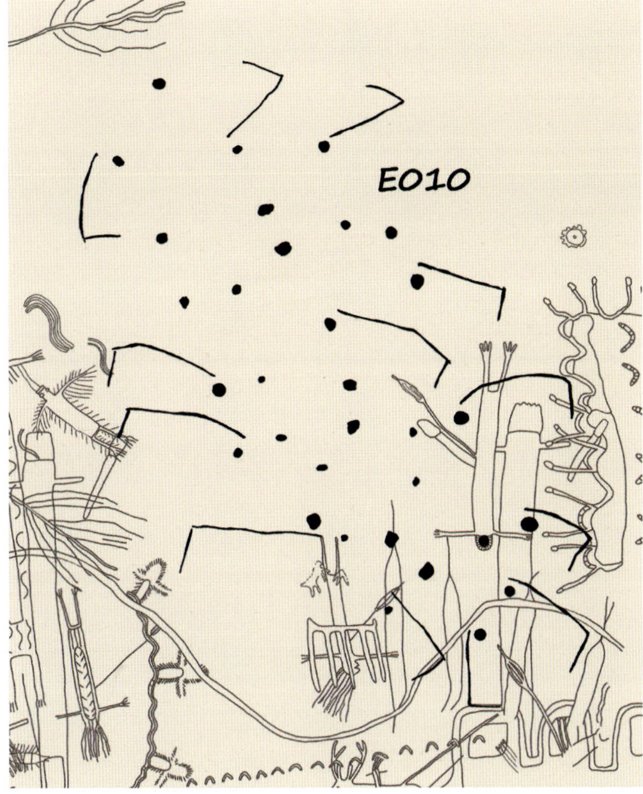

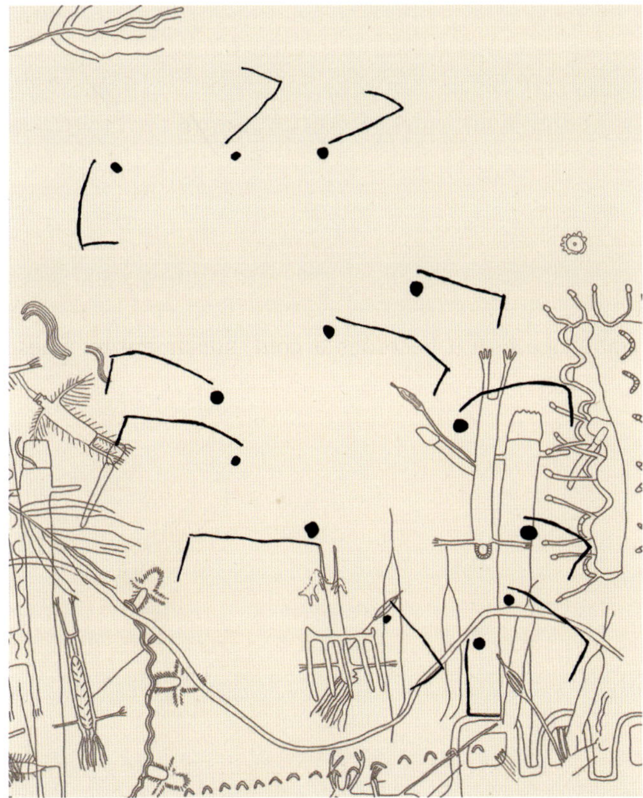

Figure 6.24. Motif VI (E010): Starry night sky. (a) Thirteen reeds or atlatls surround thirty-two black dots (stars). (b) Each of thirteen reeds or atlatls has a black dot (star) at the distal end.

The ancient Mexican philosophers imagined a vertical line of demarcation across the middle of the sky, separating the starry heavens into portions allotted to male and female souls (Nuttall 1901:39). The soul associated with the heart, which among the Nahua is referred to as the *yolia* soul, leaves the body upon death and travels to realms beyond. When a person is alive, their *yolia* soul is hot and therefore associated with the color red, but upon death the *yolia* soul is cold and black (Carrasco 1999b:13-14). The *yolia* souls of male warriors who died in sacrifice to the sun were said to dwell in the east, where just before dawn they armed themselves as if going into battle and heralded the rising of the solar deity. They traveled with him until he reached the zenith, and at midday the souls of women who died in childbirth—female warriors—took over and escorted the lunar sun to the western horizon. Collectively, these stellar warriors were known as Tzitzimime. They were conceived of as stars or star demons appearing in multiples and not acting alone (Boone 1999:200). Seler (1996:41–45) equates these stellar beings with the four hundred Mimixcoa (Cloud Snakes) who were created by and representative of Mixcoatl as food for the sun during primordial time.[41] These heroic warriors became the prototype for victims slain during the Festival of the Rising Sun (Graulich 1988:395, 1989:47).

In the *Anales de Cuauhtitlan* we learn the Mimixcoa "hollowed out their faces in black" with the cremated ashes of the moon goddess Itzpapalotl (Graulich 1997:169). As a consequence, Nahua star gods are portrayed wearing "black stellar masks" (Caso 1988:37).[42] In the codices, not only are star gods portrayed with the "stellar facial painting called darkness," their bodies are striped red and "hair set with white downy feather balls" (Seler 1902:79, 115) (figure 6.25). Graulich (1988:396) writes that white down in the hair and chalked bodies are the most characteristic adornments of victims marked for sacrifice.[43] While Seler (cited in Graulich 1988:396) argues that the white down symbolizes clouds, Graulich (1988:396) maintains that the white chalk and feathers denote victims who belonged to both heaven and earth. The two interpretations are not exclusionary, since the rain produced from clouds does belong to both regions.

Pohl (1998:196) says the star demons represent spirits of deceased gods and royal ancestors who were believed to come from the clouds bringing thunder, lightning, and rain. But they were also feared as star demons

Table 6.6.
Motif Analysis VI: Upside-down, impaled anthropomorphs filled with black dots (A008, A011, A012)

HUICHOL	NAHUA	HYPOTHETICAL MEANINGS
X	X	Black dots denote stars and the souls of the Ancestors.
X	X	Upside-down, impaled figures represent stellar Ancestors collectively identified with the cloud serpent.
X	X	Stellar Ancestors travel with the sun to its zenith.
	X	White dots of paint overlaying the red and black bodies and hair of upside-down figures denote sacrifice and clouds or vapor.
X	X	Black masks represent stellar masks.

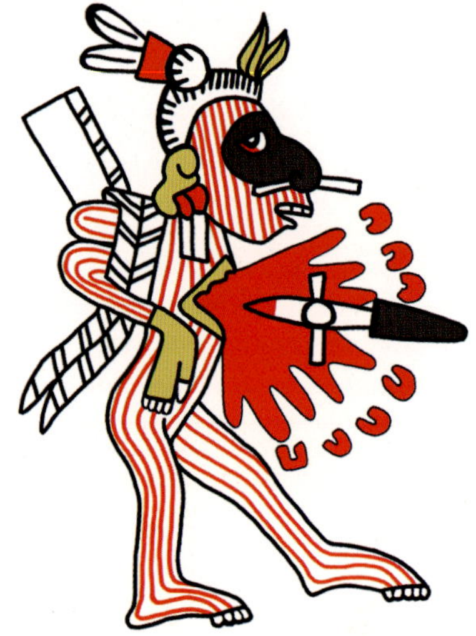

Figure 6.25. Sacrificial victim wearing black stellar mask. Redrawn from *Codex Borgia* 21 (see Díaz and Rodgers 1993).

who could descend to earth and eat people during climactic events, such as the drilling of the New Fire every fifty-two years. In the *Codex Borgia* they are portrayed falling head-first from the sky and bearing implements of punishment (Pohl 1998:196). They often are characterized by their fleshless bodies, claws, and long, tangled hair. According to Graulich (1997:255), the word *tzitzimime* can mean "disheveled hair."

Narrative Reconstruction

The upside-down figures (A008, A011, A012) on the left (east) side of the mural possess attributes comparable to those found in descriptions of Tzitzimime and the Mimixcoa (cloud serpents). Prior to the application of red paint, the three would have appeared as a collection of black dots. As stated above, the black dots filling the heavens represent the cold, stellar souls of Ancestors associated with bringing rain. In this context, they are the souls sacrificed to guide the sun across the eastern sky from sunrise until midday. They appear in the eastern region with the yellow light of dawn irradiating their bodies. And, like descriptions of Nahua stellar deities, their bodies are striped in red. They are portrayed plummeting down from the heavens, wielding implements of punishment, their disheveled hair and bodies adorned with white balls denoting them as sacrifices and the rain clouds they represent.[44] Their faces are hollowed out in black, identifying them as star gods and victims sacrificed as nourishment for the sun.

Motif Analysis VII: Food for the Sun

Three large red dots (E002) are located on the far left edge of the mural immediately above and to the left of the Hill in the East (E001) (figure 6.26). Each is pierced by a fletched dart. The stylized tips of the impaling darts are similar to the one piercing the body of the deer (Z001), whose body is filled with black dots, as well as the upside-down figures (A008, A011, A012) discussed above. Each of the three red dots is also slightly rayed, resembling a pincushion.

Formulating Hypotheses

In the Huichol story of creation, when the Ancestors emerged from the underworld, the deer who guided

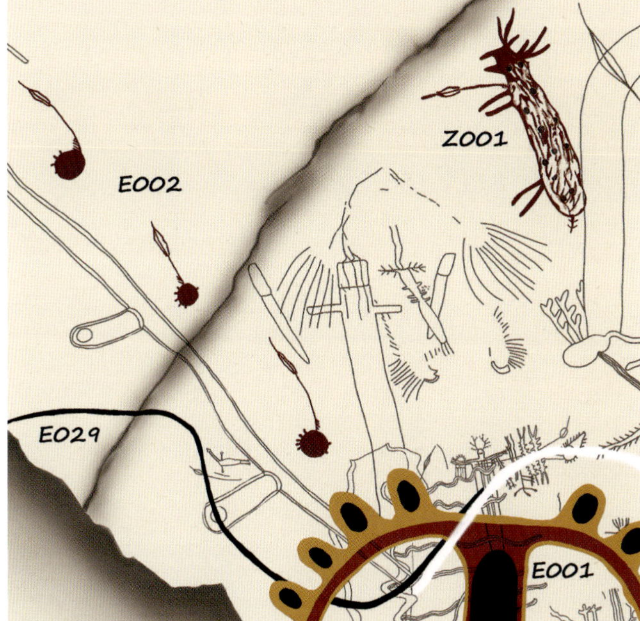

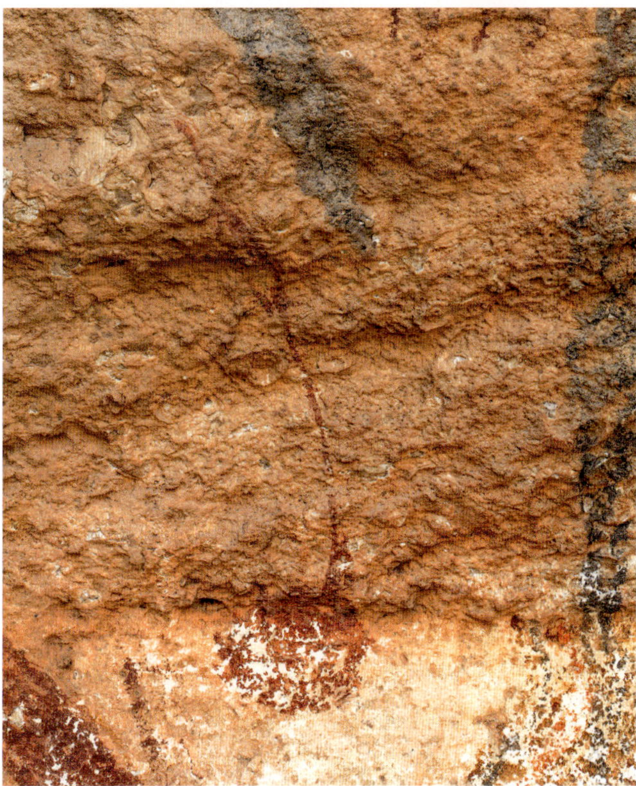

them on their journey allowed himself to be slain to provide sustenance for the sun. Through this act of self-sacrifice, his heart, which represented the souls of the Ancestors and stars, was transformed into peyote cactus. This event is reenacted annually through the ritual peyote hunt. In the last chapter I hypothesized that the red impaled dots (E002) represent the heart-soul of the deer transformed into peyote. Parallels between the events surrounding the Huichol and Nahua emergence from the underworld are notable (table 6.7).

The beautiful pictorial codex known as *Mapa de Cuauhtinchan No. 2* relates the sacred history and pilgrimage of the Chichimecs. It documents their Ancestors' emergence from the caves of Chicomoztoc, followed immediately by a series of ritual acts, including the hunting of deer and the shooting of a flowering nopal cactus with arrows (Yoneda 2007:161). The first act, however, was the drilling of a new fire inside a structure composed of thirteen arrows or reeds (figure 6.27). Olivier (2007:299) suggests this structure relates to the calendrical name of the sun, 13 Reed. Also in this opening scene, two Ancestors are portrayed falling headfirst toward two large barrel cacti. The mythical prototype of these rituals was related to the sacrifice of Mimixcoa by Itzpapalotl, the leader and deer goddess of the Chichimec who sacrificed the Mimixcoa (stars) to feed the sun at the dawn of time (Olivier 2007:299).

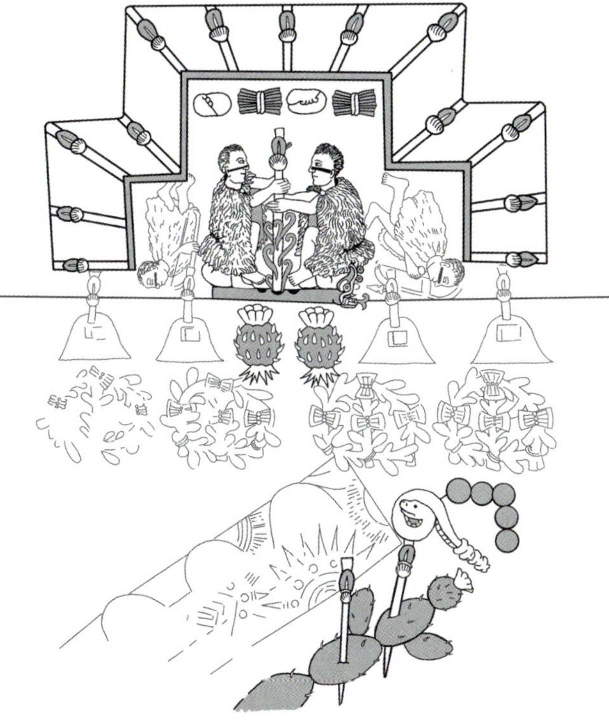

Figure 6.26. Motif VII (E002): Heart-souls of the Ancestors dwelling within the cactus (E002), which metaphorically represents the deer (Z001). The slaying of the cactus-deer fuels the sun and releases life-giving water.

Figure 6.27. *(right)* Shooting of the cactus and the drilling of a new fire at the dawn of creation. Redrawn from *Mapa de Cuauhtinchan No. 2.*

Table 6.7.
Motif Analysis VII: Impaled red dots (E002)

HUICHOL	NAHUA	HYPOTHETICAL MEANINGS
X		Heart-soul of the deer is transformed into peyote (E002) through autosacrifice and the transforming rays of the sun.
X	X	Cactus-shooting event takes place at the dawn of time when the primordial ancestors emerge from their cave birthplace in the east.
X	X	Deer and stars—both of which represent Ancestors—are associated with cactus and are slain to fuel the sun.
X	X	Slaying the cactus-deer brings rain.

One of the most familiar of these myths relates a battle between the cloud serpents and Itzpapalotl. In this story Itzpapalotl, who like other Chichimec was also a deer, pursues the Mimixcoa into a cactus and shoots them with arrows. In another version Itzpapalotl falls into a cactus while chasing one of the Mimixcoa and gets stuck. She is then shot full of arrows and her body burned. The Mimixcoa blackened their faces with her ashes. This shooting of a cactus event marked the beginning of time (Brundage 1983:209; Wake 2007; Yoneda 2007).[45] In the *Historia Tolteca-Chichimeca* the arrowing of a flowering nopal cactus takes place at dawn and marks the emergence of the Chichimec from their cave birthplace (Wake 2007:227, 235). Brundage (1983:209) argues that the slain cactus represents Mimixcoa (stellar ancestors) and sacrificial hearts offered to the sun. Similarly, Bye and Linares (2007:259) suggest the shooting of cactus portrayed in these texts refers to a mythical association with Itzpapalotl, bloodletting to feed the gods, and divination.

Although there is no direct mention of peyote in Nahua creation stories, it is well-known that they revered the cactus both for its medicinal and hallucinogenic properties (Ruiz de Alarcón 1984). They perhaps even hunted it. Davíd Carrasco (2008:235) writes that while "the Huichol are not direct descendants of the noble classes of the Aztecs, the same kind of ritual hunting for peyote was carried out by many Aztec communities." Lack of direct mention of peyote in Nahua mythology may relate to Spanish edicts against its use; more likely, in mythology and iconography it is portrayed metaphorically. What is interesting, however, is that this concept of shooting a cactus in association with creation appears to be represented in the mythologies of these two groups, but is apparently absent outside the Corachol-Aztecan linguistic community.

Narrative Reconstruction

The souls of the Ancestors, who are also deer and stars, emerge from the underworld and proceed to shoot the cactus within which they dwelled. This act of self-sacrifice fuels the sun. The slaying of the deer—the animal associated with drought—releases the rains. This is metaphorically expressed through the shooting of the cactus, which, in response, releases life-giving sustenance in the form of water.

Motif Analysis VIII: Fire, Sun, and Morning Star

To the right of the first Ancestor (A001) and emerging out of the Hill in the East (E001) is a small, antlered human figure (A006) (figure 6.28). Black dots appear at the tip of each of its nine antler tines (figure 6.29a). Unlike the five Ancestors, this small figure has fingers and toes. It also seems to be masked, giving the appearance of having eyes. It is holding an atlatl loaded with a red dart in its right hand and extra darts and a staff in its left hand. Two yellow centipede-like motifs (E039), both impaled, overlay the antlered figure's left arm (figure 6.28 and 6.29b). An elaborate red and black wrist adornment is attached to its right arm, and an elbow adornment hangs from its left arm. All black paint associated with the figure was painted first, followed by red.

The red body of A006 is sandwiched between the

black central portal of the Hill in the East and the yellow paint outlining this crenellated motif. It is also sandwiched between the black and white sinuous lines (E029) interpreted as the Flower Road, cosmic umbilicus, and cord of men. The black portion of the line begins at the far left of the panel and crosses the black body of the first Ancestor (A001) before sliding underneath the body of the small antlered figure.[46] Here, at the figure's heart, the black line stops; the white line, however, begins at the first Ancestor and runs parallel to the black line, continuing over the antlered figure and extending to the opposite end of the panel. The white and black lines run parallel for only a short distance: between the first Ancestor and the antlered figure. Thus the two are united.

Formulating Hypotheses

In chapter 5 I argued the five black and red figures are analogous to Huichol pilgrims reenacting the birth of the sun and acting as the primordial ancestors who provided fire and self-sacrifice to fuel the first sunrise. I also proposed that the elaborate anthropomorphic and enigmatic figures to whom they are connected represent the deities they are transformed into at the dawning of time. In Motif Analysis I, I suggested that these five figures are likewise analogous to Nahua primordial ancestors and penitent fire priests reenacting the birth of the sun during the New Fire Ceremony. They carry the torches blazing with the new fire to the sun god atop the Hill in the East. In the New Fire Ceremony, as in the Huichol pilgrimage, each transforms into one of the ancestral gods who participated in the sacrifice giving birth to the sun. When the priests don their ritual costumes and put on their masks, they take on the faces of gods because they become gods. As Read (1998:147) writes, ". . . it was no longer a person climbing the hill, but Quetzalcoatl or Tlaloc"—or another one of the deities associated with the dawning of time. I turn now to an analysis of these five black-bodied figures, beginning with A001, and their transformation into the deities responsible for creation and the dawn of time.

A001 is connected to A006, the small antlered figure emerging from the Hill in the East. In the preceding chapter I hypothesized that this figure is the graphic

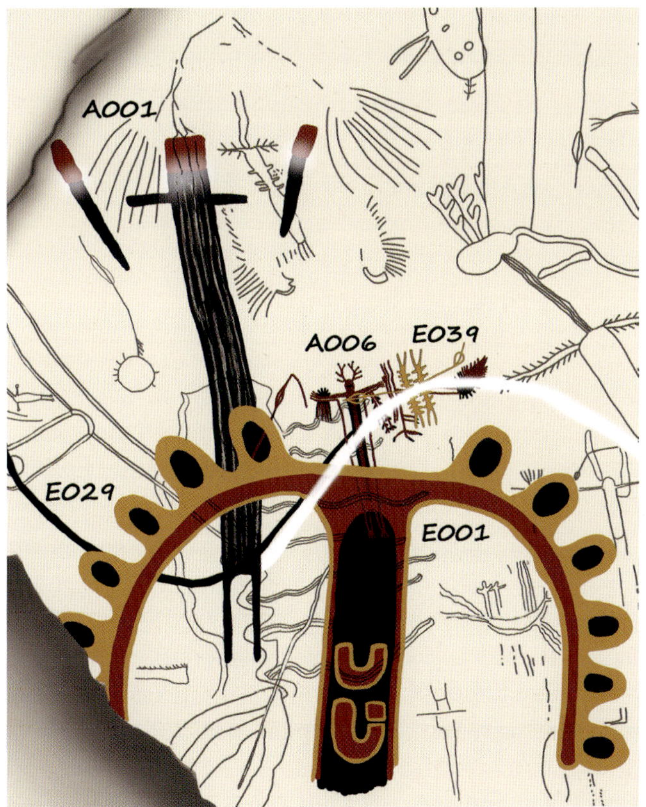

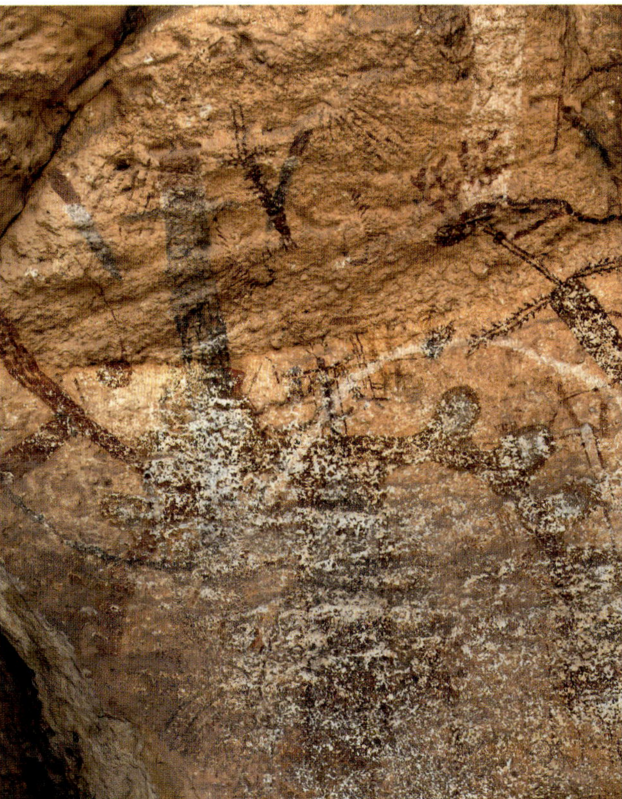

Figure 6.28. Motif VIII (A001 and A006): The divine essences of fire, sun, and Morning Star are fused into the small antlered anthropomorph (A006) emerging from the Hill in the East.

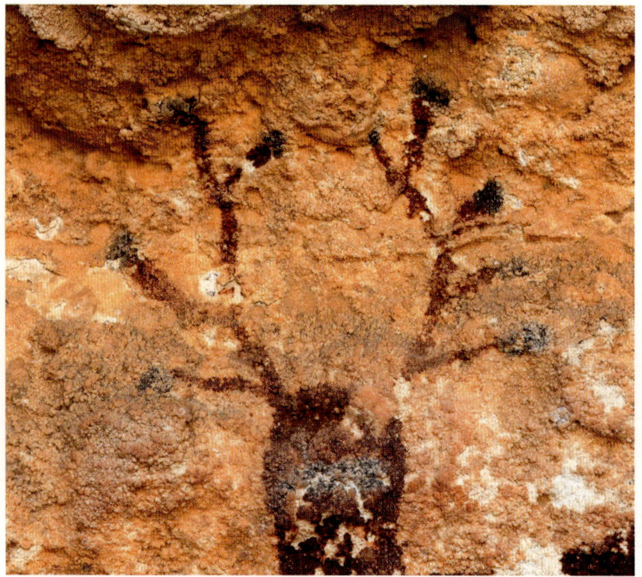

Figure 6.29. Attributes of the Fire-Sun God (A006): (a) The antlers represent the flames of the fire god. The black dots at the tip of each antler tine represent heart-souls of the Ancestors sacrificed upon the pyre of the fire god. (b) Impaled centipedes associated with the figure's left arm are equated with the resurrection of the sun from the underworld and the coming rains.

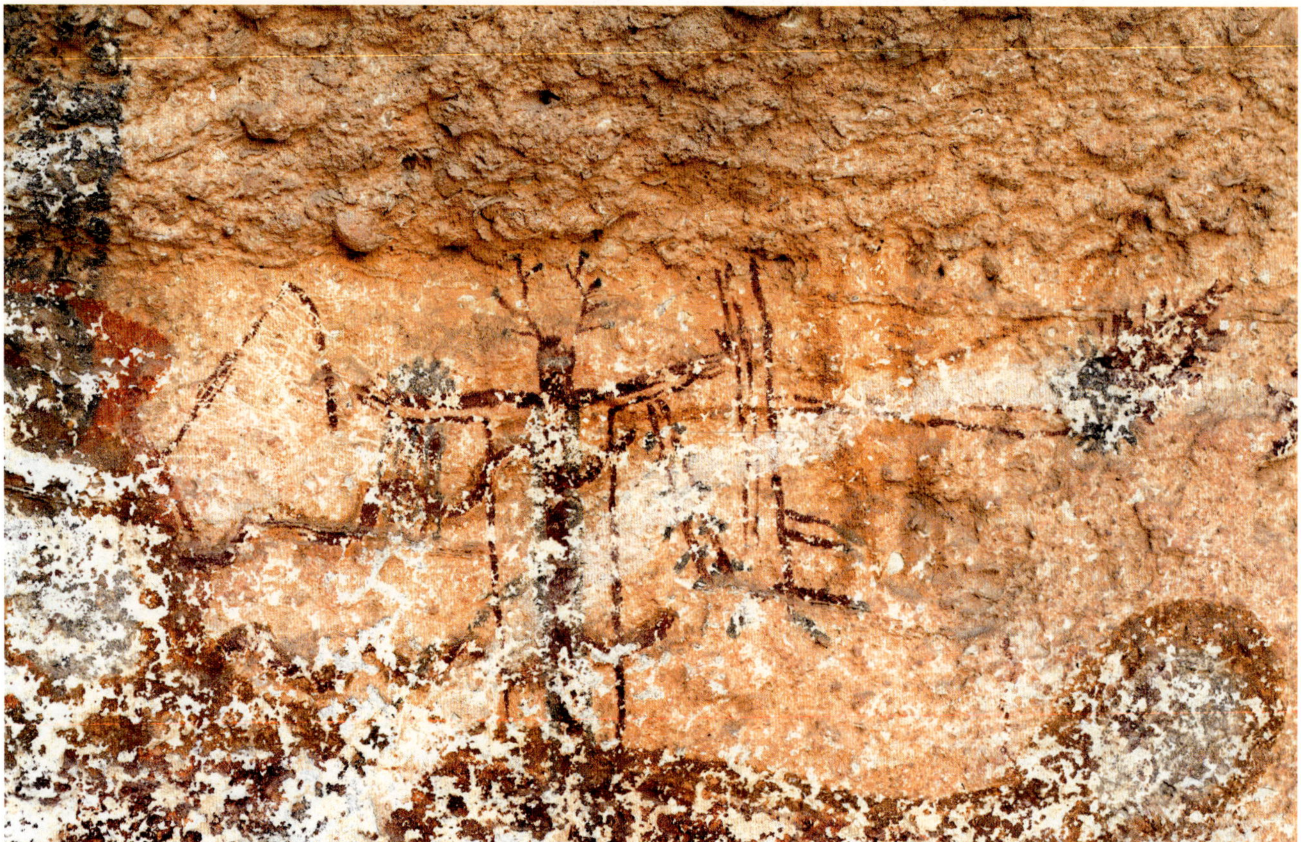

representation of a triune deity—a prototypical fire god, sun god, and deer god (Venus)—who set time into motion. The principal actors involved in the Huichol story are Tatewari, the fire god, and Kauyumari, the divine cultural hero and Venusian deity. Their counterparts in Nahua mythology are the old fire god, Xiuhtecuhtli (or Huehueteotl), and the Venusian deity, Quetzalcoatl.[47] Each hypothetical meaning proposed in chapter 5 for the antlered anthropomorph has a corollary in Nahua mythology and iconography (table 6.8).

God of fire and sun. As do the Huichol, the Nahua divide the cosmos into five world directions (*quincunx*) arranged in a cyclic sequence running east, north, west,

Table 6.8.
Motif Analysis VIII: A001 and the antlered anthropomorph (A006) emerging from the crenellated arch

HUICHOL	NAHUA	HYPOTHETICAL MEANINGS
X	X	Primordial ancestor (A001) transforms into an ancestral deity, the Fire-Sun God (A006), the dawn lord and lord of time.
X	X	Fire god dwells at the center of the earth and serves as an *axis mundi.*
X	X	Fire god is leader and father of all the deities.
X	X	Fire god transforms into the sun to become a fire-sun god.
	X	Fire-sun god puts time into motion and is lord of time.
X	X	Deer antlers denote flames of the fire god.
X	X	Venusian deer-deity retrieves the heart-souls of the Ancestors from the underworld.
X	X	Dots on antler tines denote souls of the Ancestors and water.
X	X	Venusian deity identified with wind, dawn, and deer.
	X	Black mask identifies the figure as a stellar god.
X	X	Venusian deity is a spear-throwing or shooting god.
	X	Nine antler tines are related to water and the underworld, as well as to the fire god, patron of the ninth day.
X	X	Bears centipedes (E039) to denote the rising sun, emergence from the underworld, resurrection, and arrival of rain.

south, and center.[48] Like the fire god of the Huichol, the Nahua fire god dwells at the center and serves as one of the five supports holding up the sky. Sahagún (1829:115) noted that the god of fire abides within the center of the earth among the flowers, which are *paredes almenadas* (crenellated walls) wrapped with rain clouds.[49]

This important deity, the oldest of them all, is also the mother and father of them all. The fire deity is a god of duality—both male and female, black and red, night and day—and is referred to by many different names: Xiuhtecuhtli (lord of fire, lord of time), as well as Huehueteotl (Aged God), Huehue Ilama (Ancient Man, Ancient Woman), Nauhyotecuhtli (Lord of the Group of Four), Teyacancatzin Totecuyo (Our Lord the Venerable Who Guides the Rest), and numerous other appellations (Carrasco 1999a:103; López Austin 1987:274). The old fire god is the principal god of life and, as among the Huichol, the guide of all deities (Carrasco 1999a:103, 104; Seler 1902:14).

In addition to being the god of fire and time, Xiuhtecuhtli is lord of the first hour of the first day, and the first hour of the first night (Boone 2007). It was the power of fire that was transformed into the sun at the dawn of time (Carrasco 1999a:104). When the sun rose, its rays filled the dark, wet world of primordial time with light and warmth; however, after the sun rises, he refuses to move, thus threatening the onset of an eternal dry season. In his elucidation of the *Codex Vaticanus B*, Seler (1903:150, 302) says the deer denotes drought, the dry season, and celestial fire. Xiuhtecuhtli is portrayed in the codices with a deer headdress representing the flames of the fire god (Seler 1903:17, 37) (figure 6.30). Our antlered deity rising from the crenellated Hill in the East, leading the other deities and serving as one of the five pillars, possesses the attributes of this Mesoamerican fire god.

Another attribute linking this figure to both fire and the sun is the yellow centipede-like motif (E039) over-

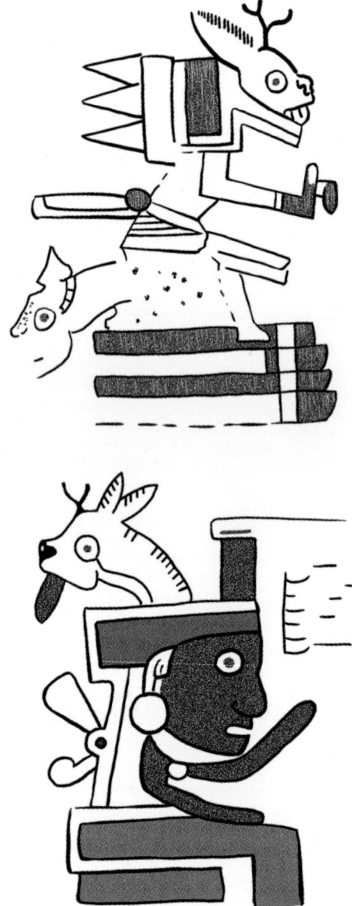

Figure 6.30. God of fire with deer antlers as flames in the *Codex Bologna*: (a) redrawn from Seler 1903:17; (b) redrawn from Seler 1903:34.

laying its left arm. In ancient Mesoamerican thought centipedes were expressions of solar fire and metaphors for entryways into the underworld. They were a "deeply rooted symbol of resurrection and apotheosis" (Looper 2009:211). Interestingly, Paulina Faba Zuleta (2004:59) has demonstrated that among the Huichol, engraved images of centipedes are directly linked with primordial ancestors emerging from the underworld and the birth of the sun. Similarly, among the Maya, centipedes are associated with the daily emergence of the sun from the underworld (Taube 2003:411). Seler (1903:75-76) equates images of centipedes in the codices with the "region or season of drought."

As recounted in *Leyenda de los soles*, the sacrifice of Nanahuatzin (avatar of Quetzalcoatl) puts an end to the perpetual rainy season, but to prevent an eternal dry season requires more sacrifices. The new sun demands to be fed with blood and heart sacrifices in order to move—to commence time as we know it today. The heart is the center of motion, and also where the *yolia*-soul is lodged (J. Furst 1995:17–22). It is the quintessential metaphor for movement, and therefore time (Graulich 1997:131).

In the White Shaman mural the serpentine line is black at the left end of the panel, but at the heart of the fire god—who is also lord of the first hour of the first day, and of the first hour of the first night—the line becomes pure white and continues to the far right end of the mural as an undulating line. As noted earlier, this line represents the ecliptic path of the sun. These two concepts, the beginning of time and the origin of the sun, are inseparably related. Time begins at the heart of the figure identified as the deity associated with putting time into motion, and through the sacrifices of men and gods, the sun is fed and equilibrium is established, alternating between day and night, dry season and rainy season. The white line, as discussed above, represents not only the path of the sun, but also the sustenance rope through which the sun is fed sacrifices. Life-giving sustenance of sacrifice flows from the bound Ancestors to the heart of the fire-sun god portrayed emerging from the Hill in the East.

Morning Star. Just as the Huichol fire god, Tatewari, shares his divine essence with Kauyumari, the Nahua fire god, Xiuhtecuhtli, shares his divine essence with Quetzalcoatl. In 1901, Eduard Seler (1998a:85) identified notable parallels between Kauyumari and Quetzalcoatl.[50] López Austin (1997:248) also has argued for a close connection between the two. In the Huichol story of creation, Kauyumari "put the world into shape" and fought with the people of the underworld to accomplish this creative act (Lumholtz 1900:12). The sacred deer god is associated with the wind, dawn, and the Morning Star/Venus. It was he who, as both sacrifice and sacrificer, shot himself with arrows (the fiery rays of the sun) so that the sun could be born and the rains would come. The parallels to Quetzalcoatl are, indeed, striking.

Quetzalcoatl was one of the creator gods present during primordial times when all was in chaos and darkness. After the watery heavens collapsed upon the earth, he helped to reestablish the firmament by separating the sky from earth and became one of the pillars holding the heavens in place. In *Leyenda de los soles*, Nanahuatzin, an avatar of Quetzalcoatl, sacrifices himself upon the pyre and descends into the underworld before rising in the east as the sun. His sacrifice, like that of Kauyumari, leads to the birth of the sun. Likely due to his ancient heritage, Quetzalcoatl is a multifaceted character with countless avatars and permutations, which can make wrapping one's mind around this important deity incredibly challenging. Brundage describes his efforts, similar to my own, to isolate the deity of Quetzalcoatl in his book *The Phoenix of the Western World.*

> When I began this work, my objective was to present only the god of Quetzalcoatl, the Feathered Serpent, to the reader. I soon found that, even more than most of the other Mesoamerican gods known to us, Quetzalcoatl kept vanishing into the images of the other gods, and those gods into others, and so on in an extensible line. As an example, Quetzalcoatl could become Xolotl, who could become Nanahuatl, who could become the fifth sun, and so on. [Brundage 1982:10]

According to Caso (1988:23), Quetzalcoatl was one of the greatest gods, whose seemingly opposite aspects were synthesized into a single deity: "He was Quetzacóatl, the god of wind, of life, and of the morning star; the planet Venus, god of twins and of monsters; and so on. According to these diverse attributes, he was known by various names: Ehécatl, Quetzacóatl, Tlahuizcalpantecuhtli, Ce Ácatl, Xólotl, etc." And, as with Kauyumari, he has the deer as an animal companion (Ingham 1984:386).

One unusual aspect of the White Shaman mural is that out of the forty-two anthropomorphs portrayed, the antlered deity is one of only three figures holding a loaded atlatl (spear-thrower). Typically, more than 50 percent of Pecos River style anthropomorphs are portrayed with atlatls, so why the discrepancy here? The answer relates back to the myth. Quetzalcoatl, as well as Xiuhtecuhtli, is patron of the ninth day of the *tonalpohualli*, and the ninth day is named *atl*. According to Seler (1902:84), the "*atl* means not only water, but also spear-throwing."[51] This brings us to another avatar of Quetzalcoatl, the divine culture hero Tlahuizcalpantecuhtli, lord of dawn, who sacrifices himself so that the sun will move and the rains will come. He is Quetzalcoatl as the Morning Star. "The Lord of Dawn was a temporary fusion of both gods; both the day represented by Quetzalcoatl and the fire represented by Xiuhtecuhtli were symbolized by the light of dawn. Quetzalcoatl was changed into fire when it was dawn; Xiuhtecuhtli was converted into dawn in the east" (López Austin 1993:150). In *Leyenda de los soles*, the lord of dawn is angered by the new sun's demand for sacrifices. He shoots at the sun but misses. The sun retaliates, "shooting at Tlahuizcalpantecuhtli, and he succeeds in hitting him because his arrows are like shafts of flame" (Bierhorst 1992:149).

In *Codex Fejérváry-Mayer*, Venus is portrayed as the spear-throwing or shooting god (Seler 1902:71). The antlered figure in the mural wielding a red atlatl loaded with a red dart is akin to the lord of dawn, the fusion of the fire god (Xiuhtecuhtli) and Morning Star (Quetzalcoatl). Above him is Venus, who in the guise of a deer sacrifices himself so that the sun will rise and time will be put into motion. For creation is impossible except through sacrifice (Séjourné 1978:59). The threat of eternal drought passes with the slaying of the deer, the emblem of drought and celestial fire. The sun will rise at dawn, but it will also set at dusk, and the rains will return. Both movement and equilibrium are established.

As noted above, the fire god and Morning Star are patrons of the number 9, which is related to the underworld and water. The figure identified as the fusion of these two important deities is adorned with an antler headdress (his flames) bearing nine antler tines. At the tip of each tine/flame is a black dot. In the previous chapter I proposed that the dots represent that which will become peyote: the flowers of Wirikuta. They are the flowery heart-souls of Ancestors (water and stars) retrieved from the underworld by the Huichol deer god and culture hero, Kauyumari. In the Nahua story, Quetzalcoatl battles the forces of the underworld to retrieve the greenstone bones, *chalchiuitl*, of the Ancestors. "*Chalchiuitl*" denotes emerald water, precious fluid, rain, and sacrificial blood (Seler 1902:109, 193), all of which are metaphorically represented by flowers (Hill 1992:130; Séjourné 1978:144–148). In both the Huichol and Nahua accounts, the divine hero brings forth the Ancestors—life-giving emerald water (human souls) from the underworld. Interestingly, in the Nahua calendar the day sign for the rain god, Tlaloc, is the deer. There are numerous parallels between the attributes of the antlered figure (A006) and Tlaloc, the ninth lord of the night. This is not surprising, given the similarities between Quetzalcoatl and Tlaloc. As Brundage (1982:155) writes, in some representations "Quetzalcoatl would seem to be almost a double of Tlaloc in his avatar Nine Rain."

In the mural life-giving water, represented by the nine black dots, is attached to the flaming antlers of the fire-sun god and lord of the dawn, another representation of the union of opposites. Among the Nahua, and arguably throughout Mesoamerica, creation is sparked through the joining of opposing forces. Laurette Séjourné (1978:99) writes, "There is proof that the dynamics of the union of opposites is at the basis of all creation, spiritual as well as material. The body 'buds and flowers' only when the spirit has been through the fire of sacrifice; in the same way the Earth gives fruit only when it is permeated by solar heat, transmuted by rain. That is to say, the creative element is not either heat or water alone, but a balance of the two."

The union of fire and water are expressed in the Nahuatl couplet combining *atl* (water) and *tlachinolli* (burning) (Séjourné (1978.105). *Atl-tlachinolli,* meaning "burning or burnt water," is a metaphor for flowering or blossoming war, and the *atl-tlachinolli* glyph is frequently associated with Quetzalcoatl, lord of dawn (Séjourné 1978:105–111). "Blossoming war" refers to the struggle between matter and spirit, which is fought within the heart of every individual. If matter wins, the spirit is destroyed. If spirit wins, "the body 'flowers' and a new light goes to give power to the sun" (Séjourné 1978:72). *Atl-tlachinolli* is signified by "two divergent currents, one of water, and one of fire—which at last unite . . . all that exists on earth is the result of the active interpenetration of these two opposed elements" (Séjourné 1978:72). In the White Shaman mural the joining of the black dots (souls and water) with the antler tines (flames) of the deity interpreted here as lord of dawn may be a graphic expression of the Nahuatl concept of burning water. It is not insignificant that this graphic couplet—a visual pun—is associated with the deity responsible for putting time into motion, who is shown here emerging from the center of the cosmos.

The Mesoamerican cosmos was conceived of as a series of thirteen celestial layers and nine watery underworlds. The Teotihuacan temple of Quetzalcoatl was modeled on the celestial cosmos and is composed of six superimposed levels. Brundage (1982:55) sees the temple as an expression of Quetzalcoatl's ascent from the eastern horizon and subsequent descent into the west, "as though the sky were a six-terraced mountain." The total number of steps, six on one side and six on the other, equals twelve, but the summit, he suggests, represents "the thirteenth level, called Omeyocan, the Place of the Two." As discussed above, the crenellated mountain from which the antlered deity is emerging has six "steps" on one side and likely six "steps" on the other. If the summit is counted as the thirteenth level, then it too may be a model of the celestial cosmos.

Narrative Reconstruction

The divine essences of fire, sun, and Morning Star are fused into the small antlered anthropomorph emerging from the Hill in the East to initiate time. As fire god he dwells at the center of the universe and serves as an *axis mundi* between the world above and the world below. His flames, graphically portrayed as deer antlers, uphold the sky and sun; attached to his antlers are the souls of the Ancestors, the life-giving waters retrieved from the bowels of the earth. They are the heart-souls sacrificed upon the pyre of the fire god in order to "flower" and give new light to the sun. This ancestral deity is mother and father of all the gods, and the union of all opposites. As Morning Star and lord of dawn, he wields the atlatl used in an act of autosacrifice. Through the slaying of the deer, which is not only his avatar but also a representation of the human soul and Venus, he puts the sun in motion, ensuring the transition from the dry season to the rainy season. He also bears the centipede to denote his resurrection and the completion of his transformation into the sun, and the subsequent arrival of the rains. Through the union of opposites—fire and water—he initiates creation and the beginning of human time, of which he is also the patron god. He is the lord of time.

Motif Analysis IX: Sweeper of the Path of the Sun

To the right of the Hill in the East (E001) is another antlered figure (A007) (figure 6.31). This conflated figure has attributes of a bird, deer, and human. It has winged arms, tail feathers, and, most unusual, two sets of antler racks with a total of sixteen tines. Just above its tail feathers is an easily missed small, oval area devoid of paint. Thin red lines project into the hole, giving the appearance of teeth (figure 6.32). The head of A007 is connected to its body by an extremely long, thin neck. The back of its head is tethered by an enigmatic red and black serpentine shape to a large red dot that terminates in a sharp, needlelike point (E049). Its right arm

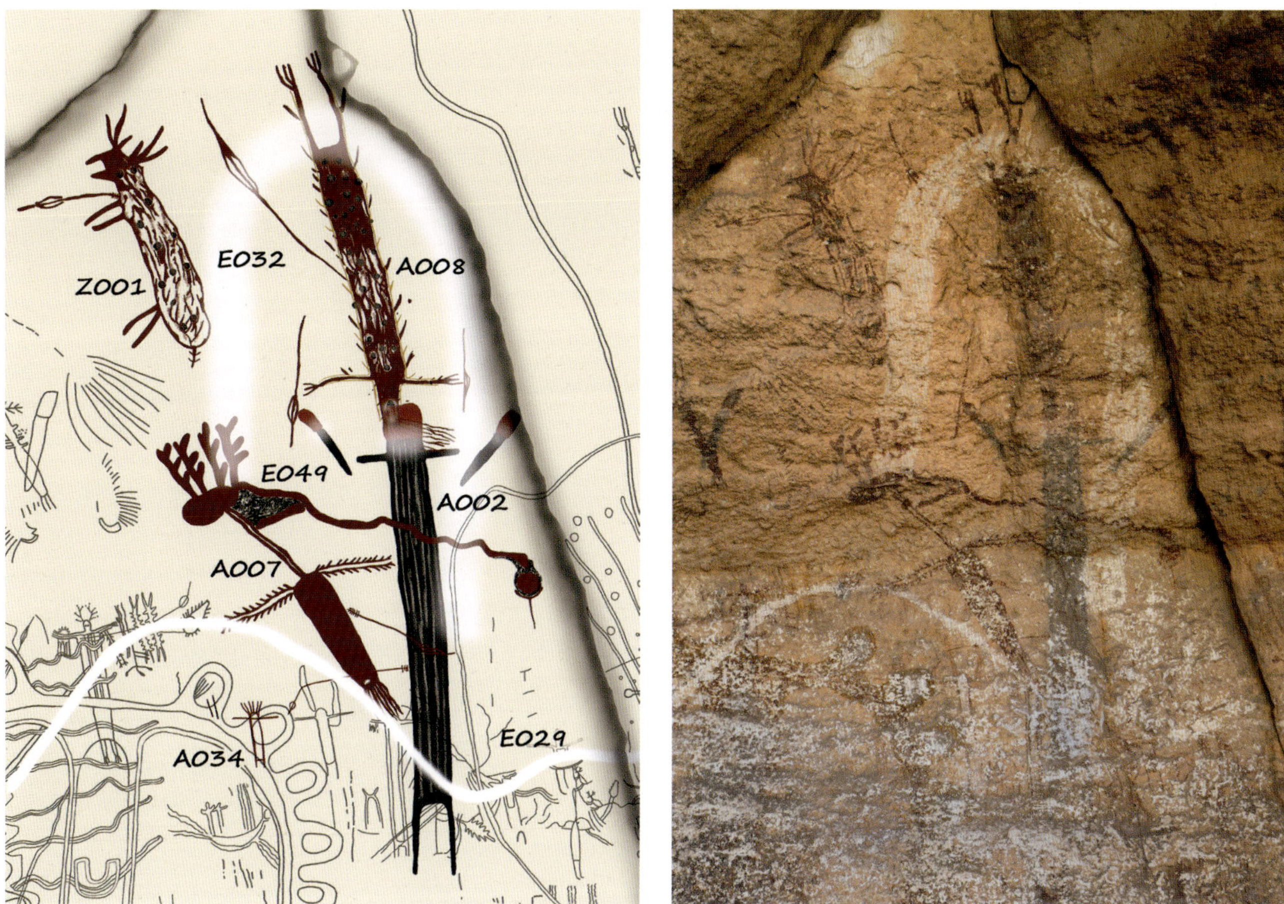

Figure 6.31. Motif IX (A002 and A007): Heralding the dawn of time, this dual-antlered Venusian deity and star demon sweeps along the ecliptic (E029). As both Morning Star and Evening Star, Venus never strays far from the sun.

and tail feathers rest on the sinuous white line (E029) interpreted as the path of the sun and Flower Road. The body of the dual-antlered figure is pierced just under its left arm by a dart with a stylized tip. Another dart, also with a stylized tip, passes through its body immediately above the "toothed" hole. The dart continues past the figure and touches the side of the second Ancestor (A002). It is loaded in an atlatl held in the left hand of a small anthropomorph with ecstatic hair (A034) (figure 6.31). This diminutive figure is sandwiched between the yellow and black solar steps of the Hill in the East.

A broad white band (E032) shoots up from the head of A007, brushing up against the hindquarters of the sacrificial deer interpreted as Venus (Z001). It then arcs, crossing the legs of one of the Mimixcoa-like star deities (A008) whose black-masked face and long, disheveled hair conjoin with the head of the second Ancestor (A002). The white band then plummets downward until it rests gently alongside A002's body; the two forms—the white band and the Ancestor's body—are equal in width. Multiple techniques were used to unite the dual-antlered figure with the second Ancestor, the star demon, the deer, and the small, left-handed anthropomorph wielding the atlatl and dart.

Formulating Hypotheses

In chapter 5 I suggested that A002, the second ancestral figure, takes on the identity of the Venusian deity and archetypical Master of the Deer, Great-Grandfather Deer Tail. This fire god is closely associated with the white-tailed hawk but is represented literally and figuratively by pairs of antler racks. Nahua mythology offers somewhat similar yet vastly more complex analogies for this motif (table 6.9).

The attributes of A007 provide a range of possible interpretations, all of which are in some way linked to Venus and rain. In Nahua mythology all twinning is an expression of the Venusian deity Xolotl, god of twins,

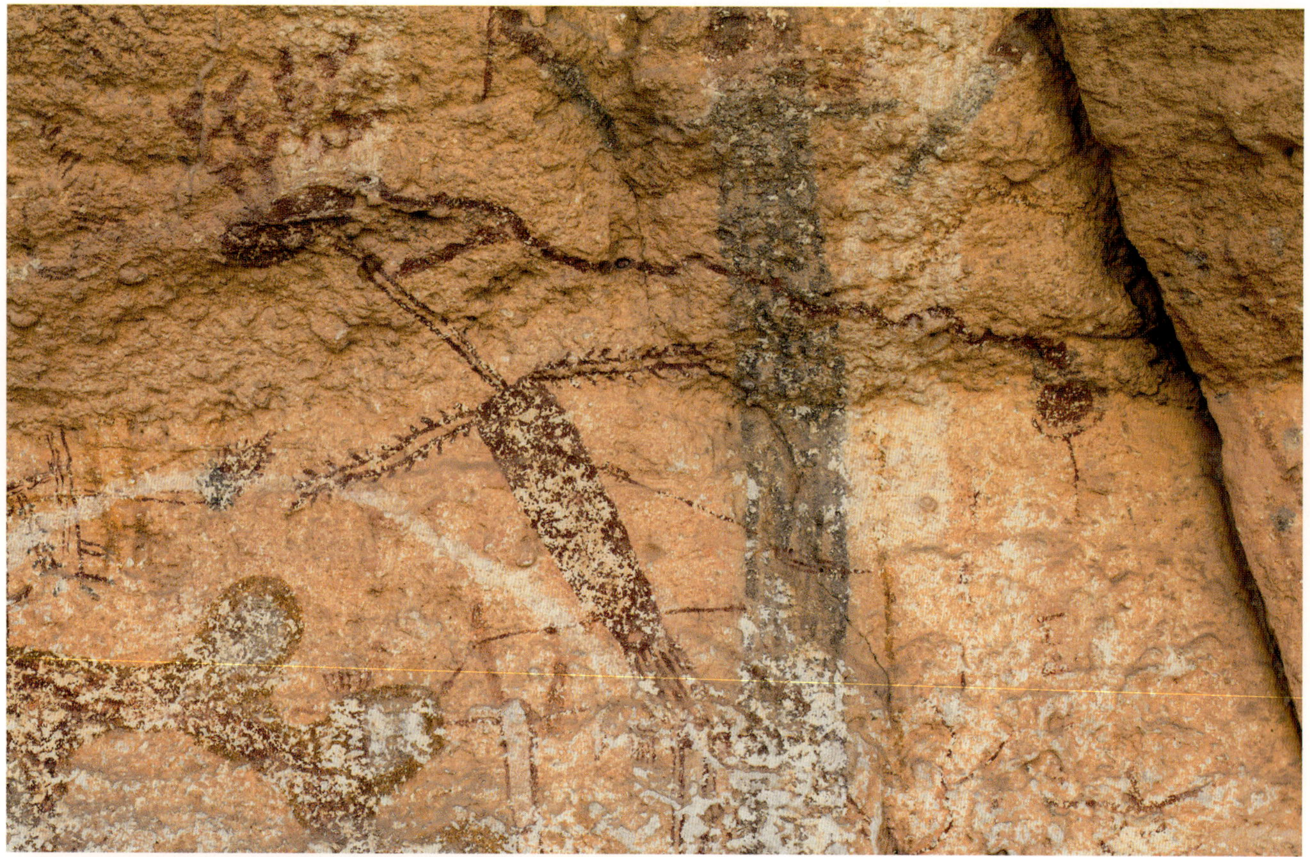

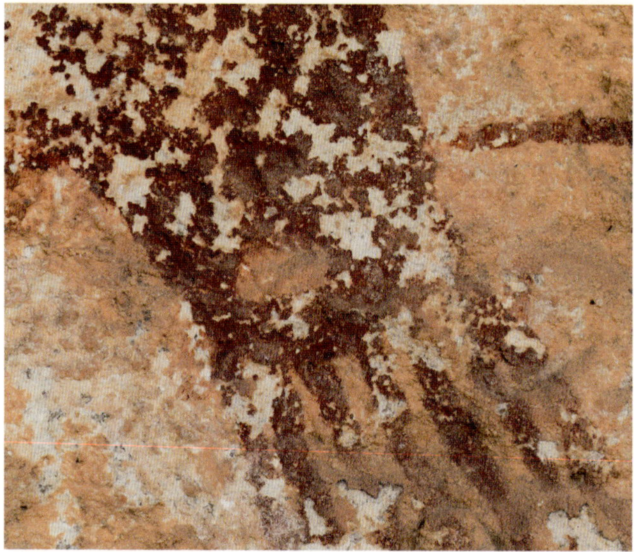

Figure 6.32. This Venusian deity consumes the heart-souls of the deer (stars) at sunrise with her *vagina dentata* and then offers herself, also a deer and a star, in sacrifice to the solar deity.

whose very name translates as "double" or "twin." This is perhaps why, as noted by Seler (1903:271), on sheet 65 of the *Codex Borgia*, "where the God of Twins and all kinds of double formations is represented, one of the thirteen day-counts belonging to this division, that of the deer, is figured with *two antlers*" (emphasis in the original). Twinning or pairing in Nahua mythology relates to the dual nature of the planet Venus. This ambivalent character possesses two identities, Morning Star and Evening Star, yet is one persona (Brundage 1983:205).

In Nahua creation myths it was either Xolotl or Ehectal-Quetzalcoatl, his twin, who compels the sun to move. Ehecatl-Quetzalcoatl, lord of the wind, is one of the many avatars of Venus and Quetzalcoatl (Milbrath 2013:16; Brundage 1982:76). The Nahuatl word for wind is *ehecatl*, and wind is quintessentially an instrument of power used by the highest gods to initiate creation (Boone 2007:174; Brundage 1982:76). In the Nahua creation story the sun is set into motion by the breath of Ehecatl-Quetzalcoatl. He is associated with the beginning of cosmic order and time, and is also the sweeper of the path of the sun (Florescano 1999:25; Sprajc 1992:226; Vogt 1969:316–318). Milbrath (1999:162) notes that Ehecatl-Quetzalcoatl as Venus is portrayed in the codices as descending down a cord that she interprets as the ecliptic.

Table 6.9.
Motif Analysis IX: Primordial ancestor (A002) and the winged, dual-antlered anthropomorph (A007)

HUICHOL	NAHUA	HYPOTHETICAL MEANINGS
X	X	Primordial ancestor (A002) transforms into an ancestral deity, the Venusian deer god/goddess and god/goddess of the hunt (A007).
X	X	A007 is an avatar of the Fire-Sun God (A006).
X	X	God/goddess of the hunt is a Venusian deity associated with both the deer and eagle/hawk.
X	X	Dual antlers (two sets) denote duality of Venus as both Morning Star and Evening Star.
	X	Toothed hole near tail feathers denotes *vagina dentata* of the Venusian goddess.
	X	Sixteen tines on dual antlers denote association with the patron of the sixteenth day, a Venusian, fire, and deer goddess.

The unique combination of two pairs of antlers and bird attributes relates to Mesoamerican Venus and rain symbolism. Ehecatl-Quetzalcoatl, in addition to guiding the sun, also announces the coming of the rains (Aguilar-Moreno 2006:148). According to Sprajc (1992:226), Ehecatl-Quetzalcoatl and the Chicchan rain serpent of the Chorti Maya are "essentially identical deities, having the same conceptual roots." The Chicchan rain deity is also associated with the planet Venus and is described as being half-feathered and half-human, sometimes wearing four horns (Milbrath 1999:36).

In the mural the four-antlered figure sweeping along the path of the sun certainly shares several attributes with this Venusian deity; however, this figure possesses other attributes that must be explored, such as its singularly red color, dart impalement, conjoining with the star demon, and the unique, albeit small and easily overlooked, "toothed hole" located just above the figure's tail feathers. This attribute, in particular, is suggestive of a myth involving Mixcoatl, a Venusian deity and god of the hunt, who is allied with a star demon, Itzpapalotl. She is a female counterpart of Mixcoatl and is portrayed in myth and iconography with attributes of a deer, which is her *nahualli*, and an eagle (Brundage 1983:173). She reportedly consumed the Mimixcoa (deer and stars) with her toothed vagina (Gingerich 1988:220). According to Brundage (1982:170), "only Itzpapalotl is confined to the role of the crepuscular light [light of dawn and dusk] and the redness of blood."[52]

As mentioned earlier, Mixcoatl is considered the father of Quetzalcoatl. There are several versions of the myth involving his role in creation—far too many to reproduce here. In *Historia de los mexicanos por sus pinturas* he captures a two-headed deer that falls from the sky. He takes this two-headed stag as his emblem and proceeds to make war on the Chichimecs (deer and stars) in order to provide food for the sun. In *Leyenda de los soles* we learn the identity of the two-headed deer: Itzpapalotl (Obsidian Butterfly), an earth-moon goddess associated with fire.[53] In this myth the star brothers of Mixcoatl, Xiuhnel and Mimich, are seduced by two bicephalic (two-headed) deer who transform themselves into female star demons (figure 6.33). Xiuhnel falls under the spell of the were-deer and is devoured by her *vagina dentata* (toothed vagina) (Gingerich 1988:220). Mimich, distraught over his brother's death, shoots the star demon after she gets stuck in a thorny cactus. He and the fire lords then burn her body, which turns into flint of different colors. Mixcoatl takes the white flint of the goddess as his emblem. This were-deer and star demon, Itzpapalotl, becomes Mixcoatl's spirit power as he wages war to feed the sun. She eats the hearts of the deer, which were the stars, to feed the sun.

Itzpapalotl is associated with celestial fire and therefore appears as a deer, and according to Graulich (1997:172), "she is bicephalic because she evokes Chantico-Cuaxolotl ('Head of Xolotl' or 'Double Head'), the goddess who lit the fire at the restoration of the

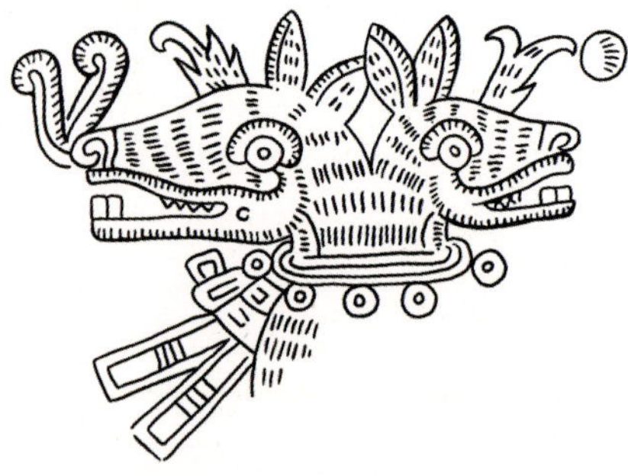

Figure 6.33. Itzpapalotl as a two-headed deer. Redrawn from Seler 1996:38.

world." She is also identified as the deer of Culhuacan, the wife of Mixcoatl, and mother of Quetzalcoatl.[54] In Mesoamerican myth and iconography married couples often represent the male and female aspects of a singular deity (Klein 2001:186).[55] Interestingly, just as Mixcoatl was the first male warrior to die in battle, Itzpapalotl was the first female warrior to be slain (Milbrath 1995:59).

The main actors and events of the myth discussed above offer possible explanations for several attributes of the four-antlered figure (A007). The dual sets of antlers suggest twinning, which is associated with the planet Venus and the deities Xolotl, Ehecatl-Quetzalcoatl, and Mixcoatl. It is Mixcoatl, however, who became a deer and had as his emblem the two-headed stag of Itzpapalotl. A007 is portrayed with two sets of antler racks bearing sixteen tines. As discussed in Motif Analysis VIII, the number of tines is significant. The figure I interpreted as a prototypical fire god and lord of time (A006) is portrayed with a rack of antlers (his flames) possessing exactly nine tines. The Nahuatl fire god, Xiuhtecuhtli, is the patron of the ninth day of the *tonalpohualli*, and the ninth day-sign, *atl* (water). As it turns out, the fire goddess Itzpapalotl is the ruler of the sixteenth day of the *tonalpohualli* and the sixteenth day-sign, vulture (Seler 1902:36).

The star demon aspect of Itzpapalotl offers the possible analogy of a toothed vagina for the hole portrayed in the vaginal region of A007. This may further explain why the upside-down figure interpreted as a star demon is conjoined with the head of the second Ancestor. The white band emerging from the head of the four-antlered figure unites the deer (Z001) and the star demon (A008) with the second Ancestor. And if crepuscular light—the soft, red glow filling the sky when the sun is below the horizon—is uniquely an attribute of this mythical character, she is appropriately located next to the Hill in the East at the dawn of the first sunrise.

With winged arms and distinctive tail feathers, she also represents a bird—but perhaps not just any bird. The type of bird may be communicated in the mural through the use of another visual pun, or visual couplet metaphor. In Nahuatl, "*in aha:ztli in cuitlapilli* 'the wings, the tail' standardly refers metonymically to the eagle" (Maxwell and Hanson 1992:144). Itzpapalotl is portrayed in myth and iconography with the attributes of not only a deer, but an eagle.

Narrative Reconstruction

Heralding in the dawn of time, this four-antlered Venusian deity and star demon is sweeping along the ecliptic (E029), poised to receive the rising sun. As god of twins, Venus—both Morning and Evening Star—never strays far from the sun. With her *vagina dentata*, she consumes the heart-souls of the deer, which are stars, at sunrise and then offers herself, also a deer and a star, in sacrifice to the sun. She/he is the first warrior to die in sacrifice to nourish the sun and put it into motion.

Motif Analysis X: Goddess of the Earth

One of the most striking figures in the White Shaman mural is the large catfish-serpent-like figure (Z003) superimposing the third Ancestor (A003) (figure 6.34). This huge creature appears to be two-headed, with whiskers at each end of its undulating body.[56] One head rests on the white ecliptic line (E029), and its body reaches upward more than twice the height of the Ancestor it superimposes. It is painted in four colors: the creature's back, turned toward the Hill in the East, is red and outlined in yellow. Its underbelly is divided into three segments: one black, one yellow, and one white. Circles devoid of paint are located at the juncture of each color, and emerging from two of the circles is a plume of red, yellow, and black lines (E016 and E017). Attached to the creature's back are three stubby red appendages outlined in yellow with a black dot at each distal end.

Formulating Hypotheses

In the preceding chapter I proposed that this catfish-serpent-like figure represents the prototypical earth goddess. The Huichol refer to her as Utuanaka, an av-

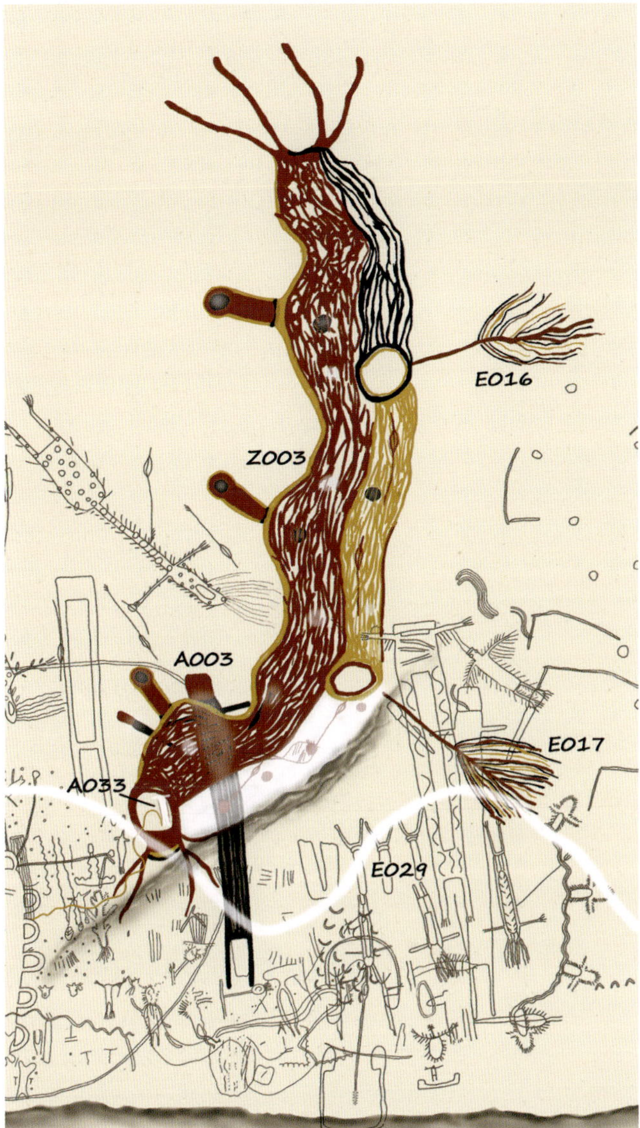

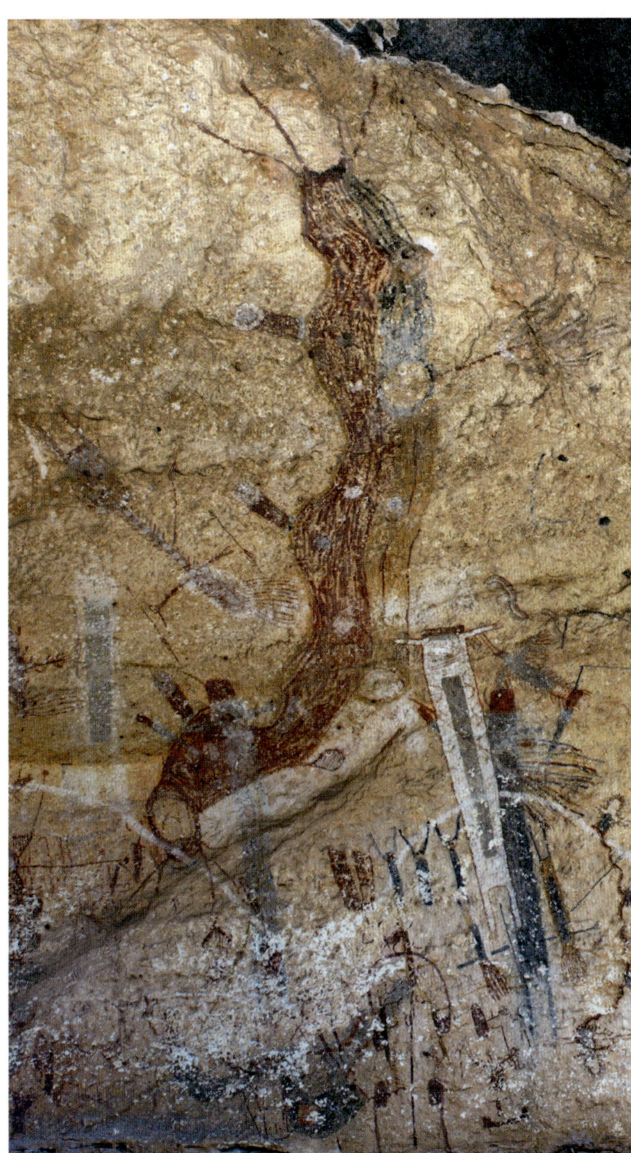

Figure 6.34. Motif X (A003 and Z003): The open mouth of the Earth Goddess (Z003) resting on the ecliptic (E029), ready to receive the sun at the transition from morning to afternoon. The three hearthstones of creation (stellar Ancestors) are established upon her back. Photo by Jean Clottes. Courtesy of Shumla Archaeological Research and Education Center.

atar of Tacutsi Nakawé, Great-Grandmother Growth—the mother of all female deities and, in some accounts, mother of all the gods. Tacutsi Nakawé is a goddess of both the earth and the moon. As earth goddess she is envisioned as the conflation of a catfish and a snake. As among the Huichol, the Nahua earth goddess is simultaneously multiple deities unfolding into a long line of avatars, including both the earth and moon deities (López Austin 1997:229, 230).[57] Also like Tacutsi Nakawé, the Nahua earth-moon deity manifests both female and male attributes, and those ascribed to Huichol and Nahua earth deities are notably similar. At the core each hypothetical meaning proposed in chapter 4 for Z003 has a corollary in Nahua accounts of this important deity (table 6.10).

According to *Historia de los mexicanos por sus pinturas,* the gods created a great fish called Cipactli and placed this beast in the primordial waters. From Cipactli's body they made the earth, which they named Tlaltecuhtli (or, in other accounts, Tlalteotl). This dual-gendered deity, who is referred to by numerous names, is sometimes envisioned as a male, but usually as a female (Klein 2001). In the creation myth recounted in *Histoire du Méchique,* Cipactli is a terrifying aquatic

Table 6.10.
Motif Analysis X: A003 and the catfish-serpent-like figure (Z003)

HUICHOL	NAHUA	HYPOTHETICAL MEANINGS
X	X	Primordial ancestor (A003) transforms into an ancestral deity, Earth Goddess (Z003).
X	X	Earth goddess associated with the underworld, night, the rainy season, and summer solstice.
X	X	Morphology denotes a bicephalous conflation of a serpent and catfish.
X	X	Colors of Z003 denote the four directions.
X	X	Circles denote junctures of the directions and portals between realms.
	X	Three appendages along the back of Z003 represent the three hearthstones of creation.
X	X	Plumelike motifs emerging from circles and impaled dots denote life-giving sustenance born from her segmented body.

beast with eyes and vicious biting mouths at each of her joints. Quetzalcoatl and Tezcatlipoca decide that creation cannot be completed with such a horrendous beast around, so they transform themselves into two giant serpents, and, working together, they split her body right down the middle. From her back they make the earth, and from her front they make the sky (López Austin 1997:14). All vegetation is then born from her segmented body.[58]

Three hearthstones were established at creation to raise the earth above the fires of the underworld, and the sky above the primordial sea. In the *Codex Chimalpopoca*, Itzpapalotl is credited with establishing these three hearthstones, whom she names Mixcoatl, Tozpan, and Ihuitl. The three stones—who are also stellar Ancestors—center the four-cornered universe and guard the fire god (Bierhorst 1992:23). This concept

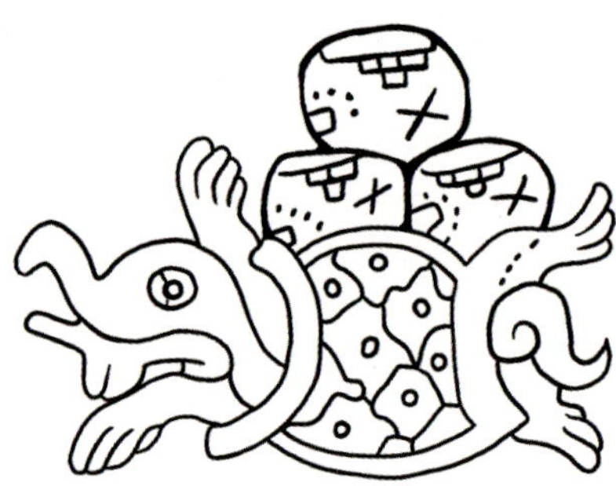

Figure 6.35. The three hearthstones of creation as depicted in the *Madrid Codex*. Redrawn from Freidel et al. 1993:82.

was especially prevalent in Maya cosmology. Freidel et al. (1993:67) determined that "these three stones of Creation are symbolic prototypes for the hearthstones used in Maya homes for over three millennia." In Maya iconography three stones or stars portrayed on a turtle's back illustrate the three hearthstones established on the back of the earth-creature (figure 6.35). The catfish-serpent-like figure interpreted here as the earth goddess (Z003) is portrayed with three stubby appendages attached to its back. At the end of each appendage is a large black dot reminiscent of the three hearthstones (stellar Ancestors) put in place at creation to support the earth and center the cosmos.

This Mesoamerican earth deity is variously conceived in myth and iconography with numerous faces and powers (López Austin 1997:229). Most often it is described as having the attributes of a monstrous reptile, a fish, or a combination of the two, and often with two heads. López Austin (1997:234) notes that "it is very common in Mesoamerican iconography to represent the Mother goddesses, and especially the earth goddess, as a two-headed serpent." In the *Codex Selden Roll*, the earth goddess is portrayed with large gaping jaws. Attached to her jaws are what Mautner (2012:259–260) has interpreted as "fangs or the drooping whiskers (called *bigoteras* in Spanish) of a water deity." The great goddess is often portrayed in dorsal view with her head upturned to confront the viewer (Carrasco 1995a:443), or, as in the *Telleriano Remensis*, she is rendered as a vo-

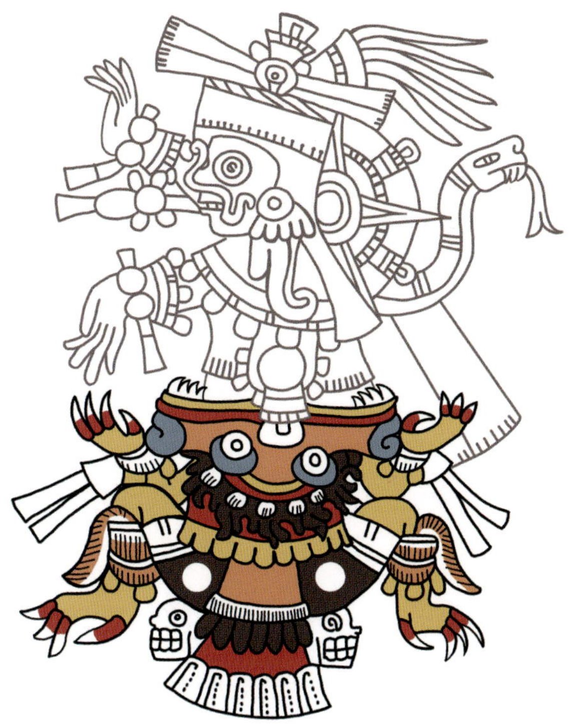

Figure 6.36. Earth Monster swallowing the solar deity. Redrawn from *Telleriano-Remensis* 20r (see Quiñones Keber 1995).

racious monster with her fanged mouth gaping wide to swallow the sun (Read and Gonzalez 2000:172) (figure 6.36).

The imposing zoomorphic figure dividing the mural vertically shares many attributes with the Mesoamerican earth goddess. She has drooping, catfish-like whiskers at both ends of her long, sinuous body, imparting an impression that she is an aquatic beast with two heads. Her cavernous mouth rests on the ecliptic as though awaiting the sun's arrival. She waits in readiness to consume the solar light as it makes its journey across the sky. But the similarities between the Lower Pecos and Mesoamerican deities do not stop there.

The body of the earth goddess (Z003) is painted in four colors: red, yellow, black, and white. In Mesoamerica, as in other parts of the world, the four cardinal directions of the earth are associated with colors. The most common of these color schemes, and apparently the earliest known, is red/east, black/west, white/north, and yellow/south (DeBoer 2005:74; MacLaury 1997). This is the color/direction scheme of the Maya, and according to Thompson (1934) and DeBoer (2005:82) it was most likely the color/direction scheme of the ancient Nahua as well.

The colors of the earth goddess are organized in typical Mesoamerican fashion. Elizabeth Boone (2007:113) explains that "the painted directional almanacs almost always refer to the four directions—east, north, south, west, generally in that order." In Mesoamerica and the American Southwest, color circuits and time sequences are typically read counter-clockwise (Boone 2007:68; DeBoer 2005:74; Edgerton 2001:305). Thus, beginning at red and moving counter-clockwise around the earth goddess in the mural, the color sequence goes east (red), north (white), south (yellow), and west (black), a seemingly odd sequence to us, yet identical to that found in the Nahua directional almanacs.

At the juncture of each color/direction is a large empty circle. This attribute also has a corollary in Nahua myth and iconography. In *Historia de los mexicanos por sus pinturas* the fourth sun is destroyed when it rains so much that the heavens fall down upon earth. The four sons of the creator couple decide to hollow out roads to the center of Cipactli in order to separate the celestial and terrestrial realms. The world was thus divided into four quarters, with a fifth "quarter" placed at the center of the cosmos. The first sheet of the *Codex Fejérváry-Mayer* presents this Mesoamerican cosmogony pictographically (figure 6.37). The fire god is portrayed in the middle of the world. Four streams of blood radiate from him toward four quadrants, each representing a cardinal direction. Also radiating outward from the center are intercardinal loops, and at the end of each loop is a circle. These circles represent the juncture of cardinal directions. Gods and other supernatural beings and forces are believed to enter the earth through portals at the four edges of the world (Carrasco 1998:67). Time is joined with space through the cardinal and intercardinal directions (Boone 2007:13). In the White Shaman mural the circles placed at each color juncture of the earth goddess may represent portals: directional junctures through which supernatural beings and forces travel, and time and space are joined.

Following that line of thought, if red represents east and white represents north, then the circle forming the monster's mouth is the juncture of these two directions, the intercardinal direction of northeast. According to Thompson (1934:222–225) and Klein (1976:2), the Nahua associated east with sunrise and north with noon. The juncture of east (red) and north (white), then, is not only the location of northeast but the transition point between morning and afternoon. The an-

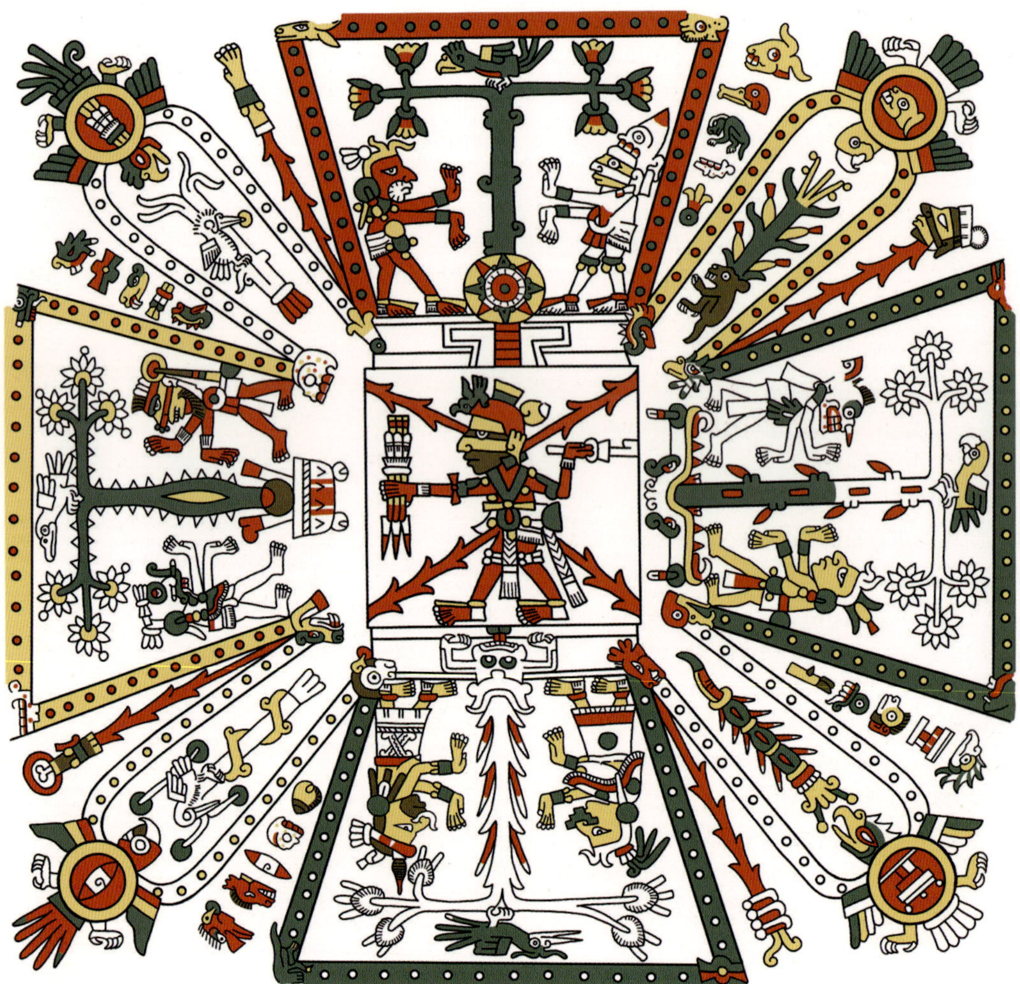

Figure 6.37. Mesoamerican cosmogony. Redrawn from the first page of the *Codex Fejérváry-Mayer.*

cient Nahua believed that "the sun rises in the morning, traverses till midday, and then returns to the east in order to start again, and that which is visible from noon till sunset is its brightness, and not the sun itself" (Phillips 1884:619). The afternoon sun is a "false" sun with characteristics of both the sun and the moon (Graulich 1997:61).

In Mesoamerica a single day, with its transition from sunrise to sunset, provides a model for a year and also for an era (Graulich 1997:265). As previously discussed, each Mesoamerican era was referred to as a "sun." In the tropics, solar zenith passage occurs at high noon, when the sun is directly overhead as it passes from the eastern to the western half of the sky. Aveni and Hartung (1981:52) note that the passage of the sun across the zenith is the moment "when all objects are rendered shadowless," and for ancient Mesoamericans, it symbolically represented the annual passage between the dry season and rainy season. Architecturally this was manifested in human-made vertical shaft features such as those at the archaeological sites of Xochicalco and Monte Alban. These vertical shafts have been interpreted as "zenith tubes" that were "deliberately designed to receive the solar image and pass it vertically into a darkened chamber" (Aveni and Hartung 1981:53). These "tubes" join space and time, capturing the sun's light when it reaches zenith. In the mural the open mouth of the earth goddess receives the sun at the transition from morning to afternoon and funnels it through her body, much like a zenith tube. The solar deity is transferred from the eastern morning sky to the western afternoon sky, where it will continue its course until sunset as the moon—a "false sun," a "lunar sun." Interestingly, in the mouth of the earth goddess there is a poorly preserved white anthropomorph (A033) outlined in red (figure 6.34). Its staff and netlike paraphernalia are barely visible inside the white underbelly of the goddess.

Zelia Nuttall (1901:38) writes that "it can be absolutely proven that the Mexican philosophers divided the heavens into two imaginary portions, and respectively identified these with the male and the female." The catfish-serpent-like figure (Z003) divides the heavens in half. From the perspective of the ancestral figures engaged in the cosmic drama portrayed in the mural, east is to the right (panel left) and west is to the left (panel right). The body of Z003 is also divided vertically. Its back is painted red and faces east, the color and direction associated with sunrise and the souls of male Ancestors. Its underbelly is painted white, yellow, and black and faces west.

Narrative Reconstruction

Represented in the eastern half of the panel are the upside-down figures interpreted as souls of male Ancestors who died in sacrifice to the sun. They are the star demons who herald the sun's rising and travel with him until reaching the zenith. The sun emerges from the Hill in the East and travels along the ecliptic escorted by these stellar Ancestors until reaching the mouth of the earth goddess. Here the sun passes through her body to emerge in the afternoon, in the western sky, as the moon, the lunar sun. This also marks the onset of the rains at the summer solstice and the transition into the nighttime of the year.

Motif Analysis XI: Moon Goddess

To the left (panel right) of the third Ancestor (A003) and superimposing the yellow underbelly of the earth goddess (Z003) is the arm of a white, humanlike figure (A015) (figure 6.38). It is outlined in red and has a wide, grayish-black band running vertically along its interior. Thin, red S-shaped lines run up and down either side of the black central band, and above it is a series of red parallel lines. The figure has no head; instead, it is capped by a slender band of red paint. This headless anthropomorph wields in its left hand two bicolored (red and black) S-shaped objects. In its right hand, although obscured by the earth goddess's body, is another

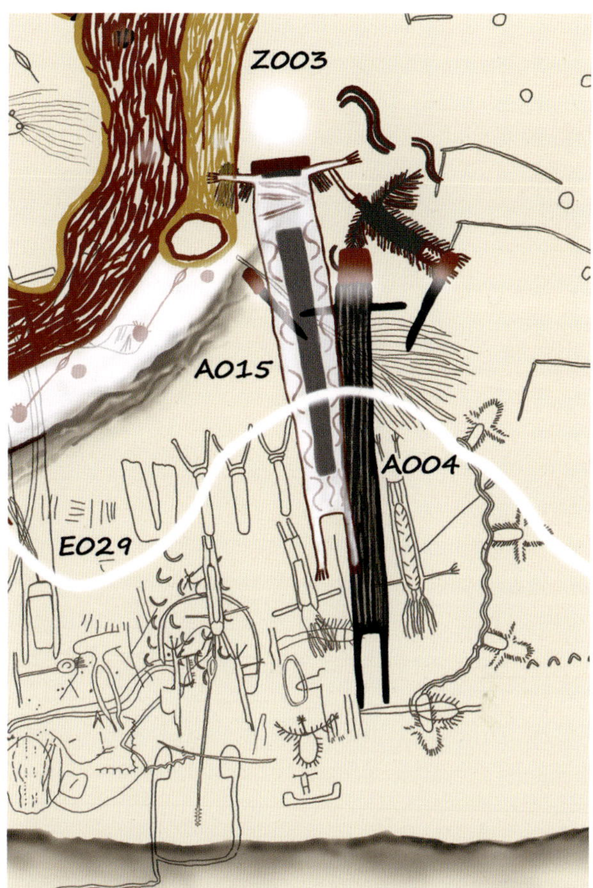

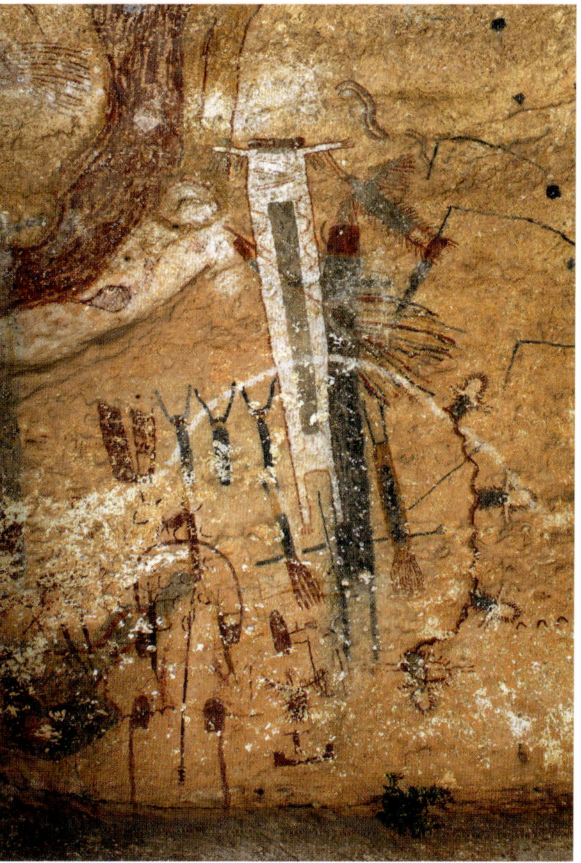

Figure 6.38. *(right)* Motif XI (A004 and A015): The white, headless Moon Goddess (A015) adorned with S-shaped *xonecuilli*, a symbol of rain, is positioned to take over as the Lunar Sun at midday. Photo by Jean Clottes. Courtesy of Shumla Archaeological Research and Education Center.

red S-shape. Attached to its left arm is a black human-bird conflation with red eyes, its entire body adorned with long red and black feathers. S-shaped objects are also associated with both "hands" of the winged figure. Attached to the white anthropomorph's right arm is a wrist adornment similar to the one on the antlered figure identified as the fire-sun god emerging from the Hill in the East. In keeping with the rule governing the order in which paint was applied, the red and black wrist adornment is overlain by the yellow underbelly of the earth goddess, but the figure's white arm overlays the yellow, thereby interweaving the two. Above the white anthropomorph is a circular area of what appears to be white paint, but it is very faint.

At least four layers of black paint were applied to the White Shaman mural before any other colors were added. The black band of the white anthropomorph, which is actually more of a dark gray color, appears to represent the deepest layer and may have been the first paint applied to the wall. The second layer of black is the arm of the fourth Ancestor (A004), which superimposes the dark gray band of A015. When the red outline and white paint of A015 were added, the arm of A004 became sandwiched between the dark gray central band and the red and white paint of A015. The two figures, A004 and A015, are thus interwoven, as are the white anthropomorph (A015) and the figure interpreted as an earth goddess (Z003).

Formulating Hypotheses

In the previous chapter I proposed that the white figure popularly known as "the White Shaman" is a prototypical moon goddess associated with the west and the winter solstice. The attributes that this figure shares with Mesoamerica moon goddesses (and gods) are stunning (table 6.11). One of the most distinctive attributes, their color, is explained in the story of the birth of the sun and moon (Phillips 1884:622).

The story goes that in the thirteenth year of the second cycle of thirteen, twenty-six years after the great flood, the gods agree to make the sun. Quetzalcoatl heats his son in a great fire from which he arises as a red, hot sun to illuminate the earth. After the fire dies out, Tlaloc, the god of rain and water, throws his son into the cinders. He arises from the ashes as the moon, and this is why it appears ashy colored. Mesoamerican lunar deities are commonly described as white or the color of the ashes from which the moon arose at creation. For example, Cihuacoatl (Snake Woman) is a lunar deity described by Sahagún's informants as "covered in white . . . She was in white, having garbed herself in white, in pure white" (Sahagún 1950–1982, bk. 1:3). Graulich (1997:98) notes that one of the sky-bearers who was put in place at creation to maintain the separation of the heavens from the earth is a lunar deity named Tenexxochitl, which translates as "Lime Flower" or "Ash Flower." The name comes from the Nahuatl

Table 6.11.
Motif Analysis XI: A004 and the headless white anthropomorph (A015)

HUICHOL	NAHUA	HYPOTHETICAL MEANINGS
X	X	Primordial ancestor (A004) transforms into an ancestral deity, the Moon Goddess (A015).
X	X	Moon goddess is avatar of earth goddess.
X	X	Associated with underworld, night, rain, and the winter solstice.
X	X	White is the color attributed to the moon goddess.
	X	Moon goddess is decapitated.
X	X	S-shaped lines in her hands and decorating her body denote serpents, rain, and sacrificial blood.
X	X	Moon goddess was responsible for saving humanity from the flood by providing a hollowed out tree or canoe.

word for limestone *(tenextetl)*, which Sahagún's informants described as being "very white."

The headless figure in the rock art, however, is not only white. She is portrayed with S-shaped red lines running vertically down the interior of her white body and S-shaped objects in each hand. In Mesoamerica, S-shaped and undulating lines are associated with serpents, which in turn symbolize lightning, clouds, and rain (Reilly 1996; Seler 1903:306; Taube 2010b:95;).[59] At the core they represent fecundity and "sacrificial blood, the mythic equivalent of rain" (Markman and Markman 1989:30).[60] Sahagún (1950–1982, bk. 1:6, 13) describes a ceremony in which the priests adorn themselves with various items made from amaranth dough.[61] One of the designs, called *xonecuilli*, is in the form of an S and covered with red amaranth or red feathers (Carrasco 1995b:9). Seler (1998a:97) argues that the Nahua *xonecuilli* is identical in form and function to the S-shape dough cakes made by the Huichol as an offering to the female deities who control rain (figure 6.39).

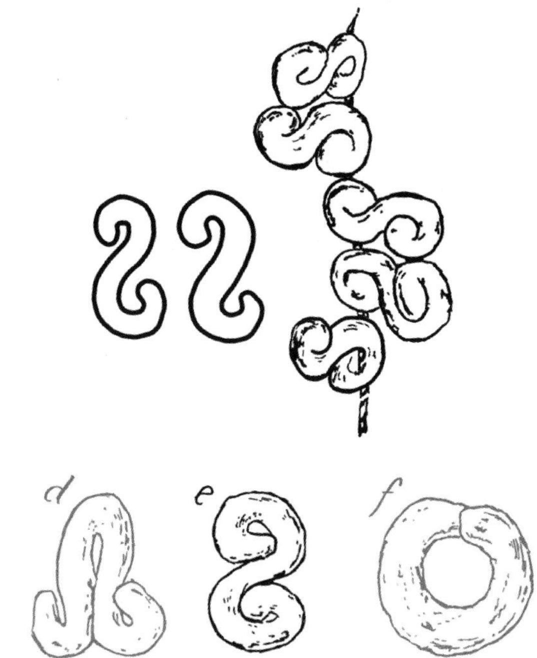

Figure 6.39. S-shaped dough cakes used in rain ceremonies: (a) Nahua "cakes" made into S-shaped *xonecuilli*. Redrawn from Seler 1998a:97. (b) Huichol S-shaped "cakes" resembling *xonecuilli*. Redrawn from Seler 1998a:97.

S-shaped weapons such as those wielded by the moon goddess in the White Shaman mural are portrayed in the codices as well. These have been interpreted as ceremonial atlatls representing lightning, serpents, and the constellation Ursa Major (Olivier 2003:206).[62] Ursa Major is associated with the lunar deity Tezcatlipoca, who is often portrayed brandishing the *xonecuilli* (Olivier 2003:266). In the Nahua flood myth, Tezcatlipoca (or his avatar Titlacahuan) command Tata and Nene to hollow out a tree and save themselves from the rising waters (Bierhorst 1992:143).

The names and iconographic representations of moon goddesses such as Coatlicue (Serpent Skirt) and Cihuacoatl (Snake Woman) attest to a close relationship between snakes and the moon. These deities are often portrayed headless, and their bodies adorned with snakes. They are so intimately associated with rain and water that the moon is envisioned as a vessel containing an invisible liquid that regulates the water on earth (Hooft 2007:137).[63] The S-shaped lines running along the body of the lunar deity in the mural may represent serpents, sacrificial blood, and rain.

The portrayal of this figure without a head further identifies her as a lunar deity and puts her at the front of a whole progeny of decapitated moon goddesses. Indeed, she may well represent the earliest surviving iconographically depicted moon goddess in all of North America. The goddess of the moon and her attendant lunar deities are often portrayed as decapitated in Mesoamerican mythology and iconography (Milbrath 1997). According to Elizabeth Boone (2007:36), artists of the *Codex Borgia* signified decapitation by painting a red band at the base of the neck to indicate where the head was severed (figure 6.40). The moon goddess in the White Shaman mural not only lacks a head, but has a narrow red band painted across her "neck"; she, too, wears the bloody "scarf" signifying decapitation. Above the red band, but detached from the body, is a large, nebulous circle of white paint resembling a moon.

We have observed a very interesting phenomenon involving this figure at sunset on winter solstices. As the sun descends into the west on this shortest day of the year, it casts a shadow on the mural that stops abruptly at the red scarf of the moon goddess (figure 6.41). Through an interplay of light and shadow, she is decapitated, thus marking the end of her reign as ruler over the nighttime of the year.

Why are lunar deities decapitated? Nobody really knows for sure (see López Austin 1997:236), but a range of possible explanations have been offered. Cecilia Klein (2008:243-244) proposes that Nahua moon goddesses are depicted as headless because Coatlicue and her four sisters (all lunar deities) sacrificed themselves upon creation so the sun would move. Milbrath (1997:185) argues that decapitation imagery in art and myth metaphorically represents lunar phases, eclipse events, and seasonal cycles. Metaphorically, the moon rules over the rainy season, and the sun rules over the dry season (Milbrath 1997:191).[64]

Narrative Reconstruction

The white moon goddess is positioned to take over as the lunar sun at midday, becoming governess of the nighttime of the year at the summer solstice. She rules until she is beheaded at the winter solstice, when the sun takes over and the days get longer. As ruler of the rainy season her body is adorned with symbols of rain, and she brandishes the S-shaped paraphernalia representing lightning, serpents, rain, and blood sacrifice. It is not the moon goddess, however, who plunges into the western horizon at dusk; it is one of her avatars, the Lunar/Setting Sun.

Motif Analysis XII: The Lunar Sun and a Stellar Sacrifice

The fifth and final Ancestor (A005) and its deity avatar (A013) are located on the far right end of the panel (figure 6.42). A005 is surrounded by approximately thirty-two black dots and thirteen enigmatic L-shapes (E010). The black dots and L-shapes were applied after the black

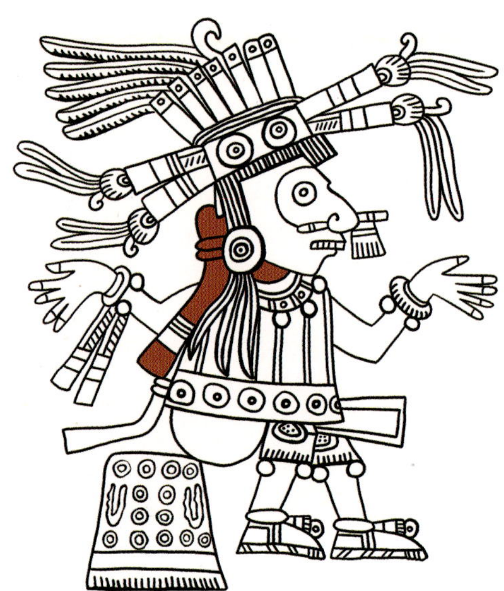

Figure 6.40. Red scarf denoting decapitation. Redrawn from *Codex Borgia* 69 (see Díaz and Rodgers 1993).

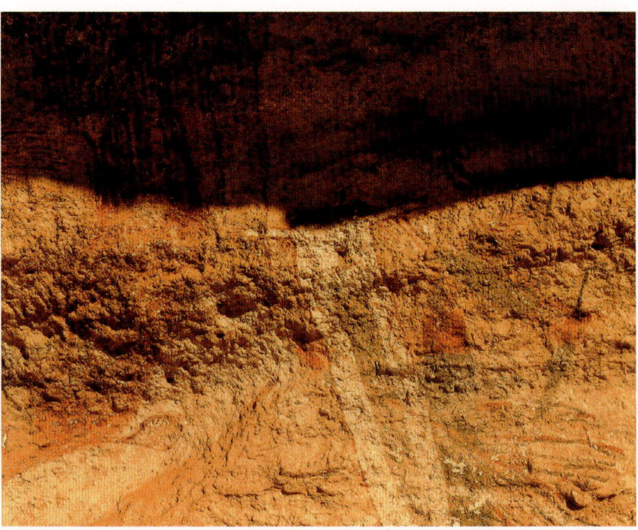

Figure 6.41. Decapitation of the Moon Goddess (A015) on the winter solstice.

body of A005, but before the red body of A013. One of the black dots, interpreted above as stars, was converted into the face or mask of a red, vertically striped anthropomorph (A013) (figure 6.43). This humanlike figure is upside-down and impaled by a dart in its left side. Surrounding the black mask is a vibrant yellow disk divided by fine red lines radiating outward like spokes on a wheel (figure 6.44). The red body of this inverted figure superimposes the torch and right arm of the fifth Ancestor, whose legs are completely obscured by a horizontal red band outlined in black (E007). I interpreted this motif above as the Land of Black and Red, the place where the blackness of night overcomes the red of the sun. At sunset on summer solstices, light from the setting sun collapses on the Land of Black and Red, leaving the rest of the mural in shadow. The same phenomenon occurs on the winter solstice with the setting of a full moon (figure 6.45).

Formulating Hypotheses

In chapter 5 I proposed that this section of the mural portrays the transformation of the fifth Ancestor (A005) into the prototypical god of the setting sun (A013), known to the Huichol as Sakaimoka, Snarer of the Deer, patron deity of the deer hunt. He is sometimes portrayed with a ring representing a deer snare encircling his head.[65] The yellow ring surrounding the black face of A013 is analogous to a deer snare and also a *nierika*, an instrument for seeing that which was before

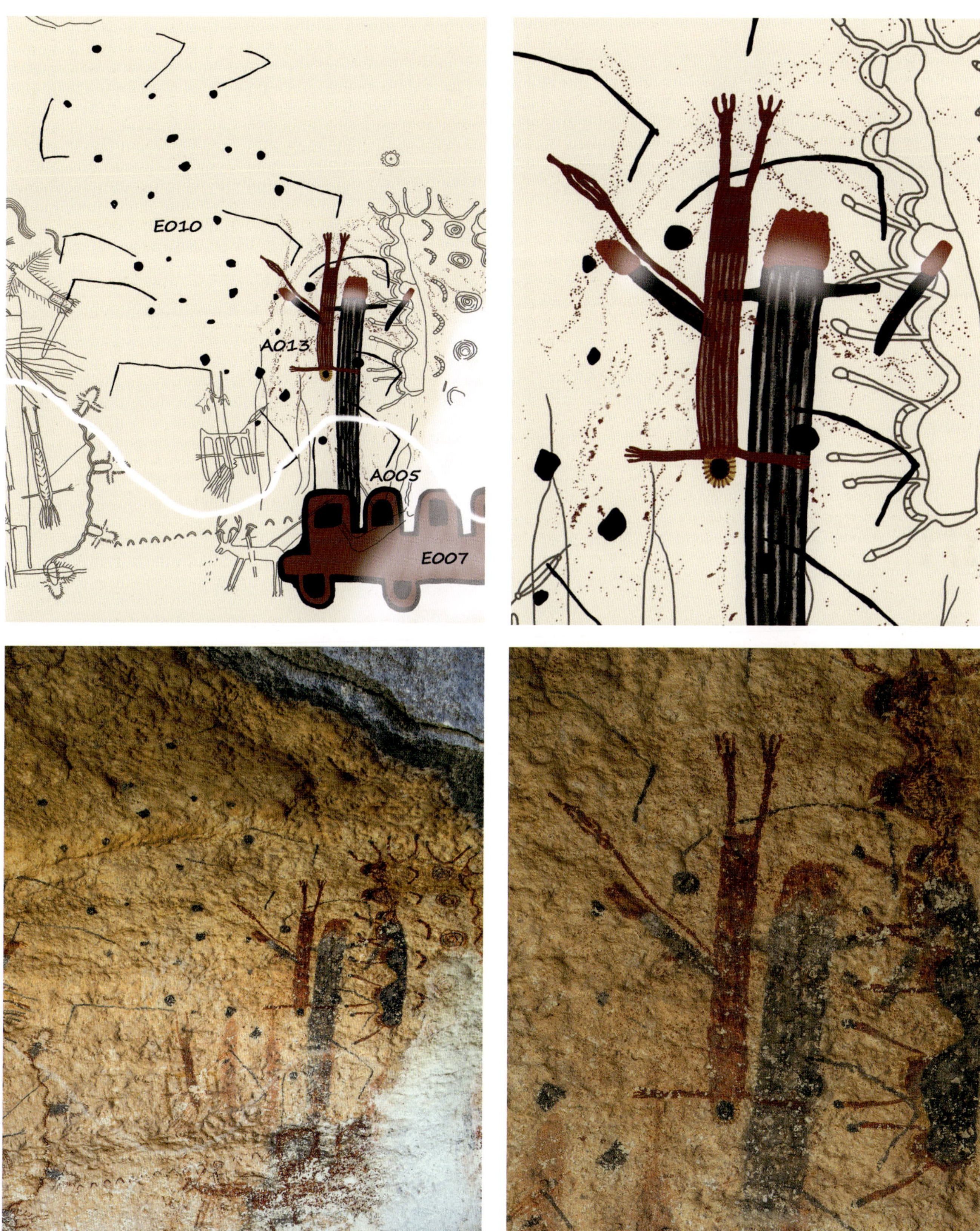

Figure 6.42. Motif XII (A005 and A013): Setting Sun is joined by a multitude of stars (E010) as he descends into the underworld (E007).

Figure 6.43. The figure's black mask and red-striped body identify him as a stellar god destined for sacrifice, while his yellow solar disk reveals his relationship with the sun.

obscured. The Huichol graphically portray *nierikas* as circles with radiating spokes, and often incorporate a mirror at the center of the image (MacLean 2005:89). *Nierikas* represent the face of the sun. Its counterpart in Nahua mythology is the obsidian mirror, an attribute associated with the setting or lunar sun, Tezcatlipoca, and his avatar Mixcoatl, god of the hunt (table 6.12).

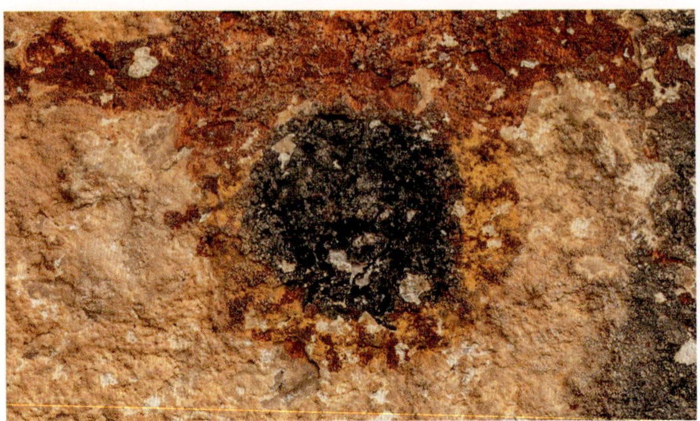

Figure 6.44. Stellar mask and solar disk of the Setting Sun.

In the monumental work *Mockeries and Metamorphoses of an Aztec God*, Guilhem Olivier (2003) provides a comprehensive overview of this intriguing deity and his many attributes, including his designation as lord of the smoking mirror. Before getting into Olivier's analysis, however, let's briefly review the mythology regarding Tezcatlipoca's important role in creation.

In *Historia de los mexicanos por sus pinturas* we learn Tezcatlipoca created fire and established the New Fire Ceremony. After the great flood destroys the fourth world and Tezcatlipoca saves Tata and Nene by instructing them to escape the rising waters in a hollowed-out tree, he works with Quetzalcoatl and the other gods to put the celestial vault back in place. Once this is accomplished, Tezcatlipoca changes himself into his avatar Mixcoatl and honors the gods by lighting a multitude of fires using his fire drill. Thus was the origin of fire (Graulich 1997:97; Phillips 1884).

The world, however, remained in darkness. The only light came from the fires, which were stars, created by

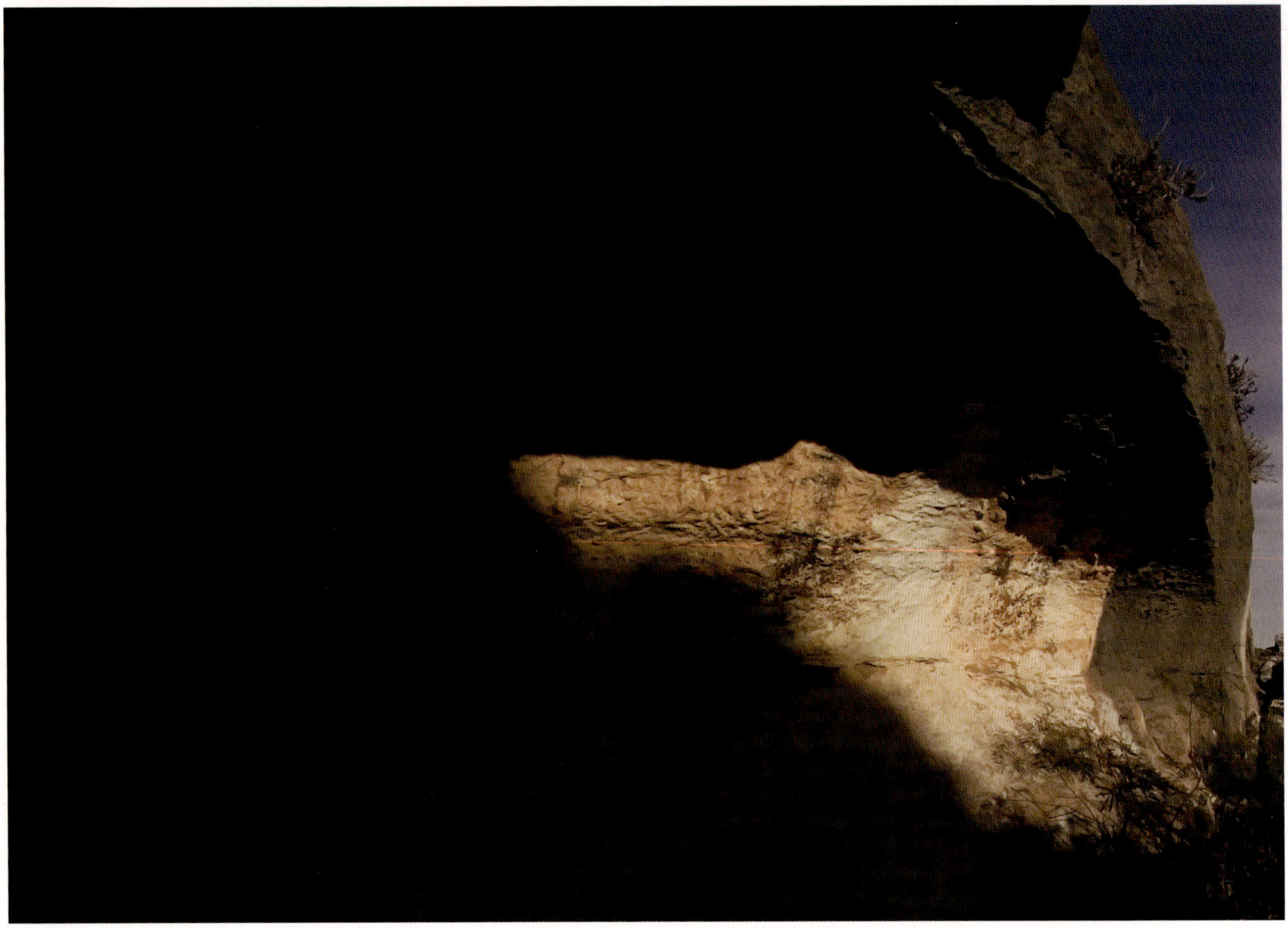

Figure 6.45. Moon setting into the Land of Black and Red on the winter solstice. Photo by Patrick Born.

Table 6.12.
Motif Analysis XII: A005 and the upside-down, impaled anthropomorph (A013) with the yellow disk encircling its black mask, surrounded by thirteen L-shapes (E010)

HUICHOL	NAHUA	HYPOTHETICAL MEANINGS
X	X	Primordial ancestor (A005) transforms into an ancestral deity, Setting Sun (A013), god of the hunt and patron deity of the deer.
	X	Creator of fire
X	X	The yellow ring around its black mask denotes a solar disk.
	X	Black mask denotes an obsidian mirror and the deity's stellar aspect.
	X	Thirteen L-shapes represent reeds, atlatl darts, starlight, and fire drills.
	X	Thirteen L-shapes denote the year the sun was born (13 Reed).
	X	Number 13 denotes association with the patron of the thirteenth day, a deity of the setting or night sun.

Tezcatlipoca-Mixcoatl. So in the year 13 Reed the gods created the sun to illuminate the earth, and Tezcatlipoca created four hundred men and five women so that the new sun would have food to eat. Nanahuatzin is sacrificed upon the great pyre created by Tezcatlipoca-Mixcoatl and is transformed into the sun. The sacrifice of Nanahuatzin is the origin of the New Fire Ceremony (Graulich 1997:97; Phillips 1884).

Tezcatlipoca, as one of the creator gods, is one of the most important Nahua deities. Of all the deities, he probably has the longest and most varied list of avatars, including the Venusian deity and patron of the hunt Mixcoatl. In addition to being the creator of fire, Tezcatlipoca-Mixcoatl is identified as a lunar deity with feminine attributes and is closely associated with the night sky and a vast array of stellar gods, including the star demon Itzpapalotl.[66] In the codices he is portrayed wearing a solar disk on his forehead (figure 6.46a). Identified as Tezcatlipoca's mirror, the disk is his most distinctive characteristic.[67] Tezcatlipoca's mirror is black and surrounded by solar rays (Graulich 1989:50). According to myth, once the sun reaches its zenith, it turns around and goes back to the east; what we see in the afternoon sky is only the true sun's reflection in Tezcatlipoca's black mirror (Graulich 1989:50). Olivier (2003:263) writes, "As an obsidian object, the black mirror belongs to the netherworld. It captures the sun in its reflection and draws it toward the earth. Being the feminine, nocturnal, and telluric element of the star, Tezcatlipoca's black mirror causes the fall of the sun." Graulich (1997:61) refers to the afternoon sun as the sun in a mirror, a false sun and a lunar sun—a star that belongs to both the sun and the moon.

The black mask or black mirror of A013 was painted prior to the striped, red body and prior to the yellow disk with red rays encircling it. In other words, before the body was painted, the mask was just one in a series of approximately thirty-two black stars in this section of the panel, but it then became the mask of A013. Nahua star gods, particularly Mixcoatl, are portrayed wearing "black stellar masks" (Caso 1988:37) (figure 6.46b). Mixcoatl is also portrayed with red stripes running vertically down his white body (Seler 1963:253). The black dots surrounding A013, including the black mask forming its mask, are analogous to the stars created by Tezcatlipoca-Mixcoatl to nourish the sun.

Surrounding this constellation of thirty-two black stars are thirteen black L-shapes resembling atlatls loaded with darts (figure 6.42). The cane (or reed) used by the Nahua in the manufacture of atlatl darts is the same reed used to signify the day-sign Reed, of which Tezcatlipoca was the patron. Among other things, atlatl darts metaphorically represent sunlight or starlight, depending upon context (Hall 1997:112). In this con-

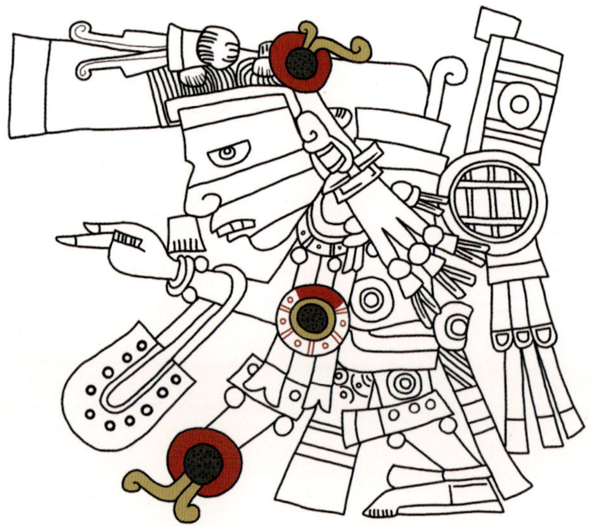

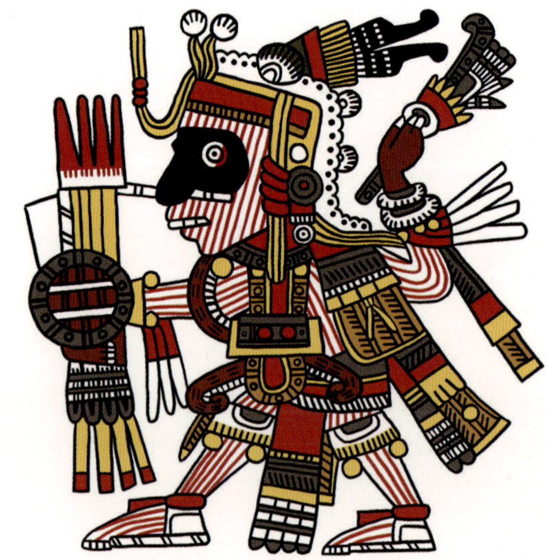

Figure 6.46. Solar mirrors and stellar masks: (a) Tezcatlipoca's mirror. Redrawn from *Codex Borgia* 21 (see Díaz and Rodgers 1993). (b) Mixcoatl's black mask and red-striped body. Redrawn from *Codex Borgia* 25 (see Díaz and Rodgers 1993).

text, with a black star located at the distal end of each dart, they would represent starlight. But the symbolism doesn't stop there. In the Nahua myth Tezcatlipoca-Mixcoatl drills a multitude of fires just prior to the birth of the sun. The reed used for drilling fire—or, in the case of Mixcoatl, drilling stars—is the same reed used for atlatls, and as an emblem of the day-sign Reed (Nuttall 1901:280; Read 1998:27). Drilling fire is deeply symbolic and is equated with the life-giving union of the dual principles of nature (Nuttall 1901:280).[68] It is perhaps a coincidence, but unlikely, that the fifth Ancestor is inserted perpendicularly into the first "bowl" of the Land of Black and Red, a motif resembling a fire board. The combining of these motifs in this location may convey a complex visual metaphor denoting both an event and a date: the birth of the sun in 13 Reed, the year both the Nahua and Maya identify with the birth of the sun.

Narrative Reconstruction

Here, at the western horizon, the Lunar/Setting Sun (A013) begins his descent into the Land of Black and Red (E007). His black mask and red-striped body identify him as a stellar god destined for sacrifice, while his yellow solar disk reveals his relationship with the sun. His descent marks the end of a day, the end of a season, and the end of an era. He is joined by the multitude of stars (E010), the fires he created to light the darkness and nourish the sun. Together they plunge to their death through a fiery act of self-sacrifice as they enter the underworld.

Motif Analysis XIII: Evening Star

Below the figure interpreted as the Setting Sun (A013) is another upside-down anthropomorph (A014) (figure 6.47). This figure has long, flowing hair, like that of the upside-down star demons in the east. Its head is in profile, facing west, exposing an open mouth. Overlying the torso of A014 is a yellow, five-pronged comb shape (E034). The middle prong superimposes and accentuates what appears to be a pointed head. A014 lacks feet but has three digits on each hand. Although poorly preserved and heavily obscured, two enigmatic yellow shapes (E048), possibly quadrupeds, superimpose the legs of A014. A fletched dart is impaling the anthropomorph's right side. One of the L-shapes interpreted above as either loaded atlatls or fire drills is touching the end of this dart. On the opposite side the tip of the distal end of another L-shape is touching the figure's stumped left leg. The two motifs, A014 and E010, are thus connected. Falling away from A014, like a collapsing row of dominoes, are four enigmatic shapes, each as tall as A014, resembling cattails (E030) (figure 6.48). The final cattail figure connects with the upside-down deer (Z006) identified in Motif Analysis V as Evening

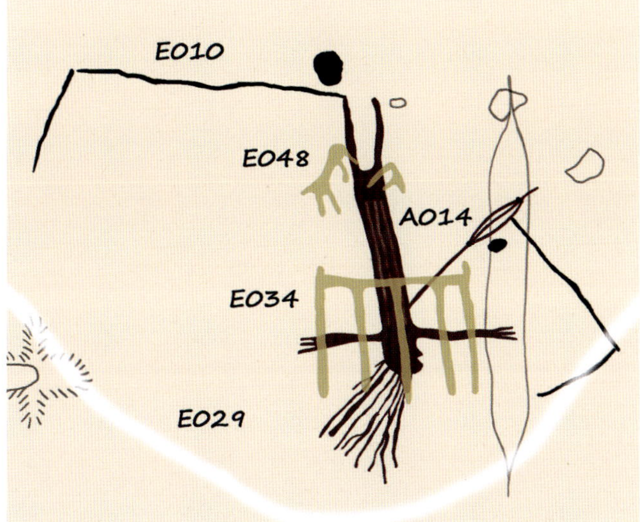

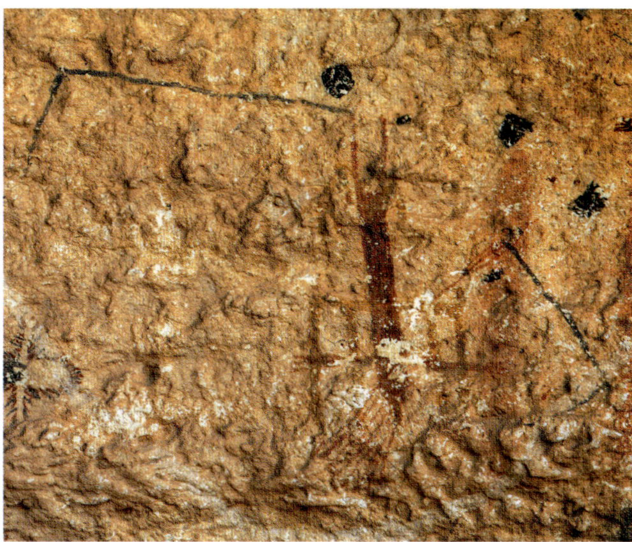

Figure 6.47. Motif XIII (A014 and E034): Evening Star (A014) descending into the underworld. The five-pronged comb (E034) painted across his torso alludes to the "fiveness" of Venus.

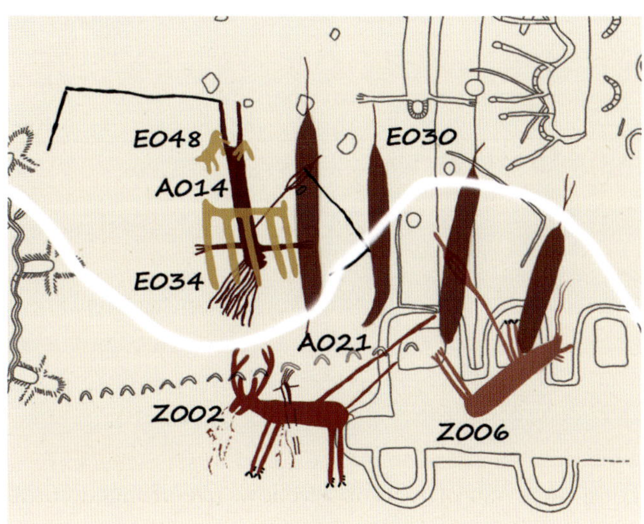

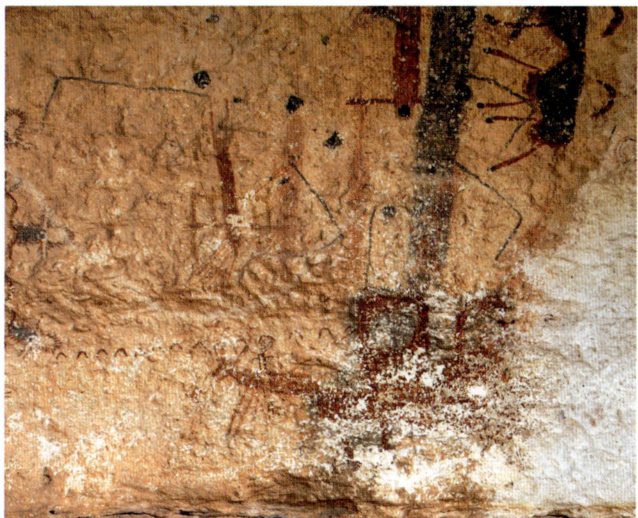

Figure 6.48. Evening Star (A014) becomes fused with the Setting Sun in the bowels of the underworld (E007) and is transformed into a deer (Z006, Z002).

Star/Night Sun in the guise of a deer. The painting sequence here follows what I identified throughout the mural: all black imagery was painted first, followed by red, yellow, and white.

Formulating Hypotheses

In chapter 5 I proposed that this cluster of motifs portrays the transformation of Evening Star into the deer who travels with the sun (or as the sun) through the underworld. The five-pronged comb, I suggested, denotes completion and the perfect sacrifice offered by the Evening Star (table 6.13). These hypothetical meanings are both clarified and expanded through a reading of Nahua mythology.

As discussed earlier, in Mesoamerican mythology gods transform themselves into other divine beings according to cycles that reproduce the model of a day, a year, or an era. Graulich (1997:180) proposes that Tezcatlipoca-Mixcoatl, who represents the setting sun, was transformed into Venus as the Evening Star. Xo-

Table 6.13.
Motif Analysis XIII: Upside-down, impaled anthropomorph (A014) overlain by a yellow, five-pronged comb shape (E034)

HUICHOL	NAHUA	HYPOTHETICAL MEANINGS
X	X	Upside-down, impaled figure represents Evening Star (A014) being sacrificed in the west and plunging into the underworld (E007).
	X	Five-pronged comb shape (E034) denotes number 5.
	X	Number 5 related to the five synodic periods of Venus
X	X	Number 5 denotes completion of a cycle and perfect sacrifice.
X	X	Evening Star (A014) transforms into or merges with the Setting Sun (A013) to become a deer (Z002).

lotl was god of the planet Venus as the Evening Star. Brundage (1982:212) equates Xolotl with Nanahuatzin, who through an act of self-sacrifice was metamorphosed into the sun. He writes, "Behind the myth was reality. What ancients of Mesoamerica saw, as all men do, was the Evening Star plunging into the vast fires of the sun after he had fallen below the horizon" (Brundage 1983:44).

During the New Fire Ceremony reenacting this cosmic event, the surrogate Nanahuatzin-Xolotl was sacrificed atop the Hill of the Star. All fires in the region were extinguished to re-create the darkness of primordial time as they awaited the drilling of the New Fire upon the chest of the sacrificial victim. The cosmos hung in the balance. If the New Fire was not drilled, chaos would follow: the world would remain in darkness, and the dreaded star demons would descend to earth. As soon as the fire priest successfully drew fire from the victim's chest, onlookers throughout the area cut their ears to join in the sacrifice. They flicked their blood toward the location where the surrogate Nanahuatzin-Xolotl and their blood sacrifice would be consumed to fuel a new dawn and new temporal period.

Xolotl is an interesting character who may even be more ancient than his "twin," Quetzalcoatl (Brundage 1983:119). In Nahuatl, one of the translations for *xolotl* is "twin." Juxtaposed, the two gods represent the planet Venus as Morning Star and Evening Star, although it is possible that at one time Xolotl represented both phases of the planet.[69] Xolotl as Evening Star is also perceived as the dog who conducts the sun into the underworld at dusk (figure 6.49). In the *Florentine Codex* (Sahagún 1950–1982, bk. 3:41) we learn that a yellow dog carries the souls of the dead across the place of Nine Waters into the underworld. Similarly, in Sahagún's version of the sun legend, Xolotl leads the star gods, who were dispatched by their bloody sacrifice, into the underworld. He travels with the Setting Sun into the underworld, where the two, the sun and Venus, are fused through a nocturnal battle to become the night sun.[70] Nahua legend recounts how the night sun is transformed in the bowels of the earth monster into a deer to mate with

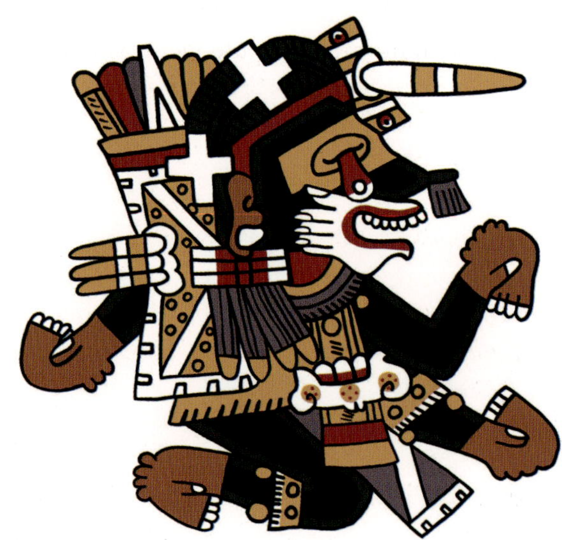

Figure 6.49. Xolotl depicted with a pointed head and attributes of a dog. Redrawn from *Codex Borgia* 10 (see Díaz and Rodgers 1993).

the moon goddess. From their union, the Morning Star is conceived. According to Caso (1988:25), ". . . it is but a mythical explanation of the death of the planet, his descent into the West, where the black and the red, the night and the day, merge, and the prophecy that he will reappear in the East as the morning star, preceding the sun."

This solar-stellar descent and transformation is portrayed in the White Shaman mural. The upside-down, impaled figure with long, flowing hair is analogous to the Evening Star (figure 6.47). A yellow figure (E048) resembling a dog, the animal double of Xolotl, overlays the legs of A014. A row of four cattail-like figures (E030) fall away from A014 and descend into the Land of Black and Red (figure 6.48). The final figure in this series is conjoined with an upside-down, impaled deer with black hooves on its front legs (Z006), which is analogous to the transformation of the night sun into a deer in the Land of Black and Red. The transformation is complete with Z002, which has black hooves on both front and back legs. The dual solar-stellar aspect of this transformation is portrayed by the anthropomorphic figure (A021) with ecstatic hair overlaying the body of the deer.

The hair of both the descending figure and the figure overlaying the deer are diagnostic attributes. The Nahua believed that at the end of the fifth and final sun, and at the end of the last fifty-two-year cycle, not only would the star demons with their disheveled hair descend to earth to devour humanity, but the sun itself would be transformed into one of the Tzitzimime. Perhaps the most significant attribute identifying A014 as the Evening Star, however, is the yellow, five-pronged comb superimposing his torso (figure 6.47). In Nahua and Maya iconography the planet Venus possesses a "fiveness" that is often depicted by symbols with five prongs. Milbrath (1999:162) says, "The five radiating elements allude to the 'fiveness' of Venus implicit in the Venus Almanac's five synodic periods."[71] Séjourné (1978:90) writes, "Since Venus-years are computed in groups of five (corresponding to eight solar years), the number 5 is also the symbol for Venus . . ." The five-pronged comb superimposing the Evening Star (A014) is similar to one of the symbols used by the Nahua to denote the number 5 (Boone 2000:43; see also Sahagún 1950–1982, bk. 4: plate 52) (figure 6.50).[72]

As noted above and illustrated in figure 6.47, two black L-shapes link this Venus figure with the larger motif (E010) of 13 reeds and 32 stars. The L-shapes encircle the stars beginning and ending with this figure whose Venus designation is denoted with a symbol for the number 5. According to Klein (1976:11 fn44), when five Venus periods have repeated 13 times, the final day coincides with both the end of the *tonalpohualli* and the 52-year cycle. This can occur only once every 104 solar cycles. The Nahua ceremonies conducted every other 52-year cycle celebrate the completion of both the critical 52-year solar cycle and the 104-year Venus cycle. When the sun and Venus simultaneously complete a cycle, the Nahua believe that the two celestial bodies engage in a mortal nocturnal combat resulting in the fusion of the two deities in the dark bowels of the earth. And just below this motif, the fusion of the two deities is portrayed by the transformation of Venus into the deer who carries the sun upon its back.

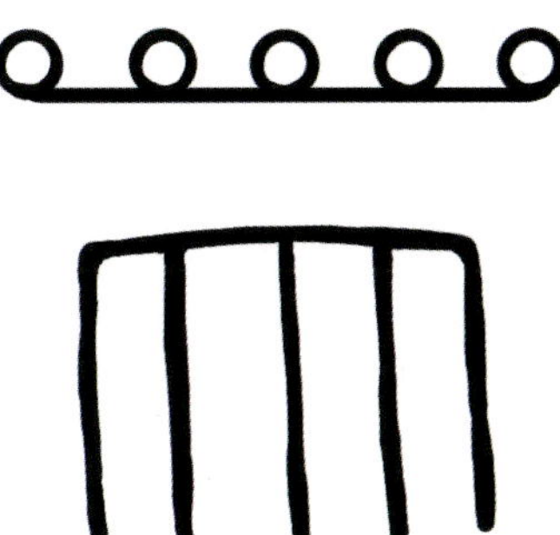

Figure 6.50. Symbols used to denote the number 5. Redrawn from the *Florentine Codex* (Sahagún 1950–1982, Illustrations, bk. 4) (see also Boone 2000:43).

Narrative Reconstruction

The Evening Star (A014) travels with the Setting Sun (A013) as they descend into the Land of Black and Red (E007). He leads the multitude of stars (E010), his progeny, whose sacrifice will fuel the movement of the sun. They are covered in a splattering of red to denote their bloody sacrifice: the death of the sun, Venus, and a multitude of stellar Ancestors. The cycle is complete, but through sacrifice, a new day and a new era dawn.

Motif Analysis XIV: Datura Hawk Moths and Transformations

The left arm and torch of A005 are overlain by a large, caterpillar-like figure (E009) (figure 6.51). This enigmat-

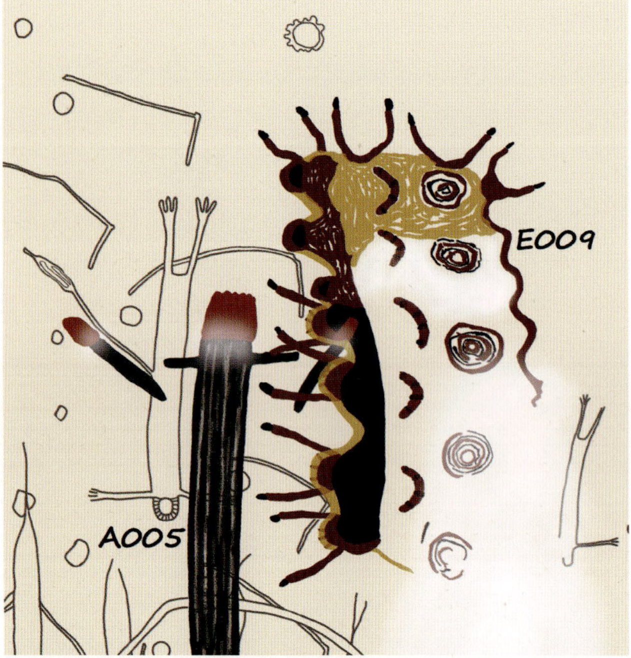

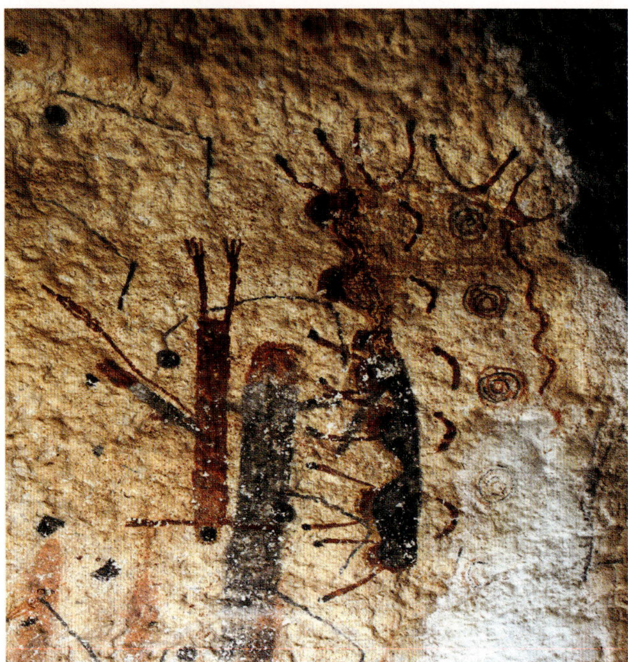

Figure 6.51. Motif XIV (E009): Datura hawk moths, caterpillars, and celestial fire.

ic figure is painted black, red, yellow, and white. Water seeping out of the wall has left a white mineral skin obscuring portions of its body; however, it is still possible to identify five sets of concentric red and black circles running the length of the figure. Five short red bars, each bearing four black dots, are paired with the concentric circles. Eight pairs of red, tendril-like shapes extend off the figure. Each of the sixteen tendrils is tipped with a black dot.

The close relationship between A005 and this caterpillar-like figure (E009) is indicated by how intricately the two images are woven together. While the black "wooden" portion of the torch held by the pilgrim is overlain by the red tendrils, the red torch tip overlays the black body of the caterpillar-like figure, and the yellow of the caterpillar overlays the red of the torch.

Formulating Hypotheses

In this and the previous chapter I propose that the avatars of the fifth ancestral figure are the Setting Sun (A013) and Evening Star (A014). These and other mythical nocturnal deities are equated with psychotropic plants in the widespread kieri complex: datura (*toloache*), morning glory (*ololiuhqui*), and solandra (*kieri*) (Aedo 2003a). Hawk moths are the principal pollinators of these night bloomers and are recognized as manifestations of the psychotropic plants of the kieri complex as well as their related deities. I believe the caterpillar-like figure intertwined with the fifth ancestral figure symbolizes a hawk moth during its larval stage (table 6.14). The relationship among the noctur-

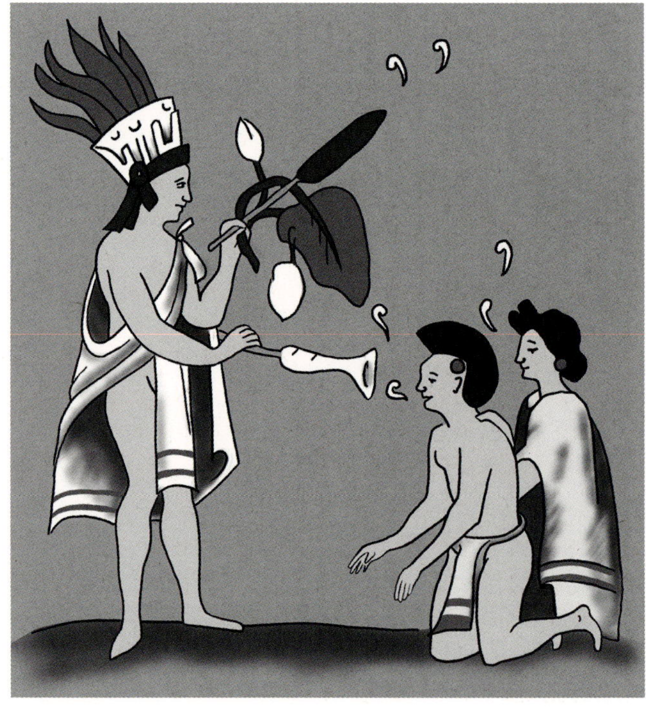

Figure 6.52. Tezcatlipoca holding datura. Redrawn from the *Florentine Codex* (Sahagún 1950–1982, Illustrations, bk. 3).

Table 6.14.
Motif Analysis XIV: Caterpillar-like figure (E009)

HUICHOL	NAHUA	HYPOTHETICAL MEANINGS
X	X	The caterpillar-like figure (E009) represents a nocturnal deity associated with psychotropic plants.
X	X	Hawk moth caterpillars are associated with nocturnal deities, in particular Setting Sun, Night Sun, and Evening Star.
X	X	Hawk moth caterpillars are associated with the west, rain, and entrance into the underworld.

nal deities, the psychotropic plants, and the hawk moth are discussed at length in chapter 5 so will not be revisited here. Instead, I turn to a discussion of the earth-moon goddess Itzpapalotl (Obsidian Butterfly), whom Ángel Aedo (2003a:242–244) has identified as an expression of the nocturnal hawk moth and as operating within the kieri complex.

Itzpapalotl, lady of the sixteenth day-count, is a fierce deity who rules over the realm of mist and rain in the west, the House of Descent, and primordial time (Seler 1903:179). She belongs to the complex of earth and moon goddesses that includes Tlazolteotl, Cihuacoatl, Coatlicue, Chimalman, and Teteoinnan, among others (Milbrath 1995:69; Yoneda 2007:175). As with other deities within the kieri complex, Itzpapalotl is represented as a radical nocturnal figure of death, desire, and madness—personifications of the extremely dangerous psychotropic plants. Her connection with these plants is also suggested by her name and association with fire. Itzpapalotl translates as either "Obsidian Butterfly" or "Clawed Butterfly"; however, as Seler (1903:221) points out, the butterfly is "a *homologue of the flower*, and like it also an expression and symbol of the flickering, that is, of *fire*." He suggests that it may be more accurate to think of her as the moth that flitters around the flames at night rather than as the flames themselves.[73]

The relationship between Itzpapalotl and moths is further evidenced in Nahuatl myths regarding stellar arrows in the form of shooting stars. Itzpapalotl was the first and most terrifying of star demons. The Nahua believe these demons release their stellar arrows among them at night. They fall to earth in the form of obsidian blades and upon impact are transformed into caterpillars. Or, worse yet, if the shooting star hits a human or

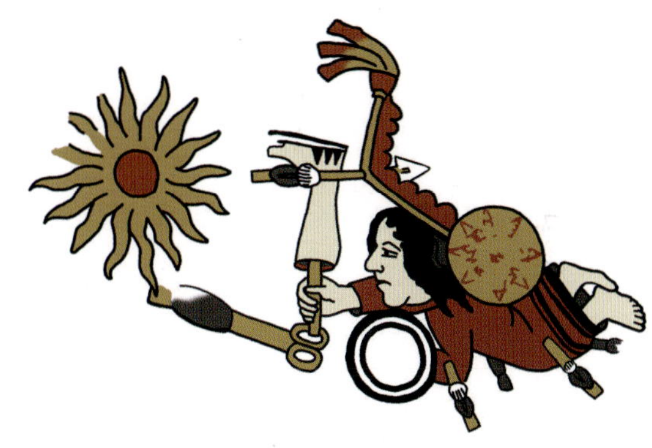

Figure 6.53. Itzpapalotl leading the Chichimecs out of the primordial world. Redrawn from *Mapa de Cuauhtinchan No. 2* (see also Carrasco and Sessions 2007).

animal, they implant a caterpillar or worm in the victim's wound. Ulrich Köhler (2002:4) states it plainly: ". . . a stellar shot results in caterpillars."

Itzpapalotl is closely allied with—and even considered to be the female counterpart of—the Chichimec god who created fire, Tezcatlipoca-Mixcoatl. Interestingly, this deity is portrayed in the *Florentine Codex* (Sahagún 1950–1982, bk. 3: plate 7) holding a plant identified as *Datura stramonium* (Olivier 2003:121) (figure 6.52). Itzpapalotl is goddess of both the fire of the hearth and the celestial red fire of dawn and dusk. Her fires glow beneath the horizon to consume the setting sun at dusk and give birth to the rising sun at dawn (Brundage 1982:168). Tezcatlipoca-Mixcoatl, as the setting sun, enters the fires of Itzpapalotl at dusk and out of this union produces his successor, the Morning Star and future sun.

In the *Mapa de Cuauhtinchan No. 2,* Itzpapalotl is represented as a mighty female warrior leading the

Chichimec pilgrims out of the primordial world to bring time into existence.[74] She carries a sun disk on her back and brandishes a trophy leg adorned with an obsidian sandal, an emblem of the night sun (figure 6.53). As leader of the Chichimec pilgrims Itzpapalotl is portrayed bringing solar power and time into human existence (Carrasco and Sessions 2007b:430).

Narrative Reconstruction

The strange caterpillar-like creature interwoven with the fifth Ancestor (A005) is analogous to the star demon and the earth-moon goddess Itzpapalotl. Sixteen tendrils project off this lady of the sixteenth day-count. She is portrayed opposite her male counterpart, the Tezcatlipoca-Mixcoatl-like deity (A013) associated with the setting sun who superimposes the fifth Ancestor's right arm. Below these two figures is the Land of Black and Red (E007), the western entrance into the underworld and the location where the two unite and are transformed. The transformation is represented by the deer with obsidian hooves carrying the anthropomorphized sun (A021) on her back. They begin their dangerous journey through the underworld to bring solar power and time into existence.

Summary

In this chapter I set out to test the hypothesis that the White Shaman mural is a graphic manifestation of ancient, interrelated, and intermeshed Mesoamerican ideas–the premise being, if Pecos River style rock art fits into the basic structure of that broader continuum, a reading of the White Shaman mural should be informed by historical accounts and ethnographic observations of Mesoamerican groups participating in that continuum. This is indeed what I found. The parallels between creation narratives of the ancient Nahua and contemporary Huichol are stunning. Although the names of the actors are different, the basic story line is virtually identical. Thus, whether informed by Nahua or Huichol mythologies, the reading of the White Shaman mural is the same. It is a visual text documenting the birth of the sun and the establishment of time. Informed by Nahua texts, however, we are presented with even greater interpretive potential through the identification of possible calendrical and numerological elements.

The congruence between the White Shaman mural and the Mesoamerican ideological universe are too marked to be attributed to mere coincidence. In the next and final chapter I address what factors could give rise to these parallels. How could people separated by both time and space share in the same ideological universe? I also examine the mural's intrinsic meaning: how that meaning is communicated through the art and how it formed part of the culture within which it was produced. In so doing, we gain insight into the framework of ideas and beliefs through which the Lower Pecos people interpreted and interacted with the world: their worldview.

THE ART OF TRANSCENDENCE

As knowledge increases, wonder deepens.
CHARLES MORGAN (1894–1958)

When I first stood before the imposing murals of the Lower Pecos Canyonlands in 1989, I was overwhelmed by wonder. I was awed by the skill required to produce paintings of this magnitude. I was impressed by the artists' use of form, color, and other elements of design to create a well-balanced composition. I tried to imagine the engineering employed to construct the scaffolding necessary to produce the murals, and how such enduring paint was created. And I wondered, what was so important to the artists that they would go to such extreme lengths to communicate their messages on rough limestone walls thousands of years ago? I certainly wasn't sure it would ever be possible to answer any of these questions, but still I wondered. Twenty-five years later, as my knowledge has increased, my wonder has deepened. I expect this will be the case the rest of my life—at least I hope so.

My appreciation of the Lower Pecos murals began as an artist, not an anthropologist, archaeologist, or historian. Today, after decades of research and countless hours of painstaking transcription, I recognize them not only as artistic masterpieces, but as literary masterpieces as well. Such is the case with the White Shaman mural. When Kim Cox and I first began researching for this manuscript, we questioned whether there would be sufficient material to fill the pages of a book devoted to one site, and a relatively small one at that. It soon became clear that the greater challenge would be keeping the text to a manageable size. Bringing it to closure has been very difficult because new patterns and stunning possibilities continue to emerge almost daily. This work must therefore be considered the first stage of what could surely be a lifetime of investigations—not only at the White Shaman site, but throughout the region. My hope is that others will become inspired to join this effort to transcribe these ancient narratives. That said, I will try to bring closure to the reporting of this first stage of investigations.

In the opening chapter I offered four proposals:

1. Pecos River style rock art in general, and the White Shaman mural specifically, is a graphic manifestation of ancient, interrelated ideas traditionally associated with complex agricultural societies in Mesoamerica and the American Southwest.
2. The White Shaman mural, much like the pre-Columbian codices, exquisitely details sophisticated cosmological and mythological concepts through the use of a graphic vocabulary.
3. The White Shaman narrative appears to relate, in stunning detail, a myth recounted by Southern Uto-Aztecan speakers, the ancient Nahua and contemporary Huichol.
4. Pecos River style rock art has far more to do with the mental conceptualization of the artist(s) than the altered state of consciousness of a shaman.

In this concluding chapter I return to these key points and propose a general myth that informed production of the White Shaman visual narrative. This reading and its resulting implications are assessed within the framework of linguistics and semiotics. I explore the underlying ideological assumptions of the society within which the narrative operated, transitioning from trying to understand *what* the visual text means to *how* it means: how meaning was communicated through the art, and how it formed part of the culture within which it was produced. I examine the mural's intrinsic meanings and seek to provide insight into the framework of ideas and beliefs through which the Lower Pecos people interpreted and interacted with the world: their worldview.

An Archaic Core

Shared cosmological beliefs permeate Native American ideologies. Alfredo López Austin (1997) maintains that historically recorded mythologies and cosmologies illustrate a durable, virtually unchangeable core of traditions and beliefs. These core concepts have endured from some point in the distant past and have shaped the ideological universe of Mesoamerica and the American Southwest into the present. Today they are manifested in the iconography and mythology of Native America. But is there evidence of these core beliefs in the rock art of the Lower Pecos, a region not only spatially removed from the area traditionally recognized as Mesoamerica (and, for that matter, the American Southwest), but temporally distant as well? If the Pecos River style rock art is part of an Archaic and, more specifically, Southern Uto-Aztecan continuum, then like all the rest of pre-Columbian Mesoamerican art, it has to fit into the basic structure of that broader continuum. This means at a minimum: (1) it must have inherent meaning, with nothing being random or arbitrary; (2) its inherent meaning is part of a larger structural meaning that directly relates to and arises out of an earlier culture and fits into the continuum that persisted into later cultures; (3) it works on several levels of interpretation; and (4) it has functional equivalents in other mythologies, cosmologies, and iconographies.

The functional equivalents for the analysis presented in the preceding chapters were sought in the mythologies, cosmologies, and iconographies of the contemporary Huichol, the ancient Nahua, and to a lesser degree other Uto-Aztecan and non-Uto-Aztecan speakers in Mesoamerica and the American Southwest. Each of these groups possesses core traditions and beliefs diagnostic of the Archaic core: concepts that persisted across linguistic, political, geographic, and cultural boundaries, even into the American Southwest. These include, among others:

1. Cyclical time as a sacred entity
2. Delimitation of the sky, earth, and underworld in the spatial layout of the cosmos
3. Supernatural and secular conflict as creative and life-sustaining forces
4. Principle of complementary dualism
5. Spoken and written language (including pictographic) as an extraordinary, powerful symbolic entity in itself, beyond its role as a means of communication
6. Replication of divine essences
7. Human body as a receptacle for two or more souls

As demonstrated in chapters 5 and 6, these core elements are exemplified in the region's rock art, and very dramatically so at the White Shaman site. Patterns in the art parallel myths and iconographies of many of these groups, with the most notable connections found in Huichol and Nahua mythology. Identification of these core traditions and beliefs in the Pecos River style rock art demonstrates that the ideological universe was already firmly established among foragers living in the Lower Pecos during the Late Archaic. That is not to say the canyons of southwest Texas and northern Mexico are the birthplace of these ideas, but rather the location of the oldest existing documented graphic expression of them. Whether this is the result of preservation bias or the first time the ideology was graphically codified has yet to be determined. Regardless, the murals provide us with a snapshot in time—a glimpse into the deeply rooted and widely shared symbolic world of indigenous Native America as it was expressed thousands of years ago. Indeed, it was the symbolic world of foragers that shaped the ideological universe of later Mesoamerican agriculturalists.

As an artist and archaeologist, I have long recognized the extraordinary complexity of Pecos River style rock art. Twenty years ago my goal was to see if it was even possible to talk about its "meaning" in a genuinely revelatory context. Through years of study I have come to realize that the true meaning of the art does not exist independent of its organizing structure. Our greatest challenge is not in deciphering the meaning of rock art; it is in recognizing the overriding principles that provided the framework for understanding its meaning and governed its production.

The White Shaman mural is a planned composition with rules governing not only the portrayal of symbolic forms, but also the sequencing of colors. The mural was first painted with black, the color of femininity and primordial time—a time of perpetual darkness. Soon after the black paint dried, the artist(s) applied red, the color associated with masculinity, fire, and blood. It is also the color of crepuscular light—the red glow appearing on the horizon just before sunrise. The next color applied was yellow—associated with the rays of the rising sun as it ushers in the dry season and overcomes the black of night and the red of predawn. And finally, the last color applied was white—associated with the zenith and the white light of midday. It is the light that renders all of creation shadowless. It is the color of sacrificial transformation and transcendence—the return to primordial time. Thus, the cycle of life continues.

Complex images painted on the walls of White Shaman Shelter in black, red, yellow, and white were woven together to form an intricate visual narrative. Each image was intentionally placed. Just as words on a page, it is a text—a visual text—communicating a narrative through a graphic vocabulary. As with the Mesoamerican codices, everything in the mural has inherent meaning; nothing is arbitrary or random, including the order in which the paint was applied. That inherent meaning is part of a larger structural meaning directly relating to and arising out of an earlier culture. Equally as complex and sophisticated, the meaning communicated through the art fits into a broader continuum that persisted into later cultures in Mesoamerica and the Southwest—up to the present day. And because it fits into that continuum, interpretation of the art is possible.

Codified on a rockshelter wall millennia ago, the White Shaman mural may represent the oldest pictorial creation narrative in North America. On a very broad level it is about cycles of time and spiritual meanings that adhere to time. It is a creation story detailing the birth of the sun and creation of time; however, the mural works on multiple levels of interpretation. Not only does it communicate an ancient creation narrative, it also metaphorically represents the heavens as viewed by people living in the Lower Pecos during the Late Archaic. The imagery relates the sun's daily cycle and the apparent path of the sun along the ecliptic throughout the year. It documents the changing seasons and the beginning and ending of ages. Beyond its portrayal of real-world cosmological events and cycles of nature, the mural also articulates the ongoing transformations of every person throughout the course of his or her life. Through austerity, transcendence is realized.

While many of the concepts represented in the White Shaman mural cross linguistic and cultural boundaries, others are distinctly Uto-Aztecan. In fact, the narrative communicated through the art stunningly relates back to the actual structure of myths and ceremonies uniquely associated with Corachol- and Nahuan-speaking peoples. At the mythological core the mural incorporates similar patterns, reveals similar, if not identical, actions and symbols, and shares a common function with mythologies of these two linguistic groups. The shared patterns are indisputable, and the parallels, only some of which were presented in the previous two chapters, are vast. While one might argue that each element individually could be coincidental, in the aggregate they are hard to deny. This begs the question— "What factors could account for such striking parallels in myth and ritual among populations separated both by time and space?"

Patterns in Myth and Language

Folkloristics

Folklorists use an approach referred to as the "historic-geographic" or "historical-geographical" method to trace a myth back to its origins. Implicit in this approach is the idea that patterns exhibited among variations of a myth told by a large number of people across time and space can be used to reconstruct the prototype (Urforms or archetypes) from which all later versions of the myth emerged.[1] The most frequently retold narrative elements reveal the kernel or core components (mythemes) of the prototype.[2]

Oicotypes (also spelled "oikotype" and "ecotype") are geographically or culturally localized variants of a narrative that diverge from their primary form. The term *ecotype* was borrowed from botany by Carl Wilhelm von Sydow to stress the fact that myths, like plants, often adapt to new environments in order to survive.[3] Variations in a similar story recounted by diverse groups represent necessary adaptations to varied social, political, cultural, ecological, and linguistic milieus. According to George Lankford (2007), an examination of these variants can be used to reveal past relationships among populations separated temporally and spatially.

> Oicotypes serve to indicate earlier linkages of tribes in belief and narrative art, and thus they can presumably point to some past time of contact and relationship. While a long way from historical precision, such patterns can nonetheless offer a sort of historical insight by suggesting now-lost relationships between people. [Lankford 2007:50]

The Huichol, Nahua, and Lower Pecos narratives appear to be geographically or culturally localized variants of the same creation story. Application of the historic-geographic approach suggests a "now-lost relationship" among these three spatially and temporally separated groups. There are at least two frameworks within which we can examine this phenomenon. The first involves the field of linguistics to trace the symbology inherent in languages passed down from one generation to the next. The second involves the field of semiotics: the study of how symbols (signs or metaphors) are acquired and operate within a culture and cross-culturally. These two perspectives also provide a framework for recognizing the mental template of whoever produced the Pecos River style rock art.

Historical Linguistics

Similar to the historic-geographic approach used by folklorists to analyze myths, historical linguists seek to reconstruct the evolution and relatedness of languages. They do this through the analysis of phonological, grammatical, and semantic changes over time. The Uto-Aztecan language of North America has been the focus of decades of research. It is the largest linguistic family in the Americas, both in terms of its geographic distribution and number of speakers.[4] The origins of the Uto-Aztecan parent or protolanguage is the subject of considerable debate, but most scholars place it somewhere in the southwestern United States or its borderlands with Mexico.[5] Both linguistic and genetic data support a Uto-Aztecan migration into Mexico from a northern homeland (Shaul 2014:183).

The Uto-Aztecan (UA) family tree is divided into two branches: Northern Uto-Aztecan and Southern Uto-Aztecan. When this branching occurred is not yet settled. While Merrill et al. (2009:21019) believe the latest date that Proto-Uto-Aztecan (PUA) was spoken was around nine thousand years ago, other scholars place the breakup of the parent language into its northern and southern components to between four thousand and five thousand years ago.[6]

Over time these branches further split into subfamilies. The Huichol language is grouped with its close linguistic relative, Cora, under a Southern Uto-Aztecan subfamily called Corachol. Classical Nahuatl, also a Southern Uto-Aztecan daughter language, belongs to the Nahuan dialect complex. Corachol and Nahua exhibit lexical and grammatical artifacts not shared with any other Uto-Aztecan language. Kaufman (2001) and Wheeler et al. (2014) believe these shared innovations are the result of contact between Corachol and Nahua speakers.[7] They suggest that the shared linguistic artifacts are Nahua borrowings from Corachol. Other linguists, however, argue these linguistic artifacts are too pervasive to be attributed to borrowing (e.g., Campbell and Langacker 1978; Hill 2001a; Shaul 2014). They maintain that the two groups are linguistically related and share a common parent language: Corachol-Aztecan (Nahuan), a subfamily of their Southern Uto-Aztecan parent. The date for the divergence of Corachol-Aztecan from its parent family has not been well established. Hill (2001b:346), however, has suggested that the spilt took place between 1000 and 500 BC.[8] In discussing homelands of these languages, Shaul (2014) writes,

> While the grammar of Nahuan suggests intrusion into central Mesoamerica, the development of Corachol could have been anywhere (in situ development, or differentiation elsewhere with subsequent migration). Nahuan shares an intermediate ancestor with Corachol (Nahuan-Corachol), so the "where" could be the historic location of Cora and Huichol. If not, the location of Nahuan-Corachol is certainly to the north of the Mesoamerican heartland. All of this suggests that UA did not develop in Mesoamerica, that the PUA homeland is not in Mesoamerica. [Shaul 2014:183]

Arguably, an understanding of the evolution and spread of the Uto-Aztecan language and its daughter languages holds tremendous potential for reconstructing the prehistory of western North America and northern Mexico (Shaul 2014). The rock art of the Lower Pecos may someday figure into this reconstruction.

Whether the linguistic artifacts of Corachol and Nahuan languages are the results of shared linguistic evolution or borrowing, the two groups were linked linguistically, geographically, or both at some point in the past. This linkage offers possible insights into the similarities in Huichol and Nahua myths. It may also illuminate the similarities between these myths and the temporally and spatially distant Pecos River style rock art.

The importance of language in the conceptual mythic framework of Native Americans cannot be overstressed. N. Scott Momaday (1970) has argued that Native American belief systems were heavily influenced by language because language, first and foremost, provides the mental construct by which people view their world. Language for the Native American, he claims, was "the dimension in which his existence is most fully accomplished. *He does not create language but is himself created within it.* In a real sense, his language is both the object and the instrument of his religious experience" (emphasis added, Momaday 1970:62). Hence, a person's worldview is, to a large extent, influenced by the structure and idiosyncrasies of their language.

Narratives are constructed by language, and the structure of the language often dictates how the story is told. Likewise, narrative art reflects not only the worldview of the artist who produced it, but the structure of the language used to relate the story.[9] One would expect, therefore, to find greater similarities in myth, customs, and symbology among populations who speak related languages than among those linguistically unrelated. Symbolism has its greatest value between people who speak the same language—people who shape and are shaped by the same language.

Semiotics

Because of the nature of semiotics, the function, meaning, and use of specific symbols by the speakers of a parent language tend to remain most closely aligned diachronically between that parent language and its daughter languages (Eco 1984). Therefore, it may be possible to determine a latest-date time frame for the initial existence of mythemes—enduring and distinguishing elements of myth. The practical application of this idea goes something like this: If a concept is pronounced among members of a parent language family, then that concept likely dates back to a time before its divergence into daughter languages. Such is the case with the Southern Uto-Aztecan concept of a Flower World. Although aspects of the Flower World complex can be found outside this linguistic group, it is fully elaborated by virtually all members of the Southern Uto-Aztecan speech community (Hill 1992:122).

As discussed here and in chapter 6, aspects of the Flower World complex appear to be woven throughout the White Shaman mural. For example, within the complex, the path of the sun is perceived as a celestial floral pathway (Flower Road) leading to a primordial mountain (Flower Mountain) filled with flowers and butterflies (heart-souls). Iconographically, the road is often portrayed as a zigzag or serpentine line, and its mountain destination as a stepped pyramid. In the White Shaman mural the white serpentine line (Flower Road) leads to the crenellated arch (Flower Mountain). This is the birthplace of peyote (heart-souls), the flower of the desert, and the sun.

The Nahua believe that through self-sacrifice, the flower of the body (heart-soul) would bloom and bring light into the world. According to Hill (1992:131) a "blooming flower" metaphorically means "bursting into flames," "to explode," and "to give off a glow." She argues this metaphorical association is widespread among Uto-Aztecan speakers and has likely been in the lexicon as far back as Proto Southern Uto-Aztecan. Earlier I suggested that the black dots attached to the antlers of the fire-sun god emerging from the primordial mountain are the heart-souls of the Ancestors—and therefore water and stars. Antlers symbolize, among other things, flames. The black dots are the souls that "bloom"; they burst forth in flame through a fiery sacrifice to fuel the rising sun.[10] They become divine fire and are transformed into peyote, the flower of the desert.

The above examples represent only a fraction of the Flower World symbolism portrayed in the mural. Its presence in the Lower Pecos Canyonlands thousands of years ago not only attests to the antiquity of the complex, but suggests that the mural may well have been created by a marginal group of Southern Uto-Aztecan speakers located east of the traditionally accepted boundary of this speech community. This is not a totally new idea. Based on similarities between the art and Uto-Aztecan myth and iconography, linguist Francisco Marcos-Marín (2013:50) proposed that Pecos River rock art is related to Southern Uto-Aztecan speakers.[11] Interestingly, the most notable parallels are not found in the myths of all Southern Uto-Aztecan groups, but in those of its daughter language, Corachol-Aztecan. Mythemes specific to mythologies of the Huichol and Nahua identified in Pecos River style rock art may provide linguists with valuable information related to the split of Corachol-Aztecan from its parent Southern Uto-Aztecan family.

As stated above, the Huichol and Nahua share a common linguistic ancestor, Corachol-Aztecan. While much of their mythology is shared with other members of the Southern Uto-Aztecan family, some aspects appear to be unique to this subgroup, such as the shooting of a cactus with an arrow to initiate time. In the rock art this mytheme appears as rayed, red dots impaled by fletched darts (E002). In Nahua and Corachol myths, a cactus embodying deer, stars, and the Ancestors is sacrificed to initiate the birth of the sun. The Nahua deer goddess, Itzpapalotl, led the ancestral pilgrims out of their cave birthplace, Chicomoztoc. She is attributed with pursuing the stellar Ancestors into a cactus, where she either shoots them with arrows or she is shot and subsequently bursts into flames, thus beginning the Nahua calendar. This mythic sacrifice provided both the food and fuel needed to put the sun into motion. The act—shooting a cactus with arrows—was reenacted in Nahua ritual and portrayed in their iconography.[12] The shooting of the cactus symbolizes the blood sacrifice that fueled the sun.

A cactus embodies deer and stellar Ancestors among the Huichol as well. In their accounts of creation, a deer leads the ancestral pilgrims through the underworld to a place where they can emerge through a cave at the top of the primordial mountain. Once they arrive, the deer allows its pursuers to shoot it with arrows and is transformed into peyote and the sun through this act of self-sacrifice. The Huichol reenact this event annually through the ritual peyote pilgrimage and hunt, during which they stalk and shoot the cactus with arrows. This ritual activity is expressed in their iconography through images of impaled deer covered with geometric symbols (dots and flowers) representing peyote and images of impaled peyote. In Pecos River style iconography dots attached to deer antler tines, impaled deer covered with dots, and impaled dots are a recurring motif.

Perhaps most stunning, however, is the presence in the White Shaman mural of what may be early expressions of the 260-day calendar. This calendrical system is based on the sacredness of its component numbers. Each number not only contains its own essence, but also is ruled over by a patron god. The age of this calendrical system is unknown, but the general consensus is that it dates back several millennia. Carolyn Tate (2012:133) suggests that its development began around 1200 BC; others argue that it could have been developed "prior to the major Archaic-to-Formative language separations . . . as early as 3500 BC" (Rice 2007:33).[13] As discussed in chapter 2, the White Shaman mural has been radiocarbon dated to 2000 ± 400 RCYBP. If accurate, this would place its production between 400 BC and AD 400, and raises the possibility that whoever created the mural was, at the very least, familiar with the 260-day calendar.

While the practice of associating days with specific concepts is shared throughout Mesoamerica, the associations identified in the White Shaman mural appear to correlate most closely with the numbered days and patron gods of the Nahua calendar. Below are some of the correlations observed in the mural.

- The figure (A006) emerging out of the primordial mountain is portrayed with an antler rack (flames) possessing nine tines. This figure appears to be a prototypical fire god ushering in the birth of the sun. Among the Nahua, the fire god, Xiuhtecuhtli, is patron of the ninth day. Attached to the nine tines are nine black dots, which I equate with water and the heart-souls of the Ancestors retrieved from the underworld at creation. The day sign for the ninth day is *atl* (water).
- The impaled deer (Z001) covered with twelve large black dots (heart-souls) located directly above the fire god is analogous to the deer whose heart was transformed into peyote at the first dawn. The Nahua medicine god, Patecatl, is patron of the twelfth day and is attributed with discovering peyote.
- Below the impaled deer is a figure (A007) with attributes of both a deer and a bird. It has two sets of antler racks with a total of sixteen tines. I proposed that this figure is analogous to the goddess of deer and fire, Itzpapalotl, who was a key player in the creation of time. In the Nahua calendar Itzpapalotl is patron of the sixteenth day.
- The upside-down figure (A013) wearing the rayed solar disk and descending into the Land of Black and Red (E007) is analogous to the lunar or setting sun deity, Tezcatlipoca. This figure is surrounded by thirteen L-shapes, which appear to be reeds loaded in atlatls. Tezcatlipoca is patron of the thirteenth day—Reed.

- The red and black horizontal band (E007) with nine crenellations—six across the top and three across the bottom—is analogous to the western, watery entrance into the underworld. The day-sign for the sixth day is Death, and for the third day, House. As discussed previously, in Mesoamerica the number 9 was almost universally associated with water and the underworld.

Are these numerological associations coincidental? I don't think so. If it were not for the fact that each of these figures possesses multiple attributes diagnostic of these particular deities, one might dismiss the numerological associations as coincidental.[14] But not only do they each possess attributes associated with these deities, their positions in the mural—their contextual locations in the narrative—further support their identification. Whether or not the people of the Lower Pecos used the same vigesimal numeration system of later Mesoamerican cultures has yet to be determined;[15] however, they clearly believed that numbers were imbued with divine essences, and it is certainly possible that these same essences were tapped into whenever and wherever the 260-day calendar was perfected.

The presence in the White Shaman mural of the pierced cactus mytheme and the possible identification of patron gods of the 260-day calendar are intriguing. These patterns suggest that at some point in the distant past there existed a relationship—perhaps linguistic, as proposed by Marcos-Marín (2013)—between the people associated with the mural's production and the people who later became the Nahua, Huichol, and Cora. This would certainly explain why the connections between the rock art and the shared symbolism of the Huichol and Nahua are so pronounced. Needless to say, there is much more work to be done before this can be definitively addressed. My intent here is simply to illuminate the patterns and demonstrate the interpretive potential afforded by Huichol and Nahua mythologies. I leave the broader linguistic implications to the linguists. Regardless, Huichol and Nahua creation stories and cosmologies appear to be variants of the prototypical myth recorded on the limestone wall of White Shaman Shelter around the beginning of the first millennium, suggesting the possibility that the Lower Pecos was a northern boundary of the Nahua homeland.

As discussed in chapter 6, the Nahuatl-speaking people encountered by the Spanish in the Basin of Mexico during the 1500s had migrated into the region from the north sometime between AD 500 and 800. These nomadic hunters and gatherers, referred to as the Chichimec, claimed Chicomoztoc (Place of Seven Caves) as their place of origin and creation, and the place they went to pray (Carrasco and Sessions 2007; Yoneda 2007:169). The *Mapa de Cuauhtinchan No. 2,* which was produced only twenty years after the conquest, pictorially recounts the story of the Chichimecs' emergence from Chicomoztoc and their ensuing pilgrimage south in search of paradise. Seven tribes emerged from the caves; among these were the Nahuatl-speaking Mexica, who later founded the great city of Tenochtitlan in AD 1325. Was the White Shaman mural produced by the ancient Chichimec, who were ancestral to the Mexica? Was White Shaman Shelter one of the cave-birthplaces associated with Chicomoztoc?

The answers to these and many more questions are contained in the visual texts archived in the canyons of southwest Texas and northern Mexico. The Lower Pecos is an untapped library. The vast body of Pecos River style rock art (spanning perhaps three thousand years) affords a unique opportunity to study the emergence and formalization of the style and, more importantly, the enduring core traditions it expresses. Indeed, intensive documentation and rigorous analyses of rock art on both sides of the border will likely translate into a rewriting of North American prehistory.

Transcendence and Transformation

There has been a long-standing debate, recently turning somewhat contentious, about why ancient people put art on rock canvases (see, for example, Bahn 2010). Much of this discussion has been centered on the spectacular Upper Paleolithic cave paintings in France and Spain. Early explanations of the paintings included art for art's sake and sympathetic magic to assist with hunting. Those explanations have enjoyed a long history (see discussion in Lewis-Williams 1995). More than forty years ago Annette Laming-Emperaire (1962) and André Leroi-Gourhan (1968) advocated a binary structuralist approach to explaining rock art, relying on what was called "an aesthetic reality." This concept saw all rock art symbolism as "images of the outside world reflected in the mind and materialized in artistic creation" (Leroi-Gourhan 1993:272). After the death of Leroi-Gourhan in 1986, however, the structuralist approach was abandoned in favor of more empirical work focused on the doctrine that the art is a result of sensory experience. This led researchers back to what was considered fundamental in the universal practice of shamanism to explain the rock art (Lewis-Williams 2002:193).[16]

This somewhat shaman-centric view of rock art has been widely advocated for at least the past thirty years. I, too, engaged this approach to some degree (Boyd 2003). It holds that most prehistoric rock art is either the result of the shamans-as-artists depicting their hallucinogenic experiences (see, for example, Whitley 1994, 2011) or that some of the symbols used in rock art depict entoptic mental images resulting from altered states of consciousness (see, for example, Lewis-Williams and Dowson 1988).[17] Nicholas Saunders (1998:6) has appropriately dubbed this type of rock art "hallucinogenically inspired iconography." As evidenced in the preceding pages, any explanation for the existence of Pecos River style rock art relying *solely* on the neuropsychological theory of visual perception (ostensibly involving shamans) is far too short-sighted.[18]

In the case of the White Shaman mural, the reason it exists is because it served a purpose very similar to that of the painted books referred to as the Mexican codices. Indeed, it is very similar to what is at the core of much of Mesoamerican art: "prayer and direct communication with and participation in the sacred realm" (Furst 1978:19). When attempting to decipher Pecos River style rock art, one must keep in mind that the imagery is not strictly visual communication, but rather a form of visual-verbal communication—or visual narrative. Any meaningful discussion of the significance of the rock art should take into consideration the oral traditions and performances that accompanied it. As with the codices, the imagery was likely read aloud and explained to onlookers who participated in the ceremony through ritual offerings, music, singing, chanting, and dance. This performance would have greatly increased the paintings' ritual significance.[19] Nahua ritual was designed around time and space, orienting the participant to the cosmos and to a sacred landscape (López Austin 1973). Through ritual performance, cosmogonic actions that were performed by gods at the beginning of time are not only commemorated, but repeated; thus human action in the present re-creates events of the past (López Austin 1973; Navarrete 2011:177).

At the White Shaman site, myth, place, and image become fused to create a time-transcending reality. Rituals performed at the rockshelter incorporated the art, which facilitated the creation of a place of metamorphosis both in terms of time and space. This took place on four separate cognitive levels. First, there was the temporal order, transitioning from day to night to day, or summer to winter to summer, in a never-ending cyclical pattern.[20] All living things are born, live, die, and are reborn from the seeds of the previous generation. The story of the White Shaman mural is structured around this temporal order of ongoing transformation.

Second, the mural also has a spatial order. From the perspective of the actors on stage—the ancestral deities looking out from the wall—east is to their right and west is to their left, with north above and south below. The world has four corners and a center. The heavens have thirteen levels, and the underworld has nine. Mountaintops and caves are settings for conversion of profane space to sacred space. The mountaintop has a connection with the heavens, and the cave has its connection with the underworld.[21] All of these are involved with the movement and transformation of souls.[22]

Third, the organization of time and space (for example, the calendrical systems and layout of sacred space) provided mechanisms for the people of the Lower Pecos to understand and control the natural sequence of events (as well as one's destiny) and to center themselves in the cosmos. It is very likely that, as with the Nahua, each day of their lives held essences manifested in the gods and their related associations. The moments of transformation in a person's life—their rites of passage—were, through ritual incorporating the artwork, assigned an orderly place in relation to the cosmos.

Fourth, there is transcendence: the opportunity to experience existence beyond the physical realm. Participants in ceremonies at the White Shaman mural could have achieved transcendence through various forms of austerity and/or altered states of consciousness that allowed them to see the world that lies beyond this one. The ultimate goal of the ritual to which the artwork belonged was transcendence through transformation from human to divine—a performance with many interconnected parts.[23]

In the physical realm participants may have ascended from water—the Pecos River below—and climbed toward the sky to encounter the essences of the gods whose images portrayed on the wall were infused with movement and life. Fire-flickered images filled with potency danced across the rockshelter. The cosmovision captured when it was originally painted into the mural was brought to life by the movement of the cosmos—the sun, the moon, and the stars—and played out in real time. The smell of incense wafted through the dancing participants. Songs, the *yolia* soul-breath of the performers, accompanied by flutes and drums, resonated down the canyon. It was pure theater—a cosmic drama in which everything was alive and everything hung in the balance.[24] Out of this sensory overload, humans transcended to the realm of the divine.

The artwork also served as the storybook for that theater: it was the organizing element. It appears to have originated out of a type of incipient writing that may have been at least partially perfected in the Lower Pecos Canyonlands. It is probable that the forms and figures in the panel have some sort of linguistic organization, and that the juxtaposition of figures formed a sort of grammar containing its own structural rules easily recognizable to people with knowledge of those rules. That is why in the artwork (similar to the Mexican codices [see Boone 2007:55]) there is no background noise that one might otherwise expect to see. Nothing in this panel is random or arbitrary; everything has its place and purpose.

This means that the art has much more to do with the mental conceptualization of the artist(s) than a shaman's altered state of consciousness.[25] Both the techniques of the composition and the messages are those of the artist-as-storyteller rather than those uniquely ascribed to shamans.[26] Ultimately, the White Shaman mural is a depiction of a culture's perception of reality.[27] Today most of us are conditioned to a material reality, but the people who painted the Pecos River style rock art perceived a world infused with a spiritual reality. It was a world in which one had to connect with one's own life force to achieve mastery of life. The harsh world we see in the Lower Pecos today was not the real world to these people. The real world was a metaphysical one—the transcendent reality depicted in the White Shaman mural—and it was the duty of the artist(s) to bring this world to life for the benefit of their community.[28] "If the good artist is master of himself and possesses a face and a heart, he will be able to achieve what is the proper end of art: 'to humanize the desires of the people,' that is, to help others to understand things human and divine and to behave in a truly human way" (León-Portilla 1980:210).

The whole notion of transcendence through transformation is, of course, a human universal fundamental to religious philosophy—whether Buddhism, Taoism, Christianity, or many others—and is present in virtually all Native American religions, which, in the end, brings us back once again to our opening discussion of shamanism. Upon entering the White Shaman rockshelter, imagine yourself walking into the Vatican's Sistine Chapel. Putting a creation story on the Sistine Chapel's ceiling required the engineering of scaffolding, the painstaking layout of the art, the making of the paint, and the very time-consuming conceptual design of an incredible genius. Viewing the rock art solely from the neurological perspective totally misses its incredible complexity and spirituality. I am not saying that shamanism played no part in the artwork. Indeed, the whole idea of transcendence through transformation is central to shamanism.[29] But just because transcendence is a necessary component of shamanism, do we have to resort to shamanism in order to explain transcendence (see Bahn 2010; Bednarik 1990)? Or, more likely, are we dealing with a mental concept universal to the Native American psyche? In terms of the artwork, it would have been much more the role of the artist to give life to the transformational process and bring the spiritual world to the people, for as Joseph Campbell (1986:*xxii*) famously pointed out, "without images . . . there is no mythology." In a myriad of ways, the art brought life to the mythology, and the mythology aided in the spiritual development of the participants, helped establish community, and was used as a teaching device for understanding natural law.

On a basic level the White Shaman mural tells a story. The method of reading that story was handed down from generation to generation, such that anyone who understood the grammar could read the painting. Then, at some point in time, everyone with that special knowledge moved on, and the message of the White Shaman mural went into a very long period of dormancy. But as those ancient artists have shown us, time always returns to its place of origin.

The headless white anthropomorph has long been seen as the visually dominating figure of the panel, and, indeed, the panel was in very recent times named for her. But she is only one of a series of interrelated figures playing out this story of creation, which may be the oldest recognized such story in all of North America. We are today separated by many generations from its creators: the original Grand Masters. The very fact that they could hand down a story to us that we can even partially understand is simply astounding to consider.

Almost eighty years ago Forrest Kirkland (1939:71) proclaimed the "outstanding artistic achievement" of Pecos River style artists. It wasn't their ability to accurately portray individual elements that impressed Kirkland, but the skillful way these elements were intentionally placed into "elaborate, beautifully balanced designs and compositions" to communicate "firmly fixed mythological ideas." Kirkland was an artist—and he was right. His perception of the people who painted the murals was shaped by the sophistication of their art. As archaeologists we too often define ancient cultures solely by their material remains. In the Lower Pecos, these remains engender images of simple foragers engaging simple tools in an often harsh and unforgiving landscape. Without the art, they are yet another little understood and little regarded Archaic population eking out a meager existence as best they could. But with the art, worlds change and wonder begins.

NOTES

CHAPTER 1

1. We recognize that the White Shaman mural is not a book in the literal sense, with multiple pages bound together by a hinge along one side. Our purpose for using the term here is to stress its function as a repository of knowledge for the people who understood its mechanism for communicating very specific and very complex ideas. As will be demonstrated in the pages that follow, the mural's message was conveyed operationally and progressively; it was not static as a work of visual art would normally be. In this fashion, its function most closely emulates a visual manuscript as opposed to simply a depiction of whatever was painted there.

2. The term *Mesoamerica,* which was first proposed by Paul Kirchhoff (1943), refers to a geographical and cultural area that extends from central Mexico into Central America. According to Kirchhoff, cultural groups within this region shared key features not found elsewhere. Based upon a suite of interrelated cultural similarities, he maintained that these groups were variations on a similar cultural theme, likely derived from a common ancestral culture; however, traditional features of Mesoamerican civilizations also appear outside of Kirchhoff's geographical boundaries for the region. In fact, its geographical borders frequently differ depending on the idea or symbol that is the point of reference. This has led some prominent Mexican scholars (e.g., Jáuregui 2008) to argue that the term should be retired from the lexicon. While I tend to agree with Jáuregui on this issue, in practicality it is difficult to avoid the term when so many authors cited herein use it.

3. To my knowledge, Lieutenant Francis Henry French and Captain Samuel Gibbs French were not related.

4. William (Bill) Sontag, under contract with Shumla Archaeological Research and Education Center, compiled a comprehensive site history for 41VV124 (White Shaman Shelter). He digitally recorded over twenty-five hours of personal interviews with past and present stakeholders of the site, and mined records housed in county offices, museums, the Texas General Land Office, and more. His unpublished manuscript is a significant contribution and is on file at Shumla.

5. See color plate 2 in *Rock Art of the Lower Pecos* (Boyd 2003).

6. It is unknown at this time if the imagery was executed by one artist or by an artist and his or her apprentice(s). In the lower registry of the mural are fine-lined, red figures that may or may not have been painted by the same artist. In some cases they are interwoven with the polychromatic figures, suggesting they were painted contemporaneously. In all cases, they follow the same rules governing production of the mural, which will be discussed in subsequent chapters.

7. In addition to peyote effigies, several items of material culture recovered from the Shumla Caves excavations are similar to paraphernalia used in peyote ceremonies by various aboriginal groups. These include rasping sticks made from either bone or wood, a rattle made from deer scapula, a pouch and reed tubes containing cedar incense, and feather plumes (La Barre 1975; Lumholtz 1900, 1902).

8. Even most skeptics, however, would concede that certain iconography familiar to us today, such as the symbol of the menorah, date back thousands of years yet retain basically the same meaning.

CHAPTER 2

1. The name of the group encountered by the expedition is variously transcribed from Castaño de Sosa's 1590 journal as Tepeguan (Foster 2008:177), Tepelguan (Schroeder and Matson 1965:50), and Depesguan (Sosa 1871:207).

2. For a comprehensive discussion on Native Americans in and around the Lower Pecos Canyonlands after Spanish contact see Kenmotsu and Wade 2002; Wade 2003; and Foster 2008.

3. In Nahuatl, *Hueyquetzales* translates to something like "people of the prominent tail feathers." This may relate to the

large anthropomorphic figures in Pecos River style rock art portrayed with hip-clusters resembling tail feathers.

4. "Images are viewed in their contextual richness, as part of an ongoing social discourse that involves their influence in social life" (Duncum 2001:107).

5. "Review of Rock Art Dates for Lower Pecos, Texas," manuscript in preparation by Karen Steelman, Lennon Bates, Carolyn Boyd, and Marvin Rowe.

6. The paint sample was collected from a Pecos River style anthropomorph at 41VV576 (Jackrabbit Shelter).

7. Schaafsma (1986:70) also sees parallels in the material culture of both regions, such as in the Grand Canyon split-twig figurine complex and clay figures recovered from Cowboy Cave, which is located near the Great Gallery mural in southern Utah.

CHAPTER 3

1. See, for example, *When Writing Met Art* (2007) by Denise Schmandt-Besserat.

2. Julio Amador Bech's book *El significado de la obra de arte* (2011) provides an excellent critique and review of Panofsky's work and presents basic concepts required for a hermeneutic approach to the interpretation of art.

3. Art historian David Gebhard from the Roswell Museum and Art Center was contracted by the National Park Service in the 1960s to assess and record the region's rock art. His recording techniques would unknowingly cause irreversible damage to the paintings and complicate efforts to radiocarbon date the art. Due to their faded condition, he elected to use kerosene to enhance the imagery. "Since we were relying on a photographic record we found it necessary to carefully clean each of the panels and in a majority of cases to coat the drawings with kerosene which appreciably helped to bring out the colors . . ." (Gebhard 1960:16). This practice was continued by Terence Grieder (1966:ii) and likely many others after.

4. For more information on the work conducted at the site and the data collected, see the *White Shaman Site Report* (2017) (www.shumla.org).

5. These paintings, as well as the site trinomial painted in 1958, are virtually invisible today. The paint is not gone, just obscured by accretions. We measured the relative moisture content of the limestone wall at various locations throughout the shelter using a protimeter. Interestingly, these heavily accreted areas returned significantly higher moisture levels than the section of the wall supporting the mural.

6. At Halo Shelter (41VV1230) and Black Cave (41VV76) we identified this same sequence for antlered anthropomorphs with black dots at the tips of their tines. The black dots were painted first, followed by the red antler tines.

7. A pXRF instrument consists of an X-ray tube source and a solid-state diode detector at angles visible in the sampling window. Primary (incident) X-rays emitted from the source strike atoms in the analyte with sufficient energy to eject low-energy inner shell electrons, creating an unstable ion. When this occurs, an electron from a higher-energy, outer orbital fills the vacancy—releasing energy in the form of secondary (fluorescent) X-rays. The energy of any given secondary X-ray is characteristic of a specific element, allowing qualitative identification of elements present in a sample. In addition, the detector also counts the number of secondary X-rays from the sample, allowing quantitative elemental concentrations to be determined.

8. See Koenig et al. 2014. This work was conducted in conjunction with Marvin Rowe (Texas A&M University–Qatar, Doha, and the Conservation Laboratory, Museum of New Mexico, Santa Fe) and Karen Steelman (Department of Chemistry, University of Central Arkansas, Conway).

9. These results agree with those of Hyman et al. (1996), who studied Pecos River pictographs in Panther Cave (41VV83) with X-ray diffraction (XRD), which yields the specific mineral (molecular) content of pigment. This process, however, is destructive. They found that all black paint was produced from manganese, and all shades of yellow and red paints were produced from a myriad of iron oxide/hydroxide minerals, including hematite (α-Fe_2O_3), maghemite (γ-Fe_2O_3), goethite (α-FeOOH), lepidocrocite (γ-FeOOH), magnetite (Fe_3O_4), and ferrihydrate (Fe_5O_7OH). In two dark red pigments analyzed by Hyman et al. (1996), both iron and manganese minerals were detected. This suggests that ancient artists either mixed iron and manganese minerals or used a naturally heterogeneous ore to produce the unique dark purple/red-colored pigment.

10. Robert Mark and Evelyn Billo with Rupestrian Cyberservices were contracted to produce the Gigapan photograph.

11. The White Shaman full-panel rendering contains 201 individual layers created in Adobe Photoshop, with each layer representing a single unit of stratification.

12. Although the archaeological evidence for the Huichol in their present location dates back to the Classic period (around 200–700 AD), "the Huichol found by the conquistadores were composite, varied societies made up of the fragments of neighboring native societies which had imploded into the mountains and canyons where a substantial Mesoamerican tradition already existed" (Weigand 1978:101). How much the belief system of the original Huichol was influenced by this amalgamation of various cultures is not known.

13. "El espíritu que alienta este trabajo se alimenta de la premisa de que el estudio minucioso de los indígenas que pueblan el Gran Nayar debe ser el punto de partida para entender el México antiguo . . ." (Aedo 2003a:221).

14. "To know something is not to be aware of the minute details of that thing but instead is to understand how that thing fits into an ever-expanding system. The Maya world is not equal to the sum of its parts. Instead, the elements making up this world must be understood as part of a gestalt, a vast system whose primary function is the regeneration and continuance of time and of the world" (Prechtel and Carlsen 1988:123).

15. "It seems to me that this multivalency is one goal of the Mesoamerican aesthetic: to provide a composition that can be understood and performed on many different levels. Attempts to decipher iconography should follow Mesoamerican epistemology and aim to see these webs of symbols as part of 'a vast system'" (Tate 2012:46).

16. "López Austin proposes a strategy for identifying the 'solid nucleus' of a symbol and a variable 'web of associations' that allows for the construction of local meanings. Such matrices of associations seem to be the fundamental way in which Mesoamerican people construct knowledge" (Tate 2012:46).

17. To a lesser degree, we examined historical accounts and ethnographies of other Uto-Aztecan-speaking peoples, including the Hopi and various small groups from the American Southwest and northwestern Mexico. Several useful early ethnographies exist pertaining to the Hopi, as well as the American group of Uto-Aztecan speakers, the Yaqui. The Maya were the only non-Uto-Aztecan group studied. Much of the modern archaeoastronomy of North America focuses on the Maya and how they viewed their world and shaped their landscape. The pioneers in this field were Anthony Aveni, Linda Schele, David Freidel, Prudence Rice, and Susan Milbrath.

18. Patricia Bass (1989) made the first attempt to analyze the Pecos River style rock art in a semiotic framework. She went into great detail describing the history of semiotic studies up until that point, and her dissertation is a good general historical reference. Our semiotic approach to the rock art is markedly different from hers.

19. A diachronic study examines change over time, whereas a synchronic study is concerned with a particular moment in time.

CHAPTER 4

1. Kaufman and Justeson (2009:223) believe that "the intercultural interaction from which a partly shared Mesoamerican cultural tradition emerged dates no earlier than about 2000 BCE." Vail and Hernández (2010) take noted exception to this theory, at least in the Mesoamerican Late Classic and most assuredly in the Postclassic. What they argue is that the similarities between Mesoamerican cosmologies were directly attributable to "direct communication among priests and scribes from distant areas who were skilled practitioners in the indigenous astronomy of Mesoamerica" (Vail and Hernández 2010:272).

2. "This use of a skirt to stand for a female generative greater-than-normal configuration is prominent in Aztec lore" (Tate 2012:190). "The gods are dynamic beings, and their changing phases can be recognized by the garments and emblems that appear in their different avatars . . . The garments and emblems constitute a code" (López Austin 1993:126).

3. The custom of putting small stones in the mouths of the dead has also been reported as occurring in south Texas during the same time period (Cox and de France 1997:29).

4. It has also been suggested by Danesi (2007:81) that semiotic cognitive codes "are characterized by opposition."

5. Schaefer (1996b:371 fn17) says the Huichol equate the cardinal directions with colors, and that red is east and black is west.

6. "The dynamic opposition between things either sunny and hot or watery and cold is inseparable from the ancient Nahuatl concept of *tlamacehua*, a divine-human covenant founded on the principles of sacrifice and constituting the origin of lunisolar time, movement, and human existence itself" (Chevalier and Sánchez Bain 2003:32).

7. Miguel León-Portilla (1988), David Freidel, Linda Schele, and Joy Parker (1993), Susan Milbrath (1999), and Prudence Rice (2007) have all argued that the Maya cosmogonic view of time dominated their artwork. Barbara Tedlock (1992) has made the same argument for the present-day Highland Maya.

8. The nineteenth-century philosopher Max Muller called this ambivalence of meanings in names "paronomy," which he believed held the key to interpreting myths (Brinton 1897:115).

9. "A major distinction, which is the one most generally noted by specialists in writing systems worldwide, is between systems that record speech, and thus called glottographic or logographic, and those that do not, and can be called semasiographic because they record meaning directly" (Boone 2011:384).

10. *Tlacuilo* is the Nahuatl term for "artist," which means "both painter and writer, and thus conveys the dual nature of the codices as images and narratives . . ." (Navarrete 2000:32 fn).

CHAPTER 5

1. After much consideration, we have elected to use the Spanish name *Huichol* to refer to the Wixáritari because it is the appellation most frequently encountered in both Spanish and English publications.

2. Peyote is a spherical, spineless, chalky blue-green cactus. The plant's geographic range is in northeastern and cen-

tral Mexico, and along the Texas borderlands, including the Lower Pecos Canyonlands (Boke and Anderson 1970; Morgan 1983). It is harvested by slicing off the small exposed crown that appears just above the surface of the ground. When dried, segments of the cactus resemble hard, brownish disks that are referred to as peyote buttons. Although more than thirty alkaloids have been chemically identified in peyote, the major active alkaloid—mescaline—is capable of producing psychic effects and hallucinations in humans (Anderson 1996). To Native Americans, however, peyote is not a hallucinogenic drug, but a medicine, a sacrament; it is the embodiment of spirit.

3. Wirikuta is approximately 500 miles south of Del Rio, Texas, and less than 400 miles from the southernmost extent of the Lower Pecos cultural area.

4. "This multiplicity of versions of an oral tradition that is at the very heart of Huichol spirituality is yet one more illustration of the truism that in mythology there is never just one 'authentic' or 'true' account but many" (P. Furst 2006:58).

5. *Mythemes* are the "gross constituent units" of myth (Lévi Strauss 1955:431). Lévi Strauss argued that myth, like language, can be broken down into constituent units representing the essential core elements or irreducible components of a myth. They are virtually unchanging and are shared and reassembled with other related mythemes in a myriad of ways.

6. According to Neurath (2005c:96 fn25), "In Huichol cosmogony the creation of the sun and peyote can be understood as simultaneous processes. In many versions the origin of peyote is narrated first, a fact that can be taken as an allusion to the Venusian character of peyote. Peyote-induced brightness of vision is equated with the light of early dawn and with the Morning Star anticipating sunrise."

7. Information from the following sources was used to create the abbreviated versions of the myths: P. Furst 1972; Furst and Anguiano 1976; Gutiérrez 2002; Lumholtz 1900; Negrín 1977; Neurath 2000a, 2000b, 2001a, 2001b, 2005a, 2005b; Preuss 1996, 1998a, 1998b; Schaefer and Furst 1996; Zingg [1938] 1977, 2004.

8. In some accounts it is the divine deer, Kauyumari, who guides the pilgrims. They are often considered to be the same.

9. According to Neurath (2005a:73), this dual aspect represents "the ethical ideal of the Huichol *mara'akame*: that of always being willing to commit self-sacrifice."

10. The deer, as leader of the hunt, "shoots himself or, respectively, allows himself to be hit" (Preuss 1996:130).

11. In an account collected by Lumholtz (1902:107–108) it was the Moon who allowed her son to be sacrificed.

12. Also called *Reu'unari* or Cerro Quemado (Burned Mountain). I will refer to the location of the first sunrise as Dawn Mountain throughout the text.

13. Some versions of the myth refer to pitch-pine trees instead of candles. Neurath (2001a:512) says, ". . . del árbol (o de la vela) que se ubica en el centro del universe y sostiene al cielo."

14. It is impossible to discuss here all of the rituals involved during the peyote hunt, much less the Huichol ceremonial cycle. The peyote hunt is one of many rituals, each equally important. It is a cycle, after all. For an overview of the rituals conducted annually, I recommend an article by Arturo Gutiérrez (2011), *Los hacedores de las lluvias.*

15. Flowers are metaphors for peyote (P. Furst 2006:82).

16. Procuring peyote (slaying the deer) is believed to prevent drought (Lumholtz 1900:18).

17. In some accounts the leader becomes Maxa Kwaxi, Great-Grandfather Deer Tail (Furst and Anguiano 1976).

18. Rites of purification and confession are not necessarily reflections of Catholic influence on Huichol religion. Peter Furst (2006:69–70) argues, "I see no reason to regard the rite as anything but purely aboriginal and pre-European. In the first place, confession was practiced in Mesoamerica long before the arrival of the Europeans: an Aztec goddess, Tlazoltéotl, to whom confessions were addressed . . . was appropriately known as 'Eater of Filth.'"

19. Fikes (2011:119) says this divine water is *cüpori* (*kupuri*) and "the word cüpori is synonymous with Ha'yorime (living water)."

20. I use the term *centrastyled* to refer to figures that have some form of design within the central area of the body or decoration along the exterior lines of the body. Modern Huichol artists depict shaman and spirit beings in a skeletonized, or centrastyled, fashion in yarn paintings. When asked why it is done that way, Ramon Medina, a Huichol shaman and artist, responded, "Because that is how it was established in the time of the ancestors" (P. Furst 1978:23).

The transformation from mortal to deity is still part of the ritual today. "To reenter this sacred land these pilgrims, or *peyoteros*, must be transformed into the deities . . . The pilgrims may lose their souls, conceptualized as fuzzy threads (*kupuri*) that connect each *peyotero* to the deity who gave him or her life" (Myerhoff 1978:57).

21. The Huichol term for *jicareros* is *xukurikate* and for *jícaras* it is *xukuri* (Kindl 2001).

22. On one level the red heads might be explained by Peter Furst (2006:157), who points out that the Huichol are said to be the descendants of the *Guachichil*, which is "a Nahuatl name said to mean 'red heads,' . . . for their custom of painting their faces red." Both Furst and the early French explorer Diguet noted this same custom among the Huichol (P. Furst 2006:157).

23. Cosmogonic sacrifices are those relating to the creation of the cosmos.

24. According to Faba Zuleta (2003:78), " . . . al pintar sus rostros con la pintura amarilla (uxa) sufren una transformación explícita en el ritual del peyote. Los Jicareros literalmente se convierten en las deidades . . ."

25. Throughout the southwestern United States (and, indeed, all over North America) one finds what appear to be human faces in rock art, mostly in the form of petroglyphs. To a large extent these are representations of masks (Markman and Markman 1989; Reagan 1935). Most Westerners think of masks in the Shakespearean sense, where the same actor can represent different characters simply by donning different masks. But that's not quite what is meant here. In well-documented historical contexts among Native Americans, the concept operates somewhat differently. Whenever a person puts on the mask, the person wearing the mask assumes the essence, if not the exact identity, of the image portrayed. "Every mask, costume, effigy, and object embodied a particular force . . . To wear it meant to take on its face (*ixtli*), to become its identity" (Read 1998:147).

This idea was carried over to the rather grisly concept of the flaying of humans. Historical accounts of the Aztecs had them dressing up individuals as gods or goddesses for elaborate ceremonies that lasted for as long as a year. During this time the individuals actually became the gods or goddesses they represented and were treated as such. At the end of the designated time period the individuals were put to death (usually beheaded), and their skins were removed from their bodies. These skins, or parts thereof, were worn by priests or beggars for a specific period of time or until they literally rotted off. The early Spanish chroniclers from whom we have learned about this practice actually commented on the smell (which, considering the source of the comment, must have been pretty rancid). The Nahua actually had a god of flaying, Xipe Totec, which indicates how significant the concept was to them.

26. "The mythology reveals that in the first times lighted candles strengthened the Sun-father. They assisted him to rise for the first dawn" (Zingg [1938] 1977:637-638).

27. "Tatewari [Grandfather Fire] is, in fact, the mara'akame (shaman) of the gods, for he led them on the first peyote hunt and thus provided the ceremonies and myths for that event in 'Ancient Times' . . . Tatewari [Grandfather Fire] cleanses man, returning him to his original condition of innocence and purity, the condition which must be regained before the peyote can be found" (Myerhoff 1974:77–78).

28. Spelled Kahuí by Negrín (1977:16). The symbolism of the white cord is repeated in the First Fruits Ceremony (*Tatei neixa*), during which children metaphorically fly to the land of peyote. White cotton balls representing the children and rain are attached along the cord. One end is attached to the three-legged drum (*tepu*) representing the mother goddess and the starting point of the journey in the west. The other end of the cord is attached to a pair of antlers, representing their final destination in the east and the deer deity, Maxa Kwaxi or Kauyumari (P. Furst 2006:61; Gutiérrez 2011; Lumholtz 1900).

29. Kelley Hays-Gilpin and Jane Hill (1999), as well as Karl Taube (2001), have demonstrated that the Mesoamerican Flower World complex has a great antiquity, "certainly prior to the break-up of proto-southern-Uto-Aztecan" (Hill 1992:138).

30. The cord, called *huicüxa* or *wikuyau*, is the spiritual lifeline or umbilical cord connecting the Huichol to the celestial mother (Fikes 2011:115).

31. " . . . de donde todo sale y a donde todo regresa" (Gutiérrez 2002:200).

32. The plant has been identified by Bauml et al. (1990) as *Mahonia trifoliolata* of the Berberidaceae family. It is commonly referred to by such names as *algerita* and *agarita*.

33. An interesting aspect of the White Shaman rockshelter is that if it were entered from below, as is done today, those coming in are traveling the path of the pilgrims, moving upward from right to left along the panel and then moving in the opposite direction upon leaving. Participants in rituals conducted here could easily have climbed up to the panel from the Pecos River, reenacting the first emergence from the watery underworld. In a ceremony closely mimicking the actions of the Ancestors and the re-creation of the universe, these facts must have been very important.

34. Although from the viewer's perspective this motif is located on the left side of the mural, from the perspective of the figures portrayed on the wall it is to the right.

35. In August 2010 the Huichol *mara'akame* (shaman) Matsihua visited the White Shaman panel. The first motif he pointed to was the red and black crenellated band (E007). Translated from Huichol, to Spanish, to English, I was told it represents the ocean. What I wanted to say was, "I am sorry, you must be confused. I think it represents the western entrance to the underworld." Thankfully, I said nothing. Later I remembered that to the Huichol, the ocean is associated with the serpent that surrounds the world, the west, and the entrance into the underworld. "Ocean" is a metaphor. The Huichol shaman possessed the cognitive code required to "read" the motif within moments of visiting the mural.

36. Significant portions of this figure are obscured by a white accretion resulting from a water seep in the limestone wall. Given its intimate relationship with water, it is likely that this natural feature was intentionally integrated into the composition.

37. The ocean in the west at sunset represents the union of opposites: fire and water. Out of this union the sun is born.

38. The combination of the black and red may also be representative of the sexual union between the female (black)

and male (red) deities that resulted in solar light (yellow). The first conception of the sun occurs at the fall equinox as a result of the union between the fire god and Earth Mother (Francisco Samaniega, personal communication, February 26, 2013).

39. The native groups found in west Mexico's Gran Nayar include the Cora, Huichol, and Mexicanero (Neurath 2005c:74). Neurath (2005c:76) argues that this "symbolic complex is not limited to Gran Nayar Indians, as indicated by the ubiquity of Venus-related symbolism in many ancient civilizations of Mesoamerica and in indigenous cultures of northwest Mexico and the North American Southwest."

40. Neurath (2005c:88) refers to the name of Morning Star in this context as "Parikuta Muyeka (He who walks at dawn)."

41. Neurath (2005c:81) points out that the Huichol language has several ways to refer to the planet Venus, including Xurawe Temai, Tamatsi Parietsika, Tunuwame, and Parikuta Muyeka.

42. Slaying with arrows is associated with metamorphosis and transformation throughout much of the ethnographic literature. Olivier (2003:145) writes, "We know that the act of shooting an arrow is the equivalent of fecundation." Ake Hultkrantz (1997:111) noted that a shooting ceremony was found in the Sun Dance of the Plains Indians where "a feather containing supernatural power 'kills' the dancers . . . The killing symbolizes the transference of supernatural powers, a transference that is so revolutionary it demands a symbolical death and renewal-of-life rite." Wissler and Duvall (1909:68–70) tell a story from the Blackfoot where shooting an arrow actually brings dead individuals back to life. Howard Martin (1977:45) relates a story from the Alabama-Coushatta Indians where one brother shooting an arrow brings his dead brothers back to life. And according to the Huichol, the slaying of the deer with arrows transforms the deer's heart into peyote.

43. According to Neurath (2005a:74), cosmogonic transformations such as this "often imply a twist in narrative logic." He uses as an example the myth of the goddess of the sea, in which the goddess throws herself against a giant rock at the extreme western edge of the cosmos to become mist and rain. She is then transformed into the rock she threw herself against. "In other words, she throws herself at herself to become herself," (Neurath 2005a:74).

44. Elder Brother Morning Star is represented as an arrow. "The notch of the arrow's shaft is considered to represent the 'horns' of Morning Star, or rather his 'antlers,' because he is also a deer" (Neurath 2005c:77).

45. "The sacred peyote itself, notwithstanding its qualitative equation with a male deer, particularly in the context of the peyote hunt, is conceived as female" (P. Furst 1996:36). Weston La Barre (1979:37–38) notes that many North American tribes believed male and female plants were different species, even though, botanically, there is only one. "Indian tribes have persistently stated that there were two kinds of peyote, but since their distinction was based on a folkloristic male/female dichotomy in a non-dioecious cactus, their contention was largely dismissed."

46. The lack of hooves may also relate to a Gran Nayar myth in which the foot or leg of Evening Star is devoured by a female monster (Neurath 2005c:83).

47. "The energy of *kupuri* blesses, or irradiates, a person's entire body, including the *iyari*" (MacLean 2012:209).

48. This is also the case for antlered anthropomorphs at Black Cave (41VV76), Halo Shelter (41VV1230), and Cedar Springs (41VV696). Using a digital microscope we were able to determine that the red antlers of anthropomorphs at these three sites overlay black dots at the tips of each tine.

49. This section of the mural is badly damaged. The legs of A006 clearly overlay the black of E001, but it is difficult to determine whether the red of A006 or the red of E001 was the next layer applied. It appears, though, that the red anthropomorph overlays the red arch. Either way, the antlered figure is sandwiched into E001 through the addition of yellow.

50. Again, damage to this section of the panel makes it difficult to determine for certain if the black line is over or under the black body of A001, but it appears to be over.

51. Lumholtz (1900:11) refers to this god as Tayau Sakaimoka, the "setting sun" and assistant to Father Sun.

52. Kauyumari "in many contexts can be considered almost the same as Tamatsi Parietsika" (Neurath 2005c:81).

53. Also spelled Tate'vali (Lumholtz 1900), Tatevalí (Zingg [1938] 1977), and Tatewarí (Schaefer and Furst 1996).

54. "The light of the moon was not sufficient to light the way of the first peyote pilgrims of the dry-season party, who were led by the greatest of the dry-season gods, Grandfather Fire. There was much danger of wild animals. So *tatevali* (Grandfather Fire) lent them fire until their quest for peyote would be successful and thus strengthen the Sun-father so he could risk the danger of shining everyday" (Zingg [1938] 1977:514).

55. I don't know if the tip of the dart is stylized like those impaling the deer and peyote. Poor preservation makes it impossible to locate the distal end of the dart.

56. Typically, over 40 percent of Pecos River style anthropomorphs are associated with a loaded atlatl. If that were the case here, more than twenty figures should be depicted thusly.

57. Valadez (1996:293) says, "The yellow face paint (uxa) the peyote pilgrims wear is said by some Huichols to represent sparks from the fire, thus helping to merge the peyoteros with the ancestor gods they represent on the sacred journey."

58. "Otra figura que encontramos representada en las pin-

turas faciales es la del ciempiés, insecto que es considerado un animal venenoso, asociado a la llegada de las lluvias . . ." (Faba Zuleta 2003:86).

59. Among the hundreds of anthropomorphic figures, it is one of only a few portrayed in this fashion.

60. In Mesoamerican iconography "sight was transmissive and procreative" (Houston et al. 2006:170). "It not only receives images from the outer world, but positively affects and changes that world through the power of sight—in short, it behaves as an 'emanating eye' that establishes communion between internal will and external result" (Houston et al. 2006:167).

61. As mentioned in the chapter 1, this is one of the most ubiquitous patterns identified in Pecos River style art.

62. "Summarizing symbols," as defined by Sherry Ortner (1973:1339), are those which are seen as summing up, expressing, and representing for the participants in emotionally powerful and relatively undifferentiated ways what the system means to them.

63. *Kupuri* was born from the Ancestors as rain (Fikes 2011:144).

64. The recycling of an individual's *kupuri* also is based on this analogy (Fikes 2011:132).

65. "The Huichol use both cüpori and antlers as synecdoche-based regenerators of life. The annual growth and shedding of antlers is predicated upon the alternation between rainy and dry seasons. When Huichol offer deer blood and antlers to accompany prayers for rain, they appear to invert this relationship of cause (rain) and effect (growth of plants producing more food for deer, which is subsequently manifested in antler growth)" (Fikes 2011:144–145). The Huichol view deer antlers as a sacred symbol that can be used to persuade the Ancestors to release the rains.

66. Fikes (2011:152) provides an ecological explanation for the relationship between antlers and rain—or, more specifically, the rainy season—as follows: "[A]ntlers are symptomatic of a natural cycle characterized by the alternation between rainy and dry seasons . . . This is the optimal time for their growth, which results from deer feeding on plants whose growth is fueled by rain. The growth of antlers is contingent upon certain conditions, primarily rain and plant growth. In this sense, antlers are a true index of the rainy season."

67. The red head of A002 clearly overlays the black mask of A008, but determining the paint sequence between the red of A002 and the red of A008 is very difficult.

68. "Las dos rocas blancas, aparentemente, representan a los dioses de las estrellas de la Mañana y de la Tarde. Se trata de figuras separadas que, frecuentemente, son identificadas una con la otra" (Preuss 1998b:324).

69. The "whiskers" might instead be bifurcated antlers.

70. Also referred to as Tacutsi (Negrín 1975) and Tako'tsi Nākawe' (Lumholtz 1900).

71. Also referred to as Yurienaka (Schaefer 2002), Tāte' Yuliana'ka (Earth Goddess) and Otegana'ka (Lumholtz 1900), and Tatei Yurinanaka (Our Mother Earth) and Tatei 'utianaka (the fish goddess) (Kindl 2000).

72. Designs in gourd bowls are not simply images but also writing. This is linked back to their creator, Tatei Utianaka: the root *utia* means "to write." When figures are applied within the gourd bowls, they are given their own life. "The important point here is the Huichol conception of the power of the written image . . . the written images that are formed of wax in these gourd bowls also have creative powers that connect with natural phenomena . . ." (Kindl 2000:55).

73. The spots are said to represent corn of all colors. Maize, peyote, and deer share a "plural identity" (Lemaistre 1996:308).

74. Other deities are equally associated with Tāte'Īpou, the two-headed serpent. Lumholtz (1900:81) stated that it is not uncommon for the same name to be given to multiple deities: "Having the same name, it is evident that these serpents are all the same to the Indian mind. There is no more contradiction in this than in the fact that there are various serpents representing one and the same god . . ."

75. Also referred to as Naaliwa'mi (Lumholtz 1900), Ni'ariwame (Neurath 2000a), Naia'ariwame (Neurath 2005c), Na'aliwaemi (Zingg [1938] 1977), N+'ariwame (Schaefer 2002), and Nariwame (Preuss 1996).

76. As determined among colors and figures engaged in a stratigraphic relationship.

77. "On the way to the godhouse of the Sun, one also passes the place where the Earth Mother Takutsi, who here, as in Aztec Mexico, is at the same time the Moon" (Preuss 1996:118).

78. Also referred to as Kewimuka (Schaefer 2002, Kindl 2000) and Tāte' Kyewimo'ka or Kyewimo'ta (Lumholtz 1900).

79. In Huichol art, S-shapes refer to rain serpents (Lumholtz 1900:47; Schaefer 1996:353).

80. "When the Huichol ancestors left the ocean, the world was still dark. Only the moon and stars lit the eternal darkness" (Neurath 2005b:590).

81. Also referred to as Sakaimo'ta and Sakaimo'ka (Lumholtz 1900) and Tsakaimúka (Zingg [1938] 1977).

82. Of the Huichol ceremony, Neurath (2001a:503) says that the most esoteric part is the initiation and reactualization of the cosmogonic sacrifices that the Ancestors suffered in the beginning. Initiation, the search to find one's *taiyari* (heart) and to acquire *nierika* (sight), means to become involved in the world of the Ancestors, to bring to life the original community of the gods, and to facilitate the continuance of the natural cycles.

83. Paul T. Kay (2005) shows a mural figure from the site of Pottery Mound that he interprets to be the caterpillar of the

hawk moth. This figure also has five sets of concentric circles on its body.

84. See also Milbrath 1999:25 and Nuttall 1901:249.

85. White paint was repeatedly applied at locations where black transitions into red, or vice versa. Note the torches and heads of each *jicarero*.

86. "Jimsonweed's [Kieri's] 'face' (aspect) was changing . . . the Sun was changing his heart"—meaning his color was changing (Zingg 2004:18). Perhaps the *iyari* of the deer, which was changed into peyote at the dawn of time, was previously the stone heart of Kieri. If so, the black dots attached to the antler tines, brought up from the underworld by the emerging sun god, may represent datura prior to transformation into peyote.

CHAPTER 6

1. Although there were many languages and countless dialects spoken throughout all of Native America, at the time of conquest Nahuatl was the *lingua franca* (Read 1998:4).

2. " . . . Chicomoztoc, sometimes conflated with Aztlan, was one of the most common sites of emergent creation referred to in the sixteenth-century manuscripts of the early colonial period" (Carrasco and Sessions 2007a:1).

3. The start of time is marked in this pictorial narrative by the ritual performance of the New Fire Ceremony (Carrasco and Sessions 2007a).

4. The Teotihuacanos were centered in the Basin of Mexico and are recognized as having extended their influence well beyond their environs, even more so than the Mexica (Read 1998).

5. The Borgia Group includes pictorial manuscripts sharing similarities in production, artistic style, content, and arrangement. The primary members of the Borgia Group are *Codex Borgia, Codex Laud, Codex Vaticanus B, Codex Cospi,* and *Codex Fejérváry-Mayer. Codex Porfirio Díaz* (which is not pre-Columbian) and *Aubin Manuscript No. 20* sometimes are included as well. The Borgia Group were produced from as far back as the Late Postclassic (preconquest) through to the Early Colonial period (Nowotny 2005).

6. Bernardino de Sahagún has been called the first true anthropologist (León-Portilla 2002b). Over an extremely long life for that time period (1499–1590) he invented anthropological techniques for documenting cultures and histories and for testing the accuracy of information given to him that are still in use today. Although he had his battles with the authorities for wanting to so thoroughly document the Nahua way of life, history has rightfully conferred on him almost mythical stature. The *Florentine Codex,* also called *Historia general de las cosas de Nueva España,* was originally begun as an aid to Franciscan friars in their attempts to convert "the heathens," but Sahagún's continuing perseverance in the face of huge obstacles gives credence to the claim that the man really was, at heart, a dedicated anthropologist trying to preserve in writing a way of life that was rapidly disintegrating.

7. See, for example, Preuss 1998d; Schaefer and Furst 1996; Myerhoff 1974; Neurath 2002; Aedo 2003a; and Carrasco 2008.

8. Legends of how the sun was born vary to some degree. What is presented here primarily follows the account documented in *Leyenda de los soles,* translated from Nahuatl by John Bierhorst (1992) with some contributions drawn from Sahagún's *Florentine Codex* (bk. 7: chap. 2).

9. Olivier (2003:277) refers to Quetzalcoatl and Tezcatlipoca as the "alpha and omega of ancient Mexican mythology."

10. In *Historia de los mexicanos por sus pinturas* (Phillips 1884:622, 648 fn25), Quetzalcoatl heated his son "red hot in a great fire" to become the sun. After the fire went out, Tlaloc (the rain god) threw his son into the ashes to become the moon.

11. "Sacrificial victims were customarily smeared with chalk and crowned with feathers" (Bierhorst 1992:148).

12. In the *Florentine Codex,* Ehecatl-Quetzalcoatl sacrifices the gods, but Xolotl tries to escape. After a lengthy pursuit, he too is slain; however, the sun still fails to move even after all the sacrifices, so Ehecatl blows the sun into movement along its path.

13. Although the New Fire Ceremony is widely attributed to the Nahua (in no small part due to Sahagún), its practice in other cultures has also been documented. J. Walter Fewkes (1906) and Frank Waters (1963:138–141) have recorded a very similar yearly practice among the Hopi (a Northern Uto-Aztecan-speaking tribe). The Zuni—who have their own distinct language group but share much of their ceremonies and religion with the Hopi—practice a similar New Fire Ceremony on the winter solstice in which "songs and dancing . . . continue until the rising of the Morning Star (Warrior to Sun Father) which is carefully watched for by men ascending the kiva ladder" (Stevenson 1904:130). For the Zuni, "it is the winter solstice that marks the starting point of the new year cycle" (Young 1992:77). It is reasonable to deduce from these examples that the original concept of the New Fire Ceremony in its Proto-Uto-Aztecan form related in some fashion to the renewal of time and the rejuvenation of the sun. Other historically recorded examples of fire ceremonies from the American Southwest may have been heavily influenced by the Hopi.

14. The earliest iconographic evidence of a New Fire Ceremony dates to the Early Classic period at Teotihuacan (see, for example, Fash et al. 2009: Uriarte 2006; von Winning 1979:19).

15. This cluster of stars was known to the Nahua as Tianquiztli, which translates as "Marketplace" (Carrasco 1999a:97).

16. Three hundred years ago the French philosopher René Descartes proposed a mind-body dichotomy that formed the basis for his concept of dualism. Many dualities, he argued, work along this oppositional scheme. Depicted in the rock art is a very similar philosophy.

17. Chevalier and Sánchez Bain (2003:46) say *tonalli* was given to the child at birth. "It was sent from the Omeyocan (Place of Duality) and was granted to the child at birth during a name-giving ceremony."

18. Jill Furst (1995:89) says the red color of a hot, flushed face provides a visual indicator of "tonalli-as-heat."

19. See Chevalier and Sánchez Bain 2003 for a discussion on healing beliefs and practices related to the hot/cold dichotomy. They write, "Healing beliefs and practices of native inspiration are constantly working at reconciling three things. The first is a sense of balance in all things, hence avoiding insults of excessive heat or cold. The second involves a recognition of the periodicity that governs regular alternations between opposite states experienced through normal activities . . . The third involves a sense of direction through time—an overall process of growth and reproduction generally heading from wetness and birth (cold) to dryness and death in the sun (hot)" (Chevalier and Sánchez Bain 2003:xv).

20. "The *tonalli* that is passed from generation to generation thus appears in the body as hair, fingernails, and blood . . . Both hair and nails possessed *tonalli*, according to the Central Mexicans" (J. Furst 1995:126).

21. "*Difrasismo* refers to a mode of expression in which a single idea is expressed by the conjunction of two or more words that are synonyms of, metaphors for, or express two qualities of the subject" (Hall 1997:95).

22. Aguilar-Moreno (2006:138) writes that "the principal of duality, of joining oppositional forces together into a cohesive whole, permeated Aztec spirituality and society, both of which were interconnected."

23. "Time, born of the feminine and the masculine, came out from the four posts and extended over the space formed by the separation of the sky from the earth" (López Austin 1997:16). See also Hooft 2007:145–146 for an excellent discussion on the union of opposites and establishment of time; she notes that the union of opposites led to the smoking of the skies and "the beginning of a new era, a new creation, the movement of the skies and, therefore, time."

24. Amos Megged (2010:136) and Kellogg (1995:175) identified it as a genealogical representation (*tlacamecayotl*, where *tlacatl* = "person or man" and *mecatl* = "rope or cord").

25. The Huichol are reported to have at one time engaged in human heart sacrifice to the sun as well. A Huichol consultant reported to Fikes (2011:226–227 fn9) that today "they feed him with their own hearts, in addition to using hearts of deer and bulls . . . Because the Huichol are now unable to provide him with children's hearts, their life is more difficult."

26. One of "the most pervasive of all concepts connected with the cult of sacrifice . . . is the equivalence of the god and the victim being sacrificed to him. We have seen something of the same identity attributed to the captor and his captive, who were supposed to be father and son" (Brundage 1983:210–211).

27. "Recall that the umbilical cord is the organ through which blood is transmitted to children and that the giving of blood in the womb, where the mother first feeds her child, is the basis of a *nakara* relationship, where parents give their children 'the heat of life.' In *nakara*, the generation of life, and its sustenance, are inseparably linked . . . when we see individuals connected to one another by an umbilical cord in the codices, the umbilical cord represents an ongoing relationship of *nakara*, as well as a tie of descent" (Monaghan 1994:95).

28. "The circle of the horizon has the association of 'year' among the Sioux and the Pawnee, and presumably in Mesoamerica as well, because of its conflation with the ecliptic and the annual movement of the sun" (Hall 1997:165).

29. According to Schele and Mathews (1999:114–115), ". . . the snake umbilicus also symbolized the ecliptic so that the planets traveled along the snake's body. The king held the double-headed snake to show he controlled this conduit to the source of power and ancestral wisdom."

30. "In Tenochtitlan, when the Mexica erected the Main Temple (Templo Mayor), they did it according to the cosmogonies of the most ancient peoples of Mesoamerica. The great pyramid, the navel of the cosmos, was built in the center of the city . . . The Main Temple had two sanctuaries . . . One of its sanctuaries was dedicated to Tláloc, the god of rain and fertility . . . and the other to Huitzilopochtli, the national Mexica god. As Johanna Broda has determined, both temples celebrated the ancient cult of the primordial mountain: Tláloc's sanctuary represents Tonacatépetl, the pristine mountain of sustenance, whereas Huitzilipochtli's sanctuary symbolizes the Coatépetl, the snake's backbone . . ." (Florescano 1999:185).

31. This same idea is found among the Hopi in their concept of the "solar ladder," which also has six steps on either side (Fewkes 1918:524).

32. "Thus Cihuacoatl's house of blackness could symbolize the cave dwelling of the new moon" (Milbrath 1997:197).

33. Carrasco (1999a:99) notes that in the New Fire Ceremony both the Hill of the Star and the Templo Mayor served as *axes mundi*.

34. Milbrath (2013:81) notes also that among the Maya, deer are believed to carry the sun swiftly across the sky during the short days of winter. They metaphorically equate deer with life-generating power, including the sun. This is powerfully manifested in the ritual Dance of Martín, conducted

annually at the beginning of the dry season to renew or recreate the world. A deer is said to have carried on its back the bundle of Martín, the most powerful object associated with renewal, from the sacred cave and place of creation. During the ceremony two dancers in the guise of deer are symbolically killed at midnight. This sacrificial act, the slaying of the deer, recharges the world with life-giving power. The dance, like the Huichol pilgrimage, is not merely a representation of creation, "but a means of returning to the dawn of time itself in order to repeat the actions of deified ancestors and gods" (Sachse and Christenson 2005:16). Xbalanque (Jaguar-Deer), one of the hero twins in the Maya creation story, becomes the moon, but also represents the Evening Star and the setting sun. And the setting sun was perceived by the Maya to be a deer (Cohodas 1975:116; Dütting and Schramm 1984:13).

35. Brundage (1983:44–45) argues that in the Nahua creation myth, the Sun, Evening Star, and Morning Star are all one.

36. Another of the names for the night sun is Yohualtecuhtli. In addition Yohualtecuhtli is a stellar deity representing the planet Venus after setting in the west (Klein 1976:10). Milbrath (2013:85), however, suggests that in some contexts this deity represents Saturn rather than Venus.

37. Graulich (1997:180) has proposed that Mixcoatl as the setting sun transformed into the Evening Star.

38. "The Evening Star was to metamorphose and to become, by an act of self-sacrifice, the sun himself" (Brundage 1983:43).

39. An accurate count of the black dots is hindered by mineral accretions. Also, it is important to remember that all black paint was applied to the limestone canvas before any other color was added. Therefore, the black mask of A013 began as one of the thirty-two black dots associated with the black L-shapes.

40. "The seemingly inappropriate procedure of figuring shining stars as black actually furnishes the strongest proof that a star group is thus represented; for, in the Maya language, 'ek' is a homonym for star and black, and a black spot was, in consequence, the most expressive sign for a star" (Nuttall 1901:35). Nuttall suggests that the Mexicans adopted this symbol from the Maya.

41. According to Payne and Closs (1986:216), the number 400 (*tzontli*) "means 'hair' or 'growth of garden herbs' and . . . signifies multitude or abundance." He maintains that the four hundred Mimixcoa "may be interpreted as an allusion to the 'multitude' of stars" (Payne and Closs 1986:219).

42. Mathiowetz et al. (2015:22) have identified striking parallels between the central Mexican star demons and Cora star warriors. During Cora ceremonies reenacting the battle between the stars and the sun, participants portraying star demons don blackened masks. "In essence, the star demons of the Cora who attack the sun appear to be historically related to remarkably similar highland Central Mexican traditions . . ." (Mathiowetz et al. 2015:22).

43. "Chalk and down (*tizatl, ihuitl*) were the most characteristic ornaments: they alone were sufficient to mark a captive doomed to perish on the sacrificial stone" (Graulich 1988:-396).

44. As discussed earlier, white paint placed at the intersection of the black (cold/wet) and red (hot/dry) indicates the location at which oppositional forces are joined; the resulting sacrifice produces a third state—in this case, clouds.

45. Brundage (1983:209) notes that "One of the details in the field of Aztec religion which has not been sufficiently described is the importance of cactus in their mythology . . ."

46. This section of the panel is badly damaged. It is difficult to know for sure if the black line is over or under the black body of A001, but it appears to be over.

47. Peter Furst (2006:247) says that Preuss "saw Káuyumari as the personified Morning Star, the Huichol equivalent of the central Mexican Quetzalcóatl."

48. According to Klein (1976:2), east and north are associated with sunrise and noon, while west and south are associated with sunset and midnight.

49. In *The Tonalamatl of the Aubin Collection*, Seler (1901:73–74) says that *paredes almenadas*, the "word for embattlement (*mixyotl, mixxotl, mixoyotl*) is in Mexican derived from the very term *mixtli*, 'Cloud,' and means the 'cloud-like' (*mixyotl*), or the 'image of the clouds.'" He maintains the stepped aspect of the *paredes almenadas* represents the thirteen layers of the clouds or heavens (Seler 1901:74, 19).

50. Zingg ([1938] 1977:246) thought that the parallels between these two divine culture heroes "may be fortuitous."

51. Eduard Seler (1903:253), referring to the *Codex Vaticanus B*, says " . . . water is the movable element, which sweeps everything away with it, and is thus an expression of the perishable nature of earthly existence." In a very Aristotelian sense, flowing water and time are metaphors for each other.

52. "Out of her crepuscular fires glowing under the horizon were born both night and day. And out of the burning of her body warriors gathered the charred bits of wood with which they painted black circles around their eyes" (Brundage 1983:168).

53. Seler (1963:140) notes that Itzpapalotl does not actually represent fire, but the moth that flitters around it. This is discussed in greater depth at the end of this chapter.

54. Chimalman was identified as the wife of Mixcoatl in *Leyenda de los soles*, but as noted by Yoneda (2007:175), Chimalman and Itzpapalotl are just different personalities of the same deity.

55. "Spranz (1973:473) finds that Itzpapalotl most strongly resembles Xiuhtecuhtli and Mixcoatl" (Milbrath 1995:70).

56. These "whiskers" may also represent antlers similar to those of Z001.

57. H. B. Nicholson (1971: Table 3) groups most of the Nahua goddesses into a single Teteoinnan (Mother of the Gods) complex.

58. Some accounts suggest that Cipactli was beheaded and that her head was taken up to the sky to become the moon (Graulich 1997:50).

59. It should come as no surprise that among the various attributes of lunar deities, especially the goddesses, is the power of fertility and reproduction (see Milbrath 1995).

60. The S-shape, in particular, was identified by Seler (1903:306) as a symbol for lightning.

61. Seler (1903:36) says cakes in the form of S-shapes are included among the offerings given to female goddesses. See also Aguilar-Moreno 2006:372 for more information on the ceremony.

62. Nuttall (1901:34-38) provides a lengthy discussion of the S-shape. She argues the *xonecuilli* represent the constellation Ursa Minor and are related to rain and the summer solstice. In contrast, other authors equate *xonecuilli* with Ursa Major and Tezcatlipoca, who is fused with the lunar deity (see discussion in Olivier 2003:234–235).

63. A horseshoe-shaped vessel symbolizes the moon in Nahua iconography (Milbrath 2013:67). Interestingly, below A015, the figure identified as the moon goddess, are two horseshoe-like shapes, one inverted over the top of the other. Also, for a detailed discussion on water snakes and other water creatures in Huastecan Nahua oral tradition, see Hooft 2007:183–197.

64. If decapitation imagery is a metaphor for observed astral events and seasonal cycles, then its portrayal in the Pecos River rock art is metaphorical, not literal. The prospect of beheading as a form of human sacrifice has always intrigued archaeologists, as well as others with a more morbid fascination with the subject. For the record, there is no archaeological evidence that supports the practice of beheading among the peoples of the Lower Pecos Canyonlands.

65. According to Lumholtz (1900:41), Sakaimoka is portrayed with a ring encircling his head to represent a snare for catching deer.

66. Milbrath (2013:109) writes that "he has so many nocturnal avatars that he may embody the night sky, including the planets, but in the astronomical narrative his most important role is as a lunar god."

67. Olivier (2003:53) says Tezcatlipoca's mirror is "a true anthroponymic glyph of the god."

68. The drilling of fire using a fire board and a drill is a procreative act equated with sexual intercourse (Graulich 1997:102). The "insertion" of the fifth Ancestor into the "bowl" of the Land of Black and Red may also be symbolic of the fire drill inserted into the bowl of the fire board.

69. For an excellent introduction to Xolotl and his numerous avatars, see Brundage (1982:197–233).

70. Klein (1976:4) says the moment the sun disappears at the western horizon, it is "converted into another deity, a solar god of the earth, death, and darkness, who passes through the underworld each night." The list of names by which this deity is referred is lengthy. "The deity, who represented the dead sun at night in the body of the female earth monster, was variously known as Xochipilli, 'Prince of Flowers,' Piltzintecuhtli, 'Lord of Princes,' Yoaltonatiuh, 'Night Sun,' Tlalchitonatiuh or Ollintonatiuh, 'Earth Sun,' and Yohualtecuhtli, the 'Lord of the Night'" (Klein 1976:4).

71. A *synodic period* refers to the time required for a planet to return to the approximately same position relative to the sun as observed from the earth. The Venus cycle is 584 days.

72. " . . . the painters of the central valleys usually linked five disks together with an underline, or occasionally they would link five strokes with a bridge . . ." (Boone 2000:43).

73. "Creo que hay que pensar en las mariposas crepusculares, las grandes falenas, que salen al anochecer y revolotean en torno a la llama" (Seler 1963:140).

74. The *Mapa de Cuauhtinchan No. 2* is an indigenous map from the sixteenth century recounting the Chichimec creation story.

CHAPTER 7

1. "The hypothetical original (Urform or archetype) that served as the prototype or model of which members of a subset (versions and variants of a type) are conceived to be derivatives can be reconstructed on the basis of a determination of the nature and number of discernible similarities and differences among subset members (versions and variants)" (Georges 1986:88–89).

2. Mesoamerican scholars have used a similar approach, perhaps more intuitive than defined, to compare mythologies and symbolism of diverse Native North American cultures, hence the identification of a "hard nucleus" or Archaic core by López Austin (1997).

3. "In the science of botany *ecotype* is a term used to denote a hereditary plant-variety adapted to a certain *milieu* . . . through natural selection amongst hereditarily dissimilar entities of the same species. When then in the field of traditions a widely spread tradition, such as a tale or a legend forms special types through isolation inside and suitability for certain culture districts, the term ecotype can also be used in the science of ethnology and folklore" (Von Sydow 1934:349). For an excellent example of the adaptability of myth, see Schaafsma and Tsosie 2009.

4. Uto-Aztecan languages are spoken as far north as Oregon and Idaho, and as far south as Nicaragua and El Salvador.

5. Catherine Fowler (1983) proposed that the Proto-Uto-Aztecan speakers came from the upper Gila River region, but with an area stretching into northern Mexico. Merrill et al. (2009) propose a Great Basin homeland, while Shaul (2014) places its origins in the southern Central Valley of California. Almost alone in her belief, the linguist Jane Hill (2001a) has proposed that Proto-Uto-Aztecan originated somewhere in central Mexico and migrated north prior to migrating back south again. Kaufman and Justeson (2009) among others (Merrill et al. 2009; Shaul 2014) have challenged this idea by showing that Hill misinterpreted the linguistic evidence that she relied upon to arrive at that theory. Hill's (2001a) theory requires that Proto-Uto-Aztecan peoples were agriculturalists. Fowler (1983) believes that they were hunters and gatherers. Hill (2012:57) returns to her idea that Proto-Uto-Aztecan originally came from "northwest Mesoamerica," although she now concedes that Proto-Uto-Aztecan people may have been hunter-gatherers who were only "in close contact with maize cultivators."

6. Relying on glottochronology, with its most recent modifications, Cecil Brown (2010) attributes the initial break-up of Proto-Uto-Aztecan (the parent language) into its northern and southern components to a time prior to 4118 BP. Silver and Miller (1997:290) have also proposed that it was "about four thousand years ago," but Marianne Mithun (1999:540) has claimed that the "languages are assumed to have diverged around 5000 years ago." Jane Hill (2012:57), reconstructing a pottery vocabulary for all Uto-Aztecan languages, believes that Proto-Uto-Aztecan broke up into its daughter languages no earlier than around 4100–4400 BP.

7. "Nawa has certain phonological traits that link it to Kora and Wichol, but the overall diachronic development trajectory of Nawa does not involve a close connection with Kora-Wichol over a very long period of time; that is, the Nawa to Kora-Wichol similarities are due to contact, not shared evolution" (Kaufman 2001:6). Wheeler et al. (2014:8) maintain that the similarities between Corachol and Nahua may be the result of "relatively recent contact, rather than indications of long-term shared evolution."

8. Beekman and Christensen (2003:136) have theorized that the earliest southern migrations of Nahuatl-speaking peoples from their territory somewhere in northern Mexico began in the sixth century AD.

9. Nuttall (1901:284) observed that "in ancient America, language powerfully influenced the choice of symbols, as may be particularly seen in the case of the serpent, the Nahuatl and Maya names for which are homonymous with duality and quadruplicity."

10. Mathiowetz (2011:295) argues that dots and concentric circles in Casas Grandes iconography are geometric depictions of flowers associated with the Flower World complex.

11. According to Marcos-Marín (2013:50), "there is reason to believe that it [the Pecos River rock art] is closer to South-Uto-Aztecan, arguably before the spilt of it into different subgroups." See also Marcos-Marín 2010.

12. "In the religious realm, these Chichimecs practiced rituals that included the preparation of offerings, the sacrifice of animals, the lighting of new fire, the piercing of cacti with arrows . . ." (Yoneda 2007:161).

13. David Stuart (2011:138) says that "the names are of great antiquity, and hearken back to the very beginnings of Mesoamerican civilization itself," and Rice (2007:32) notes that evidence of the 260-day calendar stretches "as far north as Hidalgo, Mexico, south- and east-ward into Honduras." This probably means, she claims, "that the day names originated long ago, prior to the major Archaic-to-Formative language separations—that is, perhaps as early as 3500 BC" (Rice 2007:33).

14. I didn't recognize some of the numerological associations until I was working on the conclusions. It was quite a surprise. There are any number of other correlations that can be made with other figures in the mural. These will have to wait for future publications.

15. While we have identified the repeated use of specific numbers (such as 9, 13, and 20) in other Pecos River style murals (Fate Bell-41VV74, Cedar Springs-41VV696, and 41VV90, to name a few), investigations are still in their infancy.

16. "Today . . . the shamanic interpretation is widely accepted, though healthy debate continues on just how much of the art is shamanic and in what sense it is shamanic" (Lewis-Williams 2002:194).

17. "Along with vitalized paintings, shamans almost certainly saw their own mental imagery projected onto the walls and ceilings of the shelters" (Lewis-Williams 2002:111).

18. I am not claiming that there is no value in the application of the neuropsychological model to the study of rock art; there most certainly is. It is even likely that some of the mythemes discussed here, such as the gateway serpent, have been influenced, to some degree, by hallucinatory experiences. But altered states of consciousness are only one facet of the whole of human experience that informs myth. See a lengthy critical discussion of the neuropsychological theory in Bahn 2010.

19. "During these performances, the written texts in the codices and monuments were read aloud and explained, while the oral tradition, including formalized discourses . . . as well as poems and chants . . . was solemnly recited" (Navarrete 2011:175).

20. "The cyclical nature of Native American time (rather than the linear, 'progress'-oriented nature of modern Western time) makes it possible for events of the past to occur again in the present. Because the past coexists with the pres-

ent, the past is accessible to Native Americans in a way that it is not accessible to Westerners" (Griffin-Pierce 1992:115).

21. "Across Mesoamerica, religious symbolism has important terrestrial components, and these are most frequently manifested as mountains and caves, which are the natural features considered the most sacred" (Prufer and Brady 2005:405).

22. "The process of creation is the passage through time and space" (Lopez Austin 1993:59). "Space and time are related in that they represent a relationship between objects and actions" (Prufer and Brady 2005:405).

23. "In Nahua culture, transcendence could mean the ability to commemorate the dead and the glorious past by way of a passage from one period of time to another and from one historical-mythological, earthly, or heavenly abode to the next. Moreover, transcendence could be achieved through a transition from one human cycle to the next" (Megged 2012:173).

24. "In the cosmo-magical world of the Aztecs, these images often move and are alive with divine force, participate in the ritual as much as humans do, also (in various ways) see, hear, speak, taste, and touch the social world" (Carrasco 1999a:130).

25. I use the term *artists* to refer to the people who put the artwork on the panel, but they likely performed numerous other important roles within their community. As Graña-Behrens (2012:23-24) points out, the Nahua had a term, *tlamatini,* meaning "wise men," for those who performed several roles, such as priest, soothsayer, and counselor, and also included "that of owner of sacred books, one who counted the days and watched over the prophesies."

26. Among the Nahua, the person who created the codices was called the tlacuilo, a writer/painter who had been through extensive training to learn his art. Sigal (2011:40) says, "In Nahua concepts of the tlacuilo's world, then, the tlacuilo neither reproduces a reality placed in front of him (he is not a realistic painter), nor does he simply write down what he is told. Rather, he engages in a creative, reflective, and interactive process that stresses the oral nature of the text he will produce."

27. Lankford (2007:114), discussing Paul Radin, the early nineteenth-century American ethnographer, says, "He wrote several lengthy studies of the work of the 'artist-philosopher' in native life, whose work is the transformation of traditional folklore into individual showpieces of literary art."

28. John Neihardt ([1932] 2008:67) quotes Black Elk talking about a story told to him by his father: "He said Crazy Horse dreamed and went into the world where there is nothing but the spirits of all things. That is the real world that is behind this world, and everything here is something like a shadow from that world."

29. It is the shaman who "could transcend his human limitations and gain insight into the cosmic order. In the world of the shaman, the elements that constituted man, nature, and the spiritual world were readily interchangeable" (Markman and Markman 1989:143).

BIBLIOGRAPHY

Acuña-Soto, Rodolfo, David W. Stahle, Malcolm K. Cleaveland, and Matthew D. Therrell

2002. Megadrought and Megadeath in Sixteenth Century Mexico. In *Revista Biomédica* 13(4):289–292.

Acuña-Soto, Rodolfo, David W. Stahle, Matthew D. Therrell, Sergio Gomez Chavez, and Malcolm K. Cleaveland

2005. Drought, Epidemic Disease, and the Fall of Classic Period Cultures in Mesoamerica (AD 750–950): Hemorrhagic as a Cause of Massive Population Loss. *Medical Hypotheses* 65(2):405–409.

Aedo, Ángel

2001. La región más oscura del universo: El complejo mítico asociado al kieri. Master's thesis, Escuela Nacional de Antropología e Historia, Mexico City.

2003a. La región más oscura del universo: El complejo mítico asociado al *Kieri* de los Huicholes y al *Toloatzin* de los antiguos Nahuas. In *Flechadores de estrellas: Nuevas aportaciones a la etnología de Coras y Huicholes*, edited by Jesús Jáuregui and Johannes Neurath, pp. 221–249. Instituto Nacional de Antropología e Historia, Universidad de Guadalajara.

2003b. Flores de lujuria e influjos siniestros: Fuentes nocturnas del simbolismo Huichol del cuerpo humano. *Anales de Antropología* 37:173–204.

Aguilar-Moreno, Manuel

2006. *Handbook to the Life in the Aztec World*. Oxford University Press, New York.

Alexander, Hartley Burr

1920. *Latin American Mythology*. Vol. 11 of *The Mythology of All Races*. Marshall Jones, Boston.

Amador Bech, Julio

2010. Estrategías constructivas simbolismo del paisaje y arte rupestre en los cerros de trincheras del noroeste de Sonora. In *Anales de Antropología* 44:105–157.

2011. *El significado de la obra de art*. Universidad Nacional Autónoma de México, Mexico City.

Anderson, Edward F.

1996. *Peyote: The Divine Cactus*. 2nd ed. University of Arizona Press, Tucson.

Andrews, Rhonda L., and James M. Adovasio

1980. *Perishable Industries from Hinds Cave, Val Verde County, Texas*. Ethnology Monographs 5. Department of Anthropology, University of Pittsburgh.

Arnn, John Wesley

2012. *Land of the Tejas: Native American Identity and Interaction in Texas, AD 1300 to 1700*. University of Texas Press, Austin.

Aveni, Anthony, and Horst Hartung

1981. The Observation of the Sun at the Time of Passage of the Zenith in Mesoamerica. *Archaeoastronomy* 3 (supplement to the *Journal for the History of Astronomy* 12):S51–S70.

Báez-Jorge, Félix

2000. *Los oficios de las diosas: Dialéctica de la religiosidad popular en los grupos indios de México*. Universidad Veracruzana, Xalapa, Mexico.

Bahn, Paul G.

2010. *Prehistoric Rock Art: Polemics and Progress*. Cambridge University Press.

Baird, Ellen Taylor

1985. Naturalistic and Symbolic Color at Tula, Hidalgo. In *Painted Architecture and Polychrome Monumental Sculpture in Mesoamerica*, edited by Elizabeth Hill Boone, pp. 115–144. Dumbarton Oaks, Washington, DC.

Barthes, Roland

1974. *S/Z: An Essay*. Translated by Richard Miller. Hill and Wang, New York.

Bass, Patricia Marie

1989. The Pecos Project: Semiotic Models for the Study of Rock Art. PhD dissertation, Department of Anthropology, Rice University, Houston.

Bates, Lennon, Amanda Castañeda, Carolyn Boyd, and Karen Steelman
2015. A Black Deer at Black Cave: New Pictograph Radiocarbon Date for the Lower Pecos, Texas. *Journal of Texas Archeology and History*. Online only journal, vol. 2, article 3.
Bauml, James A., Gilbert Voss, and Peter Collings
1990. *Uxa* Identified. *Journal of Ethnobiology* 10(1):99–101.
Bednarik, Robert G.
1990. On Neuropsychology and Shamanism in Rock Art. *Current Anthropology* 31:77–84.
2011. Ethnographic Analogy in Rock Art Interpretation. Auranet Library. http://www.ifrao.com/ethnographic-interpretation-of-rock-art/.
Beekman, Christopher S., and Alexander F. Christensen
2003. Controlling Doubt and Uncertainty through Multiple Lines of Evidence: A New Look at the Mesoamerican Nahua Migrations. *Journal of Archaeological Method and Theory* 10(2):111–164.
Benítez, Fernando
1975. *In the Magic Land of Peyote*. University of Texas Press, Austin.
Benítez Sánchez, José
2005a. Our Grandfather's Ladder. Translated by Richard Moszka. *Artes de México* 75:82–84.
2005b. Our Elder Brother Neighboring Wind and Our Mother Young Eagle Bring the Rainy Season. Translated by Richard Moszka. *Artes de México* 75:98–99.
Bernal-Garcia, María Elena
2007. The Dance of Time, the Procession of Space at Mexico—Tenochtitlan's Desert Garden. In *Sacred Gardens and Landscapes: Ritual and Agency*, edited by Michel Conan, pp. 69–112. Dumbarton Oaks, Washington, DC.
Bierhorst, John (editor)
1984. *The Hungry Woman: Myths and Legends of the Aztecs*. William Morrow, New York.
1992. *History and Mythology of the Aztecs: The Codex Chimalpopoca*. Translated from the Nahuatl by John Bierhorst. University of Arizona Press, Tucson.
Biesele, Megan
2013. Rock Art as an "Imagery of Ideas": Archaeology, Ethnography, and Art History in Southern Africa and Southwest Texas. In *Painters in Prehistory: Archaeology and Art of the Lower Pecos Canyonlands*, edited by Harry J. Shafer, pp. 259–269. Trinity University Press, San Antonio, Texas.
Boke, Norman H., and Edward F. Anderson
1970. Structure, Development, and Taxonomy in the Genus Lophophora. *American Journal of Botany* 57(5):569–578.
Boone, Elizabeth Hill
1994. Writing and Recording Knowledge. In *Writing without Words: Alternative Literacies in Mesoamerica and the Andes*, edited by Elizabeth Hill Boone and Walter D. Mignolo, pp. 3–26. Duke University Press, Durham, North Carolina.
1999. The "Coatlicues" at the Templo Mayor. *Ancient Mesoamerica* 10(2):189–206.
2000. *Stories in Red and Black: Pictorial Histories of the Aztecs and Mixtecs*. University of Texas Press, Austin.
2007. *Cycles of Time and Meaning in the Mexican Books of Fate*. University of Texas Press, Austin.
2011. The Cultural Category of Scripts, Signs, and Pictographies. In *Their Way of Writing: Scripts, Signs, and Pictographies in Pre-Columbia America*, edited by Elizabeth Hill Boone and Gary Urton, pp. 379–390. Dumbarton Oaks, Washington, DC.
Boone, Elizabeth Hill, and Walter D. Mignolo (editors)
1994. *Writing without Words: Alternative Literacies in Mesoamerica and the Andes*. Duke University Press, Durham, North Carolina.
Boyd, Carolyn E.
1996. Shamanic Journeys into the Otherworld of the Archaic Chichimec. *Latin American Antiquity* 7(2):152–164.
1998a. The Work of Art: Rock Art and Adaptation in the Lower Pecos, Texas Archaic. PhD dissertation, Department of Anthropology, Texas A&M University, College Station.
1998b. Pictographic Evidence of Peyotism in the Lower Pecos, Texas, Archaic. In *The Archaeology of Rock Art*, edited by Christopher Chippindale and Paul S. C. Taçon, pp. 229–246. Cambridge University Press, New York.
2003. *Rock Art of the Lower Pecos*. Texas A&M University Press, College Station.
2010. El arte rupestre de Tejas: Análisis contextual de motivos recurrentes en el área de la desembocadura del Río Pecos. *Revista Iberoamericana de Lingüística* 5:5–42.
2012. Pictographs, Patterns, and Peyote in the Lower Pecos Canyonlands of Texas. In *A Companion to Rock Art*, edited by Jo McDonald and Peter Veth, pp. 34–50. Wiley-Blackwell, New York.
Boyd, Carolyn E., Amanda M. Castañeda, and Charles W. Koenig
2013. A Reassessment of Red Linear Pictographs in the Lower Pecos Canyonlands of Texas. *American Antiquity* 78(3):456–482.
Boyd, Carolyn E., and J. Phil Dering
1996. Medicinal and Hallucinogenic Plants Identified in the Sediments and the Pictographs of the Lower Pecos, Texas Archaic. *Antiquity* 70(268):256–275.

Brinton, Daniel Garrison

1897. *Religions of Primitive Peoples.* American Lectures on the History of Religions. G. P. Putnam's Sons, New York.

Broda, Johanna

1970. Tlacaxipehualiztli: A Reconstuction of an Aztec Calendar Festival from Sixteenth Century Sources. *Revista Española de Antropología Americana* 5:197–274.

1999. The Sacred Landscape of Aztec Calendar Festivals: Myth, Nature, and Society. In *Aztec Ceremonial Landscapes,* edited by Davíd Carrasco, pp. 74–120. University Press of Colorado, Niwot.

Brotherston, Gordon

1992. *Book of the Fourth World: Reading the Native Americas Through Their Literature.* Cambridge University Press, New York.

Brown, Cecil H.

2010. Lack of Linguistic Support for Proto-Uto-Aztecan at 8900 BP. *Proceedings of the National Academy of Sciences (USA)* 107:E34.

Brown, Kenneth M.

1991. Prehistoric Economics at Baker Cave: A Plan for Research. In *Papers on Lower Pecos Prehistory,* edited by Solveig A. Turpin, pp. 87–140. Studies in Archaeology 8. Texas Archeological Research Laboratory, Austin.

Brundage, Burr Cartwright

1982. *The Phoenix of the Western World: Quetzalcoatl and the Sky Religion.* University of Oklahoma Press, Norman.

1983. *The Fifth Sun: Aztec Gods, Aztec World.* Originally published 1979. University of Texas Press, Austin.

Bryant, Vaughn M., Jr., and Richard G. Holloway

1985. A Late Quaternary Paleoenvironmental Record of Texas: An Overview of the Pollen Evidence. In *Pollen Records of the Late Quaternary North American Sediments,* edited by V. M. Bryant, Jr. and R. G. Holloway, pp. 39–70. American Association of Stratigraphic Palynologists Foundation, Dallas.

Bye, Robert A., and Edelmira Linares

2007. Botanical Symmetry and Asymmetry in the *Mapa de Cuauhtinchan No 2.* In *Cave, City, and Eagle's Nest: An Interpretive Journey through the* Mapa de Cuauhtinchan No. 2, edited by Davíd Carrasco and Scott Sessions, pp. 255–280. University of New Mexico Press, Albuquerque.

Campbell, Joseph

1986. *The Inner Reaches of Outer Space: Metaphor as Myth and Religion.* Harper, New York.

Campbell, Lyle, and Ronald W. Langacker

1978. Proto-Aztecan Vowels: Part II. *International Journal of American Linguistics* 44(3):197–210.

Campbell, Thomas N.

1958. Origin of the Mescal Bean Cult. *American Anthropologist* 60(1):156–160.

Capinera, John L.

2001. *Handbook of Vegetable Pests.* Academic Press, San Diego.

Carrasco, Davíd

1995a. Cosmic Jaws: We Eat the Gods and the Gods Eat Us. *Journal of the American Academy of Religion* 63(3):429–463.

1995b. Give Me Some Skin: The Charisma of the Aztec Warrior. *History of Religions* 35(1):1–26.

1998. *Religions of Mesoamerica: Cosmovision and Ceremonial Centers.* Originally published 1990. Waveland Press, Long Grove, Illinois.

1999a. *City of Sacrifice: The Aztec Empire and the Role of Violence in Civilization.* Beacon Press, Boston.

1999b. Uttered from the Heart: Guilty Rhetoric among the Aztecs. *History of Religions* 39(1):1–31.

2008. *Daily Life of the Aztecs.* Originally published 1998. Greenwood Press, Santa Barbara, California.

Carrasco, Davíd, and Scott Sessions

2007a. Introduction: An Interpretive Journey through the *Mapa de Cuauhtinchan No. 2.* In *Cave, City, and Eagle's Nest: An Interpretive Journey through the* Mapa de Cuauhtinchan No. 2, edited by Davíd Carrasco and Scott Sessions, pp. 1–21. University of New Mexico Press, Albuquerque.

2007b. Middle Place, Labyrinth, and Circumambulation: Cholula's Peripatetic Role in the Mapa de Cuauhtinchan No. 2. In *Cave, City, and Eagle's Nest: An Interpretive Journey through the Mapa de Cuauhtinchan No. 2,* edited by Davíd Carrasco and Scott Sessions, pp. 427–454. University of New Mexico Press, Albuquerque.

Caso, Alfonso

1988. *The Aztecs: People of the Sun.* Translated by Lowell Dunham. Originally published 1958. University of Oklahoma Press, Norman.

Cassirer, Ernst

1955. *The Philosophy of Symbolic Forms,* vol. 2: *Mythical Thought.* Yale University Press, New Haven, Connecticut.

Chandler, Daniel

2007. *Semiotics: The Basics.* 2nd ed. Originally published 2002. Routledge, New York.

Chevalier, Jacques M., and Andrés Sánchez Bain

2003. *The Hot and the Cold: Ills of Humans and Maize in Native Mexico.* University of Toronto Press, Canada.

Clendinnen, Inga

1995. *Aztecs: An Interpretation.* Originally published 1991. Cambridge University Press, United Kingdom.

Cohodas, Marvin
1975. The Symbolism and Ritual Function of the Middle Classic Ball Game in Mesoamerica. *American Indian Quarterly* 2(2):99–130.
Colas, Pierre Robert
2011. Writing in Space: Glottographic and Semasiographic Notation at Teotihuacan. *Ancient Mesoamerica* 22(1):13–25.
Cox, Kim A., and S. D. de France
1997. The Oso Dune Site (41NU37): A Late Archaic Cemetery on the Central Texas Coast. *La Tierra* 24(3):15–33.

Danesi, Marcel
2007. *The Quest for Meaning: A Guide to Semiotic Theory and Practice.* University of Toronto Press, Canada.
DeBoer, Warren R.
2005. Colors for a North American Past. *World Archaeology* 37(1):66–91.
Dering, J. Philip
1999. Earth-Oven Plant Processing in Archaic Period Economies: An Example from a Semi-Arid Savanah in South-Central North America. *American Antiquity* 64:659–674.
Diamond, Jerod
1997. *Guns, Germs, and Steel: The Fates of Human Societies.* W. W. Norton, New York.
Díaz, Gisele, and Alan Rodgers
1993. *The Codex Borgia: A Full-Color Restoration of the Ancient Mexican Manuscript.* Dover, New York.
Dibble, David S., and Dessamae Lorraine
1968. *Bonfire Shelter: A Stratified Bison Kill Site, Val Verde County Texas.* Texas Memorial Museum, Miscellaneous Papers No. 1. University of Texas, Austin.
Duncum, Paul
2001. Visual Culture: Developments, Definitions, and Directions for Art Education. *Studies in Art Education* 42(2):101–112.
Durán, Fray Diego
1971. *Book of the Gods and Rites of the Ancient Calendar.* Translated and edited by Fernando Horcasitas and Doris Heyden. Originally published 1579. University of Oklahoma Press, Norman.
Dütting, Dieter, and Matthias Schramm
1984. Venus the Moon and the Gods of the Palenque Triad. *Zeitschrift für Ethnologie* 109(1):7–74.

Eco, Umberto
1984. *Semiotics and the Philosophy of Language.* Indiana University Press, Bloomington.
Edgerton, Samuel Y.
2001. *Theaters of Conversion: Religious Architecture and Indian Artisans in Colonial Mexico.* University of New Mexico Press, Albuquerque.
Eliade, Mircea
1964. *Shamanism: Archaic Techniques of Ecstasy.* Princeton University Press, New Jersey.

Faba Zuleta, Paulina Alejandra
2003. Los rostros de nuestros antepasados: Las pinturas faciales de los jicareros (Xukurikate) huicholes de Tateikita. *Anales del Instituto de Investigaciones Estéticas* 25(82):73–92.
2004. Patrimonio, analogía etnográfica y polisemia: El caso de la gráfica rupestre del occidente de México. Thesis, Programa de Magíster en Antropología y Desarrollo, Universidad de Chile.
Fash, William L., Alexandre Tokovinine, and Barbara W. Fash
2009. The House of the New Fire at Teotihuacan and Its Legacy in Mesoamerica. In *The Art of Urbanism: How Mesoamerican Kingdoms Represented Themselves in Architecture and Imagery,* edited by William L. Fish and Leonardo López Luján, pp. 201–229. Dumbarton Oaks, Washington, DC.
Fewkes, J. Walter
1906. Hopi Shrines Near the East Mesa, Arizona. *American Anthropologist* 8(2):346–375.
1918. Sun Worship of the Hopi Indians. In *Annual Report of the Board of Regents of the Smithsonian Institution,* pp. 493–526. Government Printing Office, Washington, DC.
Fikes, Jay C.
2011. *Unknown Huichol: Shamans and Immortals, Allies against Chaos.* Altamira, Lanham, Maryland.
Fikes, Jay C., Phil C. Weigand, and Acelia García de Weigand
2004. Introduction. In *Huichol Mythology,* by Robert M. Zingg; edited by Jay C. Fikes, Phil C. Weigand, and Acelia García de Weigand, pp. xiii–xxxvi. University of Arizona Press, Tucson.
Flannery, Kent V.
2003. Theoretical Framework: Divergent Evolution. In *The Cloud People: Divergent Evolution of the Zapotec and Mixtec Civilizations,* edited by Kent V. Flannery and Joyce Marcus, pp. 1–9. Originally published 1983. Percheron Press, Clinton Corners, New York.
Florescano, Enrique
1999. *The Myth of Quetzalcoatl.* Translated by Lysa Hochroth. Johns Hopkins University Press, Baltimore, Maryland.
Foster, William C.
2008. *Historic Native Peoples of Texas.* University of Texas Press, Austin.

Fowler, Catherine S.

1983. Some Lexical Clues to Uto-Aztecan Prehistory. *International Journal of American Linguistics* 49(3):224–257.

Franck, Frederick

1973. *The Zen of Seeing: Seeing/Drawing as Meditation*. Vintage Books, London.

Freidel, David, Linda Schele, and Joy Parker

1993. *Maya Cosmos: Three Thousand Years of the Shaman's Path*. William Morrow, New York.

Fritz, Carole, and Gilles Tosello

2007. The Hidden Meaning of Forms: Methods of Recording Paleolithic Parietal Art. *Journal of Archaeological Methods and Theory* 14(1):48–80.

Furst, Jill Leslie McKeever

1995. *The Natural History of the Soul in Ancient America*. Yale University Press, New Haven, Connecticut.

Furst, Peter T.

1972. To Find our Life: Peyote among the Huichol Indians of Mexico. In *Flesh of the Gods: The Ritual Use of Hallucinogens*, edited by Peter T. Furst, pp. 136–184. Praeger, New York.

1974. Ethnographic Analogy in the Interpretation of West Mexican Tomb Art. In *The Archaeology of West Mexico*, edited by Betty Bell, pp. 132–146. Sociedad de Estudios Advanzados del Occidente de México. Ajijic, Jalisco, Mexico.

1976. Shamanistic Survivals in Mesoamerican Religion. *Actas del XLI Congreso Internacional de Americanistas* 3:149–157.

1978. The Art of "Being Huichol." In *Art of the Huichol Indians*, edited by Kathleen Berrin, pp. 18–34. Fine Arts Museum of San Francisco, Harry N. Abrams, New York.

1996. Myth as History, History as Myth: A New Look at Some Old Problems in Huichol Origins. In *People of the Peyote: Huichol Indian History, Religion and Survival*, edited by Stacy B. Schaefer and Peter T. Furst, pp. 26–60. University of New Mexico Press, Albuquerque.

2006. *Rock Crystals and Peyote Dreams: Explorations in the Huichol Universe*. University of Utah Press, Salt Lake City.

2007. *Visions of a Huichol Shaman*. Museum of Archaeology and Anthropology, University of Pennsylvania, Philadelphia.

Furst, Peter T., and M. Anguiano

1976. To Fly as Birds: Myth and Ritual Enculturation among the Huichol Indians of Mexico. In *Enculturation in Latin America: An Anthology*, edited by Johannes Wilbert, pp. 95–181. Latin American Center Publications. University of California, Los Angeles.

Furst, Peter T., and Barbara G. Myerhoff

1966. Myth as History: The Jimsonweed Cycle of the Huichols of Mexico. *Antropológica* 17:3–39.

García Garagarza, León

2012. The 1539 Trial of Don Carlos Ometochtli and the Scramble for Mount Tlaloc. In *Mesoamerican Memory: Enduring Systems of Remembrance*, edited by Amos Megged and Stephanie Wood, pp. 193–214. University of Oklahoma Press, Norman.

García-Goyco, Osvaldo

2007. The *Mapa de Cuauhtinchan No. 2* and the Cosmic Tree in Mesoamerica, the Caribbean, and the Amazon-Orinoco Basin. Translated by Scott Sessions. In *Cave, City, and Eagle's Nest: An Interpretive Journey through the* Mapa de Cuauhtinchan No. 2, edited by Davíd Carrasco and Scott Sessions, pp. 357–387. University of New Mexico Press, Albuquerque.

Gebhard, David

1960. *Prehistoric Paintings of the Diablo Region of Western Texas—A Preliminary Report*. Publications in Art and Science no. 3. Roswell Museum and Art Center, Roswell, New Mexico.

1965. Prehistoric Paintings of the Seminole Canyon Area, Val Verde County Texas. Unpublished report submitted to the National Park Service. Texas Archeological Salvage Project, University of Texas at Austin.

Georges, Robert A.

1986. The Pervasiveness in Contemporary Folklore Studies of Assumptions, Concepts and Constructs Usually Associated with the Historic-Geographic Method. *Journal of Folklore Research* 23(2/3):87–103.

Gingerich, Willard

1988. Three Nahuatl Hymns on the Mother Archetype: An Interpretive Commentary. *Mexican Studies/Estudios Mexicanos* 4(2):191–244.

Gómez-Cano, Grisel

2010. *The Return to Coatlicue: Goddesses and Warladies in Mexican Folklore*. Xlibris, Bloomington, Indiana.

Gossen, Gary

1986. Mesoamerican Ideas as a Foundation for Regional Synthesis. In *Symbol and Meaning beyond the Closed Community: Essays in Mesoamerican Ideas*, edited by Gary Gossen, pp. 1–8. Studies on Culture and Society, vol. 1. Institute for Mesoamerican Studies, State University of New York at Albany.

Grady, C. Jill, and Peter T. Furst

2011. Ethnoscience, Genetics, and Huichol Origins: New Evidence Provides Congruence. *Ethnohistory* 58(2):263–291.

Graña-Behrens, Daniel

2012. *Itzaat* and *Tlamatini*: The "Wise Man" as Keeper of

Maya and Nahua Collective Memory. In *Mesoamerican Memory: Enduring Systems of Remembrance*, edited by Amos Megged and Stephanie Wood, pp. 15–32. University of Oklahoma Press, Norman.

Graulich, Michel

1981. The Metaphor of Day in Ancient Mexican Myth and Ritual. *Current Anthropology* 22(1):45–60.

1983. Myths of Paradise Lost in Pre-Hispanic Central Mexico. *Current Anthropology* 24(5):575–588.

1988. Double Immolations in Ancient Mexican Sacrificial Ritual. *History of Religions* 27(4):393–404.

1989. Miccailhuitl: The Aztec Festivals of the Deceased. *Numen* 36(1):43–71.

1997. *Myths of Ancient Mexico.* University of Oklahoma Press, Norman.

Greco, Margaret

2011. Seeps, Springs, and the Pecos River Style Pictographs: "Renewing Reality" in Light of 25 Years. *American Indian Rock Art 37*, edited by Mavis Greer, John Greer, and Peggy Whitehead, pp. 99–114. American Rock Art Research Association, Glendale, Arizona.

Grieder, Terence

1966. Speculations on Some Pictograph Sites in the Region of Amistad Reservoir. Report to the National Park Service. Texas Archeological Salvage Project, University of Texas at Austin.

Griffin-Pierce, Trudy

1992. The Hooghan and the Stars. In *Earth and Sky: Visions of the Cosmos in Native American Folklore*, edited by Ray A. Williamson and Claire R. Farrer, pp. 110–130. University of New Mexico Press, Albuquerque.

Gutiérrez, Arturo

2000. Blood in Huichol Ritual. *Journal of the Southwest* 42(1):111–118.

2002. *La peregrinación a Wirikuta: El gran rito de paso de los huicholes.* Instituto Nacional de Antropología e Historia, Universidad de Guadalajara, Mexico.

2008. Centros ceremoniales y calendarios solares: Un sistema de transformaciones en tres comunidades huicholes. In *Las vías del noreste*, II: *Propuesta para una perspectiva sistémica e interdisciplinaria*, edited by Carlo Bonfiglioli, Arturo Gutiérrez, Marie-Areti Hers, and María Eugenia Olvarría, pp. 287–318. Universidad Nacional Autónoma de México, Mexico City.

2011. Los hacedores de las lluvias: Peregrinaciones y ceremonias de los jicareros wixaritari. *Revista de El Colegio de San Luis* 1:92–117.

Gutzeit, Emma

1931. Report of Scouting Expedition Sent Out of Witte Museum June 14–June 20, 1931. Unpublished field report on file at the Witte Memorial Museum, San Antonio, Texas.

Gutzeit, Emma, and Mary Virginia Carson

1931. Preliminary Report on Field Expedition Sent to West Texas by Witte Museum. Unpublished field report and watercolor paintings on file at the Witte Memorial Museum, San Antonio, Texas.

Hall, Robert L.

1997. *An Archaeology of the Soul: North American Indian Belief and Ritual.* University of Illinois Press, Urbana.

Hays-Gilpin, Kelley

2004. *Ambiguous Images: Gender and Rock Art.* AltaMira, Walnut Creek, California.

Hays-Gilpin, Kelley, and Jane H. Hill

1999. The Flower World in Material Culture: An Iconographic Complex in the Southwest and Mesoamerica. *Journal of Anthropological Research* 55(1):1–37.

Hernández Sánchez, Gilda

2010. Vessels for Ceremony: The Pictography of Codex-Style Mixteca-Puebla Vessels from Central and South Mexico. *Latin American Antiquity* 21(3):252–273.

Hester, T.

1980. *Digging into South Texas Prehistory.* Corona, San Antonio, Texas.

1995. The Prehistory of South Texas. *Bulletin of the Texas Archeological Society* 66:427–460.

Heyden, Doris

1972. What Is the Significance of the Mexica Pyramid? *Atti del XL Congresso Internazionale degli Americanisti* 1:109–115.

1988. Black Magic: Obsidian in Symbolism and Metaphor. In *Smoke and Mist: Mesoamerican Studies in Memory of Thelma D. Sullivan*, edited by J. K. Josserand and K. Dakin, pp. 217–236. BAR International Studies 402. British Archaeological Reports, Oxford.

Hill, Jane H.

1992. The Flower World of Old Uto-Aztecan. *Journal of Anthropological Research* 48(2):117–144.

2001a. Proto-Uto-Aztecan: A Community of Cultivators in Central Mexico? *American Anthropologist* 103(4):913–934.

2001b. Dating the Break-up of Southern Uto-Aztecan. In *Avances y balances de lenguas yutoaztecas: Homenaje a Wick R. Miller*, edited by José Luis Moctezuma Zamarrón and Jane H. Hill, pp. 345–357. Instituto Nacional de Antropología e Historia, Mexico City.

2012 Proto-Uto-Aztecan as a Mesoamerican Language. *Ancient Mesoamerica* 23(1):57–68.

Hooft, Anuschka van't

2007. *The Ways of Water: A Reconstruction of Huastecan Nahua Society through Its Oral Tradition.* Leiden University Press, Netherlands.

Houston, Stephen
1994. Literacy among the Pre-Columbian Maya: A Comparative Perspective. In *Writing without Words: Alternative Literacies in Mesoamerica and the Andes*, edited by Elizabeth Hill Boone and Walter D. Mignolo, pp. 27–49. Duke University Press, Durham, North Carolina.
Houston, Stephen, David Stuart, and Karl Taube
2006. *The Memory of Bones: Body, Being, and Experience among the Classic Maya*. University of Texas Press, Austin.
Howells, Richard, and Joaquim Negreiros
2012. *Visual Culture*. 2nd ed. Polity. Malden, Cambridge, UK.
Hultkrantz, Åke
1997. *The Attraction of Peyote: An Inquiry into the Basic Conditions for Diffusion of the Peyote Religion in North America*. Almqvist and Wiksell International, Stockholm.
Hyman, Marion, Solveig Turpin, and M. Zolensky
1996. Pigment Analysis at Panther Cave. *Rock Art Research* 13:93–103.

Ingham, John H.
1984. Human Sacrifice at Tenochtitlan. *Comparative Studies in Society and History* 26(3):379–400.

Jáuregui, Jesús
2008. ¿Quo vadis, Mesoamérica? *Boletín Oficial del INAH: Antropología* 82:3–31.
Jonghe, Edouard de
1905. Histoire du Méchique, manuscrit français inédit du XVIe siècle. In *Journal de la Société des Américanistes* n.s. 2:1-41.

Kaufman, Terrence
2001. The History of the Nawa Language Group from the Earliest Times to the Sixteenth Century: Some Initial Results. http://www.albany.edu/anthro/maldp/Nawa.pdf.
Kaufman, Terrence, and John Justeson
2009. Historical Linguistics and Pre-Columbian Mesoamerica. *Ancient Mesoamerica* 20(2):221–231.
Kay, Paul T.
2005. Datura: A Poster Presentation at the 70th annual meeting of the Society for American Anthropology, Salt Lake City, Utah. http://paultkay.info/DATURA_05_08_2006.pdf.
Keller, Angela H.
2011. A Road by Any Other Name: Trails, Paths, and Roads in Maya Thought and Language. In *Landscapes of Movement: Trails, Paths, and Roads in Anthropological Perspective*, edited by James E. Snead, Clark L. Erickson, and J. Andrew Darling, pp. 133–157. University of Pennsylvania Press, Philadelphia.
Kelley, David H.
1980. Astronomical Identities of Mesoamerican Gods. *Archaeoastronomy* 2 (supplement to the *Journal for the History of Astronomy* 11):S1–S54.
Kelley, J. Charles
1950. Atlatls, Bows and Arrows, Pictographs, and the Pecos River Focus. *American Antiquity* 16(1):71–74.
Kellogg, Susan
1995. *Law and the Transformation of Aztec Culture, 1500–1700*. University of Oklahoma Press, Norman.
Kelly, Robert L., and David H. Thomas
2013. *Archaeology*. 6th ed. Wadsworth, Cengage Learning, Belmont, California.
Kenmotsu, Nancy A., and Maria F. Wade
2002. American Indian Tribal Affiliation Study, Phase I: Ethnohistoric Literature Review. Report No. 34. Texas Department of Transportation Archeological Studies Program, Austin, and the National Park Service, Amistad National Recreation Area, Del Rio, Texas.
Kepes, Gyorgy
1965. *Education of Vision*. George Braziller, New York.
Kindl, Olivia Selena
2000. The Huichol Gourd Bowl as a Microcosm. *Journal of the Southwest* 42(1):37–60.
2001. La jícara y la flecha en el ritual huichol: Análisis iconográfico del dualismo sexual y cosmológico. *Boletín Oficial del INAH: Antropología* 64:3–20.
2005. Silent Walker: An Interview with José Benítez Sánchez. *Artes de México* 75:91–103.
Kirchhoff, Paul
1943. Mesoamérica: Sus límites geográficos, composición étnica y caracteres culturales. *Acta Americana* 1(1):92–107.
Kirkland, Forrest
1937a. A Study of Indian Pictures in Texas. *Bulletin of the Texas Archeological and Paleontological Society* 9:89–119.
1937b. A Comparison of Texas Pictographs with Paleolithic Paintings in Europe. *Central Texas Archeologist* 3:9–26.
1938. A Description of Texas Pictographs. *Bulletin of the Texas Archeological and Paleontological Society* 10:11–39.
1939. Indian Pictures in the Dry Shelters of Val Verde County, Texas. *Bulletin of the Texas Archeological and Paleontological Society* 11:47–76.
Kirkland, Forrest, and William W. Newcomb, Jr.
1967. *The Rock Art of Texas Indians*. University of Texas Press, Austin.
Klein, Cecelia F.
1976. The Identity of the Central Deity on the Aztec Calendar Stone. *Art Bulletin* 58(1):1–12.
2001. None of the Above: Gender Ambiguity in Nahua Ideology. In *Gender in Pre-Hispanic America*, edited by Ce-

celia F. Klein, pp. 183–253. Dumbarton Oaks, Washington, DC.
2008. A New Interpretation of the Aztec Statue Called Coatlicue, "Snakes-Her-Skirt." *Ethnohistory* 55(2):229–250.
Knowlton, Timothy W.
2002. Diphrastic Kennings in Mayan Hieroglyphic Literature. *Mexicon* 24(1):9–14.
2010. *Maya Creation Myths: Words and Worlds of the Chilam Balam*. University Press of Colorado, Boulder.
Koenig, Charles W., Amanda M. Castañeda, Carolyn E. Boyd, and Karen L. Steelman
2014. Portable X-Ray Fluorescence Spectroscopy of Pictographs: A Case Study from the Lower Pecos Canyonlands of Texas. *Archaeometry* 56:168–186.
Köhler, Ulrich
2002. Meteors and Comets in Ancient Mexico. In *Catastrophic Events and Mass Extinctions: Impacts and Beyond*, edited by Christian Koeberl and Kenneth G. MacLeod, pp. 1–6. Special Paper 356. Geological Society of America, Boulder, Colorado.
Kusch, Rodolfo
2010. *Indigenous and Popular Thinking in America*. Translated by María Lugones and Joshua M. Price. Duke University Press, Durham, North Carolina.

La Barre, Weston
1975. *The Peyote Cult*. 4th ed. Originally published 1938. University of Oklahoma Press, Norman.
1979. Peyotl and Mescaline. *Journal of Psychedelic Drugs* 11(1–2):33–39.
Laming-Emperaire, Annette
1962. *La signification de l'art rupestre paléolithique*. Picard, Paris.
Lankford, George E.
2007. *Reachable Stars: Patterns in the Ethnoastronomy of Eastern North America*. University of Alabama Press, Tuscaloosa.
Launey, Michel
2011. *An Introduction to Classical Nahuatl*. Translated by Christopher Mackay. Cambridge University Press, New York.
Lemaistre, Denis
1996. The Deer that is Peyote and the Deer that is Maize. Translated from the French by Karin Simoneau. In *People of the Peyote: Huichol Indian History, Religion and Survival*, edited by Stacy B. Schaefer and Peter T. Furst, pp. 308–329. University of New Mexico Press, Albuquerque.
León-Portilla, Miguel
1980. *Native Mesoamerican Spirituality: Ancient Myths, Discourses, Stories, Doctrines, Hymns, Poems from the Aztec, Yucatec, Quiche-Maya and Other Sacred Traditions*. Edited by Miguel León-Portilla. Paulist Press, Mahwah, New Jersey.
1988. *Time and Reality in the Thought of the Maya*. University of Oklahoma Press, Norman.
1990. *Aztec Thought and Culture*. Translated by Jack Emory Davis. Originally published 1963. University of Oklahoma Press, Norman.
1995. On the Meaning of Celestial Bodies in Pre-Hispanic Mexico. *Vistas in Astronomy* 39(4):451–461.
2002a. Aztec Codices, Literature and Philosophy. In *Aztecs: A Journey through the Exhibition*, edited by Eduardo Matos Moctezuma and Felipe Solíce Olguín, pp. 64–71. Royal Academy of Arts, London.
2002b. *Bernardino de Sahagún: First Anthropologist*. Translated by Mauricio J. Mixco. University of Oklahoma Press, Norman.
2006. *La filosofía Náhuatl: Estudiada en sus fuentes (Serie de cultura Náhuatl)*. Originally published 1956. Universidad Nacional Autónoma de México, Instituto de Investigaciones Históricas, Mexico City.
Leroi-Gourhan, André
1968. *The Art of Prehistoric Man in Western Europe*. Thames and Hudson, London.
1993. *Gesture and Speech*. Translated by Anna Bostock Berger. Originally published 1964. MIT Press, Cambridge, Massachusetts.
Lévi Strauss, Claude
1955. The Structural Study of Myth. In *Journal of American Folklore* 68(270):428–444.
Lewis-Williams, David
1995. Seeing and Construing: The Making and "Meaning" of a Southern African Rock Art Motif. *Cambridge Archaeological Journal* 5(1):3–23.
2002. *A Cosmos in Stone: Interpreting Religion and Society through Rock Art*. AltaMira, Walnut Creek, California.
Lewis-Williams, David, and Thomas A. Dowson
1988. The Signs of All Times: Entoptic Phenomena in Upper Paleolithic Art. *Current Anthropology* 29(2):201–245.
Lockhart, James
2001. *Nahuatl as Written: Lessons in Older, Written Nahuatl, with Copious Examples and Texts*. Stanford University Press, California.
Looper, Matthew George
2009. *To Be Like Gods: Dance in Ancient Maya Civilizations*. University of Texas Press, Austin.
López Austin, Alfredo
1973. *Hombre-Dios: Religión y política en el mundo náhuatl*. Universidad Nacional Autónoma de México, Instituto de Investigaciones Históricas, Mexico City.
1987. The Masked God of Fire. In *The Aztec Templo Mayor*, edited by Elizabeth Boone, pp. 257–291. Dumbarton Oaks, Washington, DC.

1988. *The Human Body and Ideology: Concepts of the Ancient Nahuas.* Vol. 1. Translated by Thelma Ortiz de Montellano and Bernard Ortiz de Montellano. University of Utah Press, Salt Lake City.

1993. *The Myths of the Opossum: Pathways of Mesoamerican Mythology.* Translated by Thelma Ortiz de Montellano and Bernard Ortiz de Montellano. University of New Mexico Press, Albuquerque.

1997. *Tamoanchan, Tlalocan: Places of Mist.* Translated by Thelma Ortiz de Montellano and Bernard Ortiz de Montellano. University Press of Colorado, Boulder.

2002. Cosmovision, Religion and the Calendar of the Aztecs. In *Aztecs: A Journey through the Exhibition,* edited by Eduardo Matos Moctezuma and Felipe Solíce Olguín, pp. 30–37. Royal Academy of Arts, London.

López Austin, Alfredo, and Leonardo López Luján

2009. *Monte Sagrado: Templo Mayor.* Instituto Nacional de Antropología e Historia, Mexico City.

Lord, Kenneth J.

1984. The Zooarchaeology of Hinds Cave. PhD dissertation, Department of Anthropology, Texas A&M University, College Station.

Love, Hallie N.

1999. *Watákame's Journey: The Story of the Great Flood and the New World.* Clear Light, Santa Fe, New Mexico.

Lumholtz, Carl

1900 *Symbolism of the Huichol Indians.* Memoirs of the American Museum of Natural History, New York.

1902. *Unknown Mexico. Vol. 2.* Charles Scribner's Sons, New York.

MacLaury, Robert E.

1997. *Color and Cognition in Mesoamerica: Constructing Categories as Vantages.* University of Texas Press, Austin.

MacLean, Hope

2000. The "Deified" Heart: Huichol Indian Soul-Concepts and Shamanic Art. *Antropológica* 42(1):75–90.

2001. Sacred Colors and Shamanic Vision among the Huichol Indians of Mexico. *Journal of Anthropological Research* 57(3):305–323.

2005. *Yarn Paintings of the Huichol.* Singing Deer, Quebec.

2012. *The Shaman's Mirror: Visionary Art of the Huichol.* University of Texas Press, Austin.

Madsen, William

1955. Hot and Cold in the Universe of San Francisco Tecospa, Valley of Mexico. *Journal of American Folklore* 68(268):123–139.

Magaloni Kerpel, Diana

2011. Painters of the New World. In *Colors between Two Worlds: The Florentine Codex of Bernardino de Sahagún,* edited by Gerhard Wolf and Joseph Connors, in collaboration with Louis A. Waldman, pp. 47–76. Villa I Tatti/Harvard University Center for Italian Renaissance Studies, Florence.

2014. *The Colors of the New World: Artists, Materials, and the Creation of the Florentine Codex.* Getty Research Institute, Los Angeles.

Magriñá, Laura

2001. El peyote (*hikuri*) y el kieri (*tapat*): Las culebras de agua del Valle de Matatipac. *Antropología* 64:41–50.

Marcos-Marín, Francisco

2010. Arte rupestre y lingüística amerindia: Estilos y conceptos. *Revista Iberoamericana de Lingüística* 5:43–71.

2013. The Place of Rock Art in the Linguistic History of Texas: American Indian Languages. *Dialectologia: Revista Electronica* 10:33–57.

Marcus, Joyce, Kent V. Flannery, and Ronald Spores

2003. The Cultural Legacy of the Oaxacan Preceramic. In *The Cloud People: Divergent Evolution of the Zapotec and Mixtec Civilizations,* edited by Kent V. Flannery and Joyce Marcus, pp. 36–39. Originally published 1983. Percheron, Clinton Corners, New York.

Markman, Roberta A., and Peter T. Markman

1989. *Masks of the Spirit: Images and Metaphors in Mesoamerica.* University of California Press, Berkeley.

Marmaduke, W. S.

1978. Prehistoric Culture in Trans-Pecos Texas: An Ecological Approach. PhD dissertation, Department of Anthropology, University of Texas at Austin.

Martin, Howard N.

1977. *Myths and Folktales of the Alabama-Coushatta Indians of Texas.* Encino Press, Austin, Texas.

Mathiowetz, Michael Dean

2011. The Diurnal Path of the Sun: Ideology and Interregional Interaction in Ancient Northwest Mesoamerica and the American Southwest. PhD dissertation, Department of Anthropology, University of California, Riverside.

Mathiowetz, Michael Dean, Polly Schaafsma, Jeremy Coltman, and Karl Taube

2015. The Darts of Dawn: The Tlahuizcalpantecuhtli Venus Complex in the Iconography of Mesoamerica and the American Southwest. *Journal of the Southwest* 57(1):1–102.

Mautner, Carlos Rincón

2012. Cave, Mountain, and Ancestors. In *Mesoamerican Memory: Enduring Systems of Remembrance,* edited by Amos Megged and Stephanie Wood, pp. 249–276. University of Oklahoma Press, Norman.

Maxwell, Judith M., and Craig A. Hanson

1992. *Of the Manners of Speaking That the Old Ones Had: The Metaphors of Andrés de Olmos in the TULAL Manuscript (Arte para aprender la lengua mexicana), 1547.* University of Utah Press, Salt Lake City.

McGregor, Roberta
1992. *Prehistoric Basketry of the Lower Pecos, Texas.* Monographs in World Archaeology 6. Prehistory Press, Madison, Wisconsin.
Megged, Amos
2010. *Social Memory in Ancient and Colonial Mesoamerica.* Cambridge University Press, New York.
2012. Things That Unite and Things That Divide. In *Mesoamerican Memory: Enduring Systems of Remembrance,* edited by Amos Megged and Stephanie Wood, pp. 173–192. University of Oklahoma Press, Norman.
Merrill, William L., Robert J. Hard, Jonathon B. Mabry, Gayle J. Fritz, Karen R. Adams, John R. Roney, and A. C. MacWilliams
2009. The Diffusion of Maize to the Southwestern United States and Its Impact. *Proceedings of the National Academy of the United States of America* 106(50):21019–21026.
Milbrath, Susan
1995. Gender and Roles of Lunar Deities in Postclassic Central Mexico and Their Correlations with the Maya Area. *Estudios de Cultura Nahuatl* 25:45–93.
1997. Decapitated Lunar Goddess in Aztec Art, Myth, and Ritual. In *Ancient Mesoamerica* 8(2):185–206.
1999. *Star Gods of the Maya: Astronomy in Art, Folklore, and Calendars.* University of Texas Press, Austin.
2013. *Heaven and Earth in Ancient Mexico.* University of Texas Press, Austin.
Mithun, Marianne
1999. *The Languages of Native North America.* Cambridge University Press, New York.
Momaday, N. Scott
1970. Man Made of Words. In *Indian Voices: The First Convocation of American Indian Scholars,* pp. 49–62. Indian Historian Press, San Francisco, California.
Monaghan, John
1994. The Text in the Body, the Body in the Text: The Embodied Sign in Mixtec Writing. In *Writing without Words: Alternative Literacies in Mesoamerica and the Andes,* edited by Elizabeth Hill Boone and Walter D. Mignolo, pp. 87–101. Duke University Press, Durham, North Carolina.
Morán, Elizabeth
2007. The Sacred as Everyday: Food and Ritual in Aztec Art. PhD dissertation, Department of Art History, City University of New York.
Morgan, George R.
1983. The Biogeography of Peyote in South Texas. In *Botanical Museum Leaflets* 29:73–86. Harvard University Press, Cambridge, Massachusetts.
Murray, William Breen (editor)
2007. *Arte rupestre del noreste.* Fondo Editorial de Nuevo León, Monterrey, Mexico.
Myerhoff, Barbara G.
1974. *Peyote Hunt: The Sacred Journey of the Huichol Indians.* Cornell University Press, Ithaca, New York.
1978. Peyote and the Mystic Vision. In *Art of the Huichol Indian,* edited by Kathleen Berrin, pp. 56–70. Harry N. Abrams, New York.

Nance, R.
1992. *The Archaeology of La Calsada: A Rockshelter in the Sierra Madre Oriental, Mexico.* University of Texas Press, Austin.
Navarrete, Federico
2000. The Path from Aztlan to Mexico: On Visual Narration in Mesoamerican Codices. *RES: Anthropology and Aesthetics* 37:31–48.
2011. Writing, Images, and Time-Space in Aztec Monuments and Books. In *Their Way of Writing: Scripts, Signs, and Pictographies in Pre-Columbia America,* edited by Elizabeth Hill Boone and Gary Urton, pp. 175–195. Dumbarton Oaks, Washington, DC.
Negrín, Juan
1975. *The Huichol Creation of the World.* E. B. Crocker Art Gallery, Sacramento, California.
1977. *El arte contemporáneo de los huicholes.* University of Guadalajara, Mexico.
2005. The Path of Nierika: Heart, Memory and Visions. *Artes de México* 75:80–81.
2006. What Draws the Huichol to the Pacific Ocean? http://wixarika.mediapark.net/en/documents/WhatdrawshuicholstooceanJN.pdf.
Neihardt, John G.
2008. *Black Elk Speaks: Being the Life Story of a Holy Man of the Oglala Sioux.* Originally published 1932. State University of New York Press, Albany.
Neurath, Johannes
2000a. Tukipa Ceremonial Centers in the Community of Tuapurie (Santa Catarina Cuexcomatitlán): Cargo Systems, Landscape, and Cosmovision. *Journal of the Southwest* 42(1):81–110.
2000b. El don de ver: El proceso de iniciación y sus implicaciones para la cosmovisión huichola. *Desacatos* 5:57–77.
2001a. Lluvia del desierto: El culto a los ancestros, los ritos agrícolas y la dinámica étnica de los huicholes T+ apuritari. In *Cosmovisión, ritual e identidad de los pueblos indígenas de México,* edited by Johanna Broda and Félix Báez-Jorge, pp. 485–526. Fondo de Cultura Económica, Mexico City.
2001b. El cerro del amanecer y el culto solar huichol. In *La montaña en el paisaje ritual.* Edited by Johanna Broda,

Stanislaw Iwaniszewski, and Arturo Montero, pp. 475–488. Universidad Nacional Autónoma de México, Escuela Nacional de Antropología e Historia, Universidad de Autónomo de Puebla, Mexico City.

2002. Venus y sol en la religión de coras, huicholes y mexicaneros: Consideraciones sobre la posibilidad de establecer comparaciones con las antiguas concepciones mesoamericanas. *Anales de Antropología* 36:155–177.

2005a. Ancestors in the Making: A Living Tradition. Translated by Michelle Suderman. *Artes de México* 75:71–74.

2005b. Cosmogonic Myths, Ritual Groups, and Initiation: Toward a New Comparative Ethnology of the Gran Nayar and the Southwest of the US. Translated by Donald Bahr. *Journal of the Southwest* 47(4):571–614.

2005c. The Ambivalent Character of Xurawe: Venus-Related Ritual and Mythology Among West Mexican Indians. *Archaeoastronomy* 19:74–102.

2005d. Máscaras en mascaradas: Indígenas, mestizos y dioses indígenas mestizos. *Relaciones: Estudios de historia y sociedad* 26(101):22–50.

Newcomb, William W., Jr.

1976. Pecos River Style Pictographs: The Development of an Art Form. In *Cultural Change and Continuity: Essays in Honor of James Bennett Griffin*, edited by Charles E. Cleland, pp. 175–190. Academic Press, New York.

Nicholson, Henry B.

1971. Religion in Pre-Hispanic Central Mexico. In *Handbook of Middle American Indians: Archaeology of Northern Mesoamerica*. Vol. 1. Edited by Gordon Ekholm and Igancio Bernal, and by general editor Robert Wauchope, pp. 395–446. University of Texas Press, Austin.

Nowotny, Karl Anton

2005. Tlacuilolli: *Style and Contents of the Mexican Pictorial Manuscripts with a Catalog of the Borgia Group*. Edited and translated by George A. Everett and Edward B. Sisson. University of Oklahoma Press, Norman.

Nuttall, Zelia

1901. *The Fundamental Principles of Old and New World Civilizations: A Comparative Research Based on a Study of the Ancient Mexican Religious, Sociological, and Calendrical Systems*. Archaeological and Ethnological Papers of the Peabody Museum, Vol. 2. Harvard University, Cambridge, Massachusetts.

Olivier, Guilhem

2003. *Mockeries and Metamorphoses of an Aztec God: Tezcatlipoca, Lord of the Smoking Mirror*. Translated by Michel Besson. University Press of Colorado, Boulder.

2007. Sacred Bundles, Arrows, and New Fire: Foundation and Power in the *Mapa de Cuauhtinchan No. 2*. In *Cave, City, and Eagle's Nest: An Interpretive Journey through the* Mapa de Cuauhtinchan No. 2, edited by Davíd Carrasco and Scott Sessions, pp. 281–313. University of New Mexico Press, Albuquerque.

Orellana, Margarita de

2007. Konrad T. Preuss's Mexican Adventure. Translated by Michelle Suderman. *Artes de México: Arte Antiguo Cora y Huichol* 85:73.

Ortner, Sherry B.

1973. On Key Symbols. *American Anthropologist* 75(5):1338–1346.

Páez-Riberos, L. A., J. F. Muños-Valle, L. E. Figuera, I. Nuño-Arana, L. Sandoval-Ramírez, A. González-Martín, B. Ibarra, and H. Rangel-Villalobos

2006. Y-linked Haplotypes in Amerindian Chromosomes from the Mexican Populations: Genetic Evidence to the Dual Origins of the Huichol Tribe. *Legal Medicine* 8(4):220–225.

Panofsky, Erwin

1972. *Studies in Iconology: Humanistic Themes in the Art of the Renaissance*. Originally published 1939. Icon Editions. Westview Press, Oxford.

Parsons, Mark

1986. Painted Pebbles, Style and Chronology. In *Ancient Texans*, edited by Harry J. Shafer, pp. 180–185. Texas Monthly Press, Austin.

Payne, Stanley E., and Michael P. Closs

1986. A Survey of Aztec Numbers and Their Uses. In *Native American Mathematics*, edited by Michael P. Closs, pp. 213–235. University of Texas Press, Austin.

Perrin, Michel

1996. The *Urukáme*, a Crystallization of the Soul: Death and Memory. Translated from the French by Karin Simoneau. In *People of the Peyote: Huichol Indian History, Religion and Survival*, edited by Stacy B. Schaefer and Peter T. Furst, pp. 403–428. University of New Mexico Press, Albuquerque.

Phillips, Henry

1884. Notes upon the Codex Ramirez, with a Translation of the Same: History of the Mexicans as Told by Their Paintings. *Proceedings of the American Philosophical Society* 21:616–651.

Pohl, John M.D.

1998. Themes of Drunkenness, Violence, and Factionalism in Tlaxcalan Altar Paintings. *RES: Anthropology and Aesthetics* 33:184–207.

Powell, Melissa S., and C. Jill Grady (editors)

2010. *Huichol Art and Culture: Balancing the World*. Museum of New Mexico Press, Sante Fe.

Prechtel, Martin, and Robert Carlsen

1988. Weaving and Cosmos amongst the Tzutujil Maya of Guatemala. *RES: Anthropology and Aesthetics* 15:122–132.

Preuss, Konrad Theodor

1996. Konrad Theodor Preuss (1869–1938) on the Huichols. Translated from the German by Peter T. Furst. In *People of the Peyote: Huichol Indian History, Religion and Survival,* edited by Stacy B. Schaefer and Peter T. Furst, pp. 94–135. University of New Mexico Press, Albuquerque.

1998a. La diosa de la tierra y de la luna de los antiguos mexicaneros en el mito actual. In *Fiesta, literatura y magia en el Nayarit: Ensayos sobre coras, huicholes y mexicaneros de Konrad Theodor Preuss,* edited by Jesús Jáuregui and Johannes Neurath, pp. 349–354. Instituto Nacional Indigenista, Mexico City.

1998b. El mito del diluvio entre los coras y tribus emparentadas. In *Fiesta, literatura y magia en el Nayarit: Ensayos sobre coras, huicholes y mexicaneros de Konrad Theodor Preuss,* edited by Jesús Jáuregui and Johannes Neurath, pp. 323–326. Instituto Nacional Indigenista, Mexico City.

1998c. El concepto de la estrella de la mañana según los textos recogidos entre los mexicaneros del estado de Durango, México. In *Fiesta, literatura y magia en el Nayarit: Ensayos sobre coras, huicholes y mexicaneros de Konrad Theodor Preuss,* edited by Jesús Jáuregui and Johannes Neurath, pp. 333–348. Instituto Nacional Indigenista, Mexico City.

1998d. Paralelos entre los antiguos mexicanos y los actuales indígenas huicholes. In *Fiesta, literatura y magia en el Nayarit: Ensayos sobre coras, huicholes y mexicaneros de Konrad Theodor Preuss,* edited by Jesús Jáuregui and Johannes Neurath, pp. 99–102. Instituto Nacional Indigenista, Mexico City.

Prufer, Keith M., and James E. Brady

2005. Concluding Comments. In *In the Maw of the Earth Monster: Mesoamerican Ritual Cave Use,* edited by James E. Brady and Keith M Prufer, translated by Michael A. Sandstrom, pp. 403–411. University of Texas Press, Austin.

Quiñones Keber, Eloise

1995. *Codex Telleriano-Remensis: Ritual, Divination, and History in a Pictorial Aztec Manuscript.* Includes a facsimile of the codex. University of Texas Press, Austin.

Read, Kay Almere

1998. *Time and Sacrifice in the Aztec Cosmos.* Indiana University Press, Bloomington.

Read, Kay Almere, and Jason J. Gonzalez

2000. *Mesoamerican Mythology: A Guide to the Gods, Heroes, Rituals, and Beliefs of Mexico and Central America.* Oxford University Press, New York.

Reagan, Albert B.

1935. Petroglyphs Show that the Ancients of the Southwest Wore Masks. *American Anthropologist* 37(4):707–708.

Reilly, F. Kent, III

1996. The Lazy-S: A Formative Period Iconographic Loan to Mata Hieroglyphic Writing. In *Eighth Palenque Round Table,* vol. 10, edited by Merle Greene Robertson, pp. 413–424. Pre-Columbian Art Research Institute, San Francisco.

Rice, Prudence

2007. *Maya Calendar Origins: Monuments, Mythistory, and the Materialization of Time.* University of Texas Press, Austin.

Rivera Estrada, Araceli

2012. Percepción del paisaje entre grupos cazadores: Recolectores complejos en la llanura central de Nuevo León. PhD dissertation, Escuela Nacional de Antropología e Historia, Mexico City.

Rowe, Marvin W.

2004. Radiocarbon Dating of Ancient Pictograms with Accelerator Mass Spectrometry. *Rock Art Research* 21(2):145–153.

2005. Dating Studies of Prehistoric Pictographs in North America. In *Discovering North American Rock Art,* edited by L. L. Loendorf, C. Chippindale, and D. S. Whitley, pp. 240–264. University of Arizona Press, Tucson.

2013. Radiocarbon Dates on Texas Pictographs. In *Painters in Prehistory: Archaeology and Art of the Lower Pecos Canyonlands,* edited by Harry J. Shafer, pp. 175–177. Trinity University Press, San Antonio, Texas.

Ruiz de Alarcón, Hernando

1984. *Treatise on the Heathen Superstitions That Today Live Among the Indians Native to This New Spain, 1629.* Edited and translated by J. Richard Andrews and Ross Hassig. University of Oklahoma Press, Norman.

Russ, Jon, Marion Hyman, Harry J. Shafer, and Marvin Rowe

1990. Radiocarbon Dating of Prehistoric Rock Paintings by Selective Oxidation of Organic Carbon. *Nature* 348:710–711.

Sachse, Frauke

2008. Over Distant Waters: Places of Origin and Creation in Colonial K'iche'an Sources. In *Pre-Columbian Landscapes of Creation and Origin,* edited by John E. Staller, pp. 123–160. Springer, New York.

Sachse, Frauke, and Allen J. Christenson

2005. Tulan and the Other Side of the Sea: Unraveling a Metaphorical Concept from Colonial Guatemalan Highland Sources. Mesoweb: www.mesoweb.com/articles/tulan/Tulan.pdf.

Sahagún, Bernardino de

1829. *Historia general de las cosas de Nueva España*. Vol. 2. Edited by Carlos María de Bustamante. Imprenta del Ciudadano Alejandro Valdés.

1950–1982. *General Things of New Spain, Fray Bernardino de Sahagún*. 13 vols. Translated from Nahuatl with notes and illustrations by Arthur J. O. Anderson and Charles E. Dibble. Monographs of the School of American Research. School of American Research, Santa Fe, New Mexico, and the University of Utah Press, Salt Lake City.

Sampson, Geoffrey

1985. *Writing Systems: A Linguistic Introduction*. Stanford University Press, California.

Schaafsma, Polly

1971. *The Rock Art of Utah*. Papers of Archaeology and Ethnology 65. Peabody Museum, Cambridge, Massachusetts.

1986. *Indian Rock Art of the Southwest*. School of American Research, Santa Fe, New Mexico.

Schaafsma, Polly, and Will Tsosie

2009. Xeroxed on Stone: Times of Origin and the Navajo Holy People in Canyon Landscapes. In *Landscapes of Origin in the America*, edited by Jessica Joyce Christie, pp. 15–31. University of Alabama Press, Tuscaloosa.

Schaefer, Stacy B.

1996a. The Crossing of the Souls: Peyote, Perception, and Meaning among the Huichol Indians. In *People of the Peyote: Huichol Indian History, Religion and Survival*, edited by Stacy B. Schaefer and Peter T. Furst, pp. 138–168. University of New Mexico Press, Albuquerque.

1996b. The Cosmos Contained: The Temple Where Sun and Moon Meet. In *People of the Peyote: Huichol Indian History, Religion and Survival*, edited by Stacy B. Schaefer and Peter T. Furst, pp. 332–373. University of New Mexico Press, Albuquerque.

2002. *To Think with a Good Heart: Wixárika Women, Weavers, and Shamans*. University of Utah Press, Salt Lake City.

2010. Huichol Weaving: The Zingg Collection. In *Huichol Art and Culture: Balancing the World*, edited by Melissa S. Powell and C. Jill Grady, pp. 49–63. Museum of New Mexico Press, Sante Fe.

2015. *Huichol Women, Weavers, and Shamans*. University of New Mexico Press, Albuquerque.

Schaefer, Stacy B., and Peter T. Furst

1996. Introduction. *People of the Peyote: Huichol Indian History, Religion and Survival*, edited by Stacy B. Schaefer and Peter T. Furst, pp. 1–25. University of New Mexico Press, Albuquerque.

Schele, Linda, and Peter Mathews

1999. *The Code of Kings: The Language of Seven Sacred Maya Temples and Tombs*. Touchstone, New York.

Schmandt-Besserat, Denise

2007. *When Writing Met Art: From Symbol to Story*. University of Texas Press, Austin.

Schroeder, Albert H., and Dan S. Matson

1965. *A Colony on the Move: Gaspar Castaño de Sosa's Journal, 1590-1591*. School of American Research, Santa Fe, New Mexico.

Séjourné, Laurette

1978. *Burning Water: Thought and Religion in Ancient Mexico*. Originally published 1957. Thames and Hudson, London.

Seler, Eduard

1901. *The Tonalamatl of the Aubin Collection: An Old Mexican Picture Manuscript in the Paris National Library*. Hazell, Watson, and Viney, Berlin and London.

1902. *Codex Fejérváry-Mayer: An Old Mexican Picture Manuscript in the Liverpool Free Public Museums*. T. and A. Constable, Berlin and London.

1903. *Codex Vaticanus No. 3773 (Codex Vaticanus B): An Old Mexican Pictorial Manuscript in the Vatican Library*. 2 vols. T. and A. Constable, Berlin and London.

1963. *Comentarios al Códice Borgia*. Vol. 1. Fondo de Cultura Económica, Mexico City.

1996. *Collected Works in Mesoamerican Linguistics and Archaeology*. Vol. 5. English translation of German papers from *Gesammelte Abhandlungen zur Amerikaneschen Sprach- und Alterthumskunde*, edited by Frank E. Comparato. Labyrinthos, Lancaster, California.

1998a. *Indios huicholes del estado de Jalisco*. In *Fiesta, literatura y magia en el Nayarit: Ensayos sobre coras, huicholes y mexicaneros de Konrad Theodor Preuss*, edited by Jesús Jáuregui and Johannes Neurath, pp. 63–98. Instituto Nacional Indigenista, Mexico City.

1998b. *Collected Works in Mesoamerican Linguistics and Archaeology*. Vol. 6. English translation of German papers from *Gesammelte Abhandlungen zur Amerikaneschen Sprach- und Alterthumskunde*, edited by Frank E. Comparato. Labyrinthos, Lancaster, California.

Shafer, Harry J.

1975. Clay Figurines from the Lower Pecos River Region, Texas. *American Antiquity* 40(2):148–158.

1986. *Ancient Texans: Rock Art and Lifeways along the Lower Pecos*. Texas Monthly Press, Austin.

1988. The Prehistoric Legacy of the Lower Pecos Region of Texas. *Bulletin of the Texas Archeological Society* 59:23–52.

2013. *Painters in Prehistory: Archaeology and Art of the Lower Pecos Canyonlands*. Edited by Harry J. Shafer. Trinity University Press, San Antonio, Texas.

Shafer, Harry J., and Vaughn M. Bryant, Jr.
1977. Archaeological and Botanical Studies at Hinds Cave, Val Verde County, Texas. Report submitted to the National Science Foundation. Department of Anthropology, Texas A&M University, College Station.
Shaul, David Leedom
2014. *A Prehistory of Western North America: The Impact of Uto-Aztecan Languages.* University of New Mexico Press, Albuquerque.
Sigal, Pete
2011. *The Flower and the Scorpion: Sexuality and Ritual in Early Nahua Culture.* Duke University Press, Durham, North Carolina.
Silver, Shirley, and Wick R. Miller
1997. *American Indian Languages: Cultural and Social Contexts.* University of Arizona Press, Tucson.
Sittón, Salomón Nahmad
1996. Huichol Religion and the Mexican State: Reflections on Ethnocide and Cultural Survival. Translated from the Spanish by Bonnie Glass-Coffin. In *People of the Peyote: Huichol Indian History, Religion and Survival,* edited by Stacy B. Schaefer and Peter T. Furst, pp. 471–502. University of New Mexico Press, Albuquerque.
Sobolik, Kristin D.
1996. Nutritional Constraints and Mobility Patterns of Hunter-Gatherers in the Northern Chihuahuan Desert. In *Case Studies in Environmental Archaeology,* edited by E. J. Reitz, L. A. Newsom, and S. J. Scudder, pp. 195–214. Plenum, New York.
Sosa, Gaspar Castaño de
1871. Memoria del descubrimiento que Gaspar Castaño de Sosa hizo en el Nuevo México, siendo Teniente de Gobernador y Capitan general del Nuevo Reino de Leon. In *Colección de documentos inéditos,* pp. 191–261. José María Perez, Madrid.
Soustelle, Jacques
2012. *El universo de los aztecas.* Originally published 1979. Fondo de Cultura Económica, Mexico City.
Šprajc, Ivan
1992. Venus-Rain-Maize Complex in Mesoamerica: Associated with the Evening Star? *Indiana* 12:225–257.
Steelman, Karen, Lennon Bates, Carolyn Boyd, and Marvin Rowe
N.d. Review of Rock Art Dates for Lower Pecos, Texas. Manuscript in preparation.
Stevenson, Matilda Coxe
1904. *The Zuñi Indians: Their Mythology, Esoteric Fraternities and Ceremonies.* 23rd Annual Report for the Years 1901–1902. Bureau of American Ethnology, Washington, DC.
Stewart, Omer C.
1987. *Peyote Religion: A History.* University of Oklahoma Press, Norman.
Stross, Brian
2007a. Eight Reinterpretations of Submerged Symbolism in the Mayan Popol Wuj. *Anthropological Linguistics* 49(3/4):388–423.
2007b. The Mesoamerican Sacrum Bone: Doorway to the Otherworld. *Famsi Journal of the Ancient Americas.* http://researchfamsi.org/aztlan/uploads/papers/stross-sacrum.pdf.
Stuart, David
2011. *The Order of Days: The Maya World and the Truth About 2012.* Harmony Books, New York.

Tate, Carolyn E.
2012. *Reconsidering Olmec Visual Culture: The Unborn, Women, and Creation.* University of Texas Press, Austin.
Taube, Karl A.
2001. The Breath of Life: The Symbolism of Wind in Mesoamerica and the American Southwest. In *The Road to Aztlan: Art from a Mythic Homeland,* edited by Virginia M. Fields and Victor Zamudio-Taylor, pp. 102–123. Los Angeles County Museum of Art, Los Angeles.
2003. Maws of Heaven and Hell: The Symbolism of the Centipede and Serpent in Classic Maya Religion. In *Antropología de la eternidad: La muerte en la cultura maya,* edited by Andrés Ciudad Ruiz, Mario Humberto Ruz Sosa, and María Josefa Iglesias Ponce de León, pp. 405–442. Sociedad Española de Estudios Mayas and El Centro de la Cultura Maya, Mexico City.
2004. Flower Mountain: Concepts of Life, Beauty and Paradise among the Classic Maya. *Res: Anthropology and Aesthetics* 45:69–98.
2010a. At Dawn's Edge: Tulum, Santa Rita, and Floral Symbolism in the International Style of Late Postclassic Mesoamerica. In *Astronomers, Scribes, and Priests: Intellectual Interchange Between the Northern Maya Lowlands and Highland Mexico in the Late Postclassic Period,* edited by Gabrielle Vail and Christine Hernández, pp. 145–192. Dumbarton Oaks, Washington, DC.
2010b. Gateways to Another World: The Symbolism of Supernatural Passageways in the Art and Ritual of Mesoamerica and the American Southwest. In *Painting the Cosmos: Metaphor and World View in Images from the Southwest Pueblos and Mexico,* edited by Kelley Hays-Gilpin and Polly Schaafsma, pp. 73–120. Bulletin 67. Museum of Northern Arizona, Flagstaff.
Tedlock, Barbara
1992. *Time and the Highland Maya.* Originally published 1982. University of New Mexico Press, Albuquerque.

Terry, Martin, Karen L. Steelman, Tom Guilderson, Phil Dering, and Marvin W. Rowe
2006. Lower Pecos and Coahuila Peyote: New Radiocarbon Dates. *Journal of Archaeological Science* 33(7):1017–1021.
Thompson, J. Eric S.
1934. *Sky Bearers, Colors, and Directions in Maya and Mexica Religion.* Publication 436, Contributions to American Archaeology no. 10. Carnegie Institution, Washington, DC.
1970. *Maya History and Religion.* University of Oklahoma Press, Norman.
Trigger, Bruce
2003. *Understanding Early Civilizations: A Comparative Study.* Cambridge University Press, New York.
Turpin, Solveig
1986. Toward a Definition of a Pictograph Style: The Lower Pecos Bold Line Geometrics. *Plains Anthropologist* 31(112):153–162.
1990. Rock Art and Its Contributions to Hunter-Gatherer Archaeology: A Case Study from the Lower Pecos River Region of Southwest Texas and Northern Mexico. *Journal of Field Archaeology* 17(3):263–281.
1991. Time Out of Mind: The Radiocarbon Chronology of the Lower Pecos River Region. In *Papers on Lower Pecos Prehistory.* Studies in Archeology 8. Texas Archeological Research Laboratory, University of Texas at Austin.
1994. On a Wing and a Prayer: Flight Metaphors in Pecos River Art. In *Shamanism and Rock Art in North America,* edited by Solveig Turpin, pp. 73–102. Rock Art Foundation, San Antonio, Texas.
1995. The Lower Pecos River Region of Texas and Northern Mexico. *Bulletin of the Texas Archeological Society* 66:541–560.
2010. *El arte indígena en Coahuila.* Universidad Autónoma de Coahuila, Mexico.

Uriarte, María Teresa
2006. The Teotihuacan Ballgame and the Beginning of Time. *Ancient Mesoamerica* 17(1):17–38.

Vail, Gabrielle, and Christine Hernández
2010. Introduction: Part III, Archaeoastronomy, Codices, and Cosmologies. In *Astronomers, Scribes, and Priests: Intellectual Interchange Between the Northern Maya Lowlands and Highland Mexico in the Late Postclassic Period,* edited by Gabrielle Vail and Christine Hernández, pp. 263–278. Dumbarton Oaks, Washington, DC.
Valadez, Susan Eger
1996. Wolf Power and Interspecies Communication in Huichol Shamanism. In *People of the Peyote: Huichol Indian History, Religion and Survival,* edited by Stacy B. Schaefer and Peter T. Furst, pp. 267–307. University of New Mexico Press, Albuquerque.
Viramontes Anzures, Carlos
2005. Gráfica rupestre y paisaje ritual: La cosmovisión de los recolectores-cazadores de Querétaro. Instituto Nacional de Antropología e Historia, Mexico City.
Vogt, Evon Z.
1969. *Zinacantan: A Maya Community in the Highlands of Chiapas.* Harvard University Press, Cambridge, Massachusetts.
von Sydow, Carl W.
1934. Geography and Folk-Tale Ecotypes. *Béaloideas* 4(3):344–355.
von Winning, Hasso
1979. The "Binding of the Years" and the "New Fire" in Teotihuacan. *Indiana* 5:15–32.

Wade, Maria F.
2003. *The Native Americans of the Texas Edwards Plateau, 1582–1799.* University of Texas Press, Austin.
Wake, Eleanor
2007. The Serpent Road: Iconic Encoding and the Historical Narrative of the *Mapa de Cuauhtinchan No. 2.* In *Cave, City, and Eagle's Nest: An Interpretive Journey through the* Mapa de Cuauhtinchan No. 2, edited by Davíd Carrasco and Scott Sessions, pp. 205–254. University of New Mexico Press, Albuquerque.
Waters, Frank
1963. *Book of the Hopi.* R. R. Donnelly and Sons, Harrisonburg, Virginia.
Weigand, Phil C.
1978. Contemporary Social and Economic Structure. In *Art of the Huichol Indians,* edited by Kathleen Berrin, pp. 101–115. Harry N. Abrams, New York.
Wheeler, Ward C., and Peter M. Whiteley
2014. Historical Linguistics as a Sequence Optimization Problem: The Evolution and Biogeography of Uto-Aztecan Languages. *Cladistics-:* http://dx.doi.org/10.1111/cla.12078.
Whiting, William Henry Chase
1938. Journal of William Henry Chase Whiting, 1849. In *Exploring Southwestern Trails, 1846–1854,* Southwest Historical Series 7, edited by R. P. Beiber and A. B. Bender, pp. 241–350. Arthur H. Clark, Glendale, California.
Whitley, David S.
1994. Shamanism, Natural Modeling and the Rock Art of Far Western North American Hunter-Gatherers. In *Shamanism and Rock Art in North America,* edited by Solveig Turpin, pp. 1–43. Rock Art Foundation, San Antonio, Texas.

2011. *Introduction to Rock Art Research*. 2nd ed. Left Coast, Walnut Creek, California.

Wissler, Clark, and David C. Duvall

1909. *Mythology of the Blackfoot Indians*. Anthropological Papers 2(1). American Museum of Natural History, New York.

Woolley, Chris, and Susan Milbrath

2011. "Real-Time" Climate Events in the Borgia-Group Codices: Testing Assumptions about the Calendar. *Ancient Mesoamerica* 22(1):37–51.

Yoneda, Keiko

2007. Glyphs and Messages in the *Mapa de Cuauhtinchan No. 2*: Chicomoztoc, Itzpapalotl, and 13 Flint. In *Cave, City, and Eagle's Nest: An Interpretive Journey through the* Mapa de Cuauhtinchan No. 2, edited by Davíd Carrasco and Scott Sessions, pp. 161–203. University of New Mexico Press, Albuquerque.

Young, M. Jane

1992. Morning Star, Evening Star: Zuni Traditional Stories. In *Earth and Sky: Visions of the Cosmos in Native American Folklore*, edited by Ray A. Williamson and Claire R. Farrer, pp. 75–100. University of New Mexico Press, Albuquerque.

Zingg, Robert Mowry

1977. *The Huichols: Primitive Artists*. G. E. Stechert and Company, New York. Originally published 1938. Kraus Reprint, New York.

2004. *Huichol Mythology*. Edited by Jay C. Fikes, Phil C. Weigand, and Acelia García de Weigand. University of Arizona Press, Tucson.

Zintgraff, Jim, and Solveig Turpin

1991. *Pecos River Rock Art: A Photographic Essay*. Sandy McPherson, San Antonio, Texas.

INDEX

Italic page numbers denote a diagram, illustration, or photograph.